Other Books by the Author

In Divine Company
The Trinity, Language, and Human Behavior
Theological English
Finding God in the Ordinary
The Speaking Trinity & His Worded World
Struck Down but Not Destroyed
Still, Silent, and Strong
Finding Hope in Hard Things
The Book of Giving
I Am a Human
Christmas Glory
The Great Lie
Borrowed Images

GOD OF WORDS

Essays on God and Language

by

PIERCE TAYLOR HIBBS

GOD OF WORDS
Essays on God and Language

Copyright © 2022 Pierce Taylor Hibbs. All rights reserved. Except for brief quotations in critical publications or reviews, no part of this book may be reproduced in any manner without prior written permission from the author. For more information, visit piercetaylorhibbs.com. These articles were originally published in *Westminster Theological Journal* between 2015 and 2021. They are reproduced here with permission.

ISBN: 978-1-7363411-6-2

Scripture quotations are from the ESV® Bible (The Holy Bible, English Standard Version®), copyright © 2001 by Crossway, a publishing ministry of Good News Publishers. Used by permission. All rights reserved.

Contents

Introduction	1
Imaging Communion	3
Where Person Meets Word Part 1	33
Where Person Meets Word Part 2	68
Closing the Gaps	99
Do You See how I See?	140
World through Word	171
In the Beginning was the Word	204
The Emic and Etic, Immanent and Economic	244
Metaphysics, Epistemology, and Language	275
A Linguistic Perspective on Divine Persons	325
What's in a Word? The Trinity	356

Foreword

I am happy to see more from the pen of Pierce Taylor Hibbs with regard to language and personal communication. He has thought hard and long about language, especially the language of God.

Hibbs rightly notes that the origin for personal communication is found in God himself, in his eternal existence as Father, Son, and Spirit. The Son is also called "the Word of God" (Rev. 19:13; John 1:1). Hibbs shows how God's verbal specification is a perspective on the whole world. God governs the world, in its large-shape and in its details, by speaking (Pss. 33:6, 9; 147:15–18).

In these essays Hibbs develops this perspective with fruitfulness. He understands that one of the chief ills in our culture is the suppression of the knowledge of God, which includes the suppression of his overwhelming presence in both the little and the big aspects of the world. God is present and in control. God is personal. So we are not caught in an impersonal mechanism of laws, but are held in the hand of a personal, loving God. But God's purposes and his meanings also surpass ours. Hibbs wants us not to bring God down to conform to our sinful and selfish expectations, but to grow in appreciating his glory. And this glory is a trinitarian glory, in which the Father speaks the word, in the Son, bringing it home in the power of the Holy Spirit.

I commend this book to readers, as a sound and edifying exposition.

— **Vern S. Poythress**

Introduction

When I published my first article in the *Westminster Theological Journal*, I was elated. Some of the most formative articles I'd ever read were published in the journal. I still remember asking my wife at the time of submission, "Do you really think I can do this?" Her encouragement then, as now, meant the world to me. That was back in 2015. I had no idea that I'd continue researching, writing, and publishing articles in the journal for the next six years, each article focused in some way on God's relationship to language.

I have come to see language as a perspective on all things: who God is, who we are, and what the world is like. That perspective is behind my ThM thesis from Westminster Theological Seminary, published by P&R in 2018, *The Trinity, Language, and Human Behavior*. It's also behind the more popular book *The Speaking Trinity & His Worded World: Why Language Is at the Center of Everything*. The skeleton for those books is here, in this one. The articles in this volume form the basis on which the rest of my writing has emerged. I thought it would be helpful to collect them all in one place, especially for scholars or researchers looking for bodies of work that deal with God and language, which has become a prominent area of theological study. I hope the book serves to illuminate where my mind has been, and perhaps where it is going.

– PTH

Imaging Communion
An Argument for the Existence of God Based on Speech

No one can deny that speech plays in integral role in allowing one person to commune with another. Epictetus said that silence is safer than speech,[1] but if that's the case, we don't want safety; we prefer the hazards of relationships to the seclusion of silence, and evidence of this is all around us. In the morning, we emerge from the world of disheveled dreams seeking another person to find some solace in the confusion. Throughout the day we dialogue with co-workers and use words to forge new relationships with strangers, and when we arrive at home, we stream the day's events to our family with the subtle hope that they will know where and how we have been. In the evening, we lie down and utter a final few words to our spouse before drifting into sleep again. We are always looking to join minds, and that is where speech comes into play. Speech fosters communion: it joins one mind to another, and this seems the most natural thing in the world to us.

But where does this longing for communion come from, and why does speech seem to be the perfect medium for achieving it? Is speech just a product of our ongoing communicative evolution? Are we content to say that

---

1. Epictetus, *Fragment* 29.

speech is simply a unique human faculty, regardless of where it came from and why it functions coherently? I do not think so. To say, with Noam Chomsky, that "when we study human language, we are approaching what some might call the 'human essence,'" is not so helpful.[2] Even if language is part of what it means to be human, that still does not explain our longing for communion, nor does it suggest anything of why speech functions coherently, of why it is effective in fostering communion. In fact, it leads us to the door of metaphysics: *why* do we exist this way? Evolution is not an answer to this question; it glibly skirts the issue by providing a string of how's, which brings us, eventually, back to where we started.

In the following pages, I will argue that speech, one of the most basic human behaviors, serves as evidence for God's existence. But, in contrast to other proofs for God's existence that reason inductively from creation to the Creator, I do the opposite, relying on God's revelation of himself in Scripture. Such an approach, to some, may be unhelpful. Once one plays the "Scripture card," the logical game goes foul. But does it?

The metaphysical door must be opened, and behind it lies a single word: creature. This is *what* we are, and this leads us to *why* we exist the way we do. Creatures, by definition, are bound, finite; in fact, their separation from the creator is so great that they would have no knowledge of him but by his voluntary, covenantal condescension (WCF 7.1). It pleased God to carry out this covenantal condescension through speech, not through general revelation (including reason). God's speech to us, both pre- and post-fall, enacted

---

2. Noam Chomsky, *Language and Mind*, enlarged ed. (New York: Harcourt Brace Jovanovich, 1972), 1.

something that general revelation could not; in God's perfect goodness, he "declared to [Adam and his posterity] by the word, happiness itself and the way to reach it (of which reason was ignorant)."[3]

God's special revelation via speech, then, was a divinely willed, and hence necessary, accommodation. Now, some may question whether Scripture was necessary. God could, it is suggested, simply continue to speak to his creatures and have those creatures relay the messages to the rest of creation. But we are reminded that the written word was just as necessary as the spoken word, given the context in which it occurred (post-fall). God's spoken word is without error; man's spoken words are, on the other hand, laced with them. Hence,

> Scripture is the only adequate means of guarding against the corruption of the spoken word and of making it the possession of all human beings. The sound of a voice passes away, but the written letter remains. The brevity of life, the unreliability of memory, the craftiness of the human heart, and a host of other dangers that threaten the purity of transmission all make the inscripturation of the spoken word absolutely necessary if it is to be preserved and propagated.[4]

God's speech to his creatures, both aural and thereafter written, makes all the more sense when we look at God's

---

3. Francis Turretin, "Second Topic: The Holy Scriptures," in *Thy Word Is Still Truth: Essential Writings on the Doctrine of Scripture from the Reformation to Today*, ed. Peter Lillback and Richard B. Gaffin Jr. (Phillipsburg, NJ: P&R Publishing, 2013), 346. He adds that "God can be savingly known and worshipped only by his light, just as the sun makes itself known to us only by its own light (Ps. 36:9)."

4. Herman Bavinck, "Chapter 14: Attributes of Scripture," in Lillback and Gaffin, *Thy Word Is Still Truth*, 635.

character. Because God is the self-sufficient, interpersonal, and communicative being that he is, Scripture is the best source of our knowledge of him and ourselves. A being who has spoken with himself for eternity past and will do so for eternity future would naturally use language to reveal himself—and creatures whose first behavior was to listen (Gen. 1:28) to their creator would naturally need spoken (and, given the fall) written revelation. It is this truth that repels any apology for God's existence based purely on nature, especially after the fall. Nature certainly reveals God (Rom. 1), but it reveals a God towards whom we are at enmity. We have crippled creation with sin and so when we go to nature for knowledge of God, we get it, but it isn't quite what we thought we wanted. Nature, Bavinck reminds us, speaks nothing of grace and forgiveness,[5] and so we cannot look solely to nature to develop a defense of the triune God. There we will only find a bare form of theism that hints at the character of the Christian God. If forgiveness and grace—two critical concepts for communion in a fallen world—are important to us, we must go to God's special revelation. Scripture may not be in vogue as the base for true knowledge of God, but the truth cares little for fashion. God has spoken definitively and redemptively in his word, condescending to commune with his creatures. It is that God whom we worship; it is that God whom I aim to affirm.

---

5. General Revelation "somewhat illumines the mind and restrains sin but does not regenerate the nature of human beings and the world. It can instill fear but not trust and love." Herman Bavinck, *Reformed Dogmatics*, vol. 1, *Prolegomena*, ed. John Bolt; trans. John Vriend (Grand Rapids, MI: Baker Academic 2003), 313.

The Triad of Metaphysics, Epistemology, and Language (MEL)

If we are going to talk about speech, we cannot isolate it from other human behaviors, nor can we leave out a discussion of metaphysics and epistemology.[6] For our purposes, we will keep this concise so that we can focus our attention on the argument at hand.

Simply put, language is a product of thought, and thought is a product of being.[7] Any discussion of speech,

---

6. Here I side with Kenneth Pike: "Language is behavior, i.e., a phase of human activity which must not be treated in essence as structurally divorced from the structure of nonverbal human activity. The activity of man constitutes a structural whole, in such a way that it cannot be subdivided into neat 'parts' or 'levels' or 'compartments' with language in a behavioral compartment insulated in character, content, and organization from other behavior. Verbal and nonverbal activity is a unified whole, and theory and methodology should be organized or created to treat it as such." *Language in Relation to a Unified Theory of the Structure of Human Behavior*, 2nd ed. (Paris: Mouton, 1967), 26.

7. The biblical foundation for this reasoning comes from 1 Cor. 2:11–13: "For who knows a person's thoughts except the spirit of that person, which is in him? So also no one comprehends the thoughts of God except the Spirit of God. Now we have received not the spirit of the world, but the Spirit who is from God, that we might understand the things freely given us by God. And we impart this in words not taught by human wisdom but taught by the Spirit, interpreting spiritual truths to those who are spiritual." A person's thoughts are inherently connected to his being, his spirit. Christians, Paul tells us, have received the Spirit of God, and we impart the spiritual truths we have been taught not with our own words, but with the words of the Spirit. The word, then, is the medium that takes the things "freely given us by God," i.e. God's thoughts, and communicates them to others. In sum, by God's grace we are made new creatures in Christ (being), so that we can be spiritually instructed concerning God's thoughts (thought), in order to communicate those thoughts through the Spirit's words (language). This paradigm holds for unbelievers as well, but with drastically different consequences. Their spirit is lost, and so their thoughts are confused as they try to suppress the truth (Rom. 1:18), which produces words that, at their

then, presupposes a certain metaphysic and epistemology.[8] If these are cut from the equation, we are left with a stilted notion of speech. Our epistemology, of course, is rarely declared. It shows up implicitly in our use of words, which, as we just said, reflect our thoughts. In light of this triad of metaphysics, epistemology, and language (hereafter MEL), a few things need to be said.

With regard to metaphysics, because we are made in the image of the triune God of Scripture, we are relational beings, just as God is relational in his triunity. But we are also creatures—limited, a status often forgotten or ignored by scholars studying language. The Creator-creature distinction—something that should be engrained in all of Christian thought but which is often left by the wayside—will be at the forefront of this discussion. In light of the Creator-creature distinction, speech will never be reductionistically explained via creation—not because it is too complex, but because it is rooted in an eternal being whom we cannot comprehensively understand.[9] That needs to be taken into

---

best, appear to be wise but which are, in fact, foolish (Rom. 1:22).

8. It is critical that we not separate ontology from epistemology. Van Til noted that "God's knowledge is what it is because his being is what it is." *Christian Apologetics*, 2nd ed., ed. William Edgar (Phillipsburg, NJ: P&R Publishing, 2003), 26. See also *The Defense of the Faith*, 4th ed., ed. K. Scott Oliphint (Phillipsburg, NJ: P&R Publishing, 2008), 56–57; K. Scott Oliphint, *Reasons for Faith: Philosophy in the Service of Theology* (Phillipsburg, NJ: P&R Publishing, 2006), 41, 69n22. The moment we attempt to define epistemology apart from ontology, we do so for a fictitious being; the moment we attempt to define ontology apart from epistemology, we make baseless assertions.

9. So, in a sense, yes, because it is too complex, and because, with Pike, it cannot be detached from other human behaviors. However, we can treat all of human behavior from the perspective of *creatures*. In fact, that is precisely what the biblical narrative demands that we do.

account when we explore the coherence of speech. We are *creatures* handling a *Creator's* gift.

With regard to epistemology, we think God's thoughts after him, analogically.[10] We do not think univocally (to the same extent and in the same manner as God) or equivocally (as if language were inherently unreliable, instable, and subjective). We will discuss this in more detail later on in the article, but the point to keep in mind here is that God thinks as a relational being and we do so on an analogical level.

Lastly, with regard to language, we need to remember that it is fundamentally communal. Language is the key that unlocks the doors of our minds so that we can relate to other beings.[11] It is not, first and foremost, a tool for information acquisition. It is not a self-serving social faculty. It is a behavior that allows interaction, which of course then leads to other uses such as the gathering of information and caring for one's physical and social needs.

One final caveat before examining the argument from

---

10. *The Defense of the Faith*, 4th ed., ed. K. Scott Oliphint (Phillipsburg, NJ: P&R Publishing, 2008), 62, 67, 70–71, 183, 376; *Christian Apologetics*, 2nd ed., ed. William Edgar (Phillipsburg, NJ: P&R Publishing, 2003), 77; *An Introduction to Systematic Theology: Prolegomena and the Doctrines of Revelation, Scripture, and God*, 2nd ed., ed. William Edgar (Phillipsburg, NJ: P&R Publishing, 2007), 31, 33, 42, 177–78, 185, 292, 363; *A Christian Theory of Knowledge* (Phillipsburg, NJ: Presbyterian and Reformed Publishing, 1969), 16, 17, 38, 47, 172, 278. See also paragraph twelve of John M. Frame, "A Primer on Perspectivalism," http://www.frame-poythress.org/a-primer-on-perspectivalism/; and Vern S. Poythress, *In the Beginning Was the Word: Language—A God-Centered Approach* (Wheaton, IL: Crossway, 2009), 268.

11. "The modern impersonalist worldview thinks of the human mind as a closed room. But when God created us, he intended our human minds to be open rooms in which the Father, the Son, and the Holy Spirit dwell." Vern S. Poythress, *Inerrancy and Worldview: Answering Modern Challenges to the Bible* (Wheaton, IL: Crossway, 2012), 134.

speech: any epistemology has to have a metaphysical base. If we fail to ground our thought in being, then we make, oddly enough, *groundless* assertions: superficially coherent claims that have no root in a larger metaphysical framework. Without that framework, we are like ducks whose legs are churning the pond water they wish to ignore. But the water itself is what bears them up. We cannot use our epistemological capabilities while simultaneously denying that there exists a metaphysical explanation for them—not just because a metaphysical base is logically necessary (which it is), but because that metaphysical base profoundly influences how we define our epistemology at the outset.[12] This may seem a small error, but, as Aquinas put it, "a small error at the outset can lead to great errors in the final conclusions."

---

12. A shorter way to put this would be to say that both our being and our thought is grounded in God as the *principium essendi* and the *principium cognoscendi*. God is both our ground of being and our ground for knowing.

The Argument

Now, on to the argument.

Premise 1	Every human behavior is coherent only because it is an analog of a divine behavior.
Premise 2	God is a triune being who communes with himself via speech (a divine behavior).
Premise 3	Humans commune with one another via speech.
Premise 4	Human speech presupposes the co-inherence of the Trinity.
Conclusion	Therefore, each time we speak we affirm the existence of the triune God of Scripture.

Premise 1: Every human behavior is coherent only because it is an analog of a divine behavior.

This first premise may require more extensive treatment than the others. By "coherent," we mean logical and consistent. But, when it comes to behavior, logical consistence also leads to effectiveness: the behavior accomplishes its purposed end.

God is the ultimate coherent being, supremely logical and consistent. This has to do both with his omniscience and his simplicity. With regard to the former, Francis Turretin is quite helpful:

> Concerning the intellect of God and the disquisition of his knowledge, two things above all others must be

attended to: the mode and the object. The mode consists in his knowing all things perfectly, undividedly, distinctly and immutably. . . . perfectly because he knows all things by himself or by his essence . . . . Undividedly, because he knows all things intuitively and noetically . . .
Distinctly, . . . because he most distinctively sees through all things at one glance . . . . Immutably, because with him there is no shadow of change . . .
The object of the knowledge of God is both himself . . . and all things extrinsic to him whether possible or future.[13]

The mode and object of God's knowledge cover both the *manner* and *matter* of his knowing. To put it negatively, there is no way in which God's knowledge is incomplete, restricted, or qualitatively wanting, and there exists no object of which he does not have holistic and uncompromised apprehension. Now, here is the key: God's knowledge of all things accounts for logical consistency, for "everything in the created universe . . . displays the fact that it is controlled by God, that it is what it is by virtue of the place that it occupies in the plan of God."[14] The facts comprising our knowledge can only be called such because of the "systematic relation they sustain to God."[15] His knowledge of every fact and how each one relates to his comprehensive plan to redeem the cosmos is the very ground upon which the notion of coherence is built. God does not *adhere* to the principle of coherence; he is its author.

God's simplicity also factors into the coherence of

---

13. Francis Turretin, *Institutes of Elenctic Theology*, ed. James T. Dennison Jr., trans. George Musgrave Gieger (Phillipsburg, NJ: P&R Publishing), 1:207.

14. Van Til, *Defense of the Faith*, 253. See also *A Christian Theory of Knowledge* (Phillipsburg, NJ: Presbyterian and Reformed Publishing, 1969), 37–38.

15. *Defense of the Faith*, 121.

his behavior—largely contributing to his consistency. Consistency can be a problem for beings composed of parts, for then each of those parts—an attribute—could have its own "pull," thus threatening the consistency of that being's behavior. This is not the case for the God of Scripture. Because God's characteristics are identical with his being, the fissure of doubt closes upon his consistency.[16] His behavior—no matter what it is—can only be congruous with his being, and because his being denies "all possibility of change, as much with respect to existence as to will,"[17] there is no reason to doubt the consistency of his behavior.

Now, we noted at the outset of this section that coherence leads naturally to effectiveness, and we find that God's behaviors never fail to carry out the effects he intends. This is especially germane to our discussion of speech, for throughout Scripture we find confirmations of the effectiveness of God's spoken words. In the Pentateuch, there already exists the assumption that God's speech is inescapably effective, firstly, because he does not lie: "God is not man, that he should lie, or a son of man, that he should change his mind. Has he said, and will he not do it? Or has he spoken, and will he not fulfill it?" (Num 23:19). Complementing the verity of God's words is the surety that what he says comes to fruition. The psalmist writes, "For he spoke, and it came to be; he commanded, and it stood firm" (Ps 33:9). And Isaiah (55:10–11) adds poetically,

> As the rain and the snow come down from heaven and do not return there but water the earth, making it bring forth and sprout, giving seed to the sower and bread to the eater,

---

16. Van Til, *Defense of the Faith*, 31.

17. Turretin, *Institutes*, 1:204.

so shall my word be that goes out from my mouth; it shall not return to me empty, but it shall accomplish that which I purpose, and shall succeed in the thing for which I sent it.

Throughout Jeremiah and Ezekiel, we see the clause "for I have spoken" as the cause for what is about to take place.[18] God's speech is utterly effective: what he speaks comes to be precisely as he intended, and we would expect nothing less from one whose omniscience, omnipotence, and simplicity are tied to his very being.

Now, why must every human behavior be an analog of divine behavior if it is to be coherent? We noted that the definition of "coherence" is to be "logically consistent," and that God is the very author of the concept. But how can *we* account for logical consistence if we are (1) finite, and hence cannot grasp all of known reality in order to verify logical consistency for a certain behavior; and (2) fallen, and hence noetically corrupt? In tandem with these questions is the question of effectiveness. Why are human behaviors—particularly the behavior of speech—effective in accomplishing the ends we have in mind for them?

We account for logical consistence as God's creatures by relying on his faithful and perspicuous revelation. God's revelation in Scripture accommodates us as limited creatures; it is a kind of condescending communication, if we remove the negative connotations from the former adjective. We cannot reason up to God's level of exhaustive knowledge in order to verify experientially whether or not something is logically consistent. That would be to make the creature the Creator, to replace the *Eimi* with the *eikon*, the self-sustaining God with the derivative and dependent

---

18. We understand the Hebrew *ki* in this clause to be a causal conjunction. See GKC §158.

creature.[19] As *eikonic* beings, we think God's thoughts after him on a true but creaturely level. We reason analogically, not univocally, and so we can, in reliance upon God's revelation in Scripture, verify the coherence of a human behavior. This does not mean that we understand it exhaustively, only that we know something true about what it is and how it functions.

That deals with the limitation of creatures, but what about the noetic corruption? Sadly, the human mind cannot account for logical coherence at all—that is, unless it has been redeemed by the work of Christ. At the fall, the unity of human experience and behavior was shattered like a fine glass vase, shards extending to the edges of creation's floor. Thus entered the problem of the one and many. This was not a "problem" before. It only became one in the sense that fallen creation now held unity to be at enmity with diversity—not to mention that man's one and many were now riddled with sin, which plagued his faculties and inflated his pride. But such is not the case with the triune God of Scripture, the three-in-one. Man has broken covenant with the God who holds unity and diversity together in perpetual and perfect harmony. It is only such a being who can redeem the mind of fallen man, and that is precisely how redemption goes.

The diversity of experience, riddled as it is with sin, could only be united and brought into coherence by the sovereign action of God. Creation refused to be truly *eikonic*, striving instead to piece together a notion of coherence without reference to the God of Scripture, which, based on what we have said about coherence, is the definition of

---

19. Oliphint, *Reasons for Faith*, 176–81.

absurdity.[20] We could not try to write a novel in the style of Mark Twain while at the same time denying his existence. On a cosmic scale, this is what we have been trying to do. We have rejected the notion that we are *eikonic*, refusing to image the Creator and think his thoughts after him. We have boarded the ship of univocality and set sail for a country of make-believe, but the anchor of contingency is wedged in the sand.

Yet, even before the boat was in the harbor, God had known it would play out this way. Turretin's words ring true: God's knowledge is perfect as it pertains to "all things extrinsic to him whether possible or future." He knew that in the person of Christ, the *Eimi/eikon* relationship would be restored, that the second Adam would be faithful where the first Adam fell, and that we would only rediscover what true coherence meant when we received the mind of Christ (1 Cor. 2:16).

This is where we find ourselves. We are left now only with the question of effectiveness. Why is any human behavior effective only because it is an analogue of a divine behavior?[21] The short of it is that the very idea of effectiveness presupposes teleology: a purpose in relation to a larger scheme of occurrences. Just as God's omniscience

---

20. "That which is *truly* absurd is whatever is in opposition to God. . . . Absurdity, therefore, has to be measured not in terms of what *we* can comprehend, but in terms of what God has said to us." K. Scott Oliphint, *Covenantal Apologetics: Principles and Practice in Defense of Our Faith* (Wheaton, IL: Crossway, 2013), 83–84.

21. We will not here get into the issue of the effectiveness of wicked behaviors. Suffice it to say that God uses the effectiveness of wicked behaviors (which still are only effective by his allowance) for the God of his people. We might say that wicked behavior is a corrupted or contorted analog of divine behavior, just as the serpent's deceptive speech in the Garden of Eden.

and simplicity are the grounds for the definition of coherence, so his plan for redemption is the grounds for effectiveness. It may be helpful here to make a distinction between "alleged effectiveness" and "true effectiveness." Alleged effectiveness is all around us: a child's temper tantrum is effective in altering his parents' response to him; a shopkeeper is effective in keeping people out of his shop after hours by locking the door. These actions have immediate effects, certainly, but "true effectiveness" is rooted not solely in the immediate, but in the eternal. In Luke's Gospel, the rich man was allegedly effective in storing up wealth for himself, but he was not truly effective, for his life was taken from him and his behavior was shown to be completely *ineffective* (Luke 12:16–21). He died in spiritual poverty.

So, the effectiveness of a behavior is relegated to God and his plan for history. Truly effective behaviors are only possible within that plan. When we try to build a case for effectiveness based purely on allegedly effective behavior at the creaturely level, we end up with a partial and dissatisfying view of effectiveness, perhaps resembling some form of Marxism: effectiveness is decided and executed by the powerful. If we value true effectiveness, we will accept that human behaviors are only coherent and effective because they are analogs of eternally coherent and effective divine behaviors. God's knowledge and being account for our knowledge and being; the coherence and effectiveness of his divine behaviors account for the coherence and effectiveness of our creaturely behaviors. Gaffin draws the same conclusion when examining Ps. 94:9 ("He who planted the ear, does he not hear? He who formed the eye, does he not see?"). His summary is a fitting end to our discussion of the first premise:

These questions are plainly rhetorical and, within the broader framework of biblical teaching, highlight that capacities in human beings, like hearing and seeing, do not merely derive from God but are reflective of his own divine capacities. Surely, then, by extension and in the same vein, we are to ask, "Does he who shaped the tongue not speak?" Here we are pointed to recognize this overall state of affairs: As our being itself is derived from God (we exist because he exists), and as our knowledge is an analogue of his knowledge (we know because he knows), so, too, our capacity for language and other forms of communication is derivative of his. We speak because God speaks, because he is a speaking God; that is his nature and so, derivatively, it is ours. In other words, man in his linguistic functions, as in all he is and does, is to be understood as the creature who is the image and likeness of God (Gen 1:26). In fact, should we not say that especially in his language man reflects the divine image he is?[22]

Premise 2: God is a triune being who communes with himself via speech (a divine behavior).

J. I. Packer once quipped that every biblical passage assumes two facts: that God is king and that he speaks.[23] "Kudos," we think. "Well said Packer." But the second part of his statement has ground breaking implications for our understanding of speech, especially when applied not just to creation, but to the Trinity itself.

First, we know that God speaks not just because God speaks to us, and his "his outward work (his being *ad extra*)

---

22. Richard B. Gaffin Jr., "Speech and the Image of God: Biblical Reflections on Language and Its Uses," in *The Pattern of Sound Doctrine: Systematic Theology at the Westminster Seminaries*, ed. David VanDrunen (Phillipsburg, NJ: P&R Publishing, 2004), 182–83.

23. J. I. Packer, *Knowing God* (Downers Grove, IL: IVP Books, 1975), 109.

corresponds to or images God's inner life (his being *ad intra*)," but because Scripture reveals a God who communes with himself via speech.[24] One manifestation of this truth is the doctrine of perichoresis, "the reciprocal presence and interpenetration of the three divine persons."[25] But this doctrine does not quite get at the point we are making here. There certainly is an interpenetration of the three divine persons, but we are arguing that at least one of the means by which this is achieved is through language—of some kind. Poythress reminds us,

> Not only is God a member of a language community that includes human beings, but the persons of the Trinity function as members of a language community among themselves. Language does not have as its sole purpose human-human communication, or even divine-human communication, but also divine-divine communication.[26]

Where do we find evidence for such a claim? Arguably,

---

24. Kevin J. Vanhoozer, "Triune Discourse: Theological Reflections on the Claim That God Speaks (Part 2)" in *Trinitarian Theology for the Church: Scripture, Community, Worship*, ed. Daniel J. Treier and David Lauber (Downers Grove, IL: IVP Academic, 2009), 51. More concisely, Gerald Bray states, "what God does in time reflects who and what he is in eternity." Gerald Bray, *God Is Love: A Biblical and Systematic Theology* (Wheaton, IL: Crossway, 2012), 29. Vanhoozer wants to formulate an understanding of speech based on the economic Trinity rather than the immanent Trinity, but I feel he does not go far enough with this. It is not just in the economic Trinity that we see the foundation for speech and communicative behavior, but in God's very being, beyond the work of creation.

25. Gerald O'Collins, *The Tripersonal God: Understanding and Interpreting the Trinity* (New York: Paulist Press, 1999), 206, quoted in Lane G. Tipton, "The Function of the Perichoresis and the Divine Incomprehensibility," *WTJ* 64 (2002): 290.

26. Vern S. Poythress, *In the Beginning Was the Word: Language—A God-Centered Approach* (Wheaton, IL: Crossway, 2009), 18.

throughout all of Scripture, but there are a few passages worth noting here.

In the Old Testament, God's plurality of being is first brought to the fore in the creation narrative. In addition to God bringing creation "into nothing" with the triadic medium of speech—speaker, speech, and breath— we also see God communing with himself. In Genesis 1:26, we meet the Hebrew cohortative, *na'aseh*, a verbal form that is the subject of much scholarly debate.[27] Our impetus for interpreting the form as an instance of God's inter-trinitarian dialogue (perhaps better, "trialogue") is as follows: first, aside from the fact that a speaking God would necessitate inner plurality, the only other truly viable option is that God is addressing his heavenly court.[28] But I find this view wanting on a number of levels. Why would God be addressing other creatures in a creative action that is attributed solely to his power? He certainly is not looking for approval or input from contingent beings. Is he simply announcing what he is doing? This would be a

---

27. Waltke outlines the six options we have for interpretation: (1) the plural is a remnant of ANE myth in which God is addressing other gods. This is untenable given that the Pentateuch opposes polytheism at every corner. (2) The plural is directed towards a host of previously made creatures (this still ends up relying on polytheistic tendencies that do not comport with the Genesis account). (3) The plural is honorific, like the form *Elohim*, but Waltke notes that this form is elsewhere attested by nouns, not pronouns. (4) The plural is, in Gesenius' language, "a plural of *self-deliberation*," though no other instance supports this view. (5) The plural is a reference to the Trinity. This view would be supported by later NT texts, even though Waltke argues that this violates the boundaries of grammatico-historical interpretation. (6) The plural refers to the heavenly court that surrounds God's throne. See Bruce K. Waltke, *An Old Testament Theology: A Canonical and Thematic Approach* (Grand Rapids, MI: Zondervan, 2007), 212–13.

28. See Nahum M. Sarna, *Genesis*, JPSTC (Philadelphia: The Jewish Publication Society, 1989), 12.

strange precedent, given the other grammatical structures employed to bring in other aspects of creation. Yet, it would make perfect sense if God chose to employ this particular grammatical structure exclusively in the creation of man because he was creating a being who would image himself in personal relations. This would certainly pair nicely with Genesis 2:18. Adam is not "lonely." God is not working out divine psychoanalysis. Rather, God knows that it would be "good" for Adam to commune with other creatures equal with himself because that is what God does, and God is wholly good.

Now, in response to those who would suggest that God's use of speech was strictly covenantal (i.e., he created it along with the rest of creation) there is other support. Unlike the light, which has an explicit origin in God as well as in the objects of creation,[29] linguistic or communicative behavior is, mysteriously, without a fixed origin. God simply appears on the scene and begins speaking. The repeated Hebrew grammatical structure used to introduce God's speech, *Elohim vayomer*, suggests not the genesis of language but the inveterate choice of this being to use it in creating the cosmos. Some may view it as a stretch, but we get the impression as readers that we have somehow

---

29. Here I follow those who suggest that God is a light unto himself. The light that he creates first is not earthly light, but a kind of self-referential light based upon which he creates earthly light. See Bruce K. Waltke, *Genesis: A Commentary* (Grand Rapids, MI: Zondervan, 2001), 61; Jacob Milgrom, "The Alleged 'Hidden Light,'" in *The Idea of Biblical Interpretation: Essays in Honor of James L. Kugel*, ed. Hindy Najman and Judith H. Newman (Boston: Brill, 2004), 44; and Mark S. Smith, "Light in Genesis 1:3—Created or Uncreated: A Question of Priestly Mysticism," in *Birkat Shalom: Studies in the Bible, Ancient Near Eastern Literature, and Postbiblical Judaism Presented to Shalom M. Paul on the Occasion of His Seventieth Birthday*, ed. Chaim Cohen et al. (Winona Lake, IN: Eisenbrauns, 2008), 1:127–31.

already fallen behind: "Well, of course God spoke to create. What else would he do? He is a speaking being." And, in light of the fact that art is always a few steps ahead of the wider culture,[30] we might do well to note that two of the most colossal figures in 20th century literature, C. S. Lewis and J. R. R. Tolkien, both wrote fictional creation accounts that address the issue here. Each account is unique, but one feature they both share is that God sings creation into existence: vocalization brings actualization; the sound brings the substance.[31] It would be no stretch to say that these authors pulled such a concept from the Genesis account and assumed, with the author of Genesis, that language would be God's natural medium for creation because its roots run deeper than creation itself. Language is part of who God is as an eternal, *relational* being.[32]

Other OT references to God's plurality could be explored (includingthe "angel of the Lord" passages [Gen. 21; 22; 31], Ps. 45:6–7, 110:1, and the personalization of

---

30. Francis Schaeffer discusses what he calls the "line of despair." This is a trend in thinking (originating in the 19th century) that rejected absolutes and antithesis, instead favoring dialectics and existentialism. The line of despair was realized first by philosophy, then by art, then music, then general culture, and finally in theology. The arts, according to Schaeffer, were always a few steps ahead of the broader culture. See *The God Who Is There*, in *Francis Schaeffer Trilogy* (Wheaton, IL: Crossway, 1990), 5–9.

31. For Lewis, see the end of chapter 8 and the beginning of chapter 9 in *The Magician's Nephew*. ForTolkien, see the first chapter of *The Silmarillion*, entitled "The Music of the Ainur."

32. "In short, this God who made the universe—establishing an order within the vast range of variety, with human beings as the crown of his creation, representing him as his image bearers—is relational. Communion and communication are inherent to his very being." Robert Letham, *The Holy Trinity: In Scripture, History, Theology, and Worship* (Phillipsburg, NJ: P&R Publishing, 2004), 21.

terms such as "wisdom" and "word"),[33] but I would rather focus on an NT passage that illumines God's eternal history of self-communication: John 17:4–5. In fervent prayer to his Father, Jesus Christ says, "I glorified you on earth, having accomplished the work that you gave me to do. And now, Father, glorify me in your own presence with the glory that I had with you before the world existed."

Now, beings give glory to one another via praise, and praise necessitates communicative behavior. How else would God glorify the Son if not through communicating praise? We see instances of God's praise for the Son already in other parts of the NT. Consider the striking account of Jesus's baptism, towards the beginning of his ministry: "Now when all the people were baptized, and when Jesus also had been baptized and was praying, the heavens were opened, and the Holy Spirit descended on him in bodily form, like a dove; and a voice came from heaven, 'You are my beloved Son; with you I am well pleased'" (Luke 3:21–22). God is pleased with the Son long before his climactic work of redemption on the cross, before the unparalleled event of the resurrection. In fact, God's pleasure in the Son, his praise for the Son's worth, is not merely a mark of the economic Trinity. It is rather, in Vanhoozer's terms, a mark of the *immanent* Trinity, the eternal triune community. The Son has always been praised by the Father; the Father has always communicated his praise to the Son. The Spirit also has always partaken of this glorious trialogue. God's praise for himself is the actual basis of communicative activity for his creatures.

Also in the scriptural witness, we find evidence of God's speech in the fact that God is personal, and "personality

---

33. See Letham, *The Holy Trinity*, 21–32.

does not develop nor exist in isolation, but only in association with other persons. Hence it is not possible to conceive of personality in God apart from an association of *equal* persons in Him. His contact with creatures would not account for His personality any more than man's contact with the animals would explain his personality."[34] It is these "equal persons" who commune with one another in the Godhead. In God's eternal perichoresis, he was communing with himself, and what else is language—speech—if not a means whereby one person communes with another?

The reason why we are to take "God's Trinitarian self-communication as the paradigm of what is involved in all true communication"[35] is not simply because God speaks to his creation—for, as Berkhof noted, this would not reflect God's personality; it would merely reflect his creative capabilities—his willingness to condescend and accommodate creatures. Even if we grant this route for the sake of argument, the creatures to whom he is condescending are made in his image! They presuppose analogical qualities and faculties that until that point only functioned within the Godhead.

Is it not strange that Adam has linguistic tendencies *before* the creation of Eve? This, perhaps more than anything else, may have prompted God to say, "It is not good for the man to be alone." This is not an assessment of Adam's emotional status; it is a witness to Adam's inherent, image-made capacity to commune with other persons. It is not "good"

---

34. Louis Berkhof, *Systematic Theology*, new ed. (Grand Rapids, MI: William B. Eerdmans, 1996), 85.

35. Kevin J. Vanhoozer, *Is There a Meaning in This Text? The Bible, the Reader, and the Morality of Literary Knowledge* (Grand Rapids, MI: Zondervan, 1998), 199.

for a being made in the image of the communicating God to lack an equal partner in communication. Hence, Eve enters the scene. In an act as poetic as it is sacred, a piece of Adam is removed and used to form the woman, not because women are derivative or inferior, but because the person must come from Adam's own being. Just as God's being is the commonality of the three persons, so Adam's being is the commonality for this other person: someone opposite to him (Hebrew: *neged*, Adam's counterpart or corresponding being). It would not be "good" for Adam to exist purely as a unit; communion necessitates plurality. Whereas in God this is internal, in creation it is external.

This is all the more apparent when we reflect on God as the being who brings unity and plurality into perfect harmony. God is not a fragmented being simply because he is tri-personal. In the words of the *shema*, God is still *echad* even while he his three persons: this is part of the Creator-creature distinction. We bifurcate and analyze; we try to reduce categories such as unity and plurality to mutually exclusive descriptors, like good little Aristotelians should, claiming that "paradox" is really just a fool's word for "incoherent." The truth of the matter is that this alleged paradox is the only thing that accounts for coherence in the first place. Coherence finds its fulfillment in the tri-personal God of Scripture, who alone is able to account for union and communion while simultaneously accounting for plurality.[36] All of human behavior, especially linguistic

---

36. "In every knowledge transaction, we must bring the particulars of our experience into relation with universals. So, for instance, we speak of the phenomena of physics as acting in accordance with the laws of gravitation. . . . If we study the particulars of this world as they are related to one another in time as well as in space, we observe certain historical laws. But the most comprehensive interpretation that we can give of the facts by connect-

behavior, presupposes God's eternal unity and diversity: we are separate, unique beings that are built to commune with other separate beings. The human race as a whole is revelatory of the glory of the Trinity.

In light of the scriptural witness, we can say with confidence that God is a triune being who communes with himself via speech, and that this very fact constitutes speech as a divine behavior, which we as creatures have inherited as his image-bearers.

Premise 3: Humans commune with one another via coherent speech.

If there is a premise in this argument that requires little, if any, support, it is this one. I hesitate to argue for it at all. But we can remind ourselves of a few things here.

First, though we do use speech to commune with one another, we also frequently use it for the purpose of "disunion." The fragmentation of our current society is enough evidence to convince any simpleton that we have taken the plurality inherent in God's being, and, in a sinful application to the rest of creation, have tried to make language something that fosters our own continuing isolation. We come up with pithy maxims like "the mind is a prison" in order to justify our misunderstanding of language as a faculty that is meant to bind unity with diversity together

---

ing the particulars and the universals that together constitute the universe leaves our knowledge at loose ends, unless we may presuppose God back of this world. . . . As Christians, we hold that in this universe we deal with a derivative one and many, which can be brought into fruitful relation with one another because, back of both, we have in God the original one and many [the Trinity]. If we are to have coherence in our experience, there must be a correspondence of our experience to the eternally coherent experience of God." Van Til, *Introduction to Systematic Theology*, 58–59.

in God's creatures. The mind is not a prison barring others from engaging with our thoughts or emotions; it is, perhaps, a room with a door that is often closed, but language is the key always left sitting in the lock. We know this, and we remember it every time we have a meaningful encounter with another human being via speech.

Second, the adjective "coherent" cannot be used so frequently to describe human speech, not because it lacks the ability to evoke that quality, but because language is always being used by creatures who only occasionally scratch the surface of divine coherence—the quintessence of that coherence being the person and work of Jesus Christ. Christ is the word *of* God, spoken *by* God to bring creation back into right relationship *with* God, the very designer of coherence. This is missed in part by the noetic effects of sin (going back to the MEL triad). Our knowledge of who God is and how he has redeemed the cosmos through the word of his Son and the continuing work of his Spirit has yet to percolate the tight crevices of the human mind. It takes time for a mind to heal. But we rest assured, knowing that "despite the fact that man's knowledge is categorized by self frustration, through the power and clarity of God's revelation in the world and in Scripture, he still knows things truly."[37] And when our knowledge is renewed daily as we take on the mind of Christ, we will speak with more creaturely coherence, according to God's standard for coherence (the perfect relation of the one and the many), not the world's (a bifurcated view of the one and the many).

---

37. Van Til, *Introduction to Systematic Theology*, 164.

Premise 4: Human speech presupposes the co-inherence of the Trinity.

Now that we have come this far, perhaps we can take the final premises in stride. Here again, we rely on the MEL triad.

Every coherent utterance is a microcosm of the Trinity, reflecting "the richness of [God's] inner life."[38] In terms of metaphysics, God is an eternal, relational being, and only a being who is eternally relational could account for meaningful relational behaviors in finite creatures.[39] This is because "meaningful," which includes the notion of coherence (logical consistency and effectiveness), is a label we can only give to pieces of human behavior (in this case, the behavior of speech) within a cosmic and purposeful plan. Outside the realm of a holistic plan for every detail in the cosmos, meaning is compartmentalized, and thus incoherent, since whatever logical consistency it may have is truncated. This alone disqualifies that detail from bearing the descriptor "coherent." Coherence is not an ideal form in the platonic sense; it is a concrete feature emanating from an unfathomable complex of connected relationships.[40]

---

38. John M. Frame, *Systematic Theology: An Introduction to Christian Belief* (Phillipsburg, NJ: P&R Publishing, 2013), 434. On God's speech as an essential attribute of his nature, see 522–23.

39. "Any harmonious functioning in relationships depends on the foundational harmony of God's relationships among the persons of the Trinity." Vern S. Poythress, *Redeeming Sociology: A God-Centered Approach* (Wheaton, : Crossway, 2011), 47.

40. Though I would imagine this would drive secular linguists nuts, we cannot apply the descriptor "coherent" to an isolated proposition—unless we understand that proposition to be an infinitesimal part of an unfathomably complex system that only God knows exhaustively, as if the proposition

God is the author of coherence because his being, as tri-personal, is the author of all relations in existence and as such is the only one who could account for the possibility of coherence. But more fundamental than this is that God is three persons in one being. He communes with himself in eternity and throughout redemptive history, and it is only because God does this that his image bearers can do the same. Temporal relational behavior relies on God's eternal relational behavior for its meaning and coherence.

In terms of epistemology (how we attain knowledge), "comprehensive knowledge somewhere must be the basis for true knowledge anywhere."[41] Only God has this comprehensive knowledge, and only in the Triune God of Scripture could this knowledge be centered on persons.[42] This has as its foundation the fact that God eternally reveals his being to himself: his perfect knowledge of who he is and what he does is eternally communicated in the Godhead.[43] Humans, of course, cannot bear the weight of this knowledge; they can only bear, in God's grace, a small piece of it, enough to recognize that God (Father, Son, and Holy Spirit) is Lord and that his omniscience is the only ground for our partial and analogical knowledge.

---

itself were a blade of grass in a bird's nest the size of Saturn.

41. Van Til, *Defense of the Faith*, 65.

42. Paul K. Moser has helpfully pointed out that knowledge of God is "person-centered" because God is a person. I take issue with several aspects of Moser's approach in his article, but I do find that his notion of "person-centered knowledge" is biblical and quite helpful, even when applied to the field of linguistics, since we worship the personal God of language. See Paul K. Moser, "Cognitive Inspiration and Knowledge of God," in *The Rationality of Theism*, ed. Paul Copan and Paul K. Moser (New York: Routledge, 2003), 67.

43. Frame, *Systematic Theology*, 523.

In terms of language, we must recognize that God's speech, his pure communication from one member of the Trinity to another, is the ground for our interpersonal communication. God's interpersonal communication is based on understanding, obedience, and trust. The Son has an understanding of the Father's will, obeys that will even unto his death, and trusts that God's word will stand forever, as he does. The Son's understanding, obedience, and trust allows for continual communion within the Trinity. Just as the Father declares his understanding to the Son, so the Spirit takes what has been given to the Son and applies it to creation. Understanding runs throughout the Trinity. Likewise with obedience and trust.Interpersonal communication among God's creatures also rests on understanding, obedience, and trust. When these pillars are violated, we see the nasty, corrupt potential of language: confusion (i.e., incoherence), rebellion, and deception.

Lastly, we come, yet again, to the question of effectiveness: this is the question we introduced earlier. Why is human speech effective? The short of it is, as you might have guessed,becauseGod's speech is effective. If God's word did not always attain the purpose for which he sent it (Isa. 55:10–11), then our speech would never attain the purpose we have for it. Effectiveness cannot be measured on a purely temporal scale; our behaviors are efficacious only so long as they have lasting value, and value circles back to epistemology: a knowledge of the way things truly are, a knowledge of the ultimate end of all things. The ultimate end of all things is God himself: our eternal fellowship with him or our eternal separation from him. That, ultimately, is why language is effective, because with every word we speak we are either advancing the boundary lines of God's kingdom or parrying Satan's attacks as we retreat. Philo of

Alexandria was right, every one of us is in a great battle at this very moment, either as a rebel or a dulo-rex, i.e., a servant-king of the Lord of all.[44] The effective word is either an assault on Satan's realm of evil, apathy, and incoherence, or a misuse of the Trinitarian power of language for the sake of restoration and communion.

Conclusion: Each time we speak we affirm God's existence.

As we noted before, all human behaviors are only coherent and effective because they are analogues of divine behavior. Nowhere is this more apparent than in our speech, our verbal attempts to commune with one another and with God. Speech, as a human behavior, wonderfullty reflects the necessity of the Trinity. Only in God's being, knowledge, and inter-trinitarian communication do we find solid ground for the coherence and effectiveness of human speech, which is itself an image-bearing product of our derivative being, thought, and interpersonal communication.

So the next time someone questions you about the existence of God, before you answer, understand that the person has already testified to it by uttering the question. He is relying on God's being, knowledge, and intertrinitarian speech to rebel against his creator, which, in Van Tillian terms, is like the girl climbing up on her grandfather's lap

---

44. This is a term I find helpful, since it is based on Scriptural language: from the Greek, *doûlos*, meaning "servant," and the Latin *rex*, meaning "king." A "dulo-rex" is a regenerated image-bearer, taking on the original rule of Adam in servant form, following the pattern of Christ's kingly servitude.

so that she can slap him in the face.[45] This truth, if nothing else, adds new depth to James 1:19, "let every person be quick to hear, slow to speak." For once words fall from your tongue, you have stepped into the divine limelight as a creature in covenantal relation to your speaking God.

---

45. Cornelius Van Til, "Response to Herman Dooyeweerd," in *Jerusalem and Athens: Critical Discussions on the Theology and Apologetics of Cornelius Van Til*, ed. E. R. Geehan (Phillipsburg, NJ: Presbyterian and Reformed Publishing, 1971), 98.

Where Person Meets Word Part 1
Personalism in the Language Theory of Kenneth L. Pike

Reformed theology has always championed the Trinity as the beating heart of the Christian faith. This is true not just of the mainstay historical Reformers, Luther and Calvin, but also of Dutch Calvinism, Old Princeton, and the Westminster heritage.[1] Certainly, Calvin and Melanchthon were not alone in claiming that "God's triunity was that which distinguished the true and living God from idols."[2] The true God *is* the Trinity.

Out of this tradition emerged Cornelius Van Til and his insistence that the self-contained ontological Trinity be the basis of all human experience and knowledge.[3] He

---

1. On Luther, see David Lumpp, "Returning to Wittenberg: What Martin Luther Teaches Today's Theologians on the Holy Trinity," *CTQ* 67 (2003): 232, 233-34; and Mickey Mattox, "From Faith to the Text and Back Again: Martin Luther on the Trinity in the Old Testament," *ProEccl* 15 (2006): 292. On Calvin, see T. F. Torrance, "Calvin's Doctrine of the Trinity," *CTJ* 25 (1990): 166. For an example of the Dutch Calvinist view, see Herman Bavinck, *Reformed Dogmatics*, vol. 2, *God and Creation*, ed. John Bolt, trans. John Vriend (Grand Rapids, MI: Baker Academic, 2004), 279, 329. For Old Princeton, see Charles Hodge, *Systematic Theology*, 3 vols. (Peabody, MA: Hendrickson, 2013), 1:442; and B. B. Warfield, *Biblical and Theological Studies*, ed. Samuel G. Craig (Phillipsburg, NJ: Presbyterian & Reformed, 1968), 22. For a more contemporary discussion, see Louis Berkhof, *Systematic Theology* (Grand Rapids, MI: Eerdmans, 1996), 85.

2 Scott R. Swain, "The Trinity in the Reformers," *The Oxford Handbook of the Trinity* (ed. Gilles Emery and Matthew Levering; New York: Oxford, 2011), 228.

3. "The Trinity . . . gives the most basic description possible of God as the *principium essendi* of knowledge for man" (Cornelius Van Til, *Introduction to*

claimed that "if we are to have *coherence* in our experience, there must be a correspondence of our experience to the eternally coherent experience of God. Human knowledge ultimately rests upon the internal coherence within the Godhead; our knowledge rests upon the ontological Trinity as its presupposition."[4] In other words, our experience and knowledge are grounded in the equal ultimacy of the one and many, and the perichoretic relationship of the persons in the Godhead.[5] What might this mean for our understanding of people and our use of language? Many things, certainly, but one of them must be that God's trinitarian nature is imprinted on the structure of our communicative behavior. Not only does this have critical implications for our understanding and use of language, but it also encourages us to reassess the place of the Trinity in general revelation.

Building on the foundation laid by Van Til, we can explore the trinitarian implications for language and general revelation indirectly by examining the work of Kenneth L. Pike (1912–2000), who developed a distinctly trinitarian approach to all of human behavior, especially

---

Systematic Theology: Prolegomena and the Doctrines of Revelation, Scripture, and God, ed. William Edgar [Phillipsburg, NJ: Presbyterian & Reformed, 2007], 30). "Our knowledge rests upon the ontological Trinity as its presupposition" (ibid., 59). With regards to the final reference point of all interpretation, all predication of meaning, Van Til wrote, "The Protestant principle finds this in the self-contained ontological Trinity." It is this God, we must maintain, that "is always the most basic and therefore the ultimate or final reference point in human interpretation" (Cornelius Van Til, *The Defense of the Faith*, ed. K. Scott Oliphint [Phillipsburg, NJ: Presbyterian & Reformed, 2008], 100. On this doctrine taken explicitly from Scripture, see pp. 227–28, 236, and 241).

4. Van Til, *Introduction to Systematic Theology*, 59.

5. See ibid., 58–59; Van Til, *Defense of the Faith*, 47–50.

language. What's more, Pike's thought foregrounds the inherently personal nature of God and its ramifications for our understanding of people as creatures made in his image. Given that the *imago Dei* and the internal witness of God to all people is part and parcel of a Reformed view of general revelation, what we learn from Pike has repercussions for our understanding of the traditional doctrine of general revelation as it relates to the Trinity.

In order to develop these ideas adequately, this article is broken into two parts. The overarching thesis of both parts is that the trinitarian structure of Pike's theory is not only prescriptive for our thinking about language (and all purposive behavior), it was a destination he was bound to arrive at because personalism (general revelation) and Scripture (special revelation) converge in the Trinity.

In Part 1, we will see that the trinitarian structure of Pike's language theory was in part propelled by the personalism underlying his thought. We will begin by reminding ourselves of the mystery rooted in people and the origin of their communicative behavior (the triune God), and then move on to consider Pike's tristructural view of language. Once it has been established that his approach is truly trinitarian, we will move on to examine personalism and its manifestations in his work.

In Part 2, I show how his personalism merged with his understanding of Scripture and the *imago Dei*. This tandem, alongside personalism, is the concomitant catalyst for the trinitarian shape of his theory. Finally, we will end by noting that Pike's work opens the discussion for the nuanced treatment of the Trinity in general revelation.

People, Mystery, and the Trinity

We begin with a simple point: people are not so easily pigeonholed. As much as our labels and judgments categorize and compartmentalize, they fall short of exhaustive description. We do not know others as deeply as we wish. This is part of the reason why we weep at funerals: we have not grasped the whole of someone, and the residual mystery exits the known world without being fully accounted for. Sitting before the funeral casket, we are painfully remindedofthe inanity of thinking we can exhaustively know another human being, or anything else for that matter. Mystery is an irrevocable part of existence.

The trouble is that throughout human history we have either ignored the implications of this mystery or assumed that we canstep outside its shadow when we are *not* dealing with a person. People may retain an element of mystery, but a pinecone does not—neither does an ecosystem or the structure of a particular language. These things, we assume, can be boiled down to their most basic elements; we can know them more or less comprehensively, as boasted by the rich history of theoretical formulation and empirical analysis.

Contrast this sentiment with that of Cornelius Van Til when he uttered the following words to his students several decades ago: "We certainly cannot penetrate intellectually the mystery of the Trinity, but neither can we penetrate anything else intellectually because all other things depend on the mystery of the Trinity, and therefore all other things have exactly as much mystery in them as does the Trinity."[6] This remark is quite striking, when you consider

---

6. Cornelius Van Til, "Christ and Human Thought: Modern Theology,

the implications for academic inquiry.

Van Til was pointing to the nature of reality. The world in which we live is inherently personal because it was created, is governed, and will be consummated by the *personal* God of Scripture. God is himself a person, a triune person, and every human being contains an element of mystery because he or she is made in his image.[7] This much we might accept, but the same principle applies to the rest of creation—and that is difficult for academics to swallow. Even a pinecone is grounded in the Trinity, and so we cannot know everything about it; we cannot know it exhaustively. A claim to know *anything* exhaustively— be it a person, a pinecone, or the particular syntax of a language—is a claim of divinity.[8]

Part 1" (lecture, Westminster Theological Seminary, Glenside, PA, no date).

7. "Christian theism holds that every finite person is surrounded by a completely personalistic atmosphere because, even if the world immediately around him is impersonal, this impersonal world derives its meaning from its Creator" (Van Til, *Introduction to Systematic Theology*, 230). See also Vern S. Poythress, *Inerrancy and Worldview: Answering Modern Challenges to the Bible* (Wheaton, IL: Crossway, 2012), 246 and John M. Frame, *The Doctrine of God* (Phillipsburg, NJ: Presbyterian & Reformed, 2002), 26.

With regard to man being ultimately incomprehensible, see Kallistos Ware, foreword to *Deification in Christ: Orthodox Perspectives on the Nature of the Human Person*, by Panayiotis Nellas, trans. Norman Russell (Crestwood, NY: St. Vladimir's Seminary Press, 1987], 9, quoted in Robert Letham, *The Holy Trinity: In Scripture, History, Theology, and Worship* [Phillipsburg, NJ: Presbyterian & Reformed, 2004], 460).

8. We can, however, know truth in a way analogous to the way in which God knows it. See Van Til, *Defense of the Faith*, 62, 67, 70-71, 183, 376; Cornelius Van Til, *Christian Apologetics*, ed. William Edgar (Phillipsburg, NJ: Presbyterian & Reformed, 2003), 77; Van Til, *Introduction to Systematic Theology*, 31, 33, 42, 177-78, 185, 292, 363; Cornelius Van Til, *A Christian Theory of Knowledge* (Phillipsburg, NJ: Presbyterian & Reformed, 1969), 16, 17, 38, 47, 172, 278; Vern S. Poythress, "Reforming Ontology and Logic in the

This presents a dilemma: our default response to mystery and limitation is impersonal reductionism—accompanied by fear, discomfort, or hubris.[9] Impersonal reductionism allows us to continue in the dream of control and mastery, despite its intellectual pomposity, and because we falsely frame reality so that it appears more manageable, we wander into intellectual countries we have no metaphysical, epistemological, or linguistic business traversing. Our reductionism, coupled with a vapid curiosity, brings us, paradoxically, into more mystery. And from there, pure curiosity—fascination detached from personal application—takes the reins of our inquiry. As Pascal wrote, "The chief malady of man is restless curiosity about things which he cannot understand; and it is not so bad for him to be in error as to be curious to no purpose."[10] Our precarious history with mystery and limitation, as I see it, leaves us with two responses to this dilemma: (1) We can ignore the personal and mysterious nature of life and treat any subject within it as if it wereexhaustibly knowable. This would be impersonal and unitarian at best, and certainly no place for personal, trinitarian Christian thought. (2)

Light of the Trinity: An Application of Van Til's Idea of Analogy," *WTJ* 57 (1995): 187–219; and Vern S. Poythress, *In the Beginning Was the Word: Language—A God-Centered Approach* (Wheaton, IL: Crossway, 2009), 268.

9. Consider, e.g., Plato's reduction of the universe to ideas: "The Platonic tradition . . . desires to purify concepts by separating the idea (the meaning, the content) from its embodiment in language. Plato counseled aspiring philosophers to seek to know the idea of the good, the beautiful, and the just. The idea was thought to be in its essence a transcendent idea, independent of any particular language—also independent of God. It was an impersonal idea. And so Plato's vision tacitly assumed an impersonalist universe" (Poythress, *Logic: A God-Centered Approach to the Foundation of Western Thought* [Wheaton, IL: Crossway, 2013], 161).

10. Blaise Pascal, *Pensées*, fragment 18.

We can account for the personal and mysterious nature of existence, looking to the tripersonal God of Scripture to direct and shape our perspective of the world and our methodology for inquiry. The latter option does not mean we cannot rigorously investigate and study aspects of the world with precision and draw true and lasting conclusions; it simply means that we cannot eclipse the personal nature of existence in the process or ignore that it is the trinitarian God who created it and is reflected within it.

The second response, however, is not so popular in academia, particularly in the field of linguistics. Sacrificing the possibility of exhaustive or comprehensive knowledge seems needless at the least, fatuous and barbaric at the worst. Thus, structural linguistics and transformative-generative grammar have been taken far more seriously in the last few decades than the tagmemic theory of Kenneth L. Pike, whose integrative philosophy for all of human behavior allowed for the personal nature of reality while not excluding the rigor and precision desired in understanding a meaningful event of that reality—whether linguistic or non-linguistic. It is to Pike's theory that we now turn, before coming back to the personalism that played a role in shaping it.

A Tristructural View of Language and Human Behavior

Before navigating the tributaries leading to the trinitarian structure of Pike's thought, we should provide some evidence up front concerning what exactly makes his approach to language (and to all of human behavior) trinitarian.

To start, *is* it trinitarian? Pike would probably prefer the term *tristructural*; at least, that is the term he used in an article published by *Bibliotheca Sacra* in 1958. By tristructural, he meant that "every significant unit of speech . . . is comprised simultaneously of three structures, in such a way that each of the structures includes all the substance of the unit, but each structure is formally distinct from the other two."[11] However, after even a cursory examination of his main works, it is clear that we have warrant to call it trinitarian. Certainly, the most obvious feature of his thought is his triads: the particle, wave, and field observer perspectives;[12] the grammatical, phonological, and referential hierarchies;[13] linguistic units with contrastive-identificational features, variation, and distribution;[14] events simultaneously

---

11. Kenneth L. Pike, "Language and Life 4: Tristructural Units of Human Behavior," *BSac* 115 (1958): 36.

12. Kenneth L. Pike, "Language as Particle, Wave, and Field," in *Kenneth L. Pike: Selected Writings to Commemorate the 60th Birthday of Kenneth Lee Pike*, ed. Ruth Brend (The Hague: Mouton, 1972), 129; Pike, "Towards a Theory of the Structure of Human Behavior [1956]," in *Selected Writings*, 106.

13. Kenneth L. Pike, *Linguistic Concepts: An Introduction to Tagmemics* (Lincoln, NE: University of Nebraska Press, 1982), 13–15.

14. We arrive at a contrastive-identificational awareness of a particular unit of language or human behavior, when we can tell what it is *not* like in addition to what it *is* like. "The same components which help us to see that one unit differs from another also help us to *recognize* the unit when it is no longer close to the one which we separated it from. . . . Features which are contrastive in relation to some contexts are *identificational* in others" (Pike, *Linguistic Concepts*, 42). Variation deals with "those features of a unit which may change *without causing the loss of recognizability* of the unit. The appropriate observer readily recognizes that certain changes do not affect deeper identities" (ibid., 52). Distribution provides the broader functional system within which a unit finds its meaning. "Some place must be the point of origin for the coordinates which allow one to identify oneself in a place in the larger world. Something must tell us where we are, beyond reference to our immediate environment. Reference to successively larger patterns of occurrence, to a larger *universe of discourse*, is necessary if one is to know the

structured in the manifestation, feature, and distribution mode.[15] Yet, these triads themselves are not sufficient to merit the label "trinitarian." Countless philosophers and theologians utilize triads in their theory. What makes Pike's approach unique is not simply the *matter* of his thought (the triads themselves), but the *manner* of his thought, that is, the way in which he sees them functioning. The hierarchies of grammar, phonology, and reference are overlapping and interlocking.[16] The particle, wave, and field perspectives

---

significance of a person, a thing, or a word. Knowing that I'm behind my nose does not tell me how to find the way to town. I need to be oriented in reference to a larger context, to a universe—or to a discourse. The *I* of a discourse (in relation to *you*) suggests that the speaker knows something about his social relations. But unless one goes beyond oneself and his neighbor to a hierarchically ordered outside world, he is in some sense lost within himself" (ibid., 60).

15. The manifestation mode is "the hierarchical structuring of the physical material which is present in every human behavioral event. In language, this implies structure in terms of phonemes, which in turn enter a hierarchy with syllables, stress groups, and still higher units." The feature mode is "the simultaneous identification-contrastive components of that unit, with its internal segmentation analyzed with special reference to purpose or lexical meaning wherever these are detectable. It is in reference to this mode . . . that any over-all meaning of a sentence is treated." Lastly, the distribution mode is "the breaking up of the sentence into its pertinent major and minor spot classes. Specifically, the distribution mode is . . . the correlation of spots plus the classes filling those spots" (Pike, "Towards a Theory," 114–15). A *spot* is "the place at which substitution can occur. . . . All behavior is considered to contain significant spots at which behavior occurrences can be found." A *class* is the "particular list of items which are appropriate to that spot" (ibid., 110–11). Pike would later change his terminology to *slot* and *class*. Each *slot* would then have an appropriate collection of *fillers* that could fill that behavioral slot.

16. Kenneth L. Pike, *Language in Relation to a Unified Theory of the Structure of Human Behavior*, 2nd ed. (The Hague: Mouton, 1967), 475, 566, and 567–80. For an example of overlapping hierarchies, see p. 101.

are different structural views of the same data.[17] A single unit has contrast, variation, *and* distribution.[18] One can see right away that Pike's triads reflect the God who is three-in-one, as well as what theologians refer to as the coinherence or perichoresis of the Trinity.[19] Just as the persons of the Godhead interpenetrate one another, so the various aspects of Pike's triads overlap and interlock—units of the grammatical hierarchy simultaneously substantive in levels of the phonological hierarchy, and units of the phonological hierarchy simultaneously substantive in the referential hierarchy, and so on. Critical to a well-developed understanding of a linguistic unit is its identity, variation, and distribution—focusing on only one of these features leaves us with a partial view of the data.

Mystery, too, enters into the relationship of these interlocking triads, which is also a key tenet of

---

17. "There are three views of linguistics which cover approximately the same material and which in some respects are similar, but which are different enough to allow a far richer experience if the linguist uses all three than if he uses only one" (Pike, *Linguistic Concepts*, 12).

18. Note that Pike's focus on units having contrastive-identificational features and yet having variation ultimately goes back to the perfect harmony of unity and diversity in the Godhead. A linguistic unit can have variation and yet still maintain its identity. This is the case ultimately because "each of the persons of the Trinity is exhaustive of divinity itself, while yet there is a genuine distinction between persons. Unity and plurality are equally ultimate in the Godhead" (Van Til, *Introduction to Systematic Theology*, 348). "The unit of class and the diversity of particularity both rest on the ontologically ultimate unity and diversity of God" (Poythress, "Reforming Ontology and Logic," 197). On the relation of the one and the many, see Van Til, *Defense of the Faith*, 48-49.

19. See Charles Hodge, *Systematic Theology*, 1:461-62; Frame, *Systematic Theology*, 479-81; Van Til, *Introduction to Systematic Theology*, 357; Letham, *Holy Trinity*, 178, 208; Joel R. Beeke and Mark Jones, *A Puritan Theology: Doctrine for Life* (Grand Rapids: Reformation Heritage, 2012), 90-91.

incomprehensibility of the Godhead.[20] This mystery presents itself in the fuzzy boundaries of hierarchies and their component units. For example, in discussing the "thresholds," that is, the upper and lower boundaries of a behavioreme (an identifiable unit of human behavior, such as having breakfast or driving to work), Pike suggests that the relative indeterminacy of these thresholds "is reflecting some of the ambiguity which exists, in fact, in the activity of the community itself, and that a concealing of this ambiguity in order to get 'clear cut' theory at this point would not contribute to the fidelity of description but to concealment of the facts of behavioral structure."[21] His avoidance of reductionism and discrete categories, while earning him criticism from modernist-minded scholars, is, in fact, what makes his theory more markedly trinitarian.[22]

---

20. The incomprehensibility of God can be seen in the "mysterious interpenetration of the persons of the Godhead," stressed particularly in the work of Charles Hodge and rearticulated by Van Til, who sought to guard this ancient doctrine from the threat of univocal reasoning in the form of rationalism. See Lane G. Tipton, "The Function of Perichoresis and the Divine Incomprehensibility," *WTJ* 64 (2002): 289–306. Van Til's understanding of perichoresis bears an uncanny resemblance to Pike's metaphorical use of the concept in his linguistic theory (interpenetrating hierarchies). This may be because both Van Til and Pike were familiar with the work of Charles Hodge, particularly the first volume of his *Systematic Theology*.

21. Pike, *Language*, 129. Note also that the ambiguity of these borders may reflect the fact that human community in some way resembles or at least retains the mark of the Trinity. Mystery also exists in the replaceable components of an intonation system. In an interview in the early 1990s, Pike commented that "there's something very mysterious about the way the paradigmatic handling of intonation shows replaceable components at a particular point in a system and is important in that way" (see Alan S. Kaye, "An Interview with Kenneth Pike," *Current Anthropology* 35 [1994]: 296).

22. Again, see Tipton, "The Function of Perichoresis," for Van Til's defense of but supplement to traditional orthodox trinitarianism. Van Til's defense of the incomprehensibility of the Godhead as it relates to perichoresis

While it certainly reveals patterns, human behavior is not an empirically exhaustible plexus of relations, nor is language an antidote injected into the bloodstream of mystery; it merely channels mystery from place to place in recognizable ways for finite creatures, allowing us to communicate coherently and yet keeping us from understanding the world and ourselves exhaustively.[23] Digging deeply enough into any linguistic structure or meaningful human behavior, one will inevitably run into mystery, for, as Van Til says, all that God has made reflects the mystery that is part of his tripersonal nature.[24]

Therefore, it is Pike's *manner* of thinking that set him apart from other linguists of his day. Interlocking hierarchies and perspectives are conducive to producing larger amounts of data and a depth of understanding, but not an exhaustive

---

pairs nicely with Pike's rejection of the comprehensibility of the structure of human behavior.

23. Note, e.g., how the *Word* of God—God's own speech to us—in the flesh helps us to understand and relate to God more concretely (just as language helps us relate to the world), and yet Christ is still shrouded in mystery by the paradox of his divine-human nature, just as the inner workings of language are, I argue, as mysterious as the perichoresis of God.

24. This can be traced back to the analogical nature of human reality. In our being, thought, and language, we are analogous to the trinitarian God. In terms of our being, there is classification (i.e., stability or *who we are*), instantiation (i.e., variation and uniqueness), and association (our relationships). Each of these features presupposes the other two; each is a perspective on our being. In terms of our thought, we develop categories for interpreting the world that are also classificational, instantiational, and associational, since "our conception of language . . . influences our conception of logic." In terms of our language, "Trinitarian speech is necessarily Trinitarian, trimodal, and coinherent. Human speech is dependent. Since it provides access to real knowledge of God, it is necessarily trimodal and coinherent by analogy" (see Poythress, "Reforming Ontology and Logic," 195).

mastery of syntax, morphology, or phonology. Pike knew that limitation, and he was content with it because mystery, for him, had a place in all of human behavior. Rather than spend time trying to understand an element of human behavior exhaustively in the abstract, he focused on concrete situations in which the observer needed to extract a particular understanding from a behavioral unit—no matter how small or large that unit was.

In sum, if the *manner* of our thinking should reflect our being made in the image of the triune God who has created and upholds all things by his Word, if our approach to language and thought needs "radical recasting in the light of Trinitarian ontology and logic,"[25] then Pike certainly seems to be headed in the right direction.

Personalism *Defined*

The above summary should help us to appreciate that Pike's theory *is* truly trinitarian. The question we have before us now is, how did it come about? To begin answering that question, we need to understand Pike's personalism.

Personalism as an official movement is difficult to define, not only because there are many schools and applications of it (depending on the setting, historical and geographical), but also because it carries core values common to other philosophical movements.[26] We can try to limit ourselves

---

25. Poythress, ibid., 217.

26. Personalism, according to the *Stanford Encyclopedia of Philosophy*, has roots recognizable in Europe, America, and Asia; its proponents range from F. D. E. Schleiermacher to Walt Whitman, its forebears are as diverse as Boethius, Thomas Aquinas, Immanuel Kant, Jean Lacroix, and Emmanuel Mounier. With so many figures attached to a single movement, whether to its historical foundation or contemporary expression, we must be careful in

to what Simon Blackburn calls the "older usage" of the term: "Personalism is the theistic stress on the existence of divine personality or any philosophy according to which the individual person is the starting point of theory."[27] Better yet for our context is the definition provided by Alistair Hannay, "The finite individual is somehow grounded in and seeks its fulfillment in an infinite spirit, or God, understood as personal."[28] This, in part, is in accord with the American strand of personalism brought out in the work of Borden Parker Bowne (1847–1910) and Edgar Sheffield Brightman (1871–1960), which was "both idealistic and theistic . . . and had as its foundational insight the view that all reality is ultimately personal. God is the transcendent person and the ground or creator of all other persons; nature is a system of objects either for or in the minds of persons."[29] Speaking more particularly of Bowne's personalism, we can say that it "maintains that reality is a society of selves and persons with a Supreme Person (God) at its center. Person was, for Bowne, the fundamental principle of explanation, capable of explaining all other principles but itself."[30]

However, we can and must improve and clarify these

---

committing to a definition without qualification. See "Personalism," *Stanford Encyclopedia of Philosophy*, http://plato.stanford.edu/entries/personalism/ (accessed August 3, 2014).

27. Simon Blackburn, *The Oxford Dictionary of Philosophy* (New York: Oxford University Press, 1994), 284.

28. Alistair Hannay, "Personalism," *The Oxford Companion to Philosophy*, 2nd ed., ed. Ted Honderich (New York: Oxford University Press, 2005), 692.

29. Robert Audi, ed., "Personalism," *The Cambridge Dictionary of Philosophy*, 2nd ed. (New York: Cambridge University Press, 1999), 661.

30 Rufus Burrow, Jr., *Personalism: A Critical Introduction* (St. Louis, MO: Chalice, 1999), 11.

definitions within the Reformed tradition.[31] In distinction from the so-called "Boston personalism," we affirm that all of reality is grounded in the triune, personal God who reveals himself objectively and yet personally in revelation to man as his image-bearer. In this sense, we can say that reality is ultimately personal, and that if nature is a system of objects in the minds of persons, then the ultimate mind is the mind of God.[32] Personalism in this sense is not relativism or subjectivism. When couched in the appropriate language, it is nothing more than a representation of scriptural truth. Reality is not an impersonal conglomeration of material, facts, and data; there is nothing that exists apart from God's creating and sustaining Word, and because God is personal, all of reality is as well.

Theologically, personalism falls into the field of general revelation. God "reveals himself in the history of nations

---

31. Van Til was clear in articulating the theological chasm between "Boston personalism" and what he called "orthodox personalism." Proponents of the former, namely Bowne and Brightman, ran into serious trouble because they sought to make finite personality the "fulcrum for the operations of the laws of thought. But finite personality can be thought of intelligently only on the presupposition of the idea of the self-intelligent God. And on the basis of the idea of this God alone is it possible to avoid both rationalism and irrationalism, both determinism and pure contingency, or a combination of them" (Cornelius Van Til, "Boston Personalism" [lecture delivered at Boston University School of Theology, March 6, 1956], 55–56).

32. "Man's surroundings are shot through with personality because all things are related to the infinitely personal God" (Van Til, *Christian Theory of Knowledge*, 208). Van Til is quick to point out that though there is continuity between man's mind and God's mind, there is not identity of content (Van Til, *Introduction to Systematic Theology*, 270–71). God's mind is ultimate in the sense that there can only be analogical knowledge for man, but the fact that this is the case means there is continuity between God's mind and man's mind, since "God is the original knower, and man is the derivative re-knower" (ibid., 274). For man to be a "re-knower," he must have a mind in analogical correspondence to that of his Creator.

and persons (Deut. 32:8; Pss. 33:10; 67:4; 115:16; Prov. 8:15, 16; Acts 17:26; Rom. 13:1). He also discloses himself in the heart and conscience of every individual (Job 32:8; 33:4; Prov. 20:27; John 1:3–5, 9, 10; Rom. 2:14, 15; 8:16)."[33] Or, as Calvin put it, "there is a sense of divinity engraved in the hearts of all *people*. . . . It cannot be erased from the human spirit."[34] God reveals himself not only in the world around us, but also in each person's conscience,[35] and by nature of the fact that all people are made in God's image.[36] People are walking testaments to the nature of reality as created and sustained by a triune, personal God.

The above definitions of personalism and its place in general revelation will help us to understand how Pike arrived at a trinitarian theory of language and human behavior. However, rather than move on just yet, we need to understand that Pike's personalism was not an explicit acceptance of an official movement but a manifestation of his theological convictions within the field of linguistics.

---

33. Herman Bavinck, *Reformed Dogmatics*, vol. 1, *Prolegomena*, ed. John Bolt, trans. John Vriend (Grand Rapids, MI: Baker Academic, 2003), 310.

34. John Calvin, *Institutes of the Christian Religion: 1541 French Edition*, trans. Elsie Anne McKee (Grand Rapids, MI: Eerdmans, 2009), 26; emphasis added.

35. Kelly, *Systematic Theology*, 1:144. See also Rom. 2.

36. The *imago Dei* is far too rich a subject to treat here. Suffice it to say that the *imago Dei* is reflected in everything we do as human beings. In Oliphint's words, "all that we are, think, do, and become is derivative, coming from or out of something else; we depend on, as well as mirror, the real, the Original, the *Eimi*. In classical terminology, we are 'ectypal.' The *kind* or *type* of people we are, knowledge we have, thoughts we think, things we do, is always and everywhere a copy, pattern, impression, image, taking its metaphysical and epistemological cue from the only One who truly *is*, that is, from God himself" (K. Scott Oliphint, *Reasons for Faith: Philosophy in the Service of Theology* [Phillipsburg, NJ: Presbyterian & Reformed, 2006], 178–79).

Pike has, in this sense, his own strand of personalism, which at first glance is nothing novel. Like many figures in the Reformed tradition, he is wary of treating reality as an impersonal, mechanistic system rooted in pure physicality. Yet, the uniqueness of Pike's strand of personalism comes to the fore in his embrace of observer perspectives (particle, wave, and field) and the rejection of abstract categories or concepts that are either divorced from concrete manifestation or skew the data of language by being reductionistic.[37] In light of these concepts, his critiques of other linguists were spent on those who either (1) bifurcated aspects of language that he felt must be tied together (such as form and meaning); or (2) reduced linguistics to a particular hierarchy (e.g., grammar or reference) rather than focusing on its interlocking hierarchies as perceived by observers. Both critiques are tied to his personalism—the notion that *people are central to inquiry and investigation.* This is back of Pike's critiques of the *structuralist* movement within American descriptive linguistics (a movement of which he was a part), as it was based on the foundations laid by

---

37. Rémy de Gourmont stated that "the only excuse a man has for writing is to write himself—to reveal to others the kind of world reflected in his individual mirror." Commenting on this, Pike writes, "The world mirrored in each man's mind is unique. Constantly changing, bafflingly complex, the external world is not a neat, well-ordered place replete with meaning, but an enigma requiring interpretation. This interpretation is the result of a transaction between events in the external world and the mind of the individual—between the world 'out there' and the individual's previous experience, knowledge, values, attitudes, and desire. Thus the mirrored world is not just the sum total of eardrum rattles, retinal excitations, and so on; it is a creation that reflects the peculiarities of the perceiver as well as the peculiarities of what is perceived. In a very real sense there are as many interpretations of the world as there are people in it" (Richard E. Young, Alton L. Becker, and Kenneth L. Pike, *Rhetoric: Discovery and Change* [New York: Harcourt, Brace, & World, 1970], 25). See also *Linguistic Concepts,* xi, xii, 3.

Ferdinand de Saussure, Leonard Bloomfield, and Noam Chomsky.[38]

In terms of Pike's own teaching, both theological and linguistic, we find that even from its genesis in the mid-1930s, people remained his central focus. This might be attributed to his initial experience with the Summer Institute of Linguistics (SIL), when he worked on his own among the Mixtecs, an isolated and agrarian people of Mesoamerica, translating the NT into a tongue to which he had no prior exposure.[39] In such a setting, relationships are the bedrock of survival, both physically and socially. When you are several days' journey by donkey to the closest train station, linguistic ideals and abstractions do little to fill your stomach or break the language barrier isolating you from substantive human contact. Pike cut his teeth on practical linguistics, choosing to live among a foreign people, to think in their language, and to study both its structure and pronunciation. The experience showed him early on that compartmentalizing aspects of language such as grammar and phonemics was an exercise in abstraction and did not adequately represent the linguistic community under consideration. Thus he writes, "If a language structure is to be described realistically, the interweaving of grammatical and phonemic facts must not be ignored. A language system represents a structural whole which one cannot compartmentalize mechanically without doing violence to

---

38. For examples of critiques, see Pike, *Language*, 63, 536, 355, 97, 149, 496.

39. Pike's boss at the time, W. Cameron Townsend, even had him avoid learning Spanish before living among the Mixtecs, so as to help his immersion and subsequent functionality in the language. See Eunice V. Pike, *Ken Pike: Scholar and Christian* (Dallas, TX: Summer Institute of Linguistics, 1981), 18–48.

the facts."⁴⁰

It is also important to know that Pike's personalism is related to his focus on the physical manifestation of meaning. By this we mean that "every structural unit postulated for language . . . has a physical component as its base; no exceptions are knowingly tolerated."⁴¹ In other words, units of language (morphemes, words, phrases, clauses, etc.) are *always* bound up with a particular physical manifestation; their meaning is inseparable from their form within a participant sequence of activity (e.g., a conversation, a paragraph).⁴² But because we often discuss meaning and form as if they were capable of being isolated, a question arises: How can we study, analyze, categorize, or discuss a unit of language without "doing violence to the facts"? Pike's answer is, in a word, *hypostasis*.

> Any abstraction of an activity from a normal participant sequence for purposes of viewing it, studying it, mentioning it, analyzing it, listing it, cataloging it, or discussing it as such, we shall call HYPOSTASIS of that activity. The mention of a word is an activity of hypostasis. The formation of a dictionary listing is accomplished by the hypostasis of these forms. The practicing of the passing of a football is the hypostasis, and repetition of hypostasis, of the football-passing activity of a normal game, etc.
>
> The native speaker, in quoting a word out of normal context, is performing an act of hypostasis. If he means the MEANING of that word, however, he is doing something further: he is making an abstraction from various contexts

---

40. Kenneth L. Pike, "Grammatical Prerequisites to Phonemic Analysis (1947)," in *Selected Writings*, 48.

41. Kenneth L. Pike, "Meaning and Hypostasis (1955)," in *Selected Writings*, 102.

42. Ibid., 102–3.

of some common phase of the elicitation-response characteristics of those contexts, and is giving to his abstraction a name, or "label." The physical manifestation of the label is a component of the abstracting activity, and, for that activity, fulfills the kind of function which for the non-abstracting activity of normal speech is played by the physical component of that normal speech. Activity units in which a substitute verbalization for hypostasis defining purposes replaces the verbal activity utilized in normal non-abstracting sequences, we may call 'conceptualized hypostasis' to differentiate it from hypostasis which merely repeats, out of context, an item to study it apart from that context.[43]

In more simple language, what Pike is saying is that (1) sometimes we remove a unit of language from its genuine participant context in order to study it, an act of hypostasis; (2) sometimes we talk about the *meaning* of that hypostasized unit, and in such a case we are gathering meanings from various participant contexts and creating an abstraction, a conceptualized hypostasis. For example, if we discuss the intonation and stress of the word *love* in the clause "God is love" (1 John 4:8) in hopes of showing how the intonation and stress in that clause relate to John's meaning in the larger context of the paragraph, then we are performing an act of hypostasis—temporarily treating the word in isolation from its context. If, however, we claim that *love* is "wanting what is best for another without regard for oneself," then we have taken multiple participant contexts in which that word occurs (or contexts we associate with our perceived meaning, e.g., Jesus's death on the cross) and made an abstraction—a label that encompasses the mass of specific physical manifestations we have in mind.

---

43. Ibid., 103.

Both hypostasis and conceptualized hypostasis are analytical tools, but in our use of them we must be conscious of what we are doing. We are temporarily *pretending* that a specific form can be isolated from a specific meaning in a specific physical context; we sacrifice (or at least temporarily ignore) the acute meaning in a defined participant situation in order to focus on meaning in a broader context of analysis. Yet even here we do not bifurcate form and meaning because in the process we have created a new form: either the hypostasized form and meaning in a new context or the conceptually hypostasized form and its contextually compounded meaning.

Now, why mention this in relation to personalism? Just as language units cannot be abstracted from sequences of participant activity without in some sense distorting or skewing our perception of the original data, so language cannot be separated from those who speak it without distorting or skewing our perception of its structure, function, and purpose. A linguistic unit—even a hypostasized one—is a form-meaning composite. Analogously, a speaking person is a form-meaning composite. The meaningful language a person uses cannot be separated from that person (the "form") without skewing our perception of the data. To deal with language is to deal with people.

The above discussion has, I hope, brought us to a place where we can more precisely define Pike's particular strand of personalism. For the remainder of this article, we will assume the following definition: people and their meaningful behavior in specific contexts are vital to our understanding of the structure of language and of the rest of reality. This definition will serve us well in the following section, in which we highlight manifestations of personalism in Pike's work.

Manifestations of Personalism in Pike's Work

We have already discussed certain aspects of Pike's personalism in brief, but having more evidence of personalism in its varying forms throughout his writing establishes the point and deepens our understanding of his approach to linguistics. Each of the following manifestations of personalism confirms just how pervasive the concept is in his thought.

We must first begin by establishing that, for Pike, language is a phase of human behavior that cannot be structurally divorced from other kinds of human behavior.[44] This is primarily because (1) "language behavior and nonlanguage behavior are fused in single events" and (2) "verbal and nonverbal elements may at times substitute structurally for one another in function."[45] Pike confirmed through examples that "language behavior and nonlanguage behavior are structurally so analogous that on some occasions certain of their parts are interchangeable."[46] In sum, "the complexity

---

44. Viola G. Waterhouse, *The History and Development of Tagmemics* (The Hague: Mouton, 1974), 15. In his magnum opus, Pike claims, "Language is behavior, i.e., a phase of human activity which must not be treated in essence as structurally divorced from the structure of nonverbal human activity. The activity of man constitutes a structural whole, in such a way that it cannot be subdivided into neat 'parts' or 'levels' or 'compartments' with language in a behavioral compartment insulated in character, content, and organization from other behavior. Verbal and nonverbal activity is a unified whole, and theory and methodology should be organized or created to treat it as such" (*Language*, 26). See also Pike, "Towards a Theory of the Structure of Human Behavior (1956)," in *Selected Writings*, 106.

45. Pike, *Language*, 26.

46. Ibid., 30. Pike is quick to acknowledge his teacher, Edward Sapir, for his direction in this idea. According to Sapir, "a further psychological characteristic of language is the fact that while it may be looked upon as a

of human beings reflects itself in human action,"⁴⁷ and language is one of those actions. This baseline assumption consorts well with hispersonalism: he is studying human behavior holistically, rather than atomistically.

The Emic and the Etic

Pike's personalism was also evident in the founding and use of the concepts *emic* and *etic*, ending morphemes of the words *phonemic* and *phonetic*. These are essentially two

---

symbolic system which reports or refers to or otherwise substitutes for direct experience, it does not as a matter of actual behavior stand apart from or run parallel to direct experience but completely interpenetrates with it. . . . This interpenetration is not only an intimate associative fact; it is also a contextual one. It is important to realize that language may not only refer to experience or even mold, interpret, and discover experience, but that it also substitutes for it in the sense that in those sequences of interpersonal behavior which form the greater part of our daily lives speech and action supplement each other and do each other's work in a web of unbroken pattern." Edward Sapir, *Selected Writings in Language, Culture, and Personality* (Berkeley: University of California Press, 1963; repr., London: Forgotten Books, 2012), 11–12.

In addition, Sapir suggested that linguistics could be understood as a window into the rest of human behavior (Sapir, *Selected Writings*, 166; cited in Pike, *Language*, 32). It seems Pike followed Sapir's recommendation and, using linguistics, generated a unified approach to the structure of human behavior—a fitting albeit less elegant title for his magnum opus.

47. Vern S. Poythress, *Redeeming Sociology: A God-Centered Approach* (Wheaton, IL: Crossway, 2011), 243. He continues, "One of these complexities reveals itself especially in language. Language shows multiple subsystems that we use in communication. Specifically, a language has a referential subsystem, enabling us to refer to things and to communicate content; it has a grammatical subsystem, maintaining internal structure; and it has a phonological subsystem, enabling transmission by sound." Spoken like a true student of Pike!

different ways of viewing the same data or experience.⁴⁸ We might begin by substituting the word *insider* for *emic* and *outsider* for *etic*.⁴⁹ A simple example will serve to illustrate: consider an extraterrestrial who is watching people drive in and out of a gas station. Some people, he notices, get out of their metal boxes, remove a square piece of plastic from their pockets, and insert it into a machine next to them before quickly pulling it back out. Then they push lightly on the machine, remove a hose from it, attach the hose to their metal box, and wait a few minutes. Finally, they put the hose back in its place and push lightly on the machine once more. But at this point, the alien is puzzled: after lightly pushing on the machine, some people take a small piece of paper from it, but others do not. All the alien can confirm is that this phenomenon happens; he cannot attach meaning to it from the perspective of these people. Why do they not all take a slip of paper from the machine? Is the machine withholding? Is it judging them based on their parking skill? Is the color of their metal box the deciding factor?

Imagine the same scenario from the perspective of a

---

48. Here, again, Pike incorporates the teaching of Edward Sapir, with whom he worked closely in the late 1930s, conversing with him about linguistics into the late hours of the night. Sapir wrote, "It is impossible to say what an individual is doing unless we have tacitly accepted the essentially arbitrary modes of interpretation that social tradition is constantly suggesting to us from the very moment of our birth" (Sapir, *Selected Writings*, 546).

49. Pike, *Language*, 37. Waterhouse defines the contrast between emic and etic as follows: "The etic view has to do with universals, with typology, with observation from outside a system, as well as with the nature of initial field data, and with variant forms of an emic unit. The emic view is concerned with the contrastive, patterned system of a specific language or culture or universe of discourse, with the way a participant in a system sees that system, as well as with distinctions between contrastive units" (*History and Development of Tagmemics*, 6).

person filling his car up with gas. When he sees the man next to him push a button after fueling and not receive a slip of paper, the action is instantly meaningful. He knows that the man simply does not want a receipt for the transaction. He can draw a number of conclusions about this action that the alien cannot: perhaps the man hates clutter; perhaps he wishes to help the environment by saving paper; perhaps he is in a rush and would rather not wait for a receipt to print out. And, what's more, while the person has an instant understanding of the potential meaningfulness of the action, he may be unaware of all the things that the alien observed because his rote execution blinds him to certain details. The alien considers how strange it is for a piece of plastic to go in and out of a machine and cause that machine to respond. He wants to know how this works. The person, on the other hand, probably could not care less. He has inserted and removed his card at the gas pump countless times without hesitation and without much thought. He does not think about how the magnetic strip in his card is read by the machine, or how his pin number is related to the magnetic strip, and so forth. So, both the alien and the person at the gas pump notice certain things about the same event; each perspective yields unique but useful results; each has its advantages and limitations. The alien would not survive socially in the man's culture. The man would not survive in his own culture if he thought of every single activity he performed with meticulous scrutiny. The alien's view and the man's view are complementary.

The emic and etic perspectives have varying uses for the linguist, for each offers different opportunities and advantages of analysis. The etic view structures behavioral units from an outsider's perspective, while the emic view "is domestic, leading to units which correspond to those of an insider familiar with and participating in the system."[50] The etic view can be used cross culturally, while the emic view is "monocultural" because it only perceives internal relations of a person or culture.[51] The etic view classifies types of behavior, while the emic view structures them in relation to the native system.[52] Because of their potential for broader application, etic views are more absolute, while emic views are more relative.[53] Perhaps most important,

> etic units and classifications, based on prior broad sampling or surveys (and studied in training courses) may be available before one begins the analysis of a further particular language or culture. Regardless of how much training one has, however, emic units of a language must be determined during the analysis of that language; they must be discovered, not predicted.[54]

---

50. Kenneth L. Pike, "A Stereoscopic Window on the World," *BSac* 114 (1957): 145.

51. Ibid.

52. Ibid.

53. Ibid.

54. Pike, *Language*, 37. One can discover the emic categories and units of a language by observing the responses to verbal and nonverbal behavior as they are distributed in various contexts. "Every emic unit of language behavior must be studied in reference to its distribution—distribution in reference to verbal behavior, and distribution in reference to nonverbal cultural behavior. Within the study of the distribution of language units in nonverbal contexts is included the consideration of the nonverbal responses of individuals to speech addressed to them. Just as the verbal replies of a speaker help one determine meanings of elements of communication, so the nonverbal ones do likewise. To attempt to analyze or describe language without reference to its function in eliciting responses—verbal and nonverbal—is to ignore one of the crucial kinds of evidence which is essential if the emic structure of language is to be determined, whether one is dealing with the larger units of that structure, such as the sentence, or smaller ones, such as some of the emic units of the sound system" (Pike, *Language*, 39–40).

Our understanding of a particular unit of behavior—that is, an element of experience—largely depends on who is observing that unit—either an outsider or a participant of the community in question. This is a key point at which we encounter Pike's focus on observer perspectives.[55]

Each person is part of an emic system(s), and, as such, has a perceptual grid through which he views the world—a pattern of actions and behaviors commonly understood by him. In other words, "Our own emic pattern of behavior heavily influences or controls our perceptions."[56] While we can always learn to make etic observations (such as the alien viewing people at the gas station), we carry our emic system around with us.

We can easily see how this relates to personalism. We might be tempted to simplify reality by saying that every person interprets and responds to the same events in the same way. For example, when a volcano erupts, there are not some who stand and ponder the nature of fire, and others who begin climbing the mountain to gather evidence as to what led to the eruption, and still others who sprint to safety. *Everyone* flees. Such instances encourage us to unify human responses to events. But at the same time,

---

In addition to our identification of units of human behavior and their distribution among other verbal and nonverbal units of behavior, emic units must be considered in terms of their variation. See Sapir, *Selected Writings*, 34.

55. Of course, observer perspectives come to the fore in Pike's use of particle, wave, and field.

56. Pike, "Stereoscopic Window," 148. "Each observer will also have some bias in terms of the behavior events most familiar to him—those which are emic in his own activity. These he tends to take as his point of departure, as his norms, so that cultural background may affect an etic report" (Pike, *Language*, 46).

there are innumerable events that are etically the same but elicit a variety of emic responses based on an individual's emic system. A burning house has the same physical characteristics (etic) to both the pedestrian and the fire fighter, but while the pedestrian's emic system tells him to run *from* the house, the fire fighter's emic system tells him to run *towards* it (provided he has arrived on the scene with his crew and equipment—though heroism may surface if one ignores the suggestions of one's emic system). People are unique, not just in their God-given interests and passions, but also in their experiences and perspective of the world. Pike eschewed reductionism in perception because he saw that it distorted or misperceived reality as it is experienced by *people*.

Interestingly, this emic-etic concept related not just to his understanding of people, but also to his understanding of God's revelation as a *personal* revelation:

> God has chosen to respect and work through cultural structures. . . . God chose to reveal Himself within a particular culture, through a particular culture, by means of events occurring in that particular culture. He made His message concrete by incarnating it in an emic structure, rather than by a series of lectures delivered by messengers aloof from and not a part of the revealing cultural medium.
> The "target" language in this communication leading to the written tradition in the Bible was a pair of languages of specific men—Hebrew followed later by Greek. The problems of imparting a message across an emic barrier lying between heaven's communication system—whatever that may be—and man's verbal system involved the restructuring of the initial message into the target emic system. The message restructured into human speech had to be cast into the molding limits of noun, verb, lexicon, and sentence structures—in short, into a Hebrew-Greek structural grid—while retaining its conceptual integrity and

the faithfulness of its intended impact.
. . . The choice of a particular language, culture, and finally the incarnation as a particular physical event cuts sharply across any attempt to treat the Christian essence as a mere abstract concept, as primarily an ethical code, or even as asystem of theology abstracted from everyday living. Christianity stands or falls as a living program, a way of life, concreted in the life of man by the life of God through the life of the concretely living Christ.[57]

God—the perfect translator between emic systems (indeed, the Creator of emic systems!)—revealed himself to culturally entrenched *persons*, in the *person* of Christ.

Altogether, we find personalism in the emic and etic concept on a number of levels. Firstly, it accounts for individually meaningful (and communally meaningful) behavior within a shared system of patterns and experiences. Secondly, it understands that each person (and each smaller community) is biased in some way when approaching and interpreting experience, and so we must account for that bias in our understanding of any event. If no one is a participant in *all* emic systems, then we should be wary of assigning unchecked and exhaustive objectivity to their actions, thoughts, and words. Thirdly, just as the emic and etic concept allows us to account for and strive to bridge the gaps between individual persons and people groups (geographic, cultural, social, and historical), opening the door for the requisite percipience lying at the base of communication, so also God's personal communication to us in history grounds revelation as an emically translatable message from heaven to earth by the person of Jesus

---

57. Pike, "Stereoscopic Window," 152–53, 154.

Christ.[58]

Form-Meaning Composites

We have already mentioned Pike's focus on form-meaning composites in relation to personalism, so only a few remarks are necessary here. The relationship between form and meaning stretches all the way back to Plato, who posited ideal forms in abstraction from contextually meaningful particulars with variation.[59] The danger of this practice within linguistics is that it creates an imaginary dualism. Form and meaning are never separated. There are no pure forms—such things would be meaningless.[60] Certainly, for

---

58. For a discussion of the term "born again" from an emic-etic perspective, see Kenneth L. Pike, "Prescription for Intellectuals," *Eternity* 8 (1957): 11, 44–45.

59. For a discussion of Platonic reductionism and its relation to a trinitarian view of language modeled on Pike's thought, see Poythress, *In the Beginning Was the Word*, 326–31. In explaining the delay in the study of discourse by American linguists, Pike shows that he was aware of the trail of debris left by Plato's thought. It was Plato, after all, "who predicated philosophy on a 'reality' composed of thought-features abstracted from source-particulars, from things-as-directly-known. Above all, the problem [of a delayed study of discourse] may have arisen from separating the things-in-themselves (or abstract features of things, situations, or events) from the reality of *person*—person as observer, person as reality, person as investing every 'thing-in-itself' with an *observer relation* as its discoverer, its watcher, or its deducer" (Kenneth L. Pike, *Tagmemics, Discourse, and Verbal Art* [Michigan Studies in the Humanities 3 [Ann Arbor, MI: University of Michigan Press, 1981], 3).

60. Bloomfield notes that "the study of language can be conducted without special assumptions only so long as we pay no attention to the meaning of what is spoken. This phase of language study is known as *phonetics*." Shortly thereafter he asserts, "Since we can recognize the distinctive features of an utterance only when we know the meaning, we cannot identify them on the plane of pure phonetics" (Leonard Bloomfield, *Language* [Chicago: University of Chicago Press, 1984], 75, 77). He also adds that we all operate

the sake of analysis we can temporarily talk about form and meaning *as if* they were separate. And Pike would not disagree here.[61] He would, however, protest that emic units of language can never really be treated this way in the world.

> We try very hard to avoid studying form by itself or meaning by itself. We deal with them both together. We can never discuss either of them unless, lurking somewhere in the background, is the other. Even when a person tries to talk about the isolated forms of words, he knows that they are meaningful—or he knows that somebody knows that they are meaningful—or he is not handling language. Similarly, if a person tries to make a classification of isolated possible meanings, he is likely to end up without helpful results unless somehow these meanings arise from words which are tied into some language system or systems of cultural behavior.[62]

Theoretical dichotomies that dissolve in the context

---

on the fundamental assumption "that each linguistic form has a constant and specific meaning" (ibid., 145). In practical terms, we never isolate a form from its meaning; nor do we receive a meaning without a form. "The child, for the sake of learning, must learn both meaning and sound. He must learn both the meaning of the word 'dog' and how the word sounds. How will he learn the meaning of a particular word or sentence unless he can identify its distinct sounds that distinguish that word from all the other words and sentences with quite different meanings? The sound has to be there all the time to access meaning. And conversely, the meaning has to be there for the sound to make any difference. . . . Language . . . is never pure meaning or pure sound. The sound (or a writing system or a sign language) must identify the meanings. And the meanings make the sounds significant" (Poythress, *In the Beginning Was the Word*, 263–64).

61. "For convenience, one may on occasion discuss the form and meaning aspects *as if* they were separate, while taking pains to indicate that such an expedient is a distortion which must be corrected at proper intervals and in the relevant places in the discussion" (Pike, *Language*, 63).

62. Pike, *Linguistic Concepts*, 16–17.

of real human behavior are useless, but the problem runs deeper than practicality.

When we maintain a gap between form and meaning, not only do we distort the nature of language and fail to perceive reality as it is, but we also reduce it or oversimplify it so as to make it essentially *im*personal, for what person could ever value or even acknowledge a meaningless linguistic form? And who could arrive at an understanding of formless meaning? Perhaps this is why Pike was so vigilant in guarding against it. It can be easy to see the world as a kaleidoscope of vapid forms, with nothing more than functional significance in relation to a physical environment. Or, to narrow the plane, it can be easy to treat aspects of language impersonally and reductionistically, such as how Chomsky spoke of grammar theory as "completely formal and non-semantic."[63] The trouble is that reductions of this nature exclude *people* from the process of inquiry, and this inevitably leads to deception.[64] A theorist who denies

---

63. Noam Chomsky, *Syntactic Structures* (The Hague: Mouton, 1957), 93. According to Pike, Chomsky "insists that grammatical structure be identified 'independently of any semantic consideration,' since he affirms that 'those who regard semantics as providing the basis, in some sense, for grammar' have implicit to this view the claim that 'there are semantic absolutes, identifiable in noises independently of the grammatical structure assigned to them.' . . . I affirm the necessity of dealing with form and meaning at the same time, to some degree, and deny the necessity of treating semantic elements as absolutes independent of all lexical and grammatical data" (Pike, *Language*, 149).

64. Notice that even the serpent in the Garden of Eden avoided this conundrum. He knew that language is tied to people—indeed, that all of reality is tied to people. Rather than taking an impersonal approach and questioning Eve on the semantics of God's expression, rather than introduce the possibility of lexical ambiguity, he put forward the lie that God had performed an act of personal deception ("For God knows that when you eat of it . . .").

his own personal involvement in theorizing is a wizard behind the curtain. Reality cannot be adequately analyzed or interpreted using a methodology that ignores the truth that at all times and places it is *people* who are doing the analyzing and interpreting; and because people are limited in their perception, data uncovered by such methodologies are skewed and other important disciplines are left unconsidered. So, Pike is perfectly justified in claiming that our major problem throughout history is "separating the things-in-themselves (or abstract features of things, situations, or events) from the reality of *person*—person as observer, person as reality, person as investing every 'thing-in-itself' with an *observer relation* as its discoverer, its watcher, or its deducer."[65]

A form-meaning composite, then, is more than a linguist's analytical tool; it reflects a commitment to the personal nature of reality as having always and at every point forms bound up with meaning, both of which are necessary for personal use and interpretation, that is, human behavior.

Summary

Acknowledging the personalism in the above aspects of Pike's thought helps us to understand his assumptions in the study of language and the rest of human behavior. To conclude Part 1 of this article, we can say that each of the manifestations of personalism we discussed—language as a phase of human behavior, the emic and etic perspectives, and form-meaning composites—leaves room for the personal nature of reality as ultimately mysterious, since it

---

65. Pike, *Tagmemics, Discourse, and Verbal Art*, 3.

is grounded in the triune person of God. Tying language to all of human behavior only underscores the ridiculousness of noetic exhaustion; recognizing that we cannot be emic participants in every context reflects the bounds of our experiential limitations, and thus of our etic perception of mystery for the vast number of contexts *outside* of our own emic system; and form-meaning composites point to the assumption that "both physical form and mental, meaningful, interactional thought are needed for living as persons."[66]

That Pike's thought is riddled with personalism, then, is clear enough. Yet, this alone does not account for the structure of his thought as triadic.[67] We cannot say that a focus on persons leads to a trinitarian methodology, for that would run into the problems of natural theology. Bavinck proclaims, "Over against all those who want to base the doctrine of the Trinity on rational grounds, we must undoubtedly maintain that we owe our knowledge of this doctrine solely to God's special revelation. Scripture alone is the final ground for the doctrine of the Trinity."[68] Warfield confirms,

> The doctrine of the Trinity is purely a revealed doctrine. That is to say, it embodies a truth which has never been discovered, and is indiscoverable, by natural reason. With all his searching, man has not been able to find out for himself

---

66. Kenneth L. Pike, "Person Beyond Logic in Language, Life, and Philosophy," in *The Eighteenth LACUS Forum 1991* (ed. Ruth Brend; Lake Bluff, Ill.: Linguistic Association of Canada and the United States, 1992), 25.

67. Here we are thinking particularly of his use of triads, as well as his focus on interlocking hierarchies and observer perspectives, each of which has ties to the perichoresis of the Godhead.

68. Bavinck, *Reformed Dogmatics*, 2:329.

the deepest things of God. Accordingly, ethnic thought has never attained a Trinitarian conception of God, nor does any ethnic religion present in its representations of the Divine Being any analogy to the doctrine of the Trinity.[69]

So, if Pike's personalism did not lead directly to his trinitarian approach, then what did? That is the question we will answer in Part 2.

---

69. B. B. Warfield, *Biblical and Theological Studies*, ed. Samuel G. Craig (Phillipsburg, NJ: Presbyterian & Reformed, 1968), 22.

Where Person Meets Word Part 2
The Convergence of Personalism and Scripture in the Language Theory of Kenneth L. Pike

Because the Trinity plays a principal role in Reformed theology, we must always be asking ourselves how it shapes our understanding of human behavior in general, and of theology in particular. Knowing this, Van Til was adamant that the self-contained ontological Trinity be our interpretative principle everywhere; that it be the basis of all human experience and knowledge.[1]

A seemingly endless queue, both inside and outside the Reformed tradition, has already outlined the implications of this for theology proper, and for anthropology—with Van Til close to the forefront. But the Reformed tradition in particular continues to benefit from studying the relationship between language and the Trinity. As such, the work of Kenneth L. Pike provides a rich reservoir of insight from which we might draw in learning more about how we image the triune God in our communicative behavior. And by studying what contributed to the development of Pike's trinitarian thought, we not only validate Van Til's

---

1. See Van Til, *Introduction to Systematic Theology: Prolegomena and the Doctrines of Revelation, Scripture, and God*, 2nd ed., ed. William Edgar (Phillipsburg, NJ: P&R Publishing, 2007), 30, 59; *The Defense of the Faith*, 4th ed., ed. K. Scott Oliphint (Phillipsburg, NJ: P&R Publishing, 2008), 100, 227–28, 236, and 241. This means that our experience and knowledge are grounded in the equal ultimacy of the one and many, and the perichoretic relationship of the persons in the Godhead. See Van Til, *Introduction to Systematic Theology*, 58–59; *Defense of the Faith*, 47–50.

teaching on the pivotal place of the Trinity in all human experience and thought; we also learn more about how we can understand the Trinity in relation to general revelation.

In Part 1 of this article, after briefly discussing the trinitarian associations of Kenneth L. Pike's language theory, we examined the personalism underlying it. We noted that Pike's brand of personalism, not to be confused with the broader personalism movement, was a response to general revelation.[2] In considering particular manifestations of personalism in Pike's work—language as a phase of human behavior, the emic and etic perspectives, and form-meaning composites—we found that he desired to leave room for the personal nature of reality as ultimately mysterious, since it is grounded in the triune person of God.

However, this in itself cannot explain Pike's trinitarian approach to language, for general revelation, as Bavinck and Warfield remind us, does not include the trinitarian God of redemption. Something else must have converged with Pike's personalism to lead him to his trinitarian approach. This something is none other than the Word of God—hence the title of the article: "Where Person Meets Word."

In Part 1, we introduced the thesis that the trinitarian

---

2. As noted in Part 1, Van Til was clear in articulating the theological chasm between "Boston personalism" and what he called "orthodox personalism." Proponents of Boston personalism (Bowne and Brightman) ran into serious trouble because they sought to make finite personality the "fulcrum for the operations of the laws of thought. But finite personality can be thought of intelligently only on the presupposition of the idea of the self-intelligent God. And on the basis of the idea of this God alone is it possible to avoid both rationalism and irrationalism, both determinism and pure contingency, or a combination of them." Van Til, "Boston Personalism" (lecture delivered at Boston University School of Theology, March 6, 1956), 55–56.

structure of Pike's theory is not only prescriptive for our thinking about language (and all purposive behavior); it was a destination he was bound to arrive at because personalism (general revelation) and Scripture (special revelation) converge in the Trinity. Now in Part 2, we pick up with Pike's attention to Scripture and his accompanying theological convictions. We then link this to his understanding of the *imago Dei*, and end with implications for linguistics and applications to our current understanding of general revelation.

Steeped in the Scriptures

From the moment of his birth, Kenneth Pike was steeped in the Scriptures and surrounded by the Christian faith. When he was a child, his mother sang hymns to him and his siblings, such as "The Ninety and Nine that Safely Lay in the Shelter of the Fold." Nearly every day, his father read a passage of Scripture to the family, discussed it with them, and then prayed.[3] Perhaps it was this upbringing that fostered his decision to serve in missions. While attending Gordon College of Theology and Missions (now Gordon College), he became zealous for the spread of the Gospel in China with Hudson Taylor's Chinese Inland Mission (CIM). With considerable struggle, he began studying Mandarin with CIM after his studies at Gordon, and was convinced of God's use of him in China, which crushed him all the more when CIM told him that they could not use him.

Shortly after this disappointment, Pike returned to

---

3. Eunice V. Pike, *Ken Pike: Scholar and Christian* (Dallas, TX: Summer Institute of Linguistics, 1981), 7.

Gordon College to bolster his knowledge of Greek, and there he learned from a student about a newly founded program seeking to prepare students for Bible translation. It was called "Camp Wycliffe." In June of 1935, he hitchhiked from Connecticut to Arkansas to attend the camp, paying a whopping $6 a month for room and board.

The goal of Camp Wycliffe (which would later become the Summer Institute of Linguistics), according to its founders, W. Cameron Townsend and Leonard L. Legters, was to train students in linguistics and pioneer living in order to meet the need of Bible translation in Central and South America, a region that was home to many unknown and unwritten languages and hence unreachable by most mission efforts. The students were to be trained in linguistics, travel to a remote area, learn the language of a particular people, and translate the New Testament for them. This was the segue into Pike's long and vibrant relationship with the Mixtec speaking people of Mesoamerica.

Among the Mixtecs, Pike was not simply learning a new language and growing close to the inhabitants; he was immersed in the Scriptures, telling Bible stories to natives over late-night camp fires, and eventually enlisting their help to translate those stories into Mixtec. Translation itself will bring anyone more intimate knowledge of Scripture, but for Pike, his knowledge of Scripture informed his job of translation from two fronts. On the one side, he was becoming intimately familiar with the words of Scripture by translating the emic expression of truth in first century biblical culture to a corresponding emic expression in twentieth century Mixtec culture, being careful that the expression maintained integrity to the original. On the other side, his background knowledge of Scripture was informing his understanding of translation itself. In 1957, long after he had served the Mixtec people, he reflected on translation as it relates to the message of God's Word:

> The evangelical does not view the Christianizing task as merely a cultural translation. He sees it in part as a cultural task plus an infusion of supernatural power in the individual life. A variety of Christianity which attempts the cultural phases of the task without reliance upon the power emanating from the crucifixion and resurrection of Christ as trustworthy historical events would impress the evangelical as failing to provide the tribes people with the source of supernatural power which not only leads to present cultural values, such as kindness, but also gives eternal life.[4]

In other words, his knowledge of the message of Scripture—the transformative power of the resurrected Christ—was brought to bear on his approach to translation. He was not simply learning more about Scripture by translation; he was learning more about translation by studying and implementing Scripture.

As he began to publish more regularly, it became apparent that his mind was steeped in Scripture and his profession was profoundly shaped by it. His explicitly theological writings ranged from finding God's direction in one's own life—a topic on which he was particularly qualified to speak, given his own disappointments with the CIM—to advice for intellectuals;[5] from biblical exposition to linguistic critiques grounded in the presupposition of the truth of Scripture.[6] We cannot examine all of the manifestations

---

4. Pike, "Language and Life 3: A Training Device for Translation Theory and Practice," *Bibliotheca Sacra* 114, no. 456 (October 1957): 362.

5. "God's Guidance and Your Life's Work," *His* 7, no. 1 (1947): 19–28; "Prescription for Intellectuals," *Eternity* 8 (August 1957): 11, 44–45.

6. "Living on Manna," *The Sunday School Times*, May 1, 1948, 3–4; "Why I

of Pike's Scriptural knowledge throughout his career, but we can focus on a few trends: the covenantal obligations of man, a rejection of autonomy, and the *imago dei*. The latter has particular relevance for Pike's view of language, and may be the linchpin connecting his personalism to a Trinitarian philosophy of human behavior.

The covenantal obligations of man. Pike never shied away from claiming that man was a creature in covenant with his Creator, as is evident in statements such as,

> *God holds men responsible on a spiritual plane for truth which they know on a social plane.* If in a particular culture people respond to values of right and wrong in respect to relationships between men, God will hold them responsible for the application of that same knowledge in the relationship between God and man. The social light which man has is spiritual light by cultural analogy.[7]

Why are men held responsible to God for their interpersonal behavior? Because Romans 1:20 avers that all men know God and are in relationship with him—a covenantal relationship with implications for all of life.[8] This relationship is their very livelihood; claiming

---

Believe in God," *His* 18, no. 2 (November 1957): 3–7, 32–33; "Cause and Effect in the Christian Life," *His* 20, no. 1 (1959): 32–34; "Language," in *Christ and the Modern Mind*, ed. Robert W. Smith (Downers Grove, IL: InterVarsity Press, 1972), 59–67; "The Linguist and Axioms Concerning the Language of Scripture," *Journal of the American Scientific Affiliation* 26, no. 2 (June 1974): 47–51; "The Need for the Rejection of Autonomy in Linguistics," in *The Eleventh LACUS Forum*, ed. Robert A. Hall, Jr. (S. Columbia: Hornbeam, 1985), 35–53.

7. Pike, "God's Guidance and Your Life Work," 27.

8. "Because of this Scriptural statement [Rom. 1:20], . . . we must conclude that man is morally responsible for seeing in nature that there is a God." Pike, "Why I Believe in God," 7.

independence is tantamount to a death wish. This, for Pike, is recorded in the early pages of Genesis. "In the garden of Eden (Gen 3:5) the serpent said to the woman, 'You will be like God'—that is, independent. . . . Why shouldn't a person want to be independent? Because if a person succeeds in becoming independent, he dies. . . . isolation is the road to hell."[9] Sure enough, Adam and Eve's decision to act independently of God led directly to their demise.

Of course, this was prefatory to a history of grace—a history in which we work out our dependence through our God-given free will, in accordance with special revelation.[10] In Pike's words, "we are not to be robots, incapable of—or afraid of—taking initiative. We are to be free to think and act within the general orders and principles of character revealed in the Word and impressed on our consciences by the Holy Spirit."[11]

Continuing in this covenantal history, man has moral obligations before his maker, not the least of which is his moral use of language. Pike was quick to point out that "there is a moral dimension to rhetoric. 'Mere' rhetoric can be immoral. It prostitutes form, seeks contact with elegant words for the body's sake, instead of using words to reproduce one's own moral image as God did in the

---

9. Pike, "The Sin of Independence," *His* 18, no. 8 (May 1958): 6, 7.

10. This is not to say that our will exhaustively free, and that it trumps God's own plan for us. God is utterly sovereign, but human decisions are still significant. William Edgar calls this the "double truth." Thus, we can affirm with the Westminster Confession of Faith that God "is not the instigator of sin, nor does he violate the creatures he has made. Rather than interfering with their decision-making, he *establishes* a world in which secondary causes are significant." William Edgar, *A Transforming Vision: The Lord's Prayer as a Lens for Life* (Ross-shire, Scotland: Christian Focus, 2014), 30.

11. Pike, "Man or Robot," *Eternity* 15, no. 2 (February 1964): 46.

beginning with the Word."[12] In contrast to mere rhetoric and a deceptive use of metaphor is our creative use of metaphorical language in order to join in the "struggle to build bridges over which to lead someone else to truth."[13] In this holy calling—the moral pursuit and use of language for the sake of truth—we image the God who speaks.

Yet, language is not the only sphere of our moral responsibility as covenantal creatures; we are called to *think* in a way that is obedient to God's revelation. One's choice of epistemology "is a moral choice."[14] How we think, how we attain *wisdom*, is addressed directly by God's Word: "Fear of the Lord is the beginning—and the basic assumption—of wisdom, in that it sets up the only ultimately adequate epistemological starting point."[15] It is by faith that we come to know God and are truly known. It is by faith that we acquire true wisdom. He wrote with conviction, "By *faith*—not by argument—I know that the worlds are framed by the Word of God. By *faith*—not by apologetics—I know that these Scriptures are the Word of God. By *faith*—not by intellectual proof—I know that God, a Person who knows me by name, exists."[16] This in and of itself is the greatest threat to the fortress of impersonal academia. That our morals are governed by God might be granted, but our knowledge?

To drive this point home, Pike often referred to the story of Nicodemus (John 3). Why could Nicodemus not

---

12. Pike, "Morals and Metaphor," *Interchange* 12 (1972): 228.

13. Ibid., 231.

14. Pike, "Why I Believe in God," 7.

15. Ibid.

16. Ibid., 33.

understand Jesus' message ("unless one is born of water and the Spirit, he cannot enter the kingdom of God")? Because, to use previous terminology, he needed an emic system transplant.

As a leading scholar of his culture, he already had available and had absorbed the understanding of a total view of the world [his emic system]. He was elaborately structured in the intellectual sphere. He had a total world view—a view which included a pigeon hole for the possibility of help from God—with adequate illustrations of the manner, reason, and source from which help came. His intellectual system was so tightly and coherently structured, furthermore, that it could not easily bend to accommodate contradictory or inconsistent elements [such as Jesus' claim to divinity, which flew in the face of his rigid, monotheistic assumptions].[17]

Nicodemus' perceptual grid needed to be built from scratch. Jesus told him, in effect,

> You will have to abandon your total thought system and begin to build it all over again. You will have to accept my goodness and power as primary data, and start from there. Like a baby coming into the new world, you will have to learn to live with these facts before you can understand their source or reason. You must learn to accept the revolution this makes in your whole spiritual life without being able at the moment to understand its source any more than the sailor understands the source of the wind that moves his sails.[18]

The point, however, is not that Nicodemus had made

---

17. Pike, "Language and Life 1: A Stereoscopic Window on the World," *Bibliotheca Sacra* 114, no. 454 (April 1957): 155.

18. Ibid., 156.

the wrong *intellectual* decision in developing his current emic system—his Jewish scholarly view of the world; the problem was that he made the wrong *moral* decision in adopting an emic system that was not prescribed by God's Word. What he needed was a view of the world upheld by the Word of God's power (Heb. 1:3). It was only within this emic system that Nicodemus could understand Jesus' words. Pike concluded here and elsewhere that "the intellectual needs to be told that his system as a whole must be replaced—that he must be born again. Christianity is not an accretion; it is not something added. It is a *new* total outlook which is satisfied with nothing less than penetration to the farthest corners of the mind and the understanding."[19]

This is but a sampling of the work that shows Pike's writing is riddled with the covenantal obligations of God—both linguistic and non-linguistic.

A rejection of autonomy.[20] In the middle of his career, we find that Pike grew more acutely aware of the prevalence of autonomous thought in linguistics—a problem tied to man's futile claim of independence. This awareness was

---

19. Pike, "Prescription for Intellectuals," 45.

20. We should note at the outset that Pike's rejection of autonomy, though mostly in line with Van Til's concept, does not carry the presuppositional weight of that concept as far as it must go. Presuppositions affect *all* of life, so we find ourselves in disagreement with him when he says, "an excessive commitment to a theological presupposition that demands that the nature of God always be explicitly present in every scientific model (that is, which denies to the non-Christian or to the non-theist the capacity to make any statement of true fact) would deny to science, in this extreme instance, the possibility of recognizing any truth." Pike, "Language," in *Christ and the Modern Mind*, ed. Robert W. Smith (Downers Grove, IL: InterVarsity Press, 1972), 66. With Van Til, we would affirm that there are no brute facts and even those things which the non-Christian thinks he knows to be true are false if the God who stands behind them is rejected.

drawn from the text of Scripture rather than from the irritation of a mystic. Reflecting on Jeremiah 17:7–8, he remarks, "the only tree which can bear fruit is one that seeks with its roots for water and sustenance outside itself. Similarly the only man who can bear fruit is one who trusts in God and looks to Him for character."[21] We have already discussed man's moral obligations in covenant with God, and here we encounter the very foundation for morally good actions: it is not ritualistic vigilance or elitism; it is faith and trust in the God of Scripture—abandoning all hope in self-attained goals and recognizing that at every point in his behavior man is leaning on God, and he would shatter on the existential ground if God took a step to the side.

Perhaps the most poignant expression of his rejection of autonomy is, aptly titled, "The Need for Rejection of Autonomy in Linguistics."[22] Here, Pike is programmatic in his rejection, beginning with a Van Tillian affirmation: "all items in the universe are eventually related by being inside that universe."[23] The interrelation of all things

---

21. Pike, "The Sin of Independence," 6.

22. Pike, "The Need for Rejection of Autonomy in Linguistics," in *The Eleventh LACUS Forum 1984*, ed. Robert A. Hall (Columbia, S.C.: Hornbeam Press, 1985), 35–53.

23. Ibid., 36. Cf. Van Til's statements: "Unless the plan and therewith the interpretation of thought of God be back of all facts in their relations to all other facts, no idea, no hypothesis that the human mind could make with respect to them, would have any application to them." Van Til, *Defense of the Faith*, 279. Perhaps most Attacking non-Christian epistemology, Van Til writes, "All the facts of the phenomenal world are incomprehensible to me precisely because they are what they are by virtue of the voluntary action of the will of God with respect to them. They are what they are, they occupy place in the scheme of things spatio-temporal, because God by his plan and by the execution of his plan in the works of creation and providence makes

in the universe exposes the audacity of claiming that we have exhaustive knowledge in any one area, for to know *anything* exhaustively in such a universe is to know *everything* exhaustively. The independence or self-sufficiency of any discipline, therefore, is a pretension. Even in the attempt to comprehensively describe a linguistic unit, we fall short because we are required to isolate it in order to pretend that we can arrive at holistic description.[24] This isolation, though serving our desire to be independent (which, as Pike said before, is a death wish), distorts the data because not only does it ignore its variation, but it also ignores the larger pattern in which the linguistic unit appears. "Explanation without pattern is eventually not explanation, as I see it. And description, at its best, is successive embedding patterns of something."[25]

An example might serve us well here. The sentence, "Christ walked across the sea to his disciples," is a simple one. What if we were to pick out a linguistic unit such as the verb *walked* and attempt to describe it exhaustively? There would be at least two layers to this task: (1) we would need to discuss the unit "on its own," in terms of its semantic identity, variation, and distribution, and also its lexical components (root and verbal suffix), and its phonological components (tone and stress). "Easy enough," we might think. (2) We

---

them what they are." Van Til, *Introduction to Systematic Theology*, 293. Capturing the idea eloquently for those who would isolate facts from their function in a comprehensive system, he would write in *Common Grace and the Gospel*, "a fact *is* its function" (115).

24. This means that we treat the linguistic unit apart from its variation and its distribution (its instantiations and associations) in order to manage it with a finite mind.

25. Pike, "The Need for Rejection of Autonomy in Linguistics," 37.

would need to look at its relation in each of those areas to the phrase in which it occurred ("Jesus walked"), then the total clause, then the paragraph, then the larger discourse, then the book as a whole, John's other writings in the NT, the NT as a whole, the entire Bible, which was written by men of the first century, other literature of the first century, related socio-cultural behaviors of the time, related socio-cultural behaviors of our time, the relation of the physical environment to those behaviors, the nature of the physical environment, etc. For those who want to use language in dependence on a God who knows all of these contexts and relationships exhaustively, there is little problem. We can focus on a particular context and trust that God will work through us (particulars) to establish and proclaim his truth (universal). But for those who seek to master a linguistic unit, to pretend that exhaustive description is possible, language is a labyrinth.

Given that exhaustive description of linguistic units, semantics, syntax, and any other aspect of verbal or non-verbal communication is an exercise in futility, how are we to function in the world of language? Do we throw our hands up and resign ourselves to not know anything at all—a defeated relativism? Certainly not! Linguistic inquiry must simply be carried out in awareness of the interrelation of linguistic units with the rest of human behavior, and with that human behavior finding coherence and meaning in God himself. Autonomy at every level, then, must be rejected. We must, instead, search for a method of linguistic inquiry that allows for the interrelation of every aspect of communicative behavior—and it is in tagmemics that Pike believes the foundation can be laid.

Each area of tagmemic theory accommodates this. For example, in relation to the observer perspectives (particle, wave, and field),

> we need particles for rules to apply to; patterns for particles and rules to fit into; patterns of patterns for a field view which can encompass all three complementary perspectives.
> We need, then, to reject the autonomy of any single perspective of particle, wave, or field (or any autonomous static, dynamic, or relational views. We reject, too, the autonomy of mere lists, mere rules, or mere features in a system). Instead we seek a set of simultaneous or complementary approaches. I attempt to maintain such complementarity, here, by applying particle, wave, and field perspectives, rather than approaching language or behavior through any one exclusive point of view. . . . Tagmemics insists that no unit can be understood outside of several difference kinds of simultaneous contexts.[26]

Pike's comments do not stop at the need for complementary observer perspectives in the goal of avoiding autonomous linguistic methodology. He probes more deeply, to the level of hierarchy, affirming that "inclusion in a part-whole hierarchy does not allow the autonomy of included parts";[27] nor does any of the linguistic hierarchies (grammar, phonology, and reference) function in isolation.

> An attempt to give autonomy to phonology . . . disintegrates into undefinable noises—since the relevance and boundaries of sounds depend on their occurrence, also, in lexical and grammatical hierarchical units. . . . There are phonological prerequisites to grammatical analysis or to the referential analysis of data. Words do not exist, as relevant to speech communication, except as parts of conversations, monologues, sentences, clauses, phrases. . . . Paraphrases

---

26. Ibid., 38, 39.

27. Ibid., 40.

allow the same basic content to be told in various ways. The series of events of a story, for example, can be told, in English, in reverse order, without destroying the report of the chronological sequence of those events. (One can say, for example, either 'John came home and at supper' or 'John ate supper after he came home.' The changes of clause order, and from one to two sentences, do not alter the facts of the event. The difference in focus or emphasis which are thereby attained—themselves a kind of meaning— are in tagmemics attributed to the grammatical form; the retained content is attributed to the referential structure.) On the other hand, two words may be homophonous, but referentially distinct (as are 'sea' and 'see').[28]

In addition to the rejection of the autonomy of units within hierarchies, Pike rejects the autonomy of form or meaning, a background principle for his *form-meaning composites*.[29] He rejects, narrowly, the autonomy of a constituent in a particular structure, and, broadly, the autonomy of a unit of cultural behavior.[30] In fact, he rejects

---

28. Ibid., 41–42.

29. "If matter is separated from meaning (or from relevance to an observer) an autonomy is postulated which tagmemics rejects. . . . As distinct from any analytical approach which wishes first to find and describe meanings, and then to find and describe their physical forms (with 'form' used in a physical sense), tagmemics requires that both in empirical research in natural languages and in theorizing about them, the discovery of language structures and the description of their meanings must be in part simultaneous. Word forms are relevant because of their emic relation to meanings. Meanings are emically present only if they are manifested in physical forms" (ibid., 44).

30. "Any item occurs within a slot, or position, in a larger unit which acts as part of some hierarchical context of that smaller unit, and which is of immediate relevance to it. This includes the relation of a part to the next highest layer of the immediate whole which contains it. A subject is part of

the autonomy of everything except for God: "I am not autonomous. Things are not autonomous. Ideas are not autonomous. The universe is not autonomous. Linguistics is not autonomous. We are hooked—together."[31]

The imago dei. The last trend manifesting Pike's scriptural knowledge is perhaps the linchpin binding his personalism to the Trinity. The image of God in man, for the Christian, sets up a logical series of connections—a breadcrumb trail to the Trinity.

The first in that series of connections is the truth that man is made in God's image. Pike was aware of this on multiple levels—intellectually, emotionally, and linguistically. Intellectually, man is made in the image of God in terms of his scholarly pursuits and "taxonomic" tendencies (Adam's naming of the animals is an analog of God's naming other parts of creation). "God was also a 'taxonomist' (one who names things and makes scientific classifications), the Model for one to become a scholar-linguist! Did God fail to pass on this characteristic, in spite of his Eden-orders for man to name things? Certainly not. We are called to be—amongst other things—scholars."[32] However, Pike is also quick to caution us about intellectual autonomy, stating that "the chief contamination of

---

a clause. A clause is part of a sentence. A sentence is part of a conversation, or narrative, or pattern of thought" (ibid., 46).

"Any unit in culture will have some purpose in that culture, or relevance to it. Any object under observation, or in imagination, will be relevant—from the viewpoint of the observer—to his understanding of the pattern of the world of things or thought" (ibid., 47).

31. Ibid., 49.

32. Pike, "Intellectual Initiative: The Image of God," *The Banner*, November 30, 1979, 10.

mental activity . . . comes . . . from a pervasive wish to be epistemologically 'independent'—without dependence on the Creator to spell out the limits of independence in belief, or in morals, or in academic premises."[33] So while part of the image of God in man is his intellectual pursuits, he often mars that image in trying to think and reason apart from reliance on God and his revelation in Scripture.

We are also made in the image of God emotionally. If Jesus' character included his emotional life, and his emotional life was reflective of his heavenly Father, then it makes sense to conclude that,

> God created us, including our emotional life . . . in his own image; and that, therefore, we need to take the emotional life of God seriously. God is *not* an unchanged unchanging Person in the sense of being a stolid, placid, untouched, non-sad, non-joyful, non-angry type unaffected by what He sees, hears, knows, anticipates, or experiences.[34]

We may be tempted to think at times that God's immutability means that he is incapable of feeling, but "a God who is incapable of feeling is a philosophical abstraction, not the God of the Bible."[35] Indeed, the God of the Bible feels: "from before the foundation of the earth, He was a Person; we are created in His image as persons; and we hurt as He hurt when He made us, knowing that we

---

33. Ibid.

34. Pike, "Emotion in God, and Its Image in Us," *The Banner*, November 23, 1979, 4–5.

35. Norman Anderson, quoted in Pike, "Emotion in God," 5. Scripture is clear that God's emotional expressions are no threat to his impassibility. For a discussion of this from the Reformed perspective, see Frame, *The Doctrine of God*, 608–611.

would hurt too."[36]

The third aspect of the image of God is most critical for our purposes: the use of language.[37] Man images God in his communicative behavior, as that behavior is linked to morality and to creative expression.[38] For example, in our use of metaphors, we image the God who chooses to use metaphors in his revelation, such as in John 1:1.

We are created in His image of creativity. We create metaphors because He created them:

> In the beginning was the Word—note the linguistic metaphor from John 1. Why an inspired linguistic metaphor? Because there, perhaps, above all else directly accessible to science, we can study one characteristic in which we are in the image of God—we can *talk*. And in the beginning was *the One who*

---

36. Pike, "Emotion in God, and Its Image in Us," 5.

37. Others in the Reformed tradition, such as Richard Gaffin, have pointed out language as part of the *imago dei* as well: "As our being itself is derived from God (we exist because he exists), and as our knowledge is an analogue of his knowledge (we know because he knows), so, too, our capacity for language and other forms of communication is derivative of his. We speak because God speaks, because he is a speaking God; that is his nature and so, derivatively, it is ours. In other words, man in his linguistic functions, as in all he is and does, is to be understood as the creature who is the image and likeness of God (Gen 1:26). In fact, should we not say that especially in his language man reflects the divine image he is?" Richard B. Gaffin Jr., "Speech and the Image of God: Biblical Reflections on Language and Its Uses," in *The Pattern of Sound Doctrine: Systematic Theology at the Westminster Seminaries*, ed. David Van Drunen (Phillipsburg, NJ: P&R Publishing, 2004), 182–83.

38. Pike makes a connection between language, thought, and morality: "man through his spoken or thought language can set up alternative choices in hypotheses and choose between them. Through language much of his daily judgment operates; and because of language, a set of ideals, values, morals, and views of right and wrong can be part of him. Judgment of a high type requires such a moral base, and man's moral base requires language." Pike, "Man or Robot," 9.

could talk! Not just a set of rays of energy ready for a big bang; not a pantheistic sum of non-focused non-personal elements; not a vague spirit of impersonal goodness; but the Personal-One-with-Language; One who spoke and said, 'Let us make man in our image'—to use language with creative power, bursting forth in poem, in song, in metaphor.[39]

Linguistic creativity is an *imaging* behavior. But creativity is not the only aspect of language that reveals it as part of the *imago dei*. We can also take internal counsel, a linguistic behavior analogous to that which God himself employs in Genesis 1:26.[40] So, part of the image of God "includes the

---

39. Pike, "Morals and Metaphor," 231.

40. Note the use of the Hebrew cohortative. Waltke outlines the six options we have for interpreting it: (1) the plural is a remnant of ANE myth in which God is addressing other gods. This is untenable given that the Pentateuch opposes polytheism at every corner. (2) The plural is directed towards a host of previously made creatures (this still ends up relying on polytheistic tendencies that do not comport with the Genesis account). (3) The plural is honorific, like the form elohim, but Waltke notes that this form is elsewhere attested by nouns, not pronouns. (4) The plural is, in Gesenius's language, "a plural of self-deliberation," though no other instance supports this view. (5) The plural is a reference to the Trinity. This view would be supported by later NT texts, even though Waltke argues that this violates the boundaries of grammatico-historical interpretation. (6) The plural refers to the heavenly court that surrounds God's throne. See Bruce K. Waltke, *An Old Testament Theology: A Canonical and Thematic Approach* (Grand Rapids, MI: Zondervan, 2007), 212–13. I argue for interpreting the form as an instance of God's inter-trinitarian dialogue (perhaps better, "trialogue") because, aside from the fact that a speaking God would necessitate inner plurality, the only other truly viable option is that God is addressing his heavenly court. But I find this view wanting on a number of levels. Why would God be addressing other creatures in a creative action that is attributed solely to his power? He certainly is not looking for approval or input from contingent beings. Is he simply announcing what he is doing? This would be a strange precedent, given the other grammatical structures employed to bring in other aspects of creation. Yet, it would make perfect sense if God chose to employ this particular grammatical structure exclusively in the creation of man because he was creating a being who would image himself in personal relations.

fact that man is verbal, and can talk to himself. His ability to talk to himself, to argue with himself, to propose lines of activity, tentatively, before embarking upon them, is a crucial part of his selfhood. Without it he would not be man."[41]

Yet, perhaps the kernel of our linguistic imaging is not internal counsel but external relationships—both with other humans and with the triune God.[42] Since man's communication system is analogous on some level with God's, and because this allows for divine-human communication, so the linguistic patchwork of the post-Babel world is not averse to unity via translation. We relate to others via communicative behavior because God relates to himself in this way—and, what's more, from the very founding of creation he committed himself to working within the strictures of creaturely communication.[43] What

---

This would certainly pair nicely with Gen. 2:18. Adam is not "lonely." God is not working out divine psychoanalysis. Rather, God knows that it would be "good" for Adam to commune with other creatures equal with himself because that is what God does, and God is wholly good.

41. Pike, "Language and Self Image," in *The Scientist and Ethical Decision*, ed. Charles Hatfield (Downers Grove, IL: InterVarsity Press, 1973), 69.

42 "As part of the result of man's being created in the image of God, the communication system of God and that of man are not disjoint. The implication here is that by creation God has made man's language sufficiently like his own internal communication system, whatever that may be, that man's is a pale reflection of his own and allows talk across the barrier in both directions." Pike, "The Linguist and Axioms Concerning the Language of Scripture," *Journal of the American Scientific Affiliation* 26, no. 2 (June 1974): 48.

43. "God, from the beginning, not only *allowed* man to develop his emic taxonomic language structure, but *Himself chose to work within man's emic language system in His relation to man.*. . . The incarnation of thought into man's language is not new to God; the need for it in the bodily incarnation of Christ did not catch heaven by surprise." Pike, "Christianity and Culture II:

more impetus could we have, then, for working the truth of Scripture into the diction, syntax, and structure of languages foreign to us? This, of course, is what drove Pike in his work with Bible translation.

Connecting Dots

Thus far, we have established that Pike's personalism—a mark of God's general revelation—would have pointed him toward the personal God, but not the triune God. The Trinity is purely revealed through special revelation, i.e., Scripture. Now that we have established Pike's life and thought as steeped in Scripture, we have some dots to connect (perhaps obvious to some, but necessary to make overt here); the resulting shape of those connected dots will suggest that Pike's Trinitarian approach to language and human behavior was bound to take the shape it did, and, in that sense, was beyond his control.[44]

In relation to the last manifestation of Pike's scriptural knowledge—the image of God in man—we mentioned that there was a series of logical connections leading back to the Trinity. The first was the plain proposition that man *is* made in God's image. The second conjoins with the first and blends with Pike's personalism: a constant focus on people is a constant focus on image-bearers. The third connection to make is that image-bearers obviously *image*

Incarnation in a Culture," *Journal of the American Scientific Affiliation* 31, no. 2 (June 1979): 95. Elsewhere, he says, "God plays 'intellectual hopscotch' by man's rules." Pike, "Love God with Mind—and Bless Babylon," *The Gordon Alumnus* 8, no. 4 (1979): 6.

44. In the path of human development, once general revelation collides with special revelation, there is only one destination left for the person to arrive at: the triune God of Scripture.

their Creator. We noted earlier that, in Oliphint's words,

> all that we are, think, do, and become is derivative, coming from or out of something else; we depend on, as well as mirror, the real, the Original, the Eimi. In classical terminology, we are 'ectypal.' The kind or type of people we are, knowledge we have, thoughts we think, things we do, is always and everywhere a copy, pattern, impression, image, taking its metaphysical and epistemological cue from the only One who truly is, that is, from God himself.[45]

The fourth connection is that this Creator whom we image is tripersonal—the three-in-one, unity in harmony with diversity, simplicity in consonance with complexity. From the fourth connection, we jump to our next dot: God's tripersonal markings cover creation but are invisible to the non-Christian. The latter point is especially important to make since we mentioned that God's triunity is not discoverable in nature—but the caveat I would add is that it is not discoverable in nature *before special revelation has illumined and regenerated the mind of man.* Here is where Pike's thought opens the discussion for the place of the Trinity in general revelation, and this leads us to the sixth and final dot: once man has accepted the truth of God's special revelation, traces of the Trinity are ubiquitous. It is not a Unitarian God who has created and upholds all things, but a Trinitarian God, so not only should we not be surprised to see triadic reflections all around us; *but by default, we should assume that the fingerprint of the trinitarian nature of God is everywhere.* It is not theologically permissible that reality be Trinitarian; it is theologically inescapable.

So, when did Pike see all of this? Was there a moment

---

45. K. Scott Oliphint, *Reasons for Faith: Philosophy in the Service of Theology* (Phillipsburg, NJ: P&R Publishing, 2006), 178–79.

of divine epiphany? We cannot say for sure, but we can approximate a time at which he began to be fully conscious of what he would call the *tristructural* nature of reality. In 1956, he wrote that he had been working for the last seven years on his theory of the structure of human behavior, which would put us at approximately 1947.[46] This early version of his theory contained the concepts of particle, wave, and field perspectives as well as the simultaneous modal structuring of an event—manifestation, feature, and distribution. He does not make any claims to the tristructural nature of human behavior, but the concept is clearly evident, which is telling of the collision of general and special revelation. Trinitarian seeds had already been planted and taken root by 1947, if not years before.

It was not until 1958, however, that Pike drew attention to the tristructural nature of units of human behavior.[47] Most important in this article, for our purposes, was his explicit tying of these tristructural units to the Trinity. Note how chary he is when he defines his key term—markedly reminiscent of the circumspection of the early church in defining the triunity of God:[48]

> This tristructural theory is sharply distinct from a tripartite view. In the latter, the tripartite one, a unit would

---

46. Pike, "Towards a Theory of the Structure of Human Behavior (1956)," in *Kenneth L. Pike: Selected Writings to Commemorate the 60th Birthday of Kenneth Lee Pike*, ed. Ruth Brend (Paris: Mouton, 1972), 106.

47. Pike, "Language and Life 4: Tristructural Units of Human Behavior," *Bibliotheca Sacra* 114, no. 456 (January 1958): 36–43.

48. Take, for example, the language of the Nicene Creed: [I believe] "in one Lord Jesus Christ, the only-begotten Son of God, begotten of the Father before all worlds; God of God, Light of Light, very God of very God; begotten, not made, being of one substance with the Father . . ."

be conceived as having sections like an orange, or parts; the substance of the unit could be analytically split, divided, parceled out into these sections or parts, and then the parts added together would make up the whole. If one part of a tripartite unit were removed, two parts would be left. A chain with three links might symbolize the tripartite view. In the tristructural view none of these things are true. If only one of its three structures is removed from a tristructural unit the entire unit has disappeared, since each structure includes within it all the other substance of that unit. A tristructural unit is not comprised of three parts, but of one whole, with the whole structured in three different ways at once.

A tristructural analysis is crucially different, also from a triaspectual or tridimensional view of a unit. A triaspectual approach may look at a single unit from three different angles, see it from three different vantage points, study it in relation to three different functions, even though the unit is treated as having a single set of structural parts. A tridimensional view of an object may consider it as having three dimensions at the very time that it is assumed to be solid and with no internal macroscopic parts. A cube may be viewed as having height, length, and breadth, for example, but this says nothing about the internal structure of the cube. A tristructural analysis does not look at the same set of parts from different viewpoints or in different dimensions as such, but sees a single large unit divided into three sets of hierarchically arranged subunits such that each hierarchical set comprises the whole, just as the layers of a cake and the slices of that cake each include all of the substance of the cake.[49]

Notice, as well, that Pike is not making a direct correlation to the Trinity. There is, I believe, no direct correspondence between a physical object and God's triune nature that does not tend to heresy on one end or the other (usually modalism or tritheism). Pike knows that the

---

49. Pike, "Language and Life 4," 37.

Trinity is incomprehensible, so he knows that he must use analogous language when relating human behavior to the Trinity. The finite cannot contain the infinite, nor a piece of creation the Creator. So, he is careful to talk about the "tristructural" nature of units of human behavior. We may say more broadly, however, that his tristructural approach is trinitarian in that it dimly resembles a key feature of the Trinity: perichoresis—threeness in oneness, and the interlocking and overlapping of hierarchies.

This did not keep Pike from associating his theory with the Trinity, on the other hand.[50] For instance, "in the Christian understanding of God's nature there are three persons which, in order to show the analogy, might be called personal 'structures.' Each has its own personal individuality and function without constituting a new part of God or an additional God; each is the whole."[51] Christian readers might have guessed this analogy based on the description of "tristructural" alone. But he does go a bit further in his analogy:

> If one seeks for linguistic analogies for some facts of the Christian Trinity, the identificational-contrastive structure with its basic priority of meaning and purpose and communication from individual to individual would be

---

50. "For the Christian theologian the postulation of tristructural features in human behavior may well prove to be one of the most interesting of all linguistic phenomena. If this analysis can be sustained in some detail . . . there would be available a number of illustrations of a Trinitarian type which could be used to help students grasp with more intellectual clarity some restricted components of the doctrine of a Trinitarian God (note that we *do not* say 'proofs' of the nature of deity. The knowledge of the structure of deity must come from revelation grasped by faith of it cannot come at all" (ibid., 39).

51. Ibid.

suggested as illustrative of the relationship of the person of God the Father to the Trinity as a whole—inasmuch as ultimate purpose seems to reside in Him (Eph. 1:9, 11), He has taken the initiative to communicate and to reveal Himself to us (Heb. 1:1–2), and the Sonship of Christ implies the Father's priority of rank in some sense (John 14:28; Col. 1:15). On the other hand, as the manifestation structure of linguistic units is the audible, concrete form which can be directly apprehended by us, and is the medium through which all linguistic meaning is communicated, so the second person of the Trinity, the Son, was made concretely available to the senses of man, to be seen, heard, touched (Col. 1:15; 1 John 1:1) and it was through the manifested Word become flesh (John 1:1, 14) that the purposes of God were effected (John 1:3). Similarly, as the distributional-functional structure in the sentence forms the matrix within which the words of the sentence occur, in formal units that are obscure and hard to find of themselves because of their function in making vividly present before us the more concrete sounds and lexical units, so the third person of the Trinity may perhaps be viewed as the structured distributional personal matrix for the work of God (as the Spirit works in us with the love of God which "is shed abroad in our hearts by the Holy Ghost.[52]

Here, perhaps more than anywhere else in his corpus of work, he was unabashed about the connections he saw between his theory of human behavior and the Trinity.

Conclusion and Implications for Linguistic Methodology

The convergence of Pike's personalism and his knowledge of Scripture provided him with two theological locales, yet neither of these was an end in itself in terms of Pike's

---

52. Ibid., 42–43.

tristructural approach to language. Personalism and Scripture converged in the Trinity. A focus on God's image bearers will eventually lead one back to God, and God's tripersonal nature is revealed only in Scripture. *The Trinity is where person meets Word.* And so, the relationship between general and special revelation—the former being the arena of the latter—is wondrously portrayed in Pike's own career.

However, Pike's arrival at a trinitarian approach to language and human behavior suggests something important for our understanding of general revelation as it relates to the Trinity. If all of reality is truly tristructural and reflective of the coinherence of the Trinity, then we may need to nuance our treatment of the Trinity in the context of general revelation. It seems that we can no longer say that the Trinity is not to be found in nature.[53] While we affirm with Warfield, Bavinck, and a host of other Reformed theologians that the doctrine of the Trinity "embodies a truth which has never been discovered, and is indiscoverable, by natural reason," we cannot say it is not ubiquitous in reality as a whole. It most definitely is, *yet no mind but the regenerate can see it.* Warfield spoke the truth, but perhaps there is more truth to speak. Those whose minds have been illuminated by the words of Scripture have no choice but to observe the gloriously ubiquitous trinitarian structure of human behavior—of language, thought, and even of being. If they do not see it, this is not necessarily evidence of its absence or imperceptibility; it

---

53. Indeed, when Paul tells us in Rom 1 that all men "know God," can this be any other but the Trinitarian God? It cannot be a Unitarian God—a deistic Father divorced from the Son and the Spirit. It *must* be the Trinitarian God, and yet Scripture also affirms time and again that not all men having a saving knowledge of God. So we must distinguish between salvific knowledge of the Triune God and culpable knowledge of the Triune God.

may be residual blindness to God's triune nature and the corresponding structure of reality. Pike's work suggests that the special revelation of the Trinity seems to be embedded in the general revelation surrounding us and indwelling us. But if we do not have eyes to see or ears to hear it, then it remains cloaked and cloistered. Pike's work has certainly opened the floor for this discussion in Reformed circles. While the Trinity remains a specifically revealed doctrine, more attention needs to be given to its functional place in the structure of reality and human behavior since, as Van Til affirmed, the ontological Trinity grounds all of human experience.

What are the implications of the tristructural and thus trinitarian nature of reality for linguistic methodology? In the article just referenced, Pike merely says that it is "interesting to speculate whether part of the character of man which is in the 'image of God' (Gen. 1:27) might be the 'built-in' tendency to a tristructural patterning of man's behavioral units."[54] His own thought certainly suggests this tendency, but there are also many who find Pike's approach arbitrary or forced. Surely, many would affirm that it has not been our default response as Christians to consider units of human behavior tristructurally—whether linguistic or non-linguistic. Our default response might be what Pike would call "particle-like,"[55] dividing bits of human behavior, and even the emic systems that encompass them, into discrete units, capable of being neatly defined and categorized monoperspectivally.[56] This is residue not just of modernism

---

54. Ibid., 41.

55. Or what Poythress might call "unitarian."

56. "Monoperspectival reductions of the truth frequently make one perspec-

but of Platonic and Aristotelian philosophy. It is identifiably unitarian, not trinitarian. Indeed, if we embrace Van Til's biblical axiom of thinking God's thoughts after Him, not just their *matter* but their *manner*, then there is something deeply disturbing about this trend.

Our linguistic methodology rests not simply upon usefulness in helping us understand and analyze the world around us, but in its effects on our perception. What, we might ask, does a unitarian approach to language and human behavior effect in us? An exclusion of diversity? A rejection of multiple perspectives, and, hence, a self-centered view of reality? Isolation leading to the morass of self-sufficiency? All seem likely.

The above conclusions may seem rash because they are centered in thought and perception and perhaps only secondarily to language. But linguistic methodology, we must remember, is tied to epistemology and ontology. Our language is inextricably bound up with our thought, and both our language and our thought are inextricably bound up with our being.[57] Therefore, our approach to language

---

tive into a Godlike origin for everything else." Poythress, *Redeeming Philosophy: A God-Centered Approach to the Big Questions* (Wheaton, IL: Crossway, 2014), 51.

57. I refer to this as the MEL triad: metaphysics, epistemology, and language. The biblical foundation for this reasoning comes from 1 Cor. 2:11–13: "For who knows a person's thoughts except the spirit of that person, which is in him? So also no one comprehends the thoughts of God except the Spirit of God. Now we have received not the spirit of the world, but the Spirit who is from God, that we might understand the things freely given us by God. And we impart this in words not taught by human wisdom but taught by the Spirit, interpreting spiritual truths to those who are spiritual." A person's thoughts are inherently connected to his being, his spirit. Christians, Paul tells us, have received the Spirit of God, and we impart the spiritual truths we have been taught not with our own words, but with the words of the Spirit. The word, then, is the medium that takes the things "freely given us by God," i.e. God's thoughts, and communicates them to others.

affects and informs our thought and our understanding of who we are.

Any approach to language that has not accounted for the trinitarian structure of reality may be prone to an ancient heresy of some kind—arianism, modalism, sabellianism, etc. Those heresies affected the thought and understanding of being for their adherents, and so if one aspect of our humanity—ontology, epistemology, or language—has been contaminated by a heretical view of God, it is only a matter of time before the contamination spreads. Claiming that we think analogically presupposes that we understand that our being is analogical to God's, and our language is as well, and so any approach to language that does not model itself on—or at least account for—the coinherence of the Trinity is bound to lead us astray by pointing us toward a God other than the God of the Bible.

In this light, consider, from the other side, Pike's tristructural view. What might that effect in us? Unity in diversity? An acceptance of multiple perspectives and an enriched understanding of language and life? A sense of dependency on the God who knows every emic system ever manifested in human history as well as every unit within each of those systems and its distribution to time and space? Again, all seem likely. And all seem to correspond to the biblical teaching on man's being, thought, and language.

Reality is trinitarian. Being is trinitarian. Thought is

In sum, by God's grace we are made new creatures in Christ (being), so that we can be spiritually instructed concerning God's thoughts (thought), in order to communicate those thoughts through the Spirit's words (language). This paradigm holds for unbelievers as well, but with drastically different consequences. Their spirit is lost, and so their thoughts are confused as they try to suppress the truth (Rom 1:18), which produces words that, at their best, appear to be wise but which are, in fact, foolish (Rom. 1:22).

trinitarian. Behavior is trinitarian. Language is trinitarian. These maxims stand out in Pike's theory and testify to his relationship (all facets of it) with the triune Person of Scripture, the God who is three-in-one.

Pike was a poet as much as a linguist, and he often had the boldness to end an article with a poem that encapsulated his message. The courage I take in doing the same I attribute solely to his example, though I am sure it will not have the effect that his did. Still, for the man whose focus on people and knowledge of Scripture shed biblical light on a linguistic world convinced of its own autonomy, it is worth the risk, I think:

Truth is a person we join by preposition:
In is where we dwell,
Not a stagnant proposition
Or empirical spell.

Truth is God's speech:
Father by Son through Spirit.
Deafness is breeched
For those who hear it.

Truth is not alone;
It lives in community.
Speech and thought, flesh and bone,
Bear the mark of Trinity.

Closing the Gaps
Perichoresis and the Nature of Language

"Language bends us, moves us, drives us—or blocks us, holds us, binds us in a word-made mold."
— Kenneth L. Pike, *Tagmemics, Discourse, and Verbal Art*

Marshall McLuhan wrote years ago that the western world is "intensely individualist and fragmented."[1] His words still hold water four decades later. The sad follow-up is that though we are scattered and maimed by sin far more pervasively than McLuhan could have imagined as a media theorist, we still think we are better off if we have our own space.[2] The individualism of contemporary western culture has, among other things, sown the seed of this thought and then watered it so routinely that it has broken through the soil of speculation, sprouted leaves and blossomed into an axiom. Gaps, we *think*, are good. We need space between one another, space to contemplate, space to grow spiritually in our relationship with God.

Yet, in another, ironic sense, the space we claim as necessary to social, cognitive, and spiritual fruition has

---

1. Marshall McLuhan, *Understanding Media: The Extensions of Man*, crit. ed., ed. W. Terrence Gordon (Corte Madera, CA: Ginko Press, 2003), 315.

2. McLuhan ties our fragmentation to our uncritical use of media and our naiveté about its effects on our perception and noetic processes. Our individualism he attributes to the rise of the print medium, which, he thought, was waning at the dawn of the electronic era.

also bore caverns beneath the soul. These caverns are ever collapsing, opening fissures and ravines between us and those we love, and so we use language to build bridges and reconnect. The paradoxical allegory of western humanity in the twenty-first century is that we create canyons between ourselves even as we build bridges, through language, to cross them. Gaps, we *know*, are not good.

Though we are content to use language as if it were only expedient to build and mend our bridges, the lasting answer to this "problem of gaps" lies in the nature of language itself, and, on the deepest level, in the Trinity. Language is a communing activity. God is a self-communing being. Looking to the tripersonal God of Scripture and his perichoretic self-communion, we find the heart of language and the real impetus for our use of words. Building bridges is not even the half of it. We were made to commune.

Language, God, and Humanity

I will be arguing in the following pages that the divine, perichoretic origin of language points to the solution to our problem of gaps. But what exactly *is* language? We could piece together a definition from a jigsaw of psychological and social theories, but that would be unwise. Secular linguists have nearly all made the same mistake in beginning a study of language with humanity. But all coherent and effective human behavior is rooted not in social patterns or evolutionary development, but in the self-contained ontological Trinity, in whose image we are made.[3] We start

---

3. "Language originates with God, not with man." Vern S. Poythress, *In the Beginning Was the Word: Language—A God-Centered Approach* (Wheaton, IL: Crossway, 2009), 28.

with the Trinity in every discussion. So that is where we begin here.

The persons of the Godhead dwell in perfect and eternal communion with one another. They "speak" to each other in the sense that the Father, Son, and Holy Spirit love and glorify one another without end.[4] We deduce this from Scripture, for "what God does in time reflects who and what he is in eternity."[5] At least, this holds for non-redemptive actions. We would not, for example, concur with Moltmann that, because Jesus suffers as God in history, God is a "suffering God."[6] But the actions of love and glory do not bind God to creation and redemption. These are actions that existed before time began, within the immanent Trinity.

Scripture reveals that the Father loves the Son and shows him all that he does (John 5:20). The Son loves the Father by obeying his commands to perfection, just as he instructs his followers to do (John 14:15, 21, 23). And Paul's ode to holy love (1 Cor. 13:1–13) is inextricably bound to the third person of the Trinity as the fruit *of the Spirit* (Gal. 5:22–23). In fact, "the Love-life whereby these Three mutually love each other is the Eternal Being Himself. . . .

---

4. On "mutual glorification" of the persons in the Godhead, see John Frame, *Systematic Theology: An Introduction to Christian Belief* (Phillipsburg, NJ: P&R Publishing, 2013), 480–81. See also Francis Cheynell, *The Divine Triunity of the Father, Son, and Holy Spirit* (London, 1650), 62.

5. Gerald Bray, *God Is Love: A Biblical and Systematic Theology* (Wheaton, IL: Crossway, 2012), 29.

6. Jürgen Moltmann, *The Crucified God: The Cross of Christ as the Foundation and Criticism of Christian Theology* (Minneapolis, MN: Fortress, 1993), 241; *The Trinity and the Kingdom: The Doctrine of God* (Minneapolis, MN: Fortress, 1993), 21ff.; Robert Letham, *The Holy Trinity: In Scripture, History, Theology, and Worship* (Phillipsburg, NJ: P&R Publishing, 2004), 298–305.

The entire Scripture teaches that nothing is more precious and glorious than the Love of the Father for the Son, and of the Son for the Father, and of the Holy Spirit for both."[7]

Glory lies within the Trinity in equal measure. In John 17:5 Jesus says, "glorify me in your own presence with the glory that I had with you before the world existed." In the preceding chapter he proclaimed that the Spirit also glorifies him (John 16:14). So, the Son certainly receives glory from the Father and the Spirit, and yet Jesus tells us that he longs for the Father to glorify him *so that he can glorify the Father* (John 17:1). And the reason why the Son is glorified is because he gives life to all men who are dead in sins and trespasses (Rom. 6:11). Our life is in Christ, but this life is none other than "the Spirit of life" (Rom. 8:2, 6), who is the Spirit of Christ (Rom. 8:9). Therefore, we can say that the Spirit shares in the glory of the Son as life-giver.

This divine exchange of love and glory is the highest form of communication. It is so precisely because the persons are distinct and yet united; their distinction serves their unity, and their unity complements their distinction.[8]

---

7. Abraham Kuyper, *The Work of the Holy Spirit*, trans. Henry De Vries (Chattanooga, TN: AMG Publishers, 1995), 542.

8. Augustine, *De Trinitate* 5.8; John of Damascus, *Writings*, The Fathers of the Church 37, trans. Frederic H. Chase (Washington, D.C.: The Catholic University of America Press, 1958), 182–85; John P. Egan, "Toward Trinitarian Perichoresis : Saint Gregory the Theologian, (Oration) 31.41," *Greek Orthodox Theological Review* 39, no. 1–2 (March 1, 1994): 92; Verna E. F. Harrison, "Perichoresis in the Greek Fathers," *St. Vladimir's Theological Quarterly* 35, no. 1 (January 1, 1991): 59; Douglas Kelly, *Systematic Theology: Grounded in Holy Scripture and Understood in Light of the Church*, vol. 1, *The God Who Is: The Holy Trinity* (Ross-shire, Scotland: Mentor, 2008), 494; Letham, *The Holy Trinity*, 365, 369; Dumitru Stăniloae, *The Experience of God: Orthodox Dogmatic Theology*, vol. 1, *Revelation and Knowledge of the Triune God*, ed. and trans. Ioan Ionita and Robert Barringer (Brookline, MA: Holy Cross Orthodox Press, 2000), 134.; Lane G. Tipton, "The Function of Perichoresis and the Divine

Thus, the Father, Son, and Spirit speak to one another in a more intimate way than we can imagine. We can and must affirm that "there is—and has been from all eternity—talk, sharing and communication in the innermost life of God."[9] As distinct persons, they commune and coinhere in unending reciprocity of life, love, and light.[10] We communicate to move towards communion; their communication *is* their communion. For the Trinity, language is a communicative behavior that serves unbroken unity, because there are no gaps in God. In other words, "the Father does not distance Himself from the Son and Holy Spirit, and They do not think about separating Themselves from the Father. Rather, each sees Himself in the other and is more preoccupied with the other's good and with His own."[11] By the mutual love each person has for the other persons, we learn that the Trinity is a gapless God, and yet a God who chooses to communicate with himself (internally) and with his creatures (externally). Language for the Trinity is communion par excellence, showcasing the fact that the persons of the Godhead were,

---

Incomprehensibility," *WTJ* 64 (2002): 297; T. F. Torrance, *The Christian Doctrine of God, One Being Three Persons* (Edinburgh: T&T Clark, 1996), 171–72, 175, 197; Torrance, "The Doctrine of the Holy Trinity according to St. Athanasius," *Anglican Theological Review* 71, no. 4 (September 1, 1989): 400; Cornelius Van Til, *In Defense of the Faith*, vol. 2, *A Survey of Christian Epistemology* (Phillipsburg, NJ: Presbyterian and Reformed, 1969), 78.

9. Kelly, *The God Who Is: The Holy Trinity*, 487.

10. "God is in three Persons who communicate being (or life), goodness, and light (or knowledge) among Themselves. This makes God a Trinity of Persons united in the greatest possible love." Dumitru Stăniloae, *The Holy Trinity: In the Beginning There Was Love*, trans. Roland Clark (Brookline, MA: Holy Cross Orthodox Press, 2012), 14.

11. Ibid., 42.

are, and always will be "inextricably intertwined."[12]

Now that we have some sense of what language is for the Trinity, we can move on to consider how we understand human language. Given that humans are created in God's image and likeness (Gen 1:26), we must start by affirming that human language is an imaging behavior. Gaffin notes,

> As our being itself is derived from God (we exist because he exists), and as our knowledge is an analogue of his knowledge (we know because he knows), so, too, our capacity for language and other forms of communication is derivative of his. We speak because God speaks, because he is a speaking God; that is his nature and so, derivatively, it is ours. In other words, man in his linguistic functions, as in all he is and does, is to be understood as the creature who is the image and likeness of God (Gen 1:26). In fact, should we not say that especially in his language man reflects the divine image he is?[13]

Gaffin is on to something with the word "especially." Human language is not an addendum to the *imago Dei*; language grounds it.[14] Our communication points to our

---

12. Daniel F. Stramara Jr., "Gregory of Nyssa's Terminology for Trinitarian Perichoresis," *Vigiliae Christianae* 52, no. 3 (August 1, 1998): 263.

13. Richard B. Gaffin Jr., "Speech and the Image of God: Biblical Reflections on Language and Its Uses," in *The Pattern of Sound Doctrine: Systematic Theology at the Westminster Seminaries*, ed. David VanDrunen (Phillipsburg, NJ: P&R Publishing, 2004), 182–83. See also Kenneth L. Pike, "Morals and Metaphor," *Interchange* 12 (1972): 231; Poythress, *In the Beginning Was the Word*, 29–34; John M. Frame, *The Doctrine of the Knowledge of God* (Phillipsburg, NJ: P&R Publishing, 1987), 240–41.

14. "God did not create man in isolation from a later purpose to communicate. It is not as if he created man first, and then, as an afterthought, asked himself whether it might be good to establish communication, and on what terms communication might be possible. Rather, God created man already having in mind the purposes of communication." Vern S. Poythress, "Re-

ontology and divinely patented identity: we were spoken into being by the self-communing Trinity; we *are* creatures who speak. Language, then, is not an empty vehicle, a tool for achieving eclectic social and material ends. Rather, it is what sets us apart as conscious, engaging creatures of a communicating God. This not only underscores the importance of our understanding and use of language; it demands that we expand our definition of it to include far more than a system of graphic and phonetic signs.

Kenneth L. Pike (1912–2000) defined human language in a way that gives more attention to its expansiveness than the theories of other linguists, so we will adopt his approach. Language, according to Pike, is communicative behavior rooted in a unique observer of reality.[15] Each person then works with hierarchical structures—phonology, grammar, and reference—to express particular perspectives or emotions. It should be clear by this point that our unique expressions presuppose others who can interpret and engage with us. So, language is what we do as creatures in community; its goal is always communal in nature. In

---

thinking Accommodation in Revelation," *WTJ* 76 (2014): 148.

15. "Language is not merely a set of unrelated sounds, clauses, rules, and meanings; it is a total coherent system of these integrating with each other, and with behavior, context, universe of discourse, and observer perspectives." Kenneth L. Pike, *Linguistic Concepts: An Introduction to Tagmemics* (Lincoln, NE: University of Nebraska Press, 1982), 44. For details on the particle, wave, and field observer perspectives, see Pike, "Language as Particle, Wave, and Field," in *Kenneth L. Pike: Selected Writings to Commemorate the 60th Birthday of Kenneth Lee Pike*, ed. Ruth Brend (The Hague: Mouton, 1972), 129; Kenneth L. Pike and Evelyn G. Pike, *Grammatical Analysis*, Publications in Linguistics 53 (Dallas, TX: Summer Institute of Linguistics, 1977), 5; Pike, *Linguistic Concepts*, 19ff.; Pike, *Talk, Thought, and Thing: The Emic Road toward Conscious Knowledge* (Dallas, TX: Summer Institute of Linguistics, 1993), 47–51; and Poythress, *In the Beginning Was the Word*, 52–56.

this sense, it is what we might call *communion behavior*, for its purpose is the expression of one person towards another.[16] Language is a drawing together of conscious beings made in the image of the Trinity.

But why do we have this need to draw together? Why is the plain of our community riddled with fissures and canyons? The simple answer is sin. Some have described pride as the greatest sin, and therefore suggested that Adam and Eve's choice to follow the words of the serpent was a decision of hubris: they assumed that their glory could trump that of their divine creator. This is certainly a true interpretation, but pride can be dissected into its components, and when we do so, we find that at the heart of pride is not just a misplaced value of self-worth, but a desire for autonomy. The deadliest desideratum of humanity is the will for self-government. At base, this is nothing more than a longing for space, which gives us breathing room to submit our conscience and will to no one but ourselves. Sin is a violation of covenant, a breaking of God's commands, a performance of what God forbids—yes, yes. But at its heart sin is a disruption of communion, a breaking apart of what should be united. In this light, marriage, which is the most intimate inter-personal union, is defended in marital ceremonies with the words, "What God has joined let no man separate."

Because the Trinity is the archetype of distinct persons in perfect unity, it should come as no surprise that the

---

16. "One of the purposes of language—in fact, a central, predominant purpose—is to be a vehicle for personal communication and communion between God and human beings." Poythress, *In the Beginning Was the Word*, 38. As we will see, this communion also involves the expressions of the persons of the Trinity towards one another. Before creation, these expressions, as we already discussed, would have been of love and glory.

doctrine of *perichoresis* illuminates the nature of language and provides the antidote to autonomy and isolationism. In what follows, I hope to show how *perichoresis* is related to our communicative behavior, and the closing of gaps between persons.

In order to do this, we will first need to examine *perichoresis* in its historical and theological context, and then apply it to both divine and human language.

Perichoresis

Simply put, when we speak of *perichoresis* with reference to the Trinity, we are referring to the intimate union of the divine persons, such that "each is in each, and all are in each, and all are one."[17] How exactly is each person "in" the others? The language of "coinherence" and "indwelling" is most commonly offered for clarification. Others use more eccentric terms. Turretin, for instance, suggests "the divine persons *embrace* each other and *permeate* . . . each other."[18] However, no matter what terms are used, the mystery of this truth eschews rationalistic exposition. All that is clear from Scripture, particularly the Gospel of John, is that the persons of the Godhead interpenetrate one another, and yet "while indwelling one another, do not coalesce."[19] A plethora of definitions could be added as supplements,[20]

---

17. Augustine, *De Trinitate* 6.10.

18. Francis Turretin, *Institutes of Elenctic Theology*, vol. 1, *First through Tenth Topics*, ed. James T. Dennison, Jr., trans. George Musgrave Giger (Phillipsburg, NJ: P&R Publishing, 1992), 257; emphasis added.

19. Paul M. Collins, *Trinitarian Theology: West and East—Karl Barth, the Cappadocian Fathers, and John Zizioulas* (New York: Oxford, 2001), 211.

20. For other definitions, see Augustine, *De Trinitate* 1.18; John of Damas-

but the idea is, I think, clear enough for our purposes. Once we consider the biblical roots of this teaching, we can move on to consider the historical question: how did early theologians come to understand *perichoresis* so that the term came to enjoy relative semantic stability?

Biblical Roots

The intimate communion of the Father, Son, and Holy Spirit can be found throughout Scripture, but we will limit ourselves to a few texts here, namely those commonly referenced for the teaching of *perichoresis*.

Rather than jump immediately to the Gospel of John, which is easily the most illuminating text for this teaching, we can note that the linguistic analogy introduced in John's prologue (the Son as the Word) leads us to find support for *perichoresis* in other places of Scripture. Genesis 1 is a prime example. If the Son is the Word of the Father, and if the Spirit of God is bound to the life and effectiveness of that

---

cus, *Writings*, 177; Joel R. Beeke and Mark Jones, *A Puritan Theology: Doctrine for Life* (Grand Rapids, MI: Reformation Heritage Books, 2012), 90–91; Collins, *Trinitarian Theology: West and East*, 209–15; Oliver D. Crisp, "Problems with Perichoresis," *Tyndale Bulletin* 56, no. 1 (January 1, 2005): 135–39; Egan, "Toward Trinitarian Perichoresis," 92; Frame, *Systematic Theology*, 479–81; Harrison, "Perichoresis in the Greek Fathers," 59–63; Kelly, *The God Who Is: The Holy Trinity*, 489; Michael G. Lawler, "Perichoresis: New Theological Wine in an Old Theological Wineskin," *Horizons* 22, no. 1 (March 1, 1995): 52–53; Letham, *The Holy Trinity*, 365–66; John McClean, "Perichoresis, Theosis and Union with Christ in the Thought of John Calvin," *Reformed Theological Review* 68, no. 2 (August 1, 2009): 134–35; Randall E. Otto, "The Use and Abuse of Perichoresis in Recent Theology," *Scottish Journal of Theology* 54 (2001): 366; Stramara, "Gregory of Nyssa's Terminology for Trinitarian Perichoresis," 259; Tipton, "The Function of Perichoresis and the Divine Incomprehensibility," 292; Torrance, *The Christian Doctrine of God*, 169–73; and Van Til, *A Survey of Christian Epistemology*, 78.

Word (cf. Job 33:4; Rom 8:2), then Genesis 1 is the first time we witness the divine persons' indwelling one another. God is portrayed in his unity for the creation account, but the Trinity is present as the divine Speaker, Speech, and Breath.[21] The Son, as the Speech of God (Word), indwells the Father by expressing the depth of his mind and will. The Spirit, as the power and life of this expression (1 Cor 2:11; Rom 8:9), indwells the Father and the Son in order to apply the expression felicitously to creation. Thus, even in the first divine fiat, "Let there be light," we have not simply God, but the *triune* God bringing about order and beauty by his perichoretic communion. This is attested to later in Scripture when the psalmist writes, "By the word [Son] of the Lord [Father] the heavens were made, and by the breath [Spirit] of his mouth all their host" (Ps. 33:6).[22]

However, we would be fooling ourselves to ignore the fact that John's Gospel is referenced by many theologians as the threshold to the teaching of *perichoresis*, and for good reasons. Here we find more explicit references to the indwelling and interpenetration of the divine persons. In John 10:30, Jesus says, "I and the Father are one." Here, Jesus is not claiming that he and the Father are the same person, for "then the *distinction* between Jesus and God already introduced in 1:1b would be obliterated."[23] And yet, because much of John's Gospel suggests that there are "metaphysical overtones" to what Jesus is saying,[24] this is

---

21. Letham, *The Holy Trinity*, 17–21.

22. See also Poythress, *In the Beginning Was the Word*, 19–21.

23. D. A. Carson, *The Gospel according to John*, Pillar New Testament Commentary (Grand Rapids, MI: William B. Eerdmans, 1991), 394.

24. Ibid.

far more than a statement of Jesus' likeness to the Father or even to their union in accomplishing the salvation of God's people (Jesus already alludes to the latter in other parts of John's Gospel, such as 5:17). So, in what sense are Jesus and the Father "one"? We find the answer eight verses later.

In John 10:37–38, Jesus addresses the Jewish opposition to his claim of divinity. "If I am not doing the works of my Father, then do not believe me; but if I do them, even though you do not believe me, believe the works, that you may know and understand that the Father is in me and I am in the Father." Note the reciprocal nature of Jesus' answer. The Father is in him *and* he is in the Father. The indwelling is symmetrical.[25] Carson affirms that Jesus' words here are a reference to the "mutual co-inherence" between himself and the Father, and this grounds Jesus' teaching in John 5:19ff, where he tells the people that he can do nothing "by" or "from" himself.[26] The joint working of the Father and the Son, then, is an implication of their prior and eternal indwelling. And the Spirit cannot be left out of this either, for "the Spirit, along with the Father, remained with/indwelled Jesus (1:32–33; 10:38; 14:10–11)."[27] Analogously, through Christ, we enjoy "a share in his filial relationship with the Father by the indwelling of the Holy Spirit."[28] This is especially important for our purposes because Köstenberger and Swain helpfully point

---

25. Crisp, "Problems with Perichoresis," 139–40.

26. Carson, *The Gospel according to John*, 400.

27. Andreas J. Köstenberger and Scott R. Swain, *The Father, Son and Spirit: The Trinity and John's Gospel*, New Studies in Biblical Theology (Downers Grove, IL: InterVarsity Press, 2008), 146.

28. Ibid., 146–47.

out that "identifying the Spirit's relationship to Jesus and his disciples enables us to detect the Spirit's distinctive personal activity even in places where he remains otherwise unnamed."[29] Thus, when Jesus says to Phillip, "Believe me that I am in the Father and the Father is in me" (14:11), and when he prays to the Father on behalf of believers, "Holy Father, keep them in your name, which you have given me, that they may be one, even as we are one" (17:11), what we have are not statements concerned with two persons of the Trinity, but with all three of them. Jesus is in the Father, and the Spirit is in Jesus and is the Spirit of the Father; Jesus is "one" with the Father in the Spirit. This unity, referenced again in 17:21–22, is what we might call a *trinal* unity, to borrow a term from Berkhof.[30] It is a trinitarian unity, not a monistic unity.

These Johannine passages provide the basis for the doctrine of *perichoresis*, so we can say that the notion of *perichoresis* was evident long before the terminology sprouted and took root in the early church. Yet, there were, in the first several centuries A.D., important explanations of this teaching that served to illuminate the already lucid teaching of Scripture. This is where we turn presently.

Historical Survey

Nearly every theologian who has written on *perichoresis* has provided his or her own summary of the historical use of the term, so it would be redundant to reproduce it in full

---

29. Ibid., 147.

30. Louis Berkhof, *Systematic Theology*, new ed. (Grand Rapids, MI: William B. Eerdmans, 1996), 84.

yet again.[31] A summary should suffice for our purposes.

At the risk of sounding a bit juvenile, I suggest that the history of the term *perichoresis* can best be remembered with an acronym: GMPJ (Gregory of Nazianzus, Maximus the Confessor, Pseudo-Cyril, and John of Damascus).[32] Gregory of Nazianzus (c. 325–389) first used the term *perichoresis* in reference to the relationship between the divine and human natures in Christ, attempting to explain "the exchange of titles and hence of activities and attributes" of the two natures in the one person of Christ.[33] This teaching, which Crisp helpfully titles "nature-*perichoresis*" so as to distinguish it from trinitarian "person-*perichoresis*," is closely related to what later came to be known as the *communicatio idiomatum*.[34]

Though Christ's divine and human nature are said to "interpenetrate" one another, this interpenetration is not symmetrical. As Crisp notes,

> nature-*perichoresis* involves an asymmetrical relation between the two natures of Christ. The divine nature of Christ interpenetrates his human nature without confusion and without being mingled with it. But the human nature of

---

31. I recommend Harrison's historical summary, which is efficient and clear. See Harrison, "Perichoresis in the Greek Fathers," 53–63.

32. This is certainly a simplification, since others, such as Daniel Stramara, have shown that the concept of perichoresis, if not the actual vocabulary, was evident in the work of others in the early church. See Stramara, "Gregory of Nyssa's Terminology for Trinitarian Perichoresis."

33. Harrison, "Perichoresis in the Greek Fathers," 55.

34. Crisp notes that the perichoresis of the two natures of Christ should not be confused with the *communicatio idiomatum*, since the latter explains how allegedly contradictory properties can be predicated of the same person, while the former outlines how the divine and human natures of Christ are united without introducing a *tertium quid*, a third kind of nature in the person of Christ. Crisp, "Problems with Perichoresis," 123.

Christ does not interpenetrate the divine nature in any way. . . . the divine nature of Christ interpenetrates the human nature of Christ, upholding and sustaining it at each moment of its existence.[35]

Maximus the Confessor (580–662) followed Gregory's use of the term, adding that *perichoresis* applies to the two natures of Christ as well as to their "energies."[36] While his understanding of *perichoresis* paralleled that of Gregory, Maximus extended the breadth of its meaning to include our salvation and redemption (which is linked to the Eastern teaching of deification). For Maximus, there is *perichoresis* of "the believer with (or toward) the object of belief," i.e., Christ.[37] This, of course, should be distinguished from the nature-*perichoresis* of Christ, and Maximus seems to have done so by noting that we have "an identity of *energy* with God . . . whereas in Christ the *natures* actually coinhere in each other."[38] We should note in passing that others have already shown that *perichoresis* cannot be equated to our union with Christ. The two kinds of union are of different orders, despite their initial similarities.[39]

---

35. Ibid., 130.

36. Harrison, "Perichoresis in the Greek Fathers," 56–58.

37. Ibid., 57. Gregory Nazianzen had written, in *Oration* 30, that Christ "takes on a strange form, bearing the whole of me in himself with what is mine, so as to consume the bad in himself, as fire does wax or the sun does the earth's mists, and I participate in what is his through the commingling."

38. Ibid., 58.

39. See McClean, "Perichoresis, Theosis and Union with Christ in the Thought of John Calvin"; "There is the widest difference between the mystical union of believers with God and the divine union of the persons of the Trinity in nature, or of the human and divine natures in the person of Christ." Turretin, *Institutes of Elenctic Theology*, 257; Kevin J. Vanhooz-

From Maximus we move to a writer known now as Pseudo-Cyril (c. 650), who was the first to use the term *perichoresis* in reference to the persons of the Trinity, though John of Damascus should be credited for noting that trinitarian person-*perichoresis* is logically prior to the nature-*perichoresis* in the person of Christ.[40] For Pseudo-Cyril, the persons of the Godhead "'possess coinherence in each other,' though without confusion or division."[41] Note both parts of Pseudo-Cyril's definition: unity and distinction. While some theologians are quick to comment on how *perichoresis* defends God's unity, we must be equally as vigilant to defend the real distinctions of the persons, for "the idea of Father, Son, and Spirit dwelling in each other presupposes a serious and meaningful confession of their distinctness."[42] After all, it would not make much sense to affirm unity without presupposing distinction, for without distinction unity could not exist. Unity is a perfect interrelation of distinctions, so the teaching of *perichoresis* does not merely assert a monistic unity; rather, it supports, as we said earlier, a trinal unity.

The last of the theologians usually mentioned with regards to *perichoresis* is John of Damascus (born c. 676), who often receives attention for popularizing

---

er, *Remythologizing Theology: Divine Action, Passion, and Authorship* (New York: Cambridge University Press, 2010), 151–53, 157. Speaking of John 17:22, Carson writes, "The unity of the Father and the Son is the reality against which the unity of believers is to be measured, not the reverse. And like any analogy that generates a comparison, the analogy cannot be pushed to exhaustion."

40. Harrison, "Perichoresis in the Greek Fathers," 61.

41. Ibid., 59.

42. Ibid.

the concept. As noted above, for John, "the Trinitarian *perichoresis* has ontological and conceptual priority, and he understands the Christological *perichoresis* as following the same pattern."[43] The Trinity is "known in three perfect Persons and adored with one adoration, believed in and worshiped by every rational creature, united without confusion and distinct without separation, which is beyond understanding."[44] In John, we find the basic understanding of Trinitarian *perichoresis* virtually unchanged from the time of Pseudo-Cyril.[45] John did, however, bring the concept into more prominence, perhaps by eliminating earlier subordinationism from the pen of Gregory Nazianzus and Maximus the Confessor. The latter had suggested that the Father is the Monarchy of the Trinity, and thus the cause and source of deity for the Son and the Spirit.[46] But for John, the Son "was always with the Father, being begotten of Him eternally and without beginning. For the Father never was when the Son was not, but the Father and the Son begotten of Him exist together simultaneously, because the Father could not be so called without a Son."[47] The Spirit also, as eternally proceeding from the Father and the Son, cannot be relegated to a lower seat at the Trinitarian table. If there is a "monarchy," for John it is the Trinity itself. This emphasis complements the reciprocity of the divine

---

43. Ibid., 61.

44. John of Damascus, *Writings*, 177.

45. Lawler, "Perichoresis," 52.

46. Christopher A. Beeley, *Gregory of Nazianzus on the Trinity and Knowledge of God: In Your Light We Shall See Light*, Oxford Studies in Historical Theology (New York: Oxford University Press, 2008), 201–213.

47. John of Damascus, *Writings*, 178.

persons in their interpenetration, and thus led the way for future theologians to have a firm foundation when claiming that Trinitarian *perichoresis* was perfectly symmetrical.

That, in brief, is how the term *perichoresis* entered the drama of theological history, though, as noted earlier, the concept was clear in John's Gospel, and terminology that eventually gave way to *perichoresis* can be traced to other writers of nascent Christianity, particularly Gregory of Nyssa.[48]

There is much more to say, but perhaps we can end this section by noting that theologians, both then and now, have debated whether Trinitarian *perichoresis* is static or dynamic. In other words, do the persons *rest* in one another, or are they actively and ceaselessly *interpenetrating* each other? T. F. Torrance adamantly defends the latter position, claiming that *perichoresis* "has essentially a *dynamic* and not a static sense."[49] Others suggest that since *perichoresis* accents the unity of the Godhead, it is static in nature. Collins, perhaps simplistically, suggests that the dynamic view can be tied to Orthodox theologians because they begin Trinitarian discussions with the persons, whereas the static view can be tied to the Latin West, which begins Trinitarian discussions with the one divine essence.[50] That seems difficult to validate, and, as it turns out, may serve to do nothing more than draw lines in the sand. There is no reason to have one or the other when *both* seem to be represented in Scripture (John 10:38 is a prime example of the "static" sense of

---

48. Stramara, "Gregory of Nyssa's Terminology for Trinitarian Perichoresis."

49. Torrance, *The Christian Doctrine of God*, 171.

50. Collins, *Trinitarian Theology: West and East*, 209–210.

perichoresis). In fact, a push to take either one or the other suggests a theological agenda, either aimed at underscoring God's action (e.g., Barth's notion that God has his being "in act") or at reducing divine mystery so as to rationalistically master knowledge of the Godhead. Just as unity and plurality are equally ultimate in the Godhead, so are staticism and dynamism.[51] We do well to follow the example of John of Damascus and confess that we are dealing with a mystery here, not something neatly categorized at several levels.

Perichoresis and Representation

With an understanding of the biblical roots and the theological origin of *perichoresis*, we can move on to situate the concept in our discussion of language. To do that, we must revisit a Van Tillian description of this doctrine, expressed with the language of *representation*. Van Til wrote,

> In the Trinity there is completely personal relationship without residue. And for that reason it may be said that man's actions are all personal too. Man's surroundings are shot through with personality because all things are related to the infinitely personal God. But when we have said that the surroundings of man are really completely personalized, we have also established the fact of the representational principle. All of man's acts must be representational of the acts of God. Even the persons of the Trinity are mutually representational. They are *exhaustively* representational of one another.[52]

---

51. Cornelius Van Til, *Introduction to Systematic Theology: Prolegomena and the Doctrines of Revelation, Scripture, and God*, ed. William Edgar, 2nd ed. (Phillipsburg, NJ: P&R Publishing, 2007), 364–65.

52. Van Til, *A Survey of Christian Epistemology*, 78.

Van Til is here discussing the concept of *perichoresis* with fresh vocabulary—vocabulary that is particularly helpful in discussions of language, as we will soon see. We can draw Van Til's meaning of Trinitarian representation from his discussion of our analogical representation.

Van Til defines our representation in the context of covenant. Sinful philosophy, he tells us, refuses to believe that our thought and action is valid if God is involved. All of our thought and action must be completely independent if it is to be authentic. So, for example, Romans 5 and Adam's representative headship must be left by the wayside if we want to affirm authentic and meaningful human behavior. Van Til calls this "unipersonal" thought and action.[53] It suggests that all of what we do must be done autonomously, in isolation from the triune God. It suggests further that "an act can be truly personal only if the surroundings of the person be impersonal [i.e., free of God's control, authority, and presence]."

The Christian, on the other hand, must claim that "all personal activity among men must be based upon the personality of the one ultimate person, namely, the person of God, if only it be understood that this ultimate personality of God is a triune personality."[54] Therefore, we are called to affirm not only that Adam's representational headship is valid and thus that inherited sin is a biblical truth, but also that all of our behaviors, if they are to be authentic and meaningful, must represent the trinitarian God analogically. As Van Til puts it, "Because he is a creature, man must, in his thinking, his feeling, and his

---

53. Ibid.

54. Ibid.

willing, be representative of God."⁵⁵ Anything that opposes or feigns operation in isolation from this God is actually inauthentic and void of meaning.

So, we represent the triune God when we think the Father's thoughts after him as revealed in Scripture, when we echo the words of Christ and conform to his image as we speak the truth in love (Rom. 8:29; Eph. 4:15), and when we act by and through the power of the Spirit who indwells us (Rom. 8:9–11). That, in essence, is how our analogical representation of the triune God works. But it is quite another thing when we move from creature to Creator.

Within the Trinity, the persons are "exhaustively representational" of one another. This means that in each person of the Godhead the other two persons are perfectly represented. When we look at the Father, we see the Son and Spirit represented felicitously and in full. When we look at the Son, we see the Father and the Spirit represented felicitously and in full. Likewise when we look at the Spirit. The persons of the Trinity coinhere, indwell, interpenetrate, permeate, and make room for one another to such an extent that we have no choice but to be dumbfounded at how such unity could exist without eclipsing personal distinctions. And yet in God's incomprehensibility, somehow this is the case. Exhaustive representation, like the traditional teaching of *perichoresis*, is meant to bring us to our knees in adoration, to bow our hearts and our minds to the God who dwells in intimate self-communion.

Though this exhaustive representation belongs only to the Trinity,⁵⁶ Van Til showed, as we noted earlier, that our

---

55. Ibid., 78–79.

56. "The divine persons indwell human beings in a qualitatively different way than they do one another." Vanhoozer, *Remythologizing Theology*, 153.

thought and behavior as creatures is analogically related to this. If the persons of the Godhead exhaustively represent one another, then creatures made in the image of that God analogically represent the "person" of the Godhead on a finite scale. So, "man's thought is representative of God's thought, but not exhaustively representative."[57] The same goes for the rest of coherent and meaningful human behavior, i.e., language.

Now that we have settled what Van Til meant by his "representational principle," we can move on to the climax of our discussion: how perichoresis is related to and establishes the nature of language.

Perichoresis and Language

We noted earlier that our application of perichoresis would need to be applied to both divine and human language. On the divine level, we will explore how perichoresis deepens our understanding of the trinitarian analogy of Speaker (Father), Speech (Son), and Breath (Spirit). We will then move from this level to the more specific level of God's Word, considering the interpenetration of God's meaning, control, and presence within that Word. On the human level, we will examine the creaturely analogue of speaker, speech, and breath. Then we will narrow our focus once more to look at our words and the perichoretic structure of human language in relation to grammar, phonology, and reference. Here we will draw on the linguistic theory of Kenneth Pike.

---

57. Van Til, *A Survey of Christian Epistemology*, 79.

Speaker, Speech, and Breath

The linguistic analogy for the Trinity has long been celebrated by theologians of the East and West. St. Basil has a unique focus on the Father as the divine heart from which the Son as the Word is produced. In answer to the question, "why call the Son 'the Word'?" he writes,

> Why *Word*? So that it may be understood that it proceeds from the intellect. Why *Word*? Because he was begotten without passion. Why *Word*? Because he is the image of his begetter, showing in himself the whole of the begetter, not divided from him in any way and existing perfect in himself, just as our word also reflects the whole of our thought. For what we express in words is that which we think in our heart, and that which is spoken is a reflection of the thought in the heart. For *out of the abundance of the heart* [Mt 12:34; Lk 6:45] the word is expressed.[58]

But in general, it seems apropos to draw from John's prologue the conclusion that "God the Father is speaker, God the Son is the speech, and God the Spirit is the breath carrying the speech to its destination. The Spirit is also the power who brings about its effects."[59] Though the Spirit is not mentioned explicitly in the prologue, he is present through the allusion to Genesis 1, where the Spirit hovered over the surface of the waters and then was given as the breath of life for animate creatures (Job 33:4).

When it comes to *perichoresis* of the Speaker, Speech, and Breath, we find that

---

58. Basil the Great, "Homily on the Beginning of the Gospel of John," in *On Christian Doctrine and Practice*, trans. Mark DelCogliano, Popular Patristics 47 (Yonkers, NY: St. Vladimir's Seminary Press, 2012), 254–55.

59. Poythress, *In the Beginning Was the Word*, 21.

The Father's wisdom is expressed in the Word. This expression in the Word shows that the Father dwells in the Son. The Father's thought is in the Son. In addition, the Father's word is in the Father even before he expresses it to the world. That implies that the Son dwells in the Father. And the Spirit, as the breath of God, works in power in conformity with the character of the Word. The Spirit is in the Son and the Son is in the Spirit. The Spirit carries out the purpose of the Father, and manifests the power of the Father, which implies that the Father dwells in the Spirit and the Spirit in the Father.[60]

Combining this application of *perichoresis* with Van Til's vocabulary of "exhaustive representation," we come to an ancient truth: though there is distinction in roles within the Trinity, there is intimate communion of the highest order. As Speaker, the Father perfectly represents the Son as his Word and the Spirit as his Breath carrying that Word with unparalleled power and efficacy. As Speech, the Son perfectly represents the Father as the one who clearly and eternally articulated him, and the Spirit as the life and dynamism of that holy articulation. As Breath, the Spirit perfectly represents the Father who speaks the Word, whose divine phonemes, we might say, are formed and applied in congruence with the Speaker's intention and the Word's meaning.

All this is to say the perichoretic union of Speaker, Speech, and Breath is so concentrated that there is no gap between *who* God is, *what* he says, and the *effect* of what he says. The divine linguistic community holds perfect integrity with itself. We find no gaps in the communicative behavior of the Trinity. It is for this reason—the perfect communicative behavior of the immanent Trinity—that

---

60. Ibid.

we can have such blissful trust in God's revelation, i.e., the communicative behavior of the economic Trinity.

Meaning, Control, and Presence

When we narrow our focus to God's Word in particular, we retain our dependence on and awareness of the Speaker, Speech, and Breath. God's Word manifests his meaning, control, and presence.[61] These three terms, as Poythress notes, can be linked to the Father, Son, and Spirit respectively. His explanation is particularly insightful for us:

> Meaning originates from the plan of the Father. As executor of the Father's will, the Son is closely associated with control. The Father speaks specific orders in his word, which is the Word of the Son. By means of the Son, the Father carries out his will. And the Holy Spirit is closely associated with the presence of God. In Genesis 1:2 the Spirit hovering over the waters expresses the presence of God in creation. Since the persons of the Trinity are coinherent, we expect that the three perspectives on communication, namely, meaning, control, and presence, will also be derivatively coinherent.[62]

The glimmer of *perichoresis* catches the eye when we consider the creation account, where God's Word brings a meaningful world into existence—meaningful ultimately only in relation to the Trinity who chose to create it—a world that is controlled and upheld by the Word (Heb. 1:3) and which manifests the presence of the Trinity throughout. The Word manifests God's presence by manifesting the

---

61. Ibid., 24–25 ; John M. Frame, *The Doctrine of the Word of God* (Phillipsburg, NJ: P&R Publishing, 2010), 50 67.

62. Poythress, *In the Beginning Was the Word*, 25.

triune "person,"[63] for "the word of God is *God* speaking, not a 'something' detached and unrelated to God himself."[64]

The coinherence of meaning, control, and presence in God's word again attests to the truth that there are no gaps in God. The meaning of our linguistically derived world (for all of reality is derived from God's speech) is worked out through the meaningful communication of the Father's will for creation. That meaningful will is perfectly represented in the controlled expression of the Son, who executes the Father's will, but that expression itself exudes the presence of the triune God, and the Spirit works to carry the expression to its destination and apply its effects to us as hearers. The meaning coinheres with the control coinheres with the presence. To use Augustine's words again, "each is in each, and all are in each, and all are one." Relating all of this to God as divine Speaker, Speech, and Breath, we affirm that just as there is no gap between who God is, what he says, and the effect of what he says, so there is no gap between *what* he means (meaning), *how* he means (control) it, and *whom* (Spirit) he intends to convey as his word affects his audience.

Human Speakers, Speech, and Breath

As we are creatures made in the image of the triune God, we also are, analogously, speakers who can produce speech with our breath. Our longing to do so reflects that we are made in the image of a gapless God. As Stăniloae puts it,

---

63. Here I use "person" to denote not the distinct trinitarian persons, but the Godhead in its entirety, which, as is well known, Van Til did in his *Introduction to Systematic Theology*.

64. Poythress, *In the Beginning Was the Word*, 26; emphasis added.

In the Word people meet each other and the Word of God. John the Evangelist uses the name "the Word" to show us not only the interpersonal nature of the divinity but also the will and power of God to meet humans and help them meet each other. For God placed the power and the injunction of words in each one of us so that we might have communion with each other and with the divine Word.[65]

And we might add, "with the divine *Trinity*," for we have communion with the Father through the Son by the power of the Spirit. The point is that our desire for intimate communion with one another and with God is rooted in God's intimate communion with himself. God's communion is unbroken, but sin has broken our communion, both with God and with each other. We have a desire for the unparalleled trinitarian love, but in Adam we traded that fulfilled desire for isolation and autonomy. Yet, even now

> Each person has in his word a request that includes a declaration of his love for the other and that asks for the other's response. This exchange is based on the way that the incarnate Son declares His love for the Father even in His humanity. This declaration and response would not exist without an interpersonal relationship. And the supreme origin of the offer and response is in the Trinity.[66]

We need to adjust Stăniloae's wording a bit, though he

---

65. Stăniloae, *The Holy Trinity*, 37.

66. Ibid., 54. Elsewhere he writes, "Humans too are unities of intelligences, or incorporated words, made to know God the Father through the Son, and, through words, to be united with the Word of the Father." Note again the absence of the Spirit in this statement. This is an ongoing problem in his writing.

is on to something. He seems to have left the Spirit out of the equation as the Breath of God.[67] As even he himself admits, "the Spirit is not a 'He' about whom the Father and Son speak, but each speaks of the other two inseparably. Neither the Father nor the Son speaks about the Spirit as about a third who is apart from Them, but the Father has the Spirit within Himself when He speaks with the Son, and the Son has the Spirit within Himself when He speaks with the Father, just as when He speaks with us."[68] So, our longing to communicate as speakers, by speech and with breath, is rooted in the communion of Speaker, Speech, and Breath in the Trinity.

Now, the exhaustively representational Trinity has created us in his image, and so we should expect that our ability to speak would follow in God's divine footsteps, modeling the *perichoresis* of speaker, speech, and breath analogically. This is indeed the case. In the Trinity, the Father is Speaker, the Son is Speech, and the Spirit is breath; each of God's image bearers, in turn, is a speaker who utters discourse by the breath that is within him.[69] Poythress, once again, is helpful here:

> Speech presupposes a speaker. A speech without a speaker is virtually an impossibility. . . . Thus, a speech is

---

67. The reason for this, I surmise, is the underlying subordinationism in his approach to the Trinity and his rejection of the *filioque* clause, classic of Eastern Orthodox theologians. His subordinationism leads him to focus more on the relation of the Son and the Father, and his rejection of the *filioque* seems to make him relegate the Spirit to a sort of "third wheel" in the Trinity, though he tries to deny this. See Stăniloae, *The Holy Trinity*, 25, 29–32, 36–38, 49, 54, 63–65.

68. Ibid., 65.

69. Poythress, *In the Beginning Was the Word*, 31.

dependent on a speaker, and can be coherently understood only on those terms. A speech must "dwell in" a speaker in order to be a speech. But, conversely, a speaker presupposes a speech. If we are to know what the speaker means, we cannot climb inside his head; we rely on his speech of on some alternate, speech-like mode of communication (like gestures). A speaker is accessible through his speech. He "dwells in" his speech.

. . . . The speech goes to its destination through breath, or through some breath-like medium of communication. Without a medium and a transfer, there is no speech at all. The speech must "dwell in" its breath or its medium. Conversely, without the meaning content, there is no speech at all. The breath must "dwell in" a speech and its medium in order to be a speech at all. The breath must issue from a speaker, and "dwell in" the speaker.[70]

Of course, unlike the persons of the Trinity, our speech and breath are not self-conscious persons. That is where the analogy breaks down. However, there is a sense in which a human speaker, speech, and breath is analogically tied to the persons of the Godhead as the archetype. In fact, that is precisely what we have been arguing. We can speak because the Father speaks.[71] We can speak words because the Son is the Word of the Father, and our speech is carried to its destination by our breath (or some other medium) because the Spirit carries the Father's word to its destination, even if that destination is within the immanent Trinity, i.e., the Father or the Son, or both.

---

70. Ibid., 32.

71. Frame ties this to the fact that speech is an essential attribute of the Godhead. "God's eternal inter-Trinitarian speech is a necessary divine attribute, an attribute without which God would not be God. As such, speech, like all other necessary attributes, designates the essence of God, what God really and truly is. Ultimately, God's word is God, and God is his word." Frame, *Doctrine of the Word of God*, 48.

Just as humans analogically represent the Trinity as the archetypal Speaker, Speech, and Breath in perichoretic union, so also we image the Trinity in communicating meaning, control, and presence.[72] They are manifested in the substructures of human language, namely grammar, phonology, and reference, which is where we turn presently.

Perichoresis of Grammar, Phonology, and Reference

Just as we narrowed our focus on divine speech from Speaker, Speech, and Breath to the meaning, control, and presence of the Word, we now narrow our focus to the particular structure of human words. Here again we find *perichoresis* in the nature of language via the hierarchies of grammar, phonology, and reference. This is the genius of Kenneth Pike, so we will be following him closely here.[73]

For Pike, language is what he calls "tristructural." A tristructural analysis of language "does not look at the same set of parts from different viewpoints or in different dimensions as such, but sees a single large unit divided into three sets of hierarchically arranged subunits such that each hierarchical set comprises the whole."[74] Guarding against the trinitarian heresies of tritheism and modalism, Pike is

---

72. "Without meaning, speech is empty. Without control, it does not accomplish anything, and makes no difference. Without presence, the speech is disconnected from the speaker and again loses its point. We depend on the fact that we are made in the image of God." Poythress, *In the Beginning Was the Word*, 31.

73. See also chapter 32 of Poythress' *In the Beginning Was the Word*.

74. Kenneth L. Pike, "Language and Life 4: Tristructural Units of Human Behavior," *Bibliotheca Sacra* 114, no. 456 (January 1958): 37.

clear that his approach is neither tripartite nor triaspectual or tridimensional. Once we approve of his trinitarian approach, we immediately ask, what are the hierarchies that comprise this tristructural analysis?

For Pike, there are three structured hierarchies, each composed of a certain type of unit. First, there is the *identification-contrastive* structure, tied to morphemes, i.e., meaningful lexical units. In the sentence, *I believe in Christ*, we find the morphemes *I*, *believe*, *in*, and *Christ*. These morphemes reveal the meaningful referents of the speaker; thus, the identification-contrastive structure is linked to reference.

Next, there is the *manifestation* structure, which can be tied to what Pike calls "gramemes." Gramemes are grammatical-functional roles in a defined contextual matrix. For example, *I* in the example sentence would be considered the "subject-as-actor" grameme.

Lastly, there is the *distribution* or *functional* structure, which is tied to vowels, consonants, intonation, stress, and other phonemic features of a phonetic matrix. In the previous example, among other phonetic features, we find three long vowels, a shewa (*buh* in *believe*), and a short vowel (*i* for the preposition *in*). The distribution of such features is linked to the phonological system of a language.

Now, take away the units of any of these structures— identification-contrastive (reference), manifestation (grammar), and distribution (phonology)—and you are left with nothing.[75] Each structure is distinct, and yet each comprises the whole of the linguistic piece in focus. Moreover, there is interpenetration of these structures, for they are

---

75. Pike, "Language and Life 4: Tristructural Units of Human Behavior," 37–30.

"simultaneous, overlapping, but distinct." The reference to *perichoresis* should be evident. Pike brought this out explicitly at the end of the article that we have been referencing. He first notes that "in the Christian understanding of God's nature there are three persons which, in order to show the analogy, might be called personal 'structures.' Each has its own personal individuality and function without constituting a new part of God or an additional God; each is the whole."[76] Then we can go on to associate the indentification-contrastive structure (reference) with the Father, the manifestation structure (grammar) with the Son, and the distribution structure (phonology) to the Spirit.[77]

---

76. Ibid., 39.

77. Pike and Poythress differ slightly on the relation of these hierarchies to the persons of the Trinity. Pike writes, "The identificational-contrastive structure with its basic priority of meaning and purpose and communication from individual to individual would be suggested as illustrative of the relationship of the person of God the Father to the Trinity as a whole—inasmuch as ultimate purpose seems to reside in Him (Eph. 1:9, 11) . . . . On the other hand, as the manifestation structure of linguistic units is the audible, concrete form which can be directly apprehended by us, and is the medium through which all linguistic meaning is communicated, so the second person of the Trinity, the Son, was made concretely available to the senses of man, to be seen, heard, touched (Col. 1:15; 1 John 1:1) . . . . Similarly, as the distributional-functional structure in the sentence forms the matrix within which the words of the sentence occur . . . , so the third person of the Trinity may perhaps be viewed as the structured distributional personal matrix for the work of God (as the Spirit works in us with the love of God which 'is shed abroad in our hearts by the Holy Ghost' (Rom. 5:5)." Ibid., 42–43. Thus, it would seem that Pike could relate the identificational-contrastive structure with reference and the Father, as Poythress does. See Poythress, *In the Beginning Was the Word*, 267–68. However, the above quotation by Pike makes it likely that he would associate the Son with phonology, rather than the Spirit. Poythress does the opposite, which seems more fitting since the Spirit is the breath of God: the medium that carries the Word. Still, one must remember that in the context of *perichoresis*, grammar, phonology, and reference can be viewed perspectivally, so we should not

Thus, grammar, phonology, and reference in every linguistic unit of human language is a creaturely analogue of the self-communicating Trinity, summarized in the figure below.

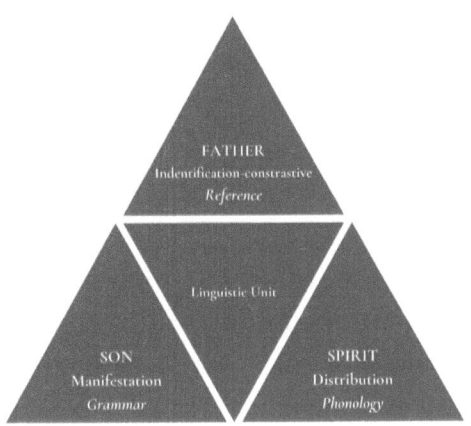

In summary, we find the concept of *perichoresis* in divine language via Speaker (Father), Speech (Son), and Breath (Spirit), as well as in the meaning, control, and presence of the Word. We also find it in human speakers, speech, and breath and in the grammatical, phonological, and referential hierarchies. All of this is well and good, but we have not yet solved "the problem of gaps" that we introduced at the start; we have not yet shown how *perichoresis* reveals the nature of language to that end.

---

expect to see elements of grammar associated with the Father or the Spirit, or elements of phonology associated with the Father, and so on. We would, on the other hand, say that each person of the Trinity has a fitting, central tie to one of these subsystems. I would concur that the Father is linked with reference, the Son with grammar, and the Spirit with phonology.

Misrepresentation and the Disruption of Analogical Perichoresis

I mentioned earlier that Van Til's language of *representation* would be particularly useful in our understanding of language. Here, in brief, is why.

The persons of the Trinity are, as Van Til put it, "exhaustively representational" of one another. Because the persons of the Godhead are exhaustively representational of one another, creatures made in the image of the Trinity are analogically representational of God in all that they do.[78]

Language, then, must also be representational. By this we mean that all of our communicative behavior represents on a finite, analogical scale the communicative behavior of the Trinity. In their communicative behavior, the persons of the Trinity exhaustively represent one another; in our communicative behavior, we image the Trinity by analogically representing ourselves. Perhaps it is for this reason that we see Scripture constantly identifying a *person* with his or her *words*, both communally and individually. The human race was a unified whole prior to Genesis 11, when "the whole earth had one language and the same words." The diffusion of language brought about not just confusion, but the separation of people groups (Gen. 11:8). Ever since that time, people groups have been identified primarily by their native language, or at least their dialect. Hence, Peter stuck out like a sore thumb among the scribes and elders of Jerusalem because his speech was phonetically unique; he was a Galilean (Matt. 23:73), and spoke as one. Every utterance marked him as a member of

---

78. Van Til, *A Survey of Christian Epistemology*, 78.

a specific geographic community.

Our words also represent us individually, ultimately because the Word of the Father is the "exact imprint of his nature" (Heb. 1:3). The Father is perfectly represented by the Son, who is the Word. Because we are creatures made in the image of the trinitarian God, our words are fitting representations of who we are. Just as God's Word reveals his personal presence, so our words express our personality, and in that sense we are present with our words.[79] Because we ourselves are present with our words, there is a sense in which our words are inextricably bound up with our person. For this reason, the psalmist writes, "Keep your tongue from evil and your lips from speaking deceit" (Ps. 34:13). *People* commit evil acts; *people* are deceptive, but our words are so deeply rooted in our personhood that the psalmist can exhort our tongues and lips as if they were *us*. Indeed, we can certainly assume this much if Christ himself says, "by your words you will be justified, and by your words you will be condemned" (Matt. 12:37). Language determines our destination as people.

Language, then, is representational of both communities and individual persons. However, language is also representational in another sense, probably more in line with what Van Til might have considered. Language is representational in the sense that we should represent the Trinitarian God in our use of words to love and honor others. For all eternity, God comprises his own linguistic

---

79. "Man's speech shows meaning, control, and presence. In this respect it images the meaning, control, and presence of God's speech." Poythress, *In the Beginning Was the Word*, 30. See also chapter 11 of John M. Frame, *The Doctrine of the Word of God* (Phillipsburg, NJ: P&R Publishing, 2010).

community of self-love and glorification.[80] While we are not called to glorify others with our words, we are called to build one another up and encourage one another (1 Thess. 5:11). This is related to glorification in that it is an uplifting behavior. When we encourage someone, we lift that person up so that he or she understands how much he or she is loved.

This means that all of our sinful communication comes from a lack of representation in speaker, speech, and breath—a *misrepresentation*. With God, there is no gap between *who* he is, *what* he says, and the *effect* his speech has on his hearers. This is not the case with us. Oftentimes who we are in Christ is not represented by what we say or how we say it. Conversely, those who are not in Christ sometimes act in ways that accord with God's law even though who they presently are, as those still "in Adam," is not represented by what they say or how they say it (Rom. 2:14). Our communication, as sinners, is riddled with misrepresentation, i.e., with gaps. Why is this the case?

Earlier, we discussed how sin disrupts communion and asserts futile self-government and autonomy. Sin is also present in marring the image of God. That image, we now know, is related to speaker, speech, and breath, as well as grammar, phonology, and reference. If human sin is a disruption or severing of communion—rather,

---

80. "The divine essence is only divine when hypostasized in three Persons, because these three have a value and a relationship between Them that deserves and is capable of absolute love." Dumitru Staniloae, *The Holy Trinity: In the Beginning There Was Love*, trans. Roland Clark (Brookline, MA: Holy Cross Orthodox Press, 2012), 17. He later writes, "The highest form of love is revealed to us in the unending love between the one and only Father of a unique Son. Yet throughout eternity the love between the Father and the Son has also been directed toward a third Person who takes joy in the love that each has for the other" (ibid., 55).

the disruption of *our* communion with the gapless, exhaustively representational triune God—then *perichoresis* may reflect this and be especially useful in helping us close the gaps between us. To put it differently, *perichoresis* may be the treatment for our diagnosis of communicative misrepresentation.

Consider this more precisely in our discussion of a speaker, speech, and breath. A problem in any of them affects all of them. There are, of course, physical effects of the Fall that have lead to problems with speakers. Not many are direct causes, mind you, but unexplainable brokenness that longs for restoration. Children and adults with lower cognitive abilities and those struggling with various forms of autism, for example, have a great deal of difficultly *as speakers*.[81] That is, they have great difficulty with, or even lack awareness of, verbal expressions and signals of nonverbal communicative behavior (gestures and body language). The challenges they encounter as speakers in turn affect their speech, or, in the absence of speech, their intended message. Likewise, the breath they long to use to send their words to a parent or loved one is frustrated and thus channeled into other expressive behaviors. Air that might have been used to articulate a request to turn off the television instead fuels anxious or methodical stimulations (sometimes referred to in the field as "stimming"). The action of the speaker is still expressing something—perhaps irritation at the sounds of the television—but many of these behaviors are difficult, if not impossible, to interpret for those unacquainted with the person affected by autism. Thus, a cognitive challenge

---

81. It has been reported that a third of children and adults with autism encounter this staggering challenge. See "10 Years of Progress: What We've Learned About Autism," Autism Speaks, http://www.autismspeaks.org/news/news-item/10-years-progress-what-we039ve-learned-about-autism.

in the speaker can and often does lead to hindrance in forming or producing an expression, in addition to impeding the reception of the message by another person. Thus, gaps open up—heart-wrenchingly painful gaps—between those who struggle to communicate and those who long to commune with them. And once those gaps open, the indwelling speech and breath meant to express the speaker's thoughts and intentions is broken.

This is only the physical side of our "speaker problems." There is also the spiritual side, and this runs even deeper. A speaker who has been redeemed in Christ by the power of the Spirit (the Speech and Breath of the divine Speaker) may be able to form communicable thoughts into verbal language and use his breath to send it to its destination in order to speak the truth in love (Eph 4:15), but what about those who are not united to Christ, and those still dealing with sin on the long road to sanctification? What happens when our speech seems nothing more than "irreverent babble" (2 Tim 2:16), when our words mainly tear down those around us (cf. Eph 4:29) or even express indifference to the struggles and joys of others?

When we fall into this category, as even the most faithful Christians do, we sow dissension and confusion with the words we articulate, and the breath that should be used to build up others in the body of Christ ends up contributing to the corrosion of communion. Our sin as speakers opens ravines that no speech or breath can bridge, save the continual intercession of the Word and the Breath of life we receive in his name. Still, on the existential level, *perichoresis* of speaker, speech, and breath for sinners is often disrupted.

When it comes to our speech, we often encounter problems related to the perichoretic ties between grammar, phonology, and reference. When one of these is disturbed, because of their mutual indwelling, it affects the other two. Consider the sentence, *Paul did not want committing sin*. Even if this sentence is pronounced with accents on the correct syllables and appropriate intonation within context, the grammatical problem is disruptive. According to the structure of English, some verbs can be followed by gerunds, some by infinitives, and some by both. Here the gerund *committing* should be replaced with the infinitive *to commit*. If not, there is semantic ambiguity, which affects the reference of the utterance. Is *committing sin* a certain type of sin that Paul did not want, or are we saying that the act of committing sin is not what Paul wanted? The referential ambiguity leads hearers of this sentence to question whether the speaker knows precisely what he wants to say, and, if he really intended to say something else, they might wonder if that might slightly change the pronunciation. For instance, perhaps the speaker originally accented the word *committing*. Sometimes English speakers accent the adjective preceding a noun to emphasize the quality (e.g., *He memorized several long passages of Scripture*). But this is probably not the speaker's intention—it would lead us to believe that Paul does not want to carry out a certain kind of sin, which, at least, is not what is implied in Rom. 7:15. If, however, the gerund is replaced by the infinitive, the stress might naturally shift to the main verb: *Paul did not want to commit sin*. With a grammatical change, the pronunciation falls into place and the referential meaning becomes clear.

We encounter problems with phonology as well. The sentence, *Why did you do that?* can be pronounced in a way that suggests either sharp criticism or simply an innocent inquiry. The pronunciation affects the meaning, and this affects how the recipient of the question views the one who asked it, the speaker. As with the grammatical problem, a problem related to pronunciation (a subsystem of phonology) introduces discord into the perichoretic relations between grammar, phonology, and reference, which in turn affects the relations of speaker, speech, and breath.

Finally, with reference to our breath, we encounter problems that are essentially related to medium. The breath we use in speech is felicitous with a certain medium, namely, spoken language. But we can use other media to communicate besides our breath. For example, we can type words on a page and use the medium of written language. The breath we used to produce sounds and send them to a destination now becomes the graphic symbols we type in a word processing document, or email. But the shift in medium introduces a whole new set of potential problems. We could use the medium inappropriately, such as when we send an email or text to someone who would have preferred that we call or meet to discuss the issue in person. The choice of medium affects the message (as McLuhan pointed out decades ago), and this in turn affects how the speaker (or writer) is perceived by the recipient of the message.

All of these disruptions in analogical *perichoresis* for human language—disruptions caused by misrepresentation—serve to introduce gaps in our communion with one another. Some gaps are larger than others. Some are small and can be closed if we make the effort to revise our communication, or apologize for poor communication, or simply for hurtful words.

Conclusion

In closing, we have learned that the doctrine of *perichoresis* shows we are bound to a God who dwells in self-communion, a God who speaks to himself and to his creatures. God's perfect self-communion is the archetype for our creaturely communion. And this is especially important to remember in a world where communion is the goal, but rarely the norm.

The nature of our language, imprinted by the Father, Son, and Holy Spirit, is thus communal. It serves to close the gaps that exist between persons as well as the gap that exists between ourselves and the tripersonal God. In God, there are no gaps. And one day, when we dwell with him in glory, gaps will be foreign to us as well. But for now, we continue speaking, leaning upon the divine Speaker, Speech, and Breath for our daily communication. The closer we come to embracing the perichoretic nature of language, the closer we will be to practicing harmony between who we are, what we say, and how we say it. The more integral that harmony becomes, the closer we will draw to the God whose personality, expression, and efficacy have brought the world into being and will one day bring all of the pieces back together so that we are one, even as he is one (John 17:21).

Do You See how I See?
The Trinitarian Roots of Human Perception

The Reformed tradition has made clear that the doctrine of the Trinity is a purely revealed doctrine. Only the radiance of Scripture could illuminate a truth so lofty. We cannot walk through the woods and recognize the Father, Son, and Holy Spirit in the venous pattern of a maple leaf—at least, not without prior knowledge of the triune God as revealed in Scripture.

Yet, the Reformed position on the place of the Trinity in general revelation seems to call for more nuanced treatment. Van Til, for instance, has always affirmed that God's triunity is the essential mark of his identity, and that all knowledge is predicated not upon a deistic god or the god of bare theism but upon the triune God of Scripture.[1] Before him, Bavinck claimed that the doctrine of the Trinity is the centerpiece of Christianity and is definitive

---

1. "The Trinity . . . gives the most basic description possible of God as the *principium essendi* of knowledge for man." Cornelius Van Til, *Introduction to Systematic Theology: Prolegomena and the Doctrines of Revelation, Scripture, and God*, 2nd ed., ed. William Edgar (Phillipsburg, NJ: P&R Publishing, 2007), 30. "Our knowledge rests upon the ontological Trinity as its presupposition" (ibid., 59). With regards to the final reference point of all interpretation, i.e., all predication of meaning, Van Til wrote, "The Protestant principle finds this in the self-contained ontological Trinity." It is this God that "is always the most basic and therefore the ultimate or final reference point in human interpretation." Van Til, *The Defense of the Faith*, 4th ed., ed. K. Scott Oliphint (Phillipsburg, NJ: P&R Publishing, 2008), 100. On this doctrine taken explicitly from Scripture, see pages 227–28, 236, and 241.

of the true God.² In other words, the bedrock of God's being is his triunity. Scripture—both the New Testament and the Old—eschews deism. Though the unity of God may be more prevalent in the Old Testament and the plurality of God more prevalent in the New, we cannot say that the God revealed in all of Scripture, and, what's more, in all of nature, is any other than the triune God. In light of this, "if the world was made by the Holy Trinity, and it also declares the glory of God, it seems reasonable to suppose that there will be hints all around us in creation that point to the Trinity."³ So, when Paul speaks of all men having a knowledge of God through what has been made (Rom 1), he must be referencing the Trinitarian God, but in what sense?⁴ How can we say that people who have not seen or accepted the light of Scripture still have knowledge of a doctrine that the Reformed tradition has adamantly defended as revealed solely in special revelation?

In the following pages, we address this question by positing a dual knowledge of the Trinity: salvific and non-salvific. We then explore one avenue in which non-salvific knowledge of the Trinity presents itself by drawing on the philosophy of Kenneth L. Pike. Ultimately, I aim to show that the presence of particle (static), wave (dynamic), and field (relational) perspectives—considered in perichoretic

---

2. Herman Bavinck, *Reformed Dogmatics*, vol. 2, *God and Creation* (ed. John Bolt; trans. John Vriend; Grand Rapids, Mich.: Baker Academic, 2004), 296.

3. Robert Letham, *The Holy Trinity: In Scripture, History, Theology, and Worship* (Phillipsburg, NJ: P&R Publishing, 2004), 435.

4. "As Calvin says, when the word God is used indefinitely it means the Triune God, and not the Father in distinction from the Son and Spirit." Charles Hodge, *Systematic Theology* (Peabody, MA: Hendrickson, 2013), 1:467.

relationship to one another—shows one way in which the trinitarian God permeates human perception. Thus, Pike's perspectives serve as an example of how people at all times and places depend on the Trinity for their coherent perception of reality, albeit none of them knows this triune God *as triune*, in a salvific sense. Non-salvific knowledge of the Triune God, then, is a blind reliance that only enforces the culpability addressed by Paul in Romans 1. For Christians, whose eyes have had the scales of sin fall away (Acts 9:18), this non-salvific knowledge serves to deepen our amazement of the ubiquity of the Trinity—for whom, through whom, and to whom are all things (Rom. 11:36).

Salvific Knowledge of the Trinity

Nearly every writer in the Reformed tradition who demands that knowledge of the Trinity only comes from Scripture is referencing *salvific* knowledge of the Trinity, i.e., discrete awareness of the Father, Son, and Holy Spirit, specifically in their redemptive roles.[5] Salvific knowledge

---

5. This includes the mainstay historical Reformers, Luther and Calvin, as well as modern and contemporary Reformed theologians such as Bavinck, Hodge, Warfield, and Berkhof. David Lumpp summarizes Luther's view on the Trinity in Scripture as follows: "Along with the parallel affirmation of the one indivisible and eternal Godhead, the internal personal distinctions can only be believed. This is what Holy Scripture teaches, Luther states casually, and to say anything less or anything else is to revert to the errors of ancient heretics, the rabbis, or the Turks. . . . Martin Luther understood that the being of the Triune God is known neither speculatively nor abstractly, but only in a relationship of trust, insofar as the God of the Gospel is revealed to sinners in the Son and through the Holy Spirit." David A. Lumpp, "Returning to Wittenberg: What Luther Teaches Today's Theologians on the Holy Trinity," *CTQ* 67, no. 3-4 (2003): 232, 233–34. Mickey Mattox, following Peura, notes that "the knowledge of God for Luther is grounded first, last, and always in the humanity of Christ. This is not to say,

of the Trinity entails the *pactum* and *ordo salutis*—that in his triunity God has planned, executed, applied, and will one day consummate his particular scheme of salvation.

Our salvific knowledge of the Trinity allows us to identify not only the redemptive work of the persons of the Godhead but also their work in creation. Thus, we come to find that each person of the triune God was involved in forging the cosmos—God the Father spoke his Word by the breath of the Holy Spirit in bringing the visible and invisible into existence.[6] He then ordered the world

---

however, that God the Father or God the Holy Spirit are not to be known, as if they could somehow be rendered superfluous by Luther's christocentrism. To the contrary, it is the Son who in his incarnate humanity opens the way to knowing God—Father, Son, and Spirit—in a saving way." The Gospel revealed in Scripture was, for Luther, what lead to a full understanding of the Triune God. See Mickey L. Mattox, "From Faith to the Text and Back Again: Martin Luther on the Trinity in the Old Testament," *Pro Eccles.* 15, no. 3 (2006): 292.

Calvin, as well, leaves perspicuous knowledge of the triune God within the courtyard of Scripture. T. F. Torrance writes that, for Calvin, "we may know God only through sharing in the knowledge of the Son by the Father and in the knowledge of the Father by the Son, and the revelation he gives us of himself through his Spirit (Matt. 11:27; Luke 10:22; 1 Cor. 2:9ff.). Practically this means that 'we must not be minded to inquire of God anywhere than in his sacred Word, or think anything of him except under the guidance of his Word, or to say anything of him except what is taken from the same Word' *(Inst.,* 1.13.21)." T. F. Torrance, "Calvin's Doctrine of the Trinity," *CTJ* 25, no. 2 (1990): 166.

For modern and contemporary assertions in line with Luther and Calvin, see Bavinck, *God and Creation*, 279, 329; Hodge, *Systematic Theology*, 1:442.; B. B. Warfield, *Biblical and Theological Studies*, ed. Samuel G. Craig (Phillipsburg, NJ: Presbyterian and Reformed, 1968), 22; Louis Berkhof, *Systematic Theology*, new ed. (Grand Rapids, MI: William B. Eerdmans, 1996), 85.

6. See Douglas Kelly, *Systematic Theology: Grounded in Holy Scripture and Understood in Light of the Church*, vol. 1, *The God Who Is: The Holy Trinity* (Ross-shire, Scotland: Mentor, 2008), 132.

through his Word and gave life to animate creatures by breathing into them (a reference to the Spirit).[7] It was no deistic god that created all that we see and do not see (Col. 1:16); it was the Trinity.

Once we have acquired salvific knowledge of the Trinity through the Word, the scratched and fractured lenses of our epistemic glasses are replaced. We look not only at all of God's dealings with man, but also every fiber of the world around us as bearing the glorious mark of the Trinity. With Calvin, we affirm that we cannot help but see this, for "there is no part of the world, however small, in which at least some spark of God's glory does not shine."[8] We must also remember, with Calvin, that in order for us to know this triune God truly, it was necessary that he open "his holy lips," for "he saw that his face and image etched into the edifice of the world were not enough."[9] Had God not spoken, we would certainly have no *conscious* knowledge that he is triune. We would rely on such a truth, no doubt, but we would be blind to it. "A blind man cannot see the light of the sun but the sun is there for all that. In fact, the blind man is blind only in relation to the light of the sun."[10] It is this blind reliance that I will call *non-salvific* knowledge of the Trinity.

It is important to note here that most Reformed theologians up to this point have used the phrase "the

---

7. Job 33:4.

8. John Calvin, *Institutes of the Christian Religion: A New Translation of the 1541 Edition*, trans. Robert White (Carlisle, PA: Banner of Truth, 2014), 10.

9. Calvin, *Institutes of the Christian Religion*, 16, 17.

10. Cornelius Van Til, *Common Grace and the Gospel* (Nutley, NJ: Presbyterian and Reformed, 1977), 214.

doctrine of the Trinity" in reference only to salvific knowledge—a perspicuous and nuanced understanding of the Father, Son, and Holy Spirit in their eternal fellowship and redemptive action. But I argue that non-salvific knowledge of the triune God should be considered within the purview of that doctrine. With Louis Berkhof, we can affirm that "the doctrine of the Trinity is very decidedly a doctrine of revelation," i.e., special revelation. But it is also foundational in general revelation.[11] And Van Til, it seems, would concur:

> Though we cannot tell why the Godhead should exist tri-personally, we can understand something of the fact, after we are told that God exists as a triune being, that the unity and the plurality of this world has back of it a God in whom unity and the plurality are equally ultimate. Thus we may say that this world, in some of its aspects at least, shows analogy to the Trinity. This world is made by God and, therefore, to the extent that it is capable of doing so, it may be thought of as revealing God as he exists. And God exists as a triune being.[12]

Though in the salvific sense non-Christians simply have no possible perception of the Trinity because "all is yellow to the jaundiced eye,"[13] it is *that* eye that provides non-salvific knowledge of the Trinity.

Non-Salvific Knowledge of the Trinity

Van Til, perhaps more than any other Reformed

---

11. Berkhof, *Systematic Theology*, 85.

12. Van Til, *Introduction to Systematic Theology*, 364–65.

13. Van Til, *Defense of the Faith*, 101.

theologian, demanded that all Christians recognize that meaning, coherence, and truth exist only as rooted in the self-contained ontological Trinity. He recurrently claimed that it is this triune God who is "the final reference point in interpretation."[14] In fact, "if we are to have *coherence* in our experience, there must be a correspondence of our experience to the eternally coherent experience of God. Human knowledge ultimately rests upon the internal coherence within the Godhead; our knowledge rests upon the ontological Trinity as its presupposition."[15]

When we pair this with his avowal that we live in a world that is "exhaustively revelational" of the triune God,[16] we cannot help but ask how the triunity of God bleeds through the fabric of general revelation—and not just the world outside of the human mind, but the human mind itself, especially as it seeks to think analogically. "Since the human mind is created by God and is therefore in itself naturally revelational of God, the mind may be sure that its system is true and corresponds on a finite scale to the system of God."[17] Is this system not trinitarian? If we cannot escape revealing the triune God in our intellectual

---

14 Ibid., 100.

15. Van Til, *Introduction to Systematic Theology*, 59.

16. Van Til, *Common Grace*, 169. Later, he notes, "the foundation of the thinking of both the Amsterdam and the Old Princeton men was that which both derived via Calvin and Paul, namely, the fact that God has unavoidably and clearly revealed himself in general and in special revelation. The whole triune God is involved in this revelation. The whole triune God testifies to man in this revelation" (186). See also Van Til's *Introduction to Systematic Theology*, 266.

17. Van Til, *Introduction to Systematic Theology*, 292.

consciousness,[18] then are we not bound to conclude that our "ectypal knowledge must inevitably show the stamp of its trinitarian archetype" and that "all human knowledge has a trinitarian structure in its source"?[19]

With others, Van Til included, I affirm that our knowledge rests upon the *internal* coherence of the Trinity, i.e., the equal ultimacy of the one and many, and the perichoretic relationship of the persons in the Godhead.[20] While Van Til would certainly echo Berkhof and claim that one of the main distinctions between men and God is that "man is uni-personal, while God is tri-personal," the fact that man's interpretation of the world around him bears the mark of his trinitarian maker seems unavoidable.[21]

Vestigia Trinitatis

This leads us into the somewhat precarious terrain of Augustine's *vestigia trinitatis*, "vestiges of the Trinity."[22] He

---

18. Van Til, *Common Grace*, 53.

19. Poythress, "Multiperspectivalism and the Reformed Faith," 191, 192. David Bentley Hart notes that we are creatures "called from nothingness to participate in the being that flows from [God], and to manifest his beauty in the depths of our nature." If this is the case, should we not assume that human perception is indelibly marked by the Trinitarian God? See David Bentley Hart, "The Mirror of the Infinite: Gregory of Nyssa on the *Vestigia Trinitatis*," *Mod. Theol.* 18, no. 4 (2002): 542.

20. See Van Til, *Introduction to Systematic Theology*, 58–59; *Defense of the Faith*, 47–50.

21. Berkhof, *Systematic Theology*, 84. "Augustine said, that as man was made in the image of the Triune God, we have reason to expect something in the constitution of our nature answering to the Trinity in the Godhead." Hodge, *Systematic Theology*, 1:478–79.

22. Augustine, *De Trinitate* 12.2.6–8.

dedicated most of one of his major works, *De Trinitate*, to surveying God's trinitarian imprints on man's nature.[23] I say "precarious" because most theologians, especially in the Reformed tradition, see a tendency in every trinitarian analogy toward either modalism or tritheism. The fear is certainly warranted, for, when pressed, each analogy certainly does lead in one of these directions by default. But we must remember two points when it comes to vestiges of the Trinity. First, we cannot ever expect exact correspondence between an analogy and its referent. If there were exact correspondence, *it would not be an analogy*! By definition, an analogy is an "aptness of proportion" or a "resemblance of relations," not an identity of relations.[24] The goal of an analogy is to draw out similarities between it and its referent in illuminating ways, not to define the referent itself. We have the creeds for just that reason. Second, we invariably encounter paradox and incongruity when trying to form an analogy from this world for the God who made it. A Trinitarian analogy is the functional equivalent of trying to explain the light of the sun with a candle. The sun is what allows the candle (both in its material composition and in our vision of it) to exist in the first place; it gives light only because the sun exists and creates its elemental environment. By its very definition

---

23. "It was especially Augustine . . . who in various ways and perspectives found the clear imprints of the Trinity in human consciousness and reason." Later in the church, this developed into the so-called psychological and sociological analogies, but it was the former that held Augustine's attention. Within man's consciousness, he found traces of God's triunity in "the trinity of being, knowing, and willing; essence, knowledge, and love; [and] mind, knowledge, and love." Bavinck, *God and Creation*, 325.

24. James A. H. Murray et al., eds., *The Oxford English Dictionary*, 2nd ed. (New York: Oxford, 1989), 1:432.

the candle is contingent and dependent on the sun, and so pales in comparison. If we try to move from the candle to the sun, we are immediately frustrated by the candle's limitation and inadequacy. Its features and relations simply *cannot* correspond sufficiently to those of the sun. Something similar might be said of our earthly analogies for the Trinity, because it is the self-contained ontological Trinity that grounds everything earthly. No analogy, then, will be adequate because we are moving from what is *ens ab alio* to what is *ens a se*.

Nevertheless, this does not mean that analogies for the Trinity are unhelpful and inappropriate. We simply need to realize the limitations outlined above. We must constantly remind ourselves, even in hyper-vigilance, that psychological analogies for the Trinity trend toward modalism and social analogies for the Trinity trend toward tritheism. If we can do that, then we can be faithful to the revelation of Scripture as we explore the depth and breadth of God's trinitarian lordship over all of creation, including the human mind.

Keeping this in the background, we move to examine a psychological analogy of the Trinity in human perception. We must begin by noting that all those who posit psychological analogies for the Trinity tread in Augustine's tracks. Indeed, Augustine himself outlined an analogy for the Trinity in human perception in terms of object, vision, and conscious attention. He writes,

> When we see some particular body, there are three things which we can very easily remark and distinguish from each other. First of all there is the thing we see, a stone or a flame or anything else the eyes can see, which of course could exist even before it was seen. Next there is the actual sight or vision, which did not exist before we sensed that object

presented to the sense. Thirdly there is what holds the sense of the eyes on the thing being seen as long as it is being seen, namely the conscious intention.[25]

These three elements—object, vision, and conscious intention—interlock and interpenetrate one another, which brings up a critical feature of all genuine vestiges of the Trinity. A vestige of the triune God cannot simply be a triad. One of its identifying markers is the perichoretic relations between the three entities of the triad, so as to reflect the coinherence or *circumcessio* of the Trinity.[26]

While Augustine's triad highlights human perception in general, there is another triad of perception that focuses more on an observer's particular choices in perceiving reality. For this, I would turn our attention to Kenneth L. Pike (1912–2000).

---

25. Augustine, *De Trinitate* 11.1.2. Augustine was well aware that such analogies were helpful but limited; he "did not intend by these analogies and images to offer a priori proof of the Trinity. On the contrary, he proceeds from faith in the Trinity; he accepts the teaching on the basis of the Word of God." In short, "though everyone can discern the imprint of the Trinity in the human spirit, only believers can recognize it as the imprint of the threefold being of God." Bavinck, *God and Creation*, 326.

26. John Frame, *Systematic Theology: An Introduction to Christian Belief* (Phillipsburg, NJ: P&R Publishing, 2013), 477–78. With regards to our knowledge of the trinitarian persons, "each of the persons bears the whole divine nature, with all the divine attributes. Each is *in* each of the others. So you cannot fully know the Son without knowing the Father and Spirit, and so on. Although the three persons are distinct, our knowledge of each involves knowledge of the others, so that for us knowledge of the Father coincides with knowledge of the Son and Spirit." John M. Frame, *Selected Shorter Writings* (Phillipsburg, NJ: P&R Publishing, 2014), 1·10

Pike's Triad of Observer Perspectives

Kenneth Pike stood out in the linguistic landscape of the twenty-first century, in part, for his tri-structural view of language. Later in his career, he expanded his linguistic observations into an integrated philosophy—stretching concepts originally applied to language in order to explain something of the nature of reality and human perception in general. In what follows, I aim to show how Pike's triad of perception is functionally necessary for every human being. Thus, it is a helpful example of how inescapable, non-salvific knowledge of the Trinity permeates reality, not just outside the mind, but within it.

In Pike's last major work, sometimes dismissed as a simplistic attempt at speculative philosophy, he reaffirms the notion of *observer perspectives*, which he had carried with him through the majority of his linguistic career.[27] The naming of these perspectives varied over the decades, but eventually settled on the terms *particle*, *wave*, and *field*.[28] Each

---

27. At the beginning of Pike's career, he used the terms *feature*, *manifestation*, and *distribution mode* to describe a unit of behavior as simultaneously having (1) "identificational-contrastive components" and "internal segmentation"; (2) "physical variants"; and (3) "relational components" such as class membership and function. See Pike, *Language in Relation to a Unified Theory of the Structure of Human Behavior* (2d ed.; The Hague: Mouton, 1967), 85–92. These were sub-classifications for viewing events in reality as segments, waves, and hierarchically structured contexts.

28. "The observer can look at the world as made up of 'things' (particles, elements, items). In some sense this is treated as the basic or normal perspective." Or "the observer can look at a series of 'discrete' events and treat the whole as a single dynamic moving entity; and any single unit can be viewed dynamically, as having beginning (initial margin), middle (nucleus), and end (final margin)." Lastly, "the observer can eliminate from the center of his attention the form or content or extension of the units as such, and focus instead on relationships between them. The unit, in this case, con

of these perspectives foregrounds the static, dynamic, and relational nature of reality, respectively. However, each of them was a different view of the same data, and they were all simultaneously in operation in the human mind. One might be in focus at any given time, but the other two are supporting and enriching that perspective. This is where we find the perichoretic activity analogous to that of the persons in the Godhead.[29]

Let us consider each of the observer perspectives and their perichoretic relations before showing how each can be linked to a person of the Trinity.

Particle. Each person "can choose to focus attention on

---

tracts to a point in a network or (or field)." Kenneth L. Pike and Evelyn G. Pike, *Grammatical Analysis*, Publications in Linguistics 53 (Dallas, TX: Summer Institute of Linguistics, 1977), 5.

Pike applied these perspectives most often to human language. The particle view considers "language as made up of PARTICLES—'things,' pieces, or parts, with sharp borders." The wave view considers "language as made up, not of parts which are separated from one another and added like bricks on a row, but rather as being made up of WAVES following one another." The field view considers "language as FUNCTIONAL, as a system with parts and classes of parts so interrelated that no parts occur apart from their function in the total whole, which in turn occurs only as the product of these parts in functional relation to a meaningful social environment." Pike, "Language as Particle, Wave, and Field," in *Kenneth L. Pike: Selected Writings to Commemorate the 60th Birthday of Kenneth Lee Pike*, ed. Ruth Brend (The Hague: Mouton, 1972), 129.

29. Pike himself saw the trinitarian reflections of this theory in the contrastive-identification, variation, and distribution of behavioral units. See Pike, "Language and Life 4: Tristructural Units of Human Behavior," *Bibl. Sacra* 114, no. 456 (1958): 42–43. See also Vern S. Poythress, *In the Beginning Was the Word: Language—A God-Centered Approach* (Wheaton, IL: Crossway, 2009), 56–57; Poythress, "Reforming Ontology and Logic in the Light of the Trinity: An Application of Van Til's Idea of Analogy," *WTJ* 57, no. 1 (1995): 191–92. Poythress' *classificational, instantiational,* and *associational* aspects draw on Pike's particle, wave, and field perspectives.

emic things or events, or on situations, or even on persons, *as if* they were semi-isolatable chunks—that is, as static particles."[30] Each of Pike's perspectives, we will see, has practical importance. In terms of the particle perspective, in order to engage with the world around us, we must view it as in some sense stable. Thus, Heraclitus' notion that the world is in constant flux, if taken to the extreme, would prevent us from actually recognizing anything in reality. My son looks different when he wakes up each morning, but every morning he is still my son. I live in a stalwart home, even though I know that time is etiolating the elements—weakening the wooden structure, eroding the stone, splitting the plaster. In the midst of this slow and ceaseless change, it is still *a thing*; it is still my home.

The particle observer perspective is requisite to functioning in the world. If our attention were always and only on the constant changes we see in the things, events, and people around us, we would eventually become hermetic—withdrawing from a reality that is unidentifiable and thus unpredictable. Without the ability to focus on stable identity, relativity would run rampant and we would retreat into utter skepticism. So, we need the particle perspective.

Wave. With the wave perspective, "a person can choose to focus attention on the same emic things, or events, or situations, or persons, as if they were in a sequence with indeterminate boarders—as sequential DYNAMIC WAVES—

---

30. Kenneth L. Pike, *Talk, Thought, and Thing: The Emic Road toward Conscious Knowledge* (Dallas, TX: Summer Institute of Linguistics, 1993), 47. See also Pike, *Linguistic Concepts: An Introduction to Tagmemics* (Lincoln, NE: University of Nebraska Press, 1982), 19; Pike, *Tagmemics, Discourse, and Verbal Art*, Michigan Studies in the Humanities 3 (Ann Arbor, MI: University of Michigan, 1981), 16. Poythress, *Redeeming Sociology: A God-Centered Approach* (Wheaton, IL: Crossway, 2011), 59; Poythress, *Redeeming Philosophy: A God-Centered Approach to the Big Questions* (Wheaton, IL: Crossway, 2014), 143–44, 163–64.

but with attention often placed on their central, or most important, components, their nuclei."[31] Again, consider the practical and universal necessity of this perspective. Our lives are not ponds; they are churning oceans—wave upon wave of experience, monotony cresting into pain or pleasure, crashing and settling into reflection with a hiss. Even our calendars are marked with the nuclei and margins. As a crude example, think of how anticipation and enthusiasm build up to Christmas day, and then fall away before rising again on New Year's Eve. Within a single week, we often have foci that we either fear or look forward to and around which the other events and discussions seem marginal, and the moment one of these foci is reached, we are pulled by the current of time into the margin of another wave.[32] Human experience is not stagnant; it is dynamic and fluent.

More importantly, none of us can focus with equal attention on everything in our physical or psychological environment. That distortion was introduced with the daguerreotype, which put all images perfectly in focus simultaneously. When we look at the world, we have to focus on something at hand and let the periphery blur into the background. We need a nucleus—at every moment of every day. Otherwise, we would be overwhelmed with stimulation and paralyzed by intellectual incontinence. To function in reality, to partake in any purposive action, we need the wave perspective.

Field. From the field perspective, "life is not merely a sensing of a sequence of bits and pieces, or of things

---

31. Pike, *Talk, Thought, and Thing,* 48.

32. For examples of waves in human activity, see Pike, *Language,* 73–82.

under change, but includes the perception of those items as points in a larger structured context, a FIELD. The points in such a field have RELATIONSHIP to one another, and those relationships help define the units themselves."³³ The necessity of this perspective is brought out not only in the coherence of reality as a functionally structured network of relationships, but also in the way in which we define elements or participants of those relationships. To perform any simple task, I must presuppose an awareness of interrelated contexts. Driving to the supermarket involves many such contexts. In getting into the car, I immediately assume awareness of a complex system of transportation and communication. I am expected to drive on the right side of the road, to not exceed the speed limit, to use a turn signal before making a turn, to follow the commands of the traffic lights, etc. I am expected to know (or learn quickly) the taxonomy of items at the supermarket and to distinguish between them, but that taxonomy itself provides the means by which I distinguish one thing from another. I know the caffeinated coffee as it contrasts with decaffeinated coffee, or a pack of coffee filters, or a box of cereal, or a frozen chicken. I rely on a system of interrelated yet contrastive elements in order to make effective decisions within that system. So, I need the field perspective.

Perichoresis. What is critical to note is that these perspectives are not isolated from one another (that would be a particle-like view of the perspectives themselves); each presupposes and interlocks with the others. When I take an apple from a pile in the produce section of the supermarket, I know it is a *thing*, a stable object with defined boarders and contrastive-identificational properties. At the same instant,

---

33. Pike, *Talk, Thought, and Thing,* 51.

I know that time is already breaking down the nutrients in the apple in a slow process of decomposition, and that if I do not eat it within a week, it will begin to rot. I also know that this apple cannot be the sole element of my diet; it deposits certain vitamins and minerals in my blood stream, but not others. So, as I pick it up, I am conscious of its adequacy in one area and its inadequacy in others, which marks it as holding a particular place in a nutritional field. This action itself—my picking up of an apple—is tacitly understood as a discrete chunk of experience with relatively fixed boarders (particle), but it is also simultaneously a marginal or nuclear element (depending on my focus) in a sequence of events (wave) and has importance relative to a network of relationships (field). In other words, "relationships interlock with stability and change. Each must be present for others to make sense."[34]

The Necessity of the Perspectives

Of course, some will claim that the above perspectives are selected arbitrarily. Who is to say that there are not other observer perspectives that we all rely upon? There are certainly many perspectives, and those outlined above are by no means exhaustive, but I would pose whether or not a perspective could be considered that is not particle, wave, or field, or some perichoretic manifestation of them. These perspectives reveal the static (unity), dynamic (diversity), and relational nature of reality, and the root of these perspectives is in *observers*. The ultimate observer, or the one whom Frame describes as "omniperspectival," is the

---

34. Poythress, *Redeeming Philosophy*, 145.

triune God himself.[35] It is this God who holds the ultimate concinnity of universals and particulars in his very being.[36] So, a set of perspectives that considers unity, diversity, and relationship to be equally ultimate seems not only necessary but felicitous for creatures made in the image of the triune God.

The particle, wave, and field perspectives also account for the rebellious thought of mankind in its myriad manifestations. I have been presupposing all along that these perspectives are necessary and universal for mankind. We could also say that they are part of our *innate* knowledge of God—triune revelation woven into the fabric of our consciousness, and "there can be no finite human consciousness that is not stirred to its depths by the revelational content within itself as well as about itself."[37] But, like all perspicuous revelation, it is suppressed by the mind, one of the many noetic effects of sin. And suppression often takes the form of distortion.

Each of Pike's observer perspectives can be and has been treated reductionistically throughout the history of human thought. Perhaps the most obvious distortion is the

---

35. John M. Frame, "A Primer on Perspectivalism," *The Works of John Frame and Vern Poythress*, http://www.frame-poythress.org/a-primer-on-perspectivalism/.

36. "Human experience of perspectives derives from an ultimate archetype, namely, the plurality of persons in the Trinity and their coinherence. This plurality of persons implies a plurality of perspectives. The indwelling of Trinitarin persons in coinherence implies the harmony and compatability of distinct perspectives, as well as the fact that one starting point in one person opens the door to all three persons." Vern S. Poythress, "Multiperspectivalism and the Reformed Faith," in *Speaking the Truth in Love: The Theology of John M. Frame*, ed. John J. Hughes (Phillipsburg, NJ: P&R Publishing, 2009), 191.

37. Van Til, *Introduction to Systematic Theology*, 312.

particle perspective, in which people have tried to reduce reality to a single aspect or compartmentalized chunks that can be classified, controlled, and rung dry of mystery. Formal logic is one example of this.[38] Post-Enlightenment empiricism and logical positivism are other examples of particle perspectives taken too far. In this sense, "both modern science and ancient philosophy, when taken as ultimate descriptions, give us forms of reductionism. They *reduce* the world to sense experience, or to matter and motion, or to some other dimension out of the world in its totality."[39] In so doing, such reductions distort or flatten reality and encourage observers to reject the God who holds the plurality of perspectives and foci to be equally ultimate with the unity of his purpose and plan.[40]

We see the same phenomenon with the wave and field perspectives. We can be so focused on change and dynamicity that we relinquish stability and coherence of context. On the other side, we can be so focused on relationships and context that we fail to see particularity, contrastive identity, and development.

---

38. Poythress, *Logic: A God-Centered Approach to the Foundation of Western Thought* (Wheaton, IL: Crossway, 2013), 73–74.

39. Poythress, *Redeeming Philosophy*, 111.

40. Poythress refers to this as "Unitarian," rather than Trinitarian thinking. Poythress, "Reforming Ontology and Logic," 202.

Observer Perspectives and the Persons of the Trinity

Pike's observer perspectives bear an analogical resemblance to the persons of the Godhead and their perichoretic relations. Keep in mind that this is an *analogical resemblance*, not a direct correlation. It would be diminutive of God, not to mention solipsistic, to claim that the Trinity is simply three perspectives of one divine being.[41] But if they are ever more than this, they are certainly not less.[42] So, sketching out the analogical connections serves not to identify the Trinitarian God but to help us further understand and enjoy the richness of his interpersonal communion.

Particle. Throughout Scripture, God the Father is described as changeless and immovable. He is the unbegotten *I am* (Exod 3:14). The world is a burning wick in the wind, but God is light eternal—unthreatened and steadfast. Certainly, the transience of creation was all too clear to the psalmist when he compared humanity to the eternally unchangeable God: "They will perish, but you will remain; they will all wear out like a garment. You will change them like a robe, and they will pass away, but you are the same, and your years have no end" (Ps 102:26–27). Berkhof addresses God's immutability in the same vein, writing that God is

> devoid of all change, not only in His Being, but also in His perfections, and in His purposes and promises. In virtue

---

41. "While in human nature there is unity person and plurality of substance (body and soul), in the divine nature there is unity of substance and plurality of persons." Letham, *The Holy Trinity*, 226–27.

42. Frame, "A Primer on Perspectivalism."

of this attribute He is exalted above all becoming, and is free from all accession or diminution and from all growth or decay in His Being or perfections. His knowledge and plans, His moral principles and volitions remain forever the same. . . . improvement and deterioration are both equally impossible.[43]

This, of course, is a description of the essence of the Godhead, not merely the Father. But we can see how this description would be especially noticeable in the Father. After all, James describes the Father as the one "with whom there is no variation or shadow due to change" (1:17). John Owen reaffirms the scriptural truth that even the Father's love, a relation to his creation, is "unchangeable."[44] Such descriptions of the Father consort well with the claim that in God "improvement and deterioration are both equality impossible." It also accords with the Father's distinct personal property of *agennetos*, unbegotten.[45]

The Father, then, can be linked to the particle perspective: the static, stable view of reality as a whole or of a constituent part of it. Whenever we view something in creation as a stable entity with relatively fixed properties, we are drawing upon remnant analogical capabilities in human consciousness that point back to the one in whom there is no shadow due to change. In other words, the

---

43. Berkhof, *Systematic Theology*, 58. Certainly, "there is change round about Him, change in the relations of men to Him, but there is no change in His being" (59).

44. Joel R. Beeke and Mark Jones, *A Puritan Theology: Doctrine for Life* (Grand Rapids, MI: Reformation Heritage Books, 2012), 106–107.

45. Francis Turretin, *Institues of Elenctic Theology*, vol. 1, *First through Tenth Topics*, ed. James T. Dennison, Jr., trans. George Musgrave Giger (Phillipsburg, NJ: P&R Publishing, 1992), 280–81.

Father's eternal, absolute stability and immutability are the ontological grounds for the temporal, relative stability of anything in creation. Whatever stability the object has is derived from the ultimate stability and immutability of the unbegotten Father.

Wave. The Son is eternally and necessarily begotten or "generated" from the Father.[46] He is *from* the Father, not in terms of time or even in terms of logic, but in terms of personal subsistence. The Son has his subsistence in the "eternal *act* of the Father."[47] Couple this with the description of the Son as the *speech* or *word* of God: "both in creation and re-creation God reveals himself by the word. By the word God creates, preserves, and governs all things, and by the word he also renews and recreates the world."[48] The Word, as Son, is the dynamism of God.

Consider also the Son's work in the incarnation. The incarnate Son is the "servant sent to effect the work of the Father, obedient even unto death and one day delivering up his kingdom to the Father."[49] Because the Son carries out the work of his Father, it is possible to view the salvific work of Christ as a wave: his life and teaching the *initial margin*, his crucifixion and resurrection the *nucleus*, and his following ascension the *final margin*. Even within that initial margin, we see the human nature of Christ in dynamic development within a field of relationships, as he "increased

---

46. Berkhof, *Systematic Theology*, 93–94. This generation is "not with respect to essence and absolutely as God, but with respect to person and reduplicatively (*reduplicative*) as Son." Turretin, *Institutes*, 1:281.

47. Berkhof, *Systematic Theology*, 93; emphasis added.

48. Bavinck, *God and Creation*, 273.

49. Ibid., 276.

in wisdom and in stature and in favor with God and man" (Luke 2:52).

So, the wave perspective can be tied to the Son. Just as the distinct personal description of the Father as unbegotten lends itself to a static view of reality, the description of the Son as eternally begotten lends itself to a dynamic view of reality. When we view reality, or some component of it, as a dynamic development—some parts peripheral and accidental (margins) while others focal and necessary (nuclei)—we are drawing upon the eternal generation of the Son, and, in the incarnation, upon his active obedience to the Father in accomplishing the plan of salvation.

Field. The Spirit *proceeds* from the Father and the Son. He is "from the Father and the Son by spiration."[50] Frame writes, "the Spirit is the member of the Trinity whom the Father and Son send, over and over again, to do their business on earth."[51] Our focus, at this point, is not merely on the procession of the Holy Spirit, but on the procession *from the Father and the Son*. The Spirit "stands in the closest possible relation to both of the other persons."[52] Hodge affirms, "the Spirit is no more said to send or to operate through the Son, than to send or operate through the Father."[53] While it is true that the Holy Spirit finds personal

---

50. Turretin, *Institutes*, 1:281. Berkhof defines "spiration" as follows: "that eternal and necessary act of the first and second persons in the Trinity whereby they, within the divine Being, become the ground of the personal subsistence of the Holy Spirit and put the third person in possession of the whole divine essence, without any division, alienation or change." Berkhof, *Systematic Theology*, 97.

51. Frame, *Systematic Theology*, 497.

52. Berkhof, *Systematic Theology*, 97.

53. Hodge, *Systematic Theology*, 478.

distinction in the Triune community via "procession," it is equally as important that the Spirit's distinction is rooted in his procession from *both* the Father and the Son.⁵⁴ As such, the Spirit associates the Father and the Son in eternal fellowship—a communion so deep and penetrating that we can only understand a glimmer of it in the penetrating communion we have analogically with the Trinity through the Spirit's work in us.⁵⁵ In other words, the deep association between the Father and the Son, a "mutual fellowship and indwelling," is what "reflects the character of God the Holy Spirit, who indwells us."⁵⁶

As the Spirit brings out the communion of the Father and the Son, so he also brings out the communion between members of the body of Christ. In Christ, we are all "being built together into a dwelling place for God by the Spirit" (Eph. 2:22).⁵⁷

---

54. The Spirit "is related to the Son as the latter is to the Father and imparts to us both the Son and the Father. He is coinherent in the Son as the Son is coinherent in him." Bavinck, *God and Creation*, 312. He we enter into the debate of the *filioque* clause, which has separated eastern and western trinitarian views for centuries. Suffice to say at this point that, with Gregory of Nazianzen, we affirm that the Spirit's procession from the Father and the Son does not infringe on the personal distinction of the Father as the "monarchy" of the Trinity, because the entire Trinity is the monarchy, the "sole principle, source, and cause" of itself. Letham, *The Holy Trinity*, 204, 366. Only this position safeguards us from subordinationism of one kind or another.

55. Poythress, "Reforming Ontology and Logic," 191.

56. Ibid., 192. "No communion with God is possible except by the Spirit. . . . By the Spirit we have communion—direct and immediate communion—with no one less than the Son and the Father themselves." Bavinck, *God and Creation*, 278.

57. "The Holy Spirit is in himself the *enhypostatic* Love and the Communion of Love in the perichoretic relations between the Father and the Son, and as such is in himself the ground of our communion with God in the

The field perspective, then, can be linked to the Holy Spirit. We sometimes view components of reality as units in a network of functional relationships—a context. In fact, we must view *every* unit that way because "no item by itself has significance. A unit becomes relevant only in relation to a context. Outside such a relationship the item will be necessarily uninterpretable by the observer."[58] This is the case even with sensory data, which are not facts in themselves, but only become facts when processed and interpreted by *someone*.[59] Such a relational view of reality is an analogical capability drawn from the Holy Spirit, who provides the relational context for the Father and the Son as he proceeds from both, and also provides the relational context for individual members of the body of Christ.

Perichoresis. The mutual indwelling of the persons in the Godhead is the archetype that provides for the ectypal perichoresis of observer perspectives. The particle, wave, and field observer perspectives interlock and presuppose one another ultimately because each of the persons of the Trinity has intimate communion and interpenetration with the others without threatening or eclipsing the personal distinctions.[60]

Love of the Father and the Son." T. F. Torrance, *The Christian Doctrine of God, One Being Three Persons* (Edinburgh: T&T Clark, 1996), 171.

58. Pike, *Linguistic Concepts*, 30.

59. With Van Til, we affirm that you cannot separate a fact from its function in a system, for "a fact *is* its function." Van Til, *Common Grace*, 115. And "the most important fact about anything in the world is its relation to God's Lordship." Frame, *Systematic Theology*, 32. Moreover, we cannot separate facts from their interpreters. See Van Til, *Defense of the Faith*, 32; John M. Frame, *The Doctrine of the Knowledge of God* (Phillipsburg, NJ: P&R Publishing, 1987), 70–72.

60. Frame, *Systematic Theology*, 479–81. Hodge notes that the "this fact—in-

So, while only the Father is unbegotten and only Son is begotten, they are each described as immutable in certain senses. We noted that in Psalm 102, the psalmist seems to be referring to God the Father when writing, "you are the same, and your years have no end" (Ps. 102:27). Yet the writer of Hebrews attributes the same description to the Son (Heb 1:12). Later in Heb 13:8, he writes, "Jesus Christ is the same yesterday and today and forever."[61] We see the immutability in the Holy Spirit as we witness him being given (or revoked), as a changeless gift, to those who accept and follow the redeeming Word of God (Ps. 51:11; Ezek. 36:26; Luke 11:13; John 20:22; Acts 2:33, 38; 5:32; 8:17, 19; 10:45; 15:8; Rom. 5:5; 1 Thess. 4:8).

While the Son is described as the dynamic Word of the Father, we find in Scripture that the Holy Spirit not only *speaks* through Christ's disciples (Mark 13:11), but also speaks directly (Acts 21:11). And though Christ is said to be the power and wisdom of God (1 Cor 1:24), the Holy Spirit is said to teach (Luke 12:12; John 14:26), and Paul prays that those in Rome would be filled with hope by the *power* of the Holy Spirit (Rom 15:13). The dynamic wisdom and power of the Word is extended not just to the Spirit, but also to the Father, who defeats Israel's enemies (2 Chro. 13:15), and silences Job with an overwhelming queue of his divine actions: laying the foundations of the world

---

timate union, communion, and inhabitation of the persons of the Trinity— is the reason why everywhere in Scripture, and instinctively by all Christians, God as God is addressed as a person, in perfect consistency with the Tripersonality of the Godhead." Hodge, *Systematic Theology*, 1:462. Bavinck suggests that "the divine being *is* tripersonal; precisely because it is the absolute, divine personality." Bavinck, *God and Creation*, 302; emphasis added. See also Kelly, *The God Who Is: The Holy Trinity*, 489–93.

61. Turretin, *Institutes*, 1:287.

(Job 38:4); building "bars and doors for the sea" (38:10); walking in the recesses of the deep (38:16); and cleaving channels for torrents of the rain (38:15), to name a few. And among God's acts of power is his implanting wisdom in his creatures. It is he who "has put wisdom in the inward parts" and "given understanding to the mind" (38:36). The Father, Son, and Spirit are each intimately involved in divine actions that are, on the surface, easily attributable to the Son as the dynamic Word and wisdom of God.

Lastly, though the Spirit binds the Father and the Son in eternal fellowship, the Father and Son also play pivotal roles in intratrinitarian and extratrinitarian communion. The Father owns the mansion with many rooms, where Christ will reunite with believers (John 14:2–3). Immediately after stating that the Father dwells in him, Jesus tells his disciples that the Holy Spirit will dwell in them. In other words, "we are drawn through the Holy Spirit into the relationship that the Son has with the Father. We are raised 'into communion with the persons of the Holy Trinity.'"[62] So, the communion fostered by the Spirit is not isolated from work of the Father and the Son. Put simply by T. F. Torrance, the biblical doctrine of perichoresis affirms that

> The Father, the Son and the Holy Spirit are distinctive Persons each with his own incommunicable properties, but they dwell *in* one another, not only *with* one another, in such an intimate way . . . that their individual characteristics instead of dividing them from one another unite them indivisibly together, the Father in the Son and the Spirit, the Son in the Father and the Spirit, and the Spirit in the Father and the Son.[63]

---

62. Letham, *The Holy Trinity*, 353.

63. Torrance, *The Christian Doctrine of God*, 172. Torrance reveals his Bar-

Let us remember that, far from being a speculative and irrelevant abstraction, perichoresis is a necessary truth in the life of believers, as it "expresses the soteriological truth of the identity between God himself and the content of his saving revelation in Jesus Christ and in the Holy Spirit, and thereby assures us that what God is toward us in Jesus Christ and in his Spirit he is inherently and eternally in himself."[64]

We need and rely upon the perichoretic relations of the Trinity, and, in an ectypal and analogous way, we need and rely upon the observer perspectives that are rooted in them. Again, this does *not* mean that the analogy of the observer perspectives is a perfect analogy for the Trinity. The observer perspectives, if taken too far, would lead to modalism (Sabellianism).[65] When understood within their limitations, however, Pike's observer perspectives shed light on the perichoretic vestiges of the Trinity we find in reality—all of which pale in comparison to the triune God

---

thian sympathies when he suggests that our knowledge of this comes only through Christ. But, as far as his definition goes, he seems to have captured *perichoresis*.

64. Ibid. See also Poythress, "Reforming Ontology and Logic," 196–97.

65. Hart helpfully reminds us, "The relationality of human persons, however essential it may be, remains a multiple reality, which must be described now in social terms, now in psychological, now in metaphysical; it is infinitely remote from that perfect indwelling, reciprocal 'containment,' transparency, recurrence, and absolute 'giving way' that is the meaning of the word *perichoresis* or *circumcessio* (adopted by Trinitarian theology long after Gregory or Augustine, and yet so perfectly suited to the theology of both). For if we forget this interval, we not only risk lapsing into either a collectivistic or solipsistic reduction of human relationality—exclusively outward or inward—but we are likely to adopt either a tritheistic or a unitarian idiom when speaking of God." Hart, "The Mirror of the Infinite," 545–46.

who dwells in unapproachable light.

Observer Perspectives and the Incomprehensibility of the Trinity

While conceptually understandable in some ways, perichoresis is ultimately mysterious and is one of the marks of God's incomprehensibility. This leads us to an important point concerning Pike's perspectives. Using all three of these perspectives harmoniously will not bring us exhaustive understanding. In fact, it should do something of the opposite: it should show us just how deep and impenetrable reality is, because it is built upon the Trinity. With Van Til, we affirm that "it is impossible for man to know himself or any of the objects of the universe about him exhaustively. For man must know himself or anything else in the created universe in relation to the self-contained God. Unless he can know God exhaustively, he cannot know anything else exhaustively."[66] The incomprehensibility of God seems to be the reason why we view the world tri-structurally. We cannot perceptually exhaust any object in reality, just as we can by no means perceptually exhaust the triune being of God.[67]

It would be misguided to then conclude that we cannot know anything truly. This is merely another way in which man's knowledge is analogical of God's knowledge. God perceives his creation as a triune being; we perceive it *tri-structurally*, to use Pike's language, as creatures made in his image. Perceiving the world with particle, wave, and field

---

66. Van Til, *Introduction to Systematic Theology*, 269.

67. Ibid., 293–95.

perspectives and leaving room for mystery is the way to true knowledge, not a barrier to it.

Returning to the Trinity in General Revelation

Pike's perspectives thus serve as another branch of Augustine's *vestigia trinitatis*. They show how the Trinity permeates the human mind. Everyone, I argue, relies on the particle, wave, and field perspectives in perichoretic relationship: everyone accounts daily for stability, change, and context. Do they see these perspectives as reflective of the triune God of Scripture? No. They rely upon them, but are blind to the God who made them. Every human in history has relied on the static, dynamic, and relational perspectives of life, just as everyone has relied on the changeless plan of the Father, the manifestation of the Son in human history, and the relational harmony between the Spirit and the Father and Son.

What does all of this mean for the Reformed tradition? First, it suggests that claiming the Trinity is only to be found in Scripture is not the full truth. The Trinity is ubiquitous; it undergirds and permeates all of reality. In short, the Trinity is present in general revelation but cannot be consciously accessed or recognized by non-Christians. As mentioned in the beginning of the article, the non-believer only has non-salvific knowledge of the Trinity, a blind reliance upon the God for whom unity and diversity are equally ultimate.

With our Reformed forebears, we can continue to proclaim that salvific knowledge of the Trinity comes from nowhere but the pages of Scripture. However, once we have seen that God as revealed in his Word, we begin to see him everywhere, upholding and guiding reality and human experience as we know it. This means, at the very least, that we must be conscious of vestiges of the Trinity in reality as we work through the spiritual, intellectual, and social problems of our day. It also means that the doctrine of perichoresis needs to receive more rigorous treatment by Reformed scholars, since the perichoretic relations of the Godhead are what account for our coherent perception of reality. Perhaps in due time, the Trinity will find its proper place in the discussion not just of special revelation, but of general revelation as well.

World through Word
Towards a Linguistic Ontology

There is a silver maple tree outside my window. The lower branches have been pruned, and the scars from the saw have turned deep brown after December rain. Do you know why that tree is there—why I can walk outside into the front yard and rest my hand on the cold bark?

Yesterday as I was sitting at a stoplight, a flock of starlings rolled in the wind like a flag as I sat waiting for the light to turn green. I thought about why they carried so well together—what was it that kept them caught up in the breeze?

Then I thought of the train line that runs through the suburbs of Philadelphia and out into the countryside where we live. The people who board it in the morning moonlight and ride the rail to some two dozen stops between Colmar and center city—how do they do it? What allows them to walk the platform, smoke a cigarette, hold a conversation?

God spoke. That is the ontological grounds for all existence and the foundation of all the coherence in our experience. Every bit of the material world, from the ground beneath us to the sky above us to the bones inside us, is there because the trinitarian God "opened his holy lips."[1] God's word is what accounts for the world. Not a

---

1. John Calvin, *Institutes of the Christian Religion: A New Translation of the 1541 Edition*, trans. Robert White (Carlisle, PA: Banner of Truth, 2014), 16. Note here that Calvin is referring to God's special revelation, not to creation. The analogy, however, is fitting for creation as well, since God spoke creation

fiber, not a quark is held together but for his speech. The same goes for the maple tree and the starlings and the passengers riding to the Market Street Station. I *am* and you *are* because he *said*. The Father spoke through the Son by the power of the Spirit; the vibrations of divine vocal chords put vigor in our veins, and set the rest of the world turning.

God's speech accounting for all that is—for all that has been and will be—means that we must have a *linguistic ontology*. And only with the Trinity is this possible. The grounds for a linguistic ontology lie only in God's trinitarian being, and these grounds are solidified by the *covenantal* and *representational* nature of reality, which, I argue, are evident because language is communal and representational on its deepest level.[2] In this article, we begin by introducing what such an ontology entails, and we end by suggesting implications that this would have for the *imago Dei*, the personalistic atmosphere of reality, and the weight of our words as speaking creatures of a speaking God.

Language and the Being of God

Two colossal questions must be answered at the outset, and then their answers must be related. The first: what is

---

into existence. In this sense, it was also necessary for God to "reopen his holy lips" when sin entered the cosmic order.

2. By "representational," we mean that because, in Van Til's terms, the persons of the Trinity are "exhaustively representational of one another," that is, each person fully indwells and interpenetrates each of the others, so God's use of language to create man requires that man be representational of the tripersonal God in all of his thoughts and behaviors. See Cornelius Van Til, *In Defense of the Faith*, vol. 2, *A Survey of Christian Epistemology* (Phillipsburg, NJ: Presbyterian and Reformed, 1969), 78.

language? It will not do to say that language is a system of graphic and phonetic signs. Kenneth L. Pike (1912–2000) showed decades ago that language is far more than this. Language is, in his words, a behavior, an activity. More precisely, it is

> a phase of human activity which must not be treated in essence as structurally divorced from the structure of nonverbal human activity. The activity of man constitutes a structural whole, in such a way that it cannot be subdivided into neat 'parts' or 'levels' or 'compartments' with language in a behavioral compartment insulated in character, content, and organization from other behavior. Verbal and nonverbal activity is a unified whole, and theory and methodology should be organized or created to treat it as such.[3]

Pike goes on to show that not only is "language behavior" bound up with "non-language behavior" in single events, but also that nonverbal elements of behavior can be (and often are) structurally substituted by elements of non-verbal behavior and vice versa.[4] Language is, then, communicative behavior. It is what we might call a *communion behavior*, in the sense that its purpose is the expression of one person towards another.[5] By its very definition, language presupposes community.

---

3. Kenneth L. Pike, *Language in Relation to a Unified Theory of the Structure of Human Behavior*, 2nd ed. (The Hague: Mouton, 1967), 26.

4. Ibid.

5. "One of the purposes of language—in fact, a central, predominant purpose—is to be a vehicle for personal communication and communion between God and human beings." Vern S. Poythress, *In the Beginning Was the Word: Language—A God-Centered Approach* (Wheaton, IL: Crossway, 2009), 38. As we will see, this communion also involves the expressions of the persons of the Trinity towards one another. Before creation, these expressions, we can biblically speculate, would have been of love and glory.

The second question: who is God? We could pour out the language of the Westminster Confession here, and we would be the wiser for it. The words of that confession are steeped in prayerful, biblical devotion, and we would be hard-pressed to find a fuller and clearer articulation of the attributes of the Godhead than what is provided in WCF 2.1–2. But the question runs deeper than God's communicable and incommunicable attributes. Yes, God is immutable, invisible, immense, and eternal; he is wise, holy, righteous, and free. But all of these attributes are given their proper weight only in God's triunity. We do well to take a reminder from Herman Bavinck: "It is in this holy trinity that each attribute of His being comes into its own, so to speak, gets its fullest content. It is only when we contemplate this trinity that we know who and what God is."[6] Elsewhere he writes, "the one name of God is only fully unfolded in that of the Father, the Son, and the Spirit."[7]

Bavinck is by no means alone here. God's trinitarian nature, warned the great Charles Hodge, was certainly not "a mere speculative or abstract truth. . . . It underlies the whole plan of salvation, and determines the character of the religion (in the subjective sense of that word) of all true Christians."[8] But as critical as the Trinity is to our salvation and religious life, it is, at base, most important that we uphold that God's *being* is triune. In other words,

---

6. Herman Bavinck, *Our Reasonable Faith*, trans. Henry Zylstra (Grand Rapids, MI: Wm. B. Eerdmans, 1956), 143.

7. Herman Bavinck, *Reformed Dogmatics*, vol. 2, *God and Creation*, ed. John Bolt, trans. John Vriend (Grand Rapids, MI: Baker Academic, 2004), 279.

8. Charles Hodge, *Systematic Theology* (Peabody, MA: Hendrickson, 2013), 1:442–43.

the identity of the three distinct Persons within the one beatific Being of God indicates that God's very Being subsists through relations. That is to say, the ontological is understood through the relational. . . . The one eternal LORD exists as a communion of holy love within Himself, and this means personal existence; that is, the inter-communion of three equally divine and holy Persons. For God to be is to be in relationship within Himself.[9]

The perichoretic communion of the persons of the Godhead is so strong that Van Til goes so far as to say that the Godhead is one person. If we walk gingerly here, we could say that just as God is both a one-conscious being and a tri-conscious being, so also he is both one person and three persons, provided we allow that "person" denotes two different things in this context.[10] Van Til's point was to show

---

9. Douglas Kelly, *Systematic Theology: Grounded in Holy Scripture and Understood in Light of the Church*, vol. 1, *The God Who Is: The Holy Trinity* (Ross-shire, Scotland: Mentor, 2008), 447.

10. Cornelius Van Til, *Introduction to Systematic Theology: Prolegomena and the Doctrines of Revelation, Scripture, and God*, ed. William Edgar, 2nd ed. (Phillipsburg, NJ: P&R Publishing, 2007), 348, 363. Here the "person" of the Godhead emerges from the doctrine of perichoresis and thus guards against God's essence being viewed as mute, impersonal, or rationalistically comprehensible; the "persons" would convey the traditional view of orthodoxy—that God is Father, Son, and Holy Spirit. Letham notes Torrance's objection to this language. The latter suggests that a "person" is defined by relations to other persons, so this is fitting for traditional orthodox understandings of "person," since the Father relates to the Son, who relates to the Spirit, who relates to the Father, and so on. If the Godhead itself is a person, to whom does the Godhead relate? Robert Letham, *The Holy Trinity: In Scripture, History, Theology, and Worship* (Phillipsburg, NJ: P&R Publishing, 2004), 180–81. Torrance, with Letham, seems to miss Van Til's underlying purpose, along with the fact that one word can have multiple denotations. Perhaps Van Til's use of person here might confuse those who are not familiar with the context, but Van Til has done nothing unorthodox here. Admittedly, he would have done well to draw out this difference in denotation,

that God's essence is not brute or impersonal. Yet, coupled with that was a desire to never see the incomprehensibility of the triune God reduced to a rationalistic formula—a product of univocal thought.[11] An implied affirmation of Van Til's argument was that God's tripersonal communion is the bedrock of his being. In other words, we might say that "God's being is in communicating," providing that we mean intra-trinitarian communication, i.e., self-communication, and not extra-trinitarian, redemptive communication.[12]

---

but surely someone with Torrance's or Letham's background could put two and two together. Tipton articulated years ago that "Van Til's Trinitarian formulation arises out of his apologetic concern to accentuate God's incomprehensibility in the context of 'univocal reasoning.'" Lane G. Tipton, "The Function of Perichoresis and the Divine Incomprehensibility," *WTJ* 64 (2002): 290–91. In other words, Van Til wants us to reason analogically about God's being, and that requires that we incorporate the teaching of perichoresis into our definition of God's essence. He did that by linking perichoresis to *both* the unity and distinctions in the Godhead, and arrived at a formula that, though innovative in its language, buttressed the orthodox teaching of the Trinity and put stronger blockades before the surging tide of univocal thought.

11. Tipton, "The Function of Perichoresis and the Divine Incomprehensibility," 290-91, 293, 297, 298–99, and 301.

12. Kevin J. Vanhoozer, *Remythologizing Theology: Divine Action, Passion, and Authorship* (New York: Cambridge University Press, 2010), 245. We would not say, however, that God has his being "in act." At least, the ontology of God is not based entirely on his action *ad extra*. It is based on who God is in himself (*ad intra*), which is faithfully but not exhaustively reflected in his works *ad extra*. In other words, we cannot take all of what God does in creation and redemption and make that essential to him, for that would tie the Creator to his creation so as to make him dependent on it. As soon as we say that God has his *being* in actions outside of himself, we have effectively collapsed the immanent Trinity—who God is apart from creation and redemption—into the economic. This not only destabilizes the being of God (God would be free to do anything, even those things contrary to his nature, e.g., commit sin or violate his covenant), it also imports into the eternal Godhead properties that belong only to the economic, redemptive work of Christ and the Spirit, thus dissolving the Creator-creature distinction. For

The latter belies Barth's later theological ontology and its host of problems, the greatest of which is a collapse of the immanent into the economic Trinity.[13] We can only affirm, then, that God *is in himself a perfectly unified tripersonal being*. In the language of T. F. Torrance, "the one being of God is to be understood in his interior relations as the Communion of the three divine persons with one another."[14]

Now we can relate the answers to our two questions. Language is communicative behavior, and God *is* the self-communicating Trinity. This means that language is a properly divine behavior. It is not the sociological capital of the human race, nor is it merely a medium for divine-human relations. As Poythress reminds us, "the persons of the Trinity function as members of a language community among themselves. Language does not have as its sole purpose human-human communication, or even divine-human communication, but also divine-divine communication."[15] Language, as communicative behavior of the Trinity, has eternal roots.

---

instance, we would not say, with Multmann, that God *is* a "suffering God." Suffering is not part of *who God is* in himself; it is only something he takes upon himself voluntarily in choosing to create and then redeem humanity, along with the rest of the cosmos.

13. For details concerning Barth's focus on election in Christ as the basis of God's triunity, and thus his distortion (if not destruction) of a truly trinitarian ontology, see James J. Cassidy, "Election and Trinity," *WTJ* 71 (2009): 66.

14. T. F. Torrance, *The Christian Doctrine of God, One Being Three Persons* (Edinburgh: T&T Clark, 1996), 136. J. B. Torrance suggests that we say God is "Being-in-Communion." See "Contemplating the Trinitarian Mystery of Christ," in *Alive to God: Studies in Spirituality, Presented to James Houston*, ed. J. I. Packer and L. Wilkinson (Downers Grove, IL: InterVarsity Press, 1992), 141.

15. Poythress, *In the Beginning Was the Word*, 18.

Language in Creation

It is with this background that we must view the creation of reality as we know it. If language is communicative behavior and the Trinity is the self-communicating tripersonal God, then the use of communicative behavior to create the cosmos must be central to a biblical, and thus a linguistic, ontology. If it is God's speech that both specifies *what* exists and *how* it exists,[16] then we must consider the centrality of language to the nature of reality as covenantal and representational. But before we get to that, we would do well to remind ourselves of the triune God's speech in creation.

Bavinck not only noticed the obligation we have as Christians to maintain that God is *essentially* trinitarian; he also saw that creation itself could not come from any other being. In noting that Scripture reveals both an internal and an external communication for God, he may have cleared the brush for us to see the necessity of creation by the Trinity.[17] His words are worth their own weight:

> Scripture . . . knows both emanation and creation, a twofold communication of God—one within and the other outside the divine being; one to the Son who was in the beginning with God and was himself God, and another to creatures who originated in time; one from the being and another by the will of God. The former is called generation; the latter, creation. By generation, from all eternity, the full image of God is communicated to the Son; by creation only a weak and pale image of God is communicated to the creature.

---

16. Vern S. Poythress, *Redeeming Philosophy: A God-Centered Approach to the Big Questions* (Wheaton, IL: Crossway, 2014), 105.

17. Herman Bavinck, *In the Beginning: Foundations of Creation Theology*, ed. John Bolt, trans. Vriend, John (Grand Rapids, MI: Baker Books, 1999), 39.

Still the two are connected. Without generation creation would not be possible. If in an absolute sense God could not communicate himself to the Son, he would be even less able, in a relative sense, to communicate himself to his creature. If God were not triune, creation would not be possible.[18]

God's inter-trinitarian speech, in other words, is requisite for his extra-trinitarian speech. The two are linked, one serving as the archetype and the other as the ectype, for which human speech is a distant echo, an ectype of an ectype. Put differently,

> God the Father expresses his character in his speech, that is, in his Son who is the Word. The constant character of God and the faithfulness of God the Father are manifested in the fact that the Word is in accordance with this character. . . . This original speech within the Trinity is the archetype for speech that creates the world external to God. The world is distinct from God and is a manifestation of the faithfulness and creativity of God. In this respect, the world images the fact that the Son is distinct from the Father and is a manifestation of the faithfulness of God in the creativity of the Son.[19]

In light of the fact that God's internal communication with the Son grounds the external communication that brought creation into being, the act of creation reveals that God is an *essentially* "relational being,"[20] i.e., a communicative being. Verbal manifestations from the mouth of God confirm that "communion and communication are

---

18. Ibid.

19. Vern S. Poythress, *Triperspectivalism and the Mystery of the Trinity* (unpublished), 117.

20. Letham, *The Holy Trinity*, 19.

inherent" for him.[21] Thus, when God exercised his divine linguistic power at the dawn of creation, that power was and is "intrinsically and undeviatingly personal within the fullness of personal Being in the Holy Trinity."[22] Creation is thus thoroughly relational and personal because it has its origin and existence in the speech of the Trinity.

However, we find ourselves in a world that is not only relational and personal, but also covenantal and representational *because it was created through the communicative behavior of the Trinity, i.e., language.* In other words, all of reality is covenantal and representational because language is covenantal and representational, and this must be factored into—in fact, it must *define*—our ontology. From the biblical perspective, more foundational than the traditional Aristotelian categories of "substance" and "accidents" are the covenantal and representational functions of all things within God's plan for history. A linguistic ontology is also a divinely purposive ontology. We will discuss this in relation to Aristotle's popular categories after establishing in what sense language is covenantal and representational.

Language as Covenantal and Representational

Language as covenantal. Tomes have been written on the centrality of covenant for theology. But in our context the word "covenant" takes on a strikingly warmer connotation than is typical. Suzerain treaties, lords and vassals, kings and their kingdoms—that's all well and good, but what

---

21. Ibid., 428.

22. Torrance, *The Christian Doctrine of God*, 207.

is a covenant? Essentially, it is a linguistic agreement, an exchange of promises, a verbalized expression of relationship. In creation, this relationship took shape when order was drawn from chaos. God's divine fiats established an order that he would keep. As Kline puts it, "God dictated into existence a covenantal kingdom order, and implicit in the structuring-defining words spoken by the beneficent Creator was his oath commitment to maintain by faithful providential oversight the good world he had made and given its meaning."[23] Why use what Kline calls a "covenantal kingdom order"? Because covenant presupposes relationship, and God is a relational being.

What is most important for our purposes is not merely the fact that creation is covenantal, but that this covenantal structure had to be implemented and established by language, God's communicative behavior. Covenant is a *voluntary* (on God's part) relational structure that emerges from God's *essential*, and hence necessary, inter-trinitarian communion. In other words, covenant is not necessary to God's being, but communion is, and covenant can only be drawn from communion. God's inner communication allows for his outer communication with creation, which itself came into being by his speech.

God's communal, covenantal speech then leads us to two conclusions: (1) this speech and its ensuing implications "furnishes the only completely personalistic interpretation of reality";[24] and (2) all of reality is *ontologically* bound to the covenantal community, which involves essentially two

---

23. Meredith G. Kline, *Kingdom Prologue: Genesis Foundations for a Covenantal Worldview* (Overland Park, KS: Two Age Press, 2000), 15–16.

24. Van Til, *A Survey of Christian Epistemology*, 2:98. This is why Van Til concludes that every person has a "covenantal personality" (95).

parties: God and everything else. Humans, however, are the primary party in the latter group, as image-bearing stewards of the rest of creation. Put differently, the covenantal speech of God reveals that his creation of humanity and of the cosmos was an essentially personal act that welded all of reality to the Trinity via divine communicative behavior.

Because God speaks the cosmos into a covenantal relationship with himself, a linguistic ontology not only demands that reality is a product of God's speech, but also that it is covenantally bound to him. We might find this easy to understand with regards to people, since theologians have a history of discussing our covenantal obligations to our creator. But this also applies to the rest of reality as well. Throughout Scripture, we find the language of covenant used analogically with the natural world, affirming that every speck of material is covered with an ancient and holy conversation, *through which it has come into being*. Creation responds in covenantal submission to the self-communicating God who called it out of nothing. The psalmist writes that trees clap their hands at the wonder of God (Ps. 148:9), and the mountains and hills "burst into song" (Isa. 55:12). Jesus responds to Pharisaic resistance to his royal reception in Jerusalem by affirming that if the disciples were mute at his coming, then "the very stones would cry out" (Luke 19:40). Here we see both praise (clapping and singing) and a witnessing to God's glorious dominion—covenantal responses. Moreover, these responses (praise and witness), we can biblically speculate, were not alien to the persons of the Godhead in eternity past. God was always in a trinitarian circle of self-love (or self-affirmation, i.e., a type of witnessing) and glorification (John 17:5). So, the covenantal dimension of reality is an echo of God's inter-trinitarian communion. Language, by its very nature, is covenantal (for us) and communal (properly and eternally for God, and analogously for his creation).

Language as representational. Language is also *representational*, which complements the covenantal nature of God's creative speech. We must at the outset state clearly what we mean by "representational." We do not mean that language represents thoughts, though this is certainly true, nor that language represents or signifies objects, which, again, is also true. Rather, we mean to predicate something quite unique about language. To understand this, we must first clarify what Cornelius Van Til meant by saying that the trinitarian God is representational. Then we can apply this to language, since language (i.e., communicative behavior) is essential to God's nature.[25]

For Van Til, the persons of the Trinity are exhaustively *representational* of one another. What did he mean by this? At heart, this was nothing more than a unique expression of the ancient teaching of *perichoresis* or *circumcessio*, which affirmed that the persons of the Trinity interpenetrate and indwell one another. Prime proof texts for this teaching include John 10:30, "I and the Father are one," John 14:9, where Jesus tells Philip that anyone who has seen him has seen the Father, and Jesus' high priestly prayer in John 17. In these texts, the writer has in mind the Son and the Father, but the Spirit is also included elsewhere in John's Gospel. For example, John tells us that Christ is "the truth" (John 14:6), but he leaves for his followers "the Spirit of truth" (John 14:17).

---

25. On speech, or in a broader sense, language, as an essential attribute of God, see John Frame, *Systematic Theology: An Introduction to Christian Belief* (Phillipsburg, NJ: P&R Publishing, 2013), 522–23.

Seeing the biblical validity of this teaching, Van Til wrote that "the persons of the Trinity are mutually representational. They are *exhaustively* representational of one another."[26] In other words, the persons of the Godhead interpenetrate and indwell one another to such a degree that when one of these persons is in focus, the other two are exhaustively represented as well.[27] This does not blur the personal distinctions among the Father, Son, and Holy Spirit; it merely accents their intimacy and the equal ultimacy of unity and diversity in the Godhead.[28]

Van Til then linked this representational feature of the Godhead to humanity. If the persons of the Godhead are exhaustively representational of one another, and if the triune God created us after his own "image and likeness," then our every thought and action must be representative of the tripersonal God. Put differently, "because he is a creature, man must, in his thinking, his feeling and his willing, be representative of God. There is no other way open for him. He could, in the nature of the case, think nothing at all unless he thought God's thoughts after him, and this is representational thinking."[29]

Yet, our "representational" behavior goes beyond our

---

26. Van Til, *A Survey of Christian Epistemology*, 78. He restates this several pages later: "The foundation of the representative principle among men is the fact that the Trinity exists in the form of a mutually exhaustive representation of the three Persons that constitute it" (96).

27. In Torrance's words, "in the Holy Trinity the Father is not properly Father apart from the Son and the Spirit, ad Son is not properly Son apart from the Father and the Spirit, and the Spirit is not properly Spirit apart from the Father and the Son." Torrance, *The Christian Doctrine of God*, 206.

28. Van Til, *A Survey of Christian Epistemology*, 96.

29. Ibid., 78–79.

thinking. It extends to the whole personality.

> The foundation of all personal activity among men must be based upon the personality of one ultimate person, namely, the person of God, if only it be understood that this ultimate personality of God is a triune personality. In the Trinity there is completely personal relationship without residue. And for that reason it may be said that man's actions are all personal too. Man's surroundings are shot through with personality because all things are related to the infinitely personal God. But when we have said that the surroundings of man are really completely personalized, we have also established the fact of the representational principle. All of man's acts must be representational of the acts of God.[30]

In sum, because the persons of the Godhead are exhaustively representational of one another, creatures made in the image of the Trinity are analogically representational of God in all that they do.

Language, then, must also be representational. By this we mean that all of our communicative behavior represents on a finite, analogical scale the communicative behavior of the Trinity. In their communicative behavior, the persons of the Trinity exhaustively represent one another; in our communicative behavior, we image the Trinity by analogically representing ourselves. Perhaps it is for this reason that we see Scripture constantly identifying a *person* with his or her *words*, both communally and individually. The human race was a unified whole prior to Genesis 11, when "the whole earth had one language and the same words." The diffusion of language brought about not just confusion, but the separation of people groups (Gen. 11:8). Ever since that time, people groups have been

---

30. Ibid., 78.

identified primarily by their native language, or at least their dialect. Hence, Peter stuck out like a sore thumb among the scribes and elders of Jerusalem because his speech was phonetically unique; he was a Galilean (Matt. 23:73), and spoke as one. Every utterance marked him as a member of a specific geographic community.

Our words also represent us individually, ultimately because the Word of the Father is the "exact imprint of his nature" (Heb. 1:3). The Father is perfectly represented by the Son, who is the Word. Because we are creatures made in the image of the trinitarian God, our words are fitting representations of who we are. Just as God's Word reveals his personal presence, so our words express our personality, and in that sense we are present with our words.[31] Because we ourselves are present with our words, there is a sense in which our words are inextricably bound up with our person. For this reason, the psalmist writes, "Keep your tongue from evil and your lips from speaking deceit" (Ps. 34:13). *People* commit evil acts; *people* are deceptive, but our words are so deeply rooted in our personhood that the psalmist can exhort our tongues and lips as if they were *us*. Indeed, we can certainly assume this much if Christ himself says, "by your words you will be justified, and by your words you will be condemned" (Matt. 12:37). Language determines our destination as people.

Language, then, is representational of both communities and individual persons. However, language is also representational in another sense, probably more in line with what Van Til might have considered. Language

---

31. "Man's speech shows meaning, control, and presence. In this respect it images the meaning, control, and presence of God's speech." Poythress, *In the Beginning Was the Word*, 30. See also chapter 11 of John M. Frame, *The Doctrine of the Word of God* (Phillipsburg, NJ: P&R Publishing, 2010).

is representational in the sense that we should represent the Trinitarian God in our use of words to love and honor others. For all eternity, God comprises his own linguistic community of self-love and glorification.[32] While we are not called to glorify others with our words, we are called to build one another up and encourage one another (1 Thess. 5:11). This is related to glorification in that it is an uplifting behavior. When we encourage someone, we lift that person up so that he or she understands how much he or she is loved.

We could end this section with Van Til's words, "One either maintains that human personal thought and action is representative, covenantal thought and action, because man is enveloped at every point by the claims of God; or, one, in effect, maintains that human personal thought and action is autonomous."[33] However, more needs to be said about the implications of language as a representational behavior.

First, language is far more than a system of signification—a variegation of phonemes and graphemes that point to reality. With Pike, we would affirm that language is communicative behavior, but, fundamentally, it is also an "imaging behavior": it marks us as creatures

---

32. "The divine essence is only divine when hypostasized in three Persons, because these three have a value and a relationship between Them that deserves and is capable of absolute love." Dumitru Staniloae, *The Holy Trinity: In the Beginning There Was Love*, trans. Roland Clark (Brookline, MA: Holy Cross Orthodox Press, 2012), 17. He later writes, "The highest form of love is revealed to us in the unending love between the one and only Father of a unique Son. Yet throughout eternity the love between the Father and the Son has also been directed toward a third Person who takes joy in the love that each has for the other" (ibid., 55).

33. Van Til, *A Survey of Christian Epistemology*, 78.

of the God who speaks *with himself*, and also with his creatures. We might even say that language, more than any other personal behavior, brands our souls with God's image. But it does not stop there. Language is central to the being of God as one who communes with himself— the Father with the Son, the Son with Spirit, the Spirit with the Father, etc.[34] Think of it this way: if it is true, as Scripture suggests, that "language originates with God, not with man," and that God in his tripersonality is essentially a communicating being, then language is not merely one among many aspects of our representational activity.[35] It is, at heart, the representational activity that shimmers with the eternal glory of God's trinitarian being. Language is not merely, in Samuel Jonson's words, "the dress of thought." It is the ontological basis of reality, since God not only spoke reality into being, but also has his being in personal self-communion.

Here is where John Zizioulas' work is so helpful. Greek and Roman usage of the word "person" (*prosopon* and *persona*, respectively) had been detached from substance, from ontology, until the time of nascent Christianity, when the early church struggled to articulate how God could be both three and one. The Greek writer Hippolytus was perhaps the first to take a Greek word formerly used with reference to substance, *hypostasis*, and identify it with *prosopon*, in what

---

34. "Man in his linguistic functions, as in all he is and does, is to be understood as the creature who is the image and likeness of God (Gen 1:26). In fact, should we not say that especially in his language man reflects the divine image he is?" Richard B. Gaffin Jr., "Speech and the Image of God: Biblical Reflections on Language and Its Uses," in *The Pattern of Sound Doctrine: Systematic Theology at the Westminster Seminaries* (ed. David VanDrunen; Phillipsburg, N.J.: P&R Publishing, 2004), 183.

35. Poythress, *In the Beginning Was the Word*, 28.

Zizioulas describes as a "revolutionary" development.[36] Based on this development and its ensuing ontological implications, Zizioulas concludes that an ontology was born not in the line of Platonic or Aristotelian metaphysics, but in the line of the triune being of God. This new, trinitarian ontology meant that,

> for someone *to be* and *to be in relation* becomes identical. For someone or something to *be*, two things are simultaneously needed: being itself (*hypostasis*) and *being in relation* (i.e., being a person). It is only in relationship that identity appears as having an ontological significance, and if any relationship did not imply such an ontologically meaningful identity, then it would be no relationship. Here is certainly an ontology derived from the being of God.[37]

Such an ontology can be further refined. What else is central to communion, to relationship, but communicative behavior, i.e., language? Creation presupposes communion, and communion presupposes language. Thus, our view of God's being demands that language be taken as the basis of ontology, not a component of it. Language is not a tree on the landscape of creation; it is what brought the landscape into being and what holds it together. This gives a whole new meaning to John 1:1 and Hebrews 1:3. "In the beginning was the Word," that is, "in the beginning was *the One who could talk!* Not just a set of rays of energy ready for a big bang; not a pantheistic sum of non-focused non-personal elements; not a vague spirit of impersonal goodness; but

---

36. John D. Zizioulas, *Being as Communion: Studies in Personhood and the Church* (Crestwood, NY: St. Vladimir's Seminary Press, 1985), 39.

37. Ibid., 88.

the Personal-One-with-Language."[38] This "personal-One-with-Language" is the same who "upholds the universe by the word of his power." Language always *was* in God, and it was this speaking, self-communing Trinity who spoke in order to bring about and sustain reality. This, surely, warrants a *linguistic ontology*.

Second, and following from the first point, the representational nature of language sheds light on the nature of sin. In the hearts of all people lies a deadly desideratum: a yearning to be self-governing and independent, in a word, autonomous. While language is a communing behavior, sin is an isolating behavior. The root of sin, as reflected in Van Til's own statement, is autonomy. Sin is an isolationist movement. It separates us from the tripersonal God in whom we have our being. Thus, all of the current malformation and corruption of language is, at root, related to our sinful desire for self-government. Just as Adam and Eve chose to act on their own, trusting in the *non-representational*, counterfeit language of the serpent, so we constantly try to act outside the model of linguistic love and encouragement rooted in the Trinity. We abuse, misuse, and ignore the weight of words not merely because we are careless or uninformed or limited in our understanding of an idea, but because we have followed the words of another. We have, like Eve, taken the serpent's words—words which led to mistrust and estrangement between man and God—and set ourselves in ethical hostility towards the God who chose to speak us into fellowship with himself.

But our ethical hostility could not, and cannot, disrupt or dissolve our metaphysical bond with the self-communing

---

38. Kenneth L. Pike, "Morals and Metaphor," *Interchange* 12 (1972): 231.

Trinity.³⁹ We are creatures bound to speak, both to God and to one another. We have gone on doing so for millennia without turning back in faithfulness to the one whose words gave us our being. We tread upon the world of the Word while we spit in the face of the speaker. How painfully poetic, then, that our restoration could only come from God speaking again, through the person of his Son (Heb. 1:2).

Covenant and Representation over Substance and Accidents

We have seen that language is covenantal and representational, and because the trinitarian God used language to create all of reality, everything visible and invisible is also covenantal and representational. This summarizes what we have called a linguistic ontology. Far from being novel, it is thoroughly biblical, taken directly from the pages of Scripture. However, if we grant it any novelty, perhaps it lies in the rejection of *being* as an abstraction, instead defining being only as it relates to God's linguistically revealed, personal purpose. A linguistic ontology, then, is also a purposive ontology. In other words, everything in reality has its being in covenantal and representational relation to the purposes of the Trinity. There is no such thing as "bare being."

Admittedly, this flies in the face of centuries of

---

39. As Van Til noted, our ethical hostility toward God cannot erase our metaphysical dependence upon and imaging of him. "Because man is a creature of God, it is impossible that he should ever be alienated from God metaphysically. He can never actually become the independent being that he thinks he is. Even the king's heart is in the hand of God as the watercourses." Van Til, *A Survey of Christian Epistemology*, 197.

philosophical assumptions based on Aristotelian metaphysics. Frederick Copleston notes that Aristotle's *Metaphysics* "has had a tremendous influence on the subsequent thought of Europe,"[40] and Aristotle's understanding of being is also what undergirds most current conceptions of logic.[41] The problem, however, is that Aristotelian metaphysics and logic are based on an impersonal view of reality, rejecting the triune God of Scripture and the covenantal and representational nature of reality.[42] This not only opposes a linguistic ontology, but also invalidates itself, for what can we truly predicate of being without presupposing a foundation of eternal, divine purpose? In other words, how could we possibly be satisfied with saying *what* and *how* something is without saying *why* it is in relation to God's redemptive plan?[43]

---

40. Frederick Copleston, *A History of Philosophy*, vol. 1, *Greece and Rome: From the Pre-Soctratics to Plotinus* (New York: Image Books, 1946), 287.

41. Vern S. Poythress, *Logic: A God-Centered Approach to the Foundation of Western Thought* (Wheaton, IL: Crossway, 2013), 28.

42. "Philosophy in most of its forms, from the time of Aristotle, clings to the foundational conception that logic is impersonal, and that certain modes of valid reasoning can be construed as mechanistic forms independent of the language of God." Ibid., 82.

43. Note here that Aristotle, and Plato before him, was not ignorant of purposiveness (or teleology) in his substance/accidents or form/matter distinction. Frame reminds us, "For Aristotle, the combination of form and matter in individual things injects an element of purposiveness or teleology into everything. Form is what each thing is, but it is also the purpose of the thing: for Aristotle, the nature and purpose of a thing are the same. So the form of bread defines it as food, a statue as art. Recall that for Plato, too, purpose and essence were closely related: everything partook of Goodness and therefore was good for something. So form is not just what things are; it is also what they should be, what they strive to be. Form is a normative category as well as a descriptive one." John M. Frame, *A History of Western Philosophy and Theology* (Phillipsburg, NJ: P&R Publishing, 2015), 71.

To review Aristotle's ontology, we need only remind ourselves that Aristotle, like his predecessors, was concerned with metaphysics as a self-contained science. "Metaphysical science is concerned with being as such [and] is the study of being *qua* being."[44] His goal was to study unchangeable *substances*, for everything in reality is either a substance or "an affection" or "accident" of a substance.[45] In other words, a substance is the essential identifying marker that makes a thing what it is, whereas an accident is an additional property of a thing, which can be removed without altering the identity. A mug, for example, in terms of its substance, is a container for liquid; that is its essence. But it can have many accidental features: it can be blue, red, tall, short, wide, or narrow, etc. The study of being, then, was a matter of boiling down features of reality to substance and accidence.

We would first take issue with the impersonal nature of Aristotle's endeavor. The study of being *qua* being, in the form of substance and accidents, is utterly impersonal. We have already concurred with Van Til that "man's surroundings are shot through with personality because all things are related to the infinitely personal God." So, leaving the tripersonal God out of the study of being would prove detrimental; breaking down components of the world into substances and accidents will not tell us the true nature of reality.

However, Aristotle's categories of substance and accidents have a far more troubling problem. To define being without reference to God's ultimate divine purpose

---

44. Copleston, *Greece and Rome*, 290.

45. Ibid., 291.

is, in effect, to walk away in the middle of a conversation. What is being without God's ultimate purpose? What is a substance or an accident without reference to God's comprehensive plan for all of reality? Consider the mug. We cannot restrict ourselves to defining the substance of a mug because a mug does not exist in isolation from the rest of reality. There is no such thing as pure, self-contained "mugness." A mug holds a liquid; a person holds a mug and probably purchased the coffee grinds that comprise the liquid; coffee is grown on plantations, which produce plants from the ground, which is also where the sediment of clay is found, which was baked at a high temperature to solidify the shape of the mug. Everything is connected. But even more important than this web of functional connections is the purpose, the ultimate goal, toward which those functions are pointing. The mug holds liquid that provides nutrients and energy for the person drinking from it, but what is that person doing? He or she is connected to a complex web of purposes each day, and those purposes are futile and meaningless if opposed to the trinitarian God and his ultimate purpose for all of reality. Thus, when Van Til says "a fact *is* its function,"[46] he is saying that things *are* not what they are abstractly. They are ontologically defined in terms of their function in God's creative and redemptive speech.

The element of "speech" is critical here, for Aristotle does try to posit the existence of a god. He traces all of being back to an ultimate "unmoved mover,"[47] but what can such an entity reveal about the purpose of reality apart

---

46. Cornelius Van Til, *Common Grace and the Gospel* (Nutley, NJ: Presbyterian and Reformed, 1977), 115.

47. Copleston, *Greece and Rome*, 291.

from communicative behavior? Such a being is mute and is posited merely to avoid an infinite regression. Any substance or accident understood in relation to such a being would be floating in an ultimately irrational and functionally stunted environment. If we wish to understand being, we must account for divine purpose, and we cannot account for divine purpose aside from the verbal revelation of the trinitarian God.

A linguistic ontology, then, as a divinely purposive ontology, fills the holes left by an impersonal Aristotelian metaphysic, and it does so by accounting for the personal nature of reality in relation to the speech of the Trinity. Only with this ontology can we truly arrive at a sound, biblical understanding of being, and of the purpose for being.

Conclusion: Implications of a Linguistic Ontology

Because a linguistic ontology has not yet been introduced in these terms,[48] it will undoubtedly face resistance in the broader philosophical (and even within the Christian philosophical) community. So we might preclude that resistance with a few comments. I restrict myself to discussing four implications: (1) the mystery of the Trinity; (2) language and the *imago Dei*; (3) the personalistic atmosphere of reality; and (4) the weight of our words.

The mystery of the Trinity. One might say that a single

---

48. Vern Poythress has laid the groundwork for this with *In the Beginning Was the Word*, and he discusses language as a perspective on the world in chapters 9 and 10 of *Redeeming Philosophy*, and chapters 18 and 19 of *Triperspectivalism and the Mystery of the Trinity*.

page in Van Til's *Introduction to Systematic Theology* has started a windstorm in trinitarian debates. He wrote,

> It is sometimes asserted that we can prove to men that we are not asserting anything that they ought to consider irrational, inasmuch as we say that God is one in essence and three in person. We therefore claim that we have not asserted unity and trinity of exactly the same thing.
> Yet this is not the whole truth of the matter. We do assert that God, that is, the whole Godhead, is one person.[49]

He goes on to say that (1) "this is a mystery that is beyond our comprehension," and (2) that God is one "in whom unity and . . . plurality are equally ultimate."[50] Van Til's purpose in setting out such a description of the Godhead was to protect God's incomprehensibility.[51] He was not denying the creedal statement, "one essence, three persons." He was merely showing that we have, for nearly two millennia, assumed that we can exhaustively understand what this means. To put it bluntly, Van Til may have been suggesting that the uncritical acceptance of Aristotelian categories has led us to a univocal approach to the triune God, rather than an analogical one. Too many theologians have uttered the creedal formula without a wink, drawing the sap from a doctrine that should be steeped in mystery, awe, and adoration.

A linguistic ontology avoids this problem by restating the personal and ultimately mysterious nature of being, for all of reality is rooted in the speech of the Trinity, the

---

49. Van Til, *Introduction to Systematic Theology*, 363.

50. Ibid., 364–65.

51. Tipton, "The Function of Perichoresis and the Divine Incomprehensibility," 290–91, 295, 298–99.

one in whom unity and plurality are equally ultimate—the one in whom "one essence" carries just as much weight as "three persons." If we follow Van Til and are consistently analogical in our approach to reality, then we can more earnestly guard ourselves against the slinking serpent of univocism, once again proclaiming that we can never exhaustively (univocally) or rationalistically comprehend the Trinity. And following this course, we must also affirm that our linguistic world has a depth no one can fathom. A linguistic ontology shows that, whether we like it or not, the Lord of reality is beyond human comprehension, and we are made in his linguistic image. This leads us to the next implication.

Language and the imago Dei. In light of a linguistic ontology, it is high time that the Christian community give language its rightful place not merely as part of the *imago Dei*, but as the center of it. Language is definitive to who we are as creatures of the self-communing trinitarian God. It is not an addendum to the classical categories of knowledge, righteousness, and holiness, nor is it an afterthought to man's reflection of God in his societal and familial relations. All of these things presuppose the centrality of language, of communicative behavior. We cannot receive or pass along knowledge apart from communicative behavior, whether that be God's communicative behavior toward us as revealed in Scripture or our expression and application of the truth of Scripture for others around us. Similarly, we cannot partake of the righteousness conferred upon us in Christ without using language to commune with other image bearers in self-sacrifice and love, thus showing we are a kingdom of priests and a holy nation of the triune God (Exod 19:6). Our societal and familial relations, as well, require the centrality of communicative behavior. We commune with others in society and with our own family members through language after the fashion of the self-communing Trinity, in an analogical and creaturely sense.

With language central to the *imago Dei*, perhaps the Reformed tradition, along with the rest of Christendom, will begin to focus on the importance of our view of language not just for apologetics or biblical studies or systematic theology, but for our entire theological system. Language is at the root, and it must receive extensive treatment if we are to live with Christian integrity in a world that has pawned language off as a biological-evolutionary development of the human species. The further the world gets from understanding the centrality of language not just to humanity, but to God and to the entire created realm, the more lost they will be in the glass-bead games of philosophers and theologians who use the very trinitarian behavior that marks us as image bearers to turn the gospel into mere information, rather than to reveal to the world the personal, life-changing message that it is.

The personalistic atmosphere of reality. Given that every part of our personality is meant to be representational of the ultimate tripersonality of God, all of human behavior must be seen as occurring in a thoroughly personalistic atmosphere. In other words, there is no part of reality, by virtue of its spoken and sustained relation to the trinitarian God, that is not personal in the deepest sense. In Van Til's language,

> If the Persons of the Trinity are representationally exhaustive of one another, human thought is cast on representational lines too. There would in that case be no other than a completely personalistic atmosphere in which human personality could function. Accordingly, when man faced any fact whatsoever, he would *ipso facto* be face to face with

God. It is metaphysically as well as religiously true that man must live and cannot but live *coram deo* always. . . . A finite personality could function in none other than a completely personalistic atmosphere, and such an atmosphere can be supplied to him only if his existence depends entirely upon the exhaustive personality of God.[52]

Van Til's words seem hyperbolic, but we should expect nothing less if we have a linguistic ontology. If all of reality was spoken by the tripersonal God, what else could it be but thoroughly personal? Following in Van Til's line of conjecture, if a single quark of the cosmos were impersonal, that would be enough to suggest that God did not speak creation into being. It is all or nothing. Either God spoke and everything is permeated by its meaningful relation to God's personal plan, or else God did not speak and nothing holds anything more than a fleeting and illusory relation to anything else.

This means that we must, as Pike did, factor persons into our view of language and the rest of reality. Pike was bent on reserving a place in his theory of language for persons, persons who make choices as to how they will see and describe the world.[53] He warned that "an attempted philosophical deletion of mind and of free observer choice may lead to an 'unlivable' life."[54] Or, at the least, it would

---

52. Van Til, *A Survey of Christian Epistemology*, 97.

53. This comes out even in his definition of language: "Language is not merely a set of unrelated sounds, clauses, rules, and meanings; it is a total coherent system of these integrating with each other, and with behavior, context, universe of discourse, and observer perspectives." Kenneth L. Pike, *Linguistic Concepts: An Introduction to Tagmemics* (Lincoln, NE: University of Nebraska Press, 1982), 44.

54. Pike, "Person beyond Logic, in Language, Life, and Philosophy," in *The Eighteenth LACUS Forum 1991*, ed. Ruth M. Brend (Lake Bluff, IL: Linguistic

lead to a life lived in a lie. And this is precisely where a linguistic ontology is so crucial. If it is true that "a person does not live in an abstraction away from things or from other people,"[55] then it is equally as true that all theories and disciplines must cater to the place of the individual in the knowing process. But this does not lead to relativism. The ultimate "person" of the Trinity is the one to whom all things are intimately related and by whom all things are known and defined. Nothing exists in isolation from God. How then, more precisely, can we articulate the connection of all things to the mind of God? In what sense, exactly, do all things exist only in relation to his mind and plan? If we hold to a linguistic ontology, the answer to these questions is that God knows and defines reality as a product of his own speech. All things are tied to the mind of God, and so we cannot know things truly but for God's speech to us. What a beautiful circle of language! God as the ultimate and absolute tripersonality speaks to us as derivative, speaking creatures. All of our knowledge of reality, then, depends upon this God's communication to us. A linguistic ontology is thus also bound up with a revelational epistemology.

Given that God's personal speech accounts for both reality itself and for our true but limited knowledge of reality, we must factor people into to every theory and every academic discipline if we are to form a truly biblical and trinitarian approach to whatever it is under consideration. But there will be much resistance to this because people are mysterious and ultimately incomprehensible. As Kallistos Ware wrote, "the human being is made in God's image

---

Association of Canada and the United States, 1992), 23.

55. Ibid., 24.

and likeness; since God is beyond understanding, his icon within humanity is also incomprehensible."[56] But, given the exhaustively personalistic atmosphere in which we find ourselves, this applies to more than just humans; it applies to all of creation! Van Til's words to his students have yet to make ripples on the pond of Protestantism: "We certainly cannot penetrate intellectually the mystery of the Trinity, but neither can we penetrate anything else intellectually because all other things depend on the mystery of the Trinity, and therefore all other things have exactly as much mystery in them as does the Trinity."[57] That is a striking claim, but true. If the trinitarian God spoke reality into being, then we cannot assume that this reality is exhaustibly knowable, for then the mind of God would be exhaustively knowable. We must factor into our explanation and exploration of any topic the tripersonal God of the Bible and his personal, linguistic revelation of himself in all of creation. And we must factor in God's image-bearers at the start of any academic or popular investigation.

The weight of words. The final implication of a linguistic ontology is helping us to understand how weighty our words can be. It has become a mark of theological piety to refer to the weakness of words—to speak of them as nothing more than signifiers of deeper, inexpressible truths. Samuel Johnson, the great poet and playwright, wrote, "I am not yet so lost in lexicography, as to forget that words are the

---

56. See Ware, forward to *Deification in Christ: Orthodox Perspectives on the Nature of the Human Person*, by Panayiotis Nellas (trans. Norman Russell; Crestwood, N.Y.: St. Vladimir's Seminary Press, 1987), 9, quoted in Letham, *The Holy Trinity*, 460.

57. Cornelius Van Til, "Christ and Human Thought: Modern Theology, Part 1" (lecture, Westminster Theological Seminary, Glenside, PA, no date).

daughters of earth, and that things are the sons of heaven. Language is only the instrument of science, and words are but the signs of ideas." Language, he quipped, was nothing more than "the dress of thought."

Let me be the first to say, yes, the way in which we often use words *suggests* they are little more than scant dressings for what really matters: objects, ideas, feelings, and emotions. All too often, words seem referentially specious and expressively anemic; they arbitrarily and imprecisely signify reality, and they are void of power because they are used by creatures who lack the foresight, determination, and aptitude (spiritual and intellectual) to see them through.

But let me also be the first to say, no. When God spoke us into existence, reflections of his communicative nature were left in our blood. We communicate with power and beauty because God speaks. We have no choice in the matter. We are creatures who must be taken at their words, just as the trinitarian God asked that we take him at his word, both in creation and in redemption. Put differently, we take God at his word because he took us at his Word. But we also take each other at our words because the trinitarian God spoke us *through* words.

I say, enough with false theological piety. It too often functions as a guise for our lazy and haphazard use of language. We are communicative beings! Language is what we do. Christians, above all others, should be the most careful, the most precise, the most cogent, the most eloquent communicators in the world. This does not demand that every Christian be a poet, or a novelist, or a renowned speaker. It simply means that we are called to think deeply about our communication.

I have little doubt that a linguistic ontology will be mocked by some, and ignored as intellectual child's play by many. But there is little we can do in the face of such a truth but praise the trinitarian God, who chose the simple things of the world to shame the wise. It may be that in making and sustaining the world through the Word, God is doing far more than exercising his power. He is calling us to see all of life through language.

In the Beginning was the Word
John 1:1–5 and a Revelational Theory of Metaphor

"The necessity of special revelation appears not only with respect to man's failure to know and react to spiritual things right, but also with respect to his inability to interpret 'natural' things aright."
– Cornelius Van Til, *Introduction to Systematic Theology*

I am Nicodemus . . . and so are you. Every Christian has rapped on the door of Christ in the middle of the night, sought an answer to a simple question, and ended up reborn. The rest of life, we might say, is about understanding and living out that second birth.

Nicodemus approached Jesus after nightfall with the hope of learning more about him. Before he encountered Jesus, he had carried with him a perceptual grid for reality: a way of understanding the world both physically and spiritually. Everything he perceived and understood was bound together with all the glorious complexity of a Jackson Pollock painting. He knew about fish and finances, death and daylight, sacrifice and sapience. All of what he experienced in his embodied existence was expressed on a single canvas of perception, stretched as tightly as the skin around his knuckles when he struck the wood on the door of the Word.

Of course, the encounter did not go as Nicodemus might have imagined. He came to admit Jesus' divine influence, but then found himself puzzled at this teacher's claim that he must be born again in order to see and enter the kingdom of God (John 3:3, 5). Why could Nicodemus not see the kingdom? In essence, Nicodemus did not have Christ at the center of his perceptual canvas. "You need a new canvas," in effect, is what Jesus told Nicodemus.

> You will have to abandon your total thought system and begin to build it all over again. You will have to accept my goodness and power as primary data, and start from there. Like a baby coming into the new world, you will have to learn to live with these facts before you can understand their source or reason. You must learn to accept the revolution this makes in your whole spiritual life without being able at the moment to understand its source any more than the sailor understands the source of the wind that moves his sails.[1]

The point is that "Christianity is not an accretion; it is not something added. It is a *new* holistic outlook which is satisfied with nothing less than penetration to the farthest corners of the mind and the understanding."[2] An encounter with the person of Christ meant that Nicodemus would receive a blank canvas, with Christ's portrait at the center.

Today, we encounter the same Christ in the words of the Bible. Special revelation is not simply an addendum to our mainly functional view of reality; it recalibrates all of what we know about anything—from sociology and science to literature and linguistics. The aim of this article is to set

---

1. Kenneth L. Pike, "Language and Life 1: A Stereoscopic Window on the World," *Bibliotheca Sacra* 114, no. 454 (April 1957): 56.

2. Kenneth L. Pike, "Prescription for Intellectuals," *Eternity* 8 (August 1957): 45.

out one of the ways in which special revelation, namely John 1:1–5, helps us re-envision language, particularly metaphor.

Far from being a tangential triviality, a biblical view of metaphor is critical to our understanding of created reality as a whole, for metaphor was not absent at the dawn of creation, as John's Gospel intimates: "In the beginning was the Word." Poythress notes that "the presence of the Word before the Father is not only the source of human metaphorical language; it is the source of the world. God created the world through his Word. We therefore expect that the world itself is shot through with metaphor."[3]

That reality is bound up with metaphor should be no threat to Christians. Certainly, when Derrida and Nietzsche referred to reality as metaphorical, they meant to disparage our trust in the referential nature of words, but this was an outgrowth of their godless view of language. Derrida, for example, understood language as a rigidly horizontal system of différence.[4] By différence, he meant that words are signifiers that can only be traced to other signifiers in a never ending labyrinth of language.[5] We cannot get outside of language to access absolute reality. We can never say what *is* because our words only refer (or *defer*) to other words. Metaphor, however, tells us what something *is* and

---

3. Vern S. Poythress, *In the Beginning Was the Word: Language—A God-Centered Approach* (Wheaton, IL: Crossway, 2009), 284–85.

4. "Différance speaks simultaneously of the tendency of words to differentiate themselves (i.e., "to differ") from other words and of necessity, "to defer" to other words in order to situate their proper meaning." David Guretzki, "Barth, Derrida, and Différance: Is There a Difference?," *Didaskalia* 53 (Spring 2002): 55.

5. Kevin J. Vanhoozer, "A Lamp in the Labyrinth: The Hermeneutics of 'Aesthetic' Theology," *Trinity Journal* 8 (1987): 25, 38–39.

is not, and so is emblematic of our imprisonment within a purely horizontal system of expression.

> Derrida reads the history of Western philosophy as the systematic repression of metaphor; metaphysics, in particular, represses the "is not." Where metaphor "transfers" meaning from one domain to another, so metaphysics transfers a concrete image to the realm of abstract truth. "Meta" is that movement that carries words beyond. For Derrida, such "transgression" is the original philosophical sin: the metaphorical "as" is mistaken for the metaphysical "is." .
> . . The problem, as Derrida sees it, is that all language—indeed, all of reality—is, so to speak, metaphorical in nature; "is and is not" is thus truer to the *différence* behind things.⁶

Nietzsche is similar in his derisive view of language and his affirmation of metaphor. Because Nietzsche assumed God was dead, he made the logical conclusion that ultimate meaning does not exist. The only meaning we have is manmade, namely through metaphors, which "create relations between things."⁷ In suggesting that reality is metaphorical, Nietzsche claims that we create coherence and relationships in order to cope with and function in a world that is summarily Godless, and, therefore, meaningless.

These views are in stark contrast to what the Christian means by saying that metaphor is bound up with reality. We are neither saying that we are trapped in language nor that we create relations in a meaningless world. Rather, based on the Trinitarian metaphor that the Son is the Word of the

---

6. Kevin J. Vanhoozer, *Is There a Meaning in This Text? The Bible, the Reader, and the Morality of Literary Knowledge* (Grand Rapids, MI: Zondervan, 1998), 130.

7. Ibid.

Father, we acknowledge that all of our words are measured against the standard of that original Word, who gives us life and light.[8] Metaphor, then, enlightens and enlivens us more deeply than we know. All of life, not merely biological but also spiritual, is linked with the metaphor of the Son as the creative and redemptive Word of the Father. Yet, while this metaphor certainly serves to illuminate God's communication with us and our communication with one another in general, it also accounts more particularly for our use of metaphor. Van Til himself articulated this in a striking passage from his *Introduction to Systematic Theology*. We all use metaphor, he claimed, based on our own experience in attempting to draw relations between what we know and what we wish to know more deeply. Christ himself used this phenomenon in his own communication.

> When Christ spoke of the vine and the branches, he did not hesitate to use that figure as symbolic of the relation of himself to the church. It is of great interest and of great importance to ask ourselves on what ground Christ was able to do this. Christ was not just a clever human being who saw interesting parallels to human experience in nature. Christ was the Logos of creation as well as the Logos of redemption. The things of nature were adapted by him to the things of the Spirit. The lower was made for the higher. The lower did not just exist independently of the higher. And because all things are made by God, that is, through the eternal Logos of creation, we too can use symbolism and analogy and know that, though we must always look for the *tertium comparationis* (the third element, the point of comparison, which explains the relation of the symbol to reality) in all symbolism, nevertheless it

---

8. Vern S. Poythress, "Reforming Ontology and Logic in the Light of the Trinity: An Application of Van Til's Idea of Analogy," *WTJ* 57, no. 1 (March 1, 1995): 193.

is at bottom true. Without a revelational foundation all symbolism and all art in general would fall to the ground.[9]

Metaphor, of course, is in the family of analogy and symbolism. Van Til is capitalizing on his firm faith in the Trinity and drawing a conclusion about language. God is a relational being, and metaphor is a means of expressing linguistic relation.[10] How fitting, then, for John to speak of the Son with a linguistic metaphor, and how powerful metaphors can be *because of this!* We will explore the implications of the Son as the Word of the Father in more detail later. For now, it is sufficient to keep in mind that the Christian has a Trinitarian, revelational grounding for metaphor.

Lastly, at the outset, we must admit that metaphor as a topic of linguistic and philosophical inquiry, has carved itself a canyon in academic history. But our intention is not to repel down the precipice and survey the riches that can be gained from comparing one theory of metaphor to a plethora of others. The aim of this article is not comparative; it is constructive. We are concerned to see how the Bible shapes our view of metaphor, and we will

---

9. Cornelius Van Til, *Introduction to Systematic Theology: Prolegomena and the Doctrines of Revelation, Scripture, and God*, ed. William Edgar, 2nd ed. (Phillipsburg, NJ: P&R Publishing, 2007), 124–25.

10. "The identity of the three distinct Persons within the one beatific Being of God indicates that God's very Being subsists through relations. That is to say, the ontological is understood through the relational. . . . The one eternal LORD exists as a communion of holy love within Himself, and this means personal existence; that is, the inter-communion of three equally divine and holy Persons. For God to be is to be in relationship within Himself." Douglas Kelly, *Systematic Theology: Grounded in Holy Scripture and Understood in Light of the Church*, vol. 1, *The God Who Is: The Holy Trinity* (Ross-shire, Scotland: Mentor, 2008), 447.

do so by using the thought of Kenneth Pike. For the sake of clarity, however, we will contrast our revelational theory of metaphor with a popular secular perspective, tension theory, in order to show more concretely how it is unique. I hope to establish that special revelation—the Bible—has a definitive role in helping us understand metaphor—along with the rest of reality.

Metaphor

A few initial comments are in order before we outline the tenets of tension theory. First, we must have some basic sense of what a metaphor is and what it does. On the broadest level, a metaphor is simply an instance of when "comparative language is used so that what is unknown may be understood in terms of what is known."[11] Thus, every metaphor has two parts, and various theories label these parts differently: the vehicle and the tenor, the source and the target, or, as in tension theory, the subsidiary and principal subject.[12] The relationship between these two parts helps us understand one or the other in a deeper sense than we had before. For example, the metaphor PEOPLE ARE PLANTS helps us understand how the features and stages of plant life illuminate the features and stages of human life.[13]

---

11. Peter Cotterell and Max Turner, *Linguistics and Biblical Interpretation* (Downers Grove, IL: IVP Academic, 1989), 299. "The essence of metaphor is understanding and experiencing one thing in terms of another." George Lakoff and Mark Johnson, *Metaphors We Live By* (Chicago: University of Chicago Press, 2003), 5.

12. See Ibid., 300; George Lakoff and Mark Turner, *More than Cool Reason: A Field Guide to Poetic Metaphor* (Chicago: University of Chicago Press, 1989), 63–65.

13. Lakoff and Turner, *More than Cool Reason*, 12–14.

It is important to note here that the parts of a metaphor always have correspondences: sets of features that seem integrally related to and yet clearly distinct from one another. People and plants both die, but people do not exit the world by having their roots cut, unless we are speaking, once again, metaphorically. The more correspondences between the parts, the richer the metaphor.

Yet metaphors do more than compare; they create.[14] Lakoff and Turner suggest that metaphor "exercises our minds so that we can extend our normal powers of comprehension beyond the range of the metaphors we are brought up to see the world through."[15] Extending our powers of comprehension means that our understanding will grow not just qualitatively but quantitatively. In other words, metaphors can extend meaning through comparison, but they can also create, or perhaps better, *reveal* new meaning by juxtaposing two things that had not previously been placed in relation to one another.[16]

Yet, whether a metaphor compares or creates meaning (or both), it is still a linguistically delivered *relationship*

---

14. Here we use "create" in a limited, creaturely sense, for, as Van Til pointed out, our goal as creatures is not to be creatively constructive but "receptively reconstructive." Van Til, *Introduction to Systematic Theology*, 213. God is the only one who has "created" in a proper sense, so we might think of metaphorical creation as the uncovering of what God has already created.

15. Ibid., 214.

16. Douglas Berggren refers to this with the terms epiphor and diaphor. He quotes Philip Wheelwright, who suggests that epiphor occurs through pictorial comparison (calling someone "hawk nose"), structured ratios ("the foot of the mountain"), or emotion-like textures ("brooding mountains"). Diaphor, Max Black suggests, is "the creation of new meaning by juxtaposition and synthesis." See Douglas Berggren, "The Use and Abuse of Metaphor 1," *The Review of Metaphysics* 16, no. 2 (December 1962): 241–42.

between words or concepts we would not commonly pair with one another. Metaphor, in this sense, is relational. It not only relates word or concepts but also the people who seek to understand or build upon them in a given context to convey truth.[17] Metaphors, we might say, are the linguistic bridges we build between words and concepts in order to convey meaning and commune with others.[18]

Tension Theory

With a basic understanding of metaphor, we can now outline tension theory so that we have something with which to compare a revelational theory of metaphor.

Tension theory uses the labels of *subsidiary* and *principal subject* to refer to the parts of a metaphor.[19] In the previous example, PEOPLE ARE PLANTS, people, with all of their attendant behavior, would be the principal subject and plant life the subsidiary subject; both of these subjects are brought into relationship by the word "plants," which Berggren calls the *sign focus* of the metaphor.[20] The sign focus, then, always has two referents; it is, in Wheelwright's terminology, an instance of "plurisignation," meaning that we must keep both signifiers in mind in order for the metaphor to work. Later, Berggren refers to this ability to

---

17. Metaphors "may carry truth judged relative to the joint expectancies of speaker-hearer acting within the same frame of reference of expectancies, intent, and literary genre." Kenneth L. Pike, *Linguistic Concepts: An Introduction to Tagmemics* (Lincoln, NE: University of Nebraska Press, 1982), 104.

18. On metaphors as bridges, see Kenneth L. Pike, "Morals and Metaphor," *Interchange* 12 (1972): 228–31.

19. Berggren, "The Use and Abuse of Metaphor 1," 238.

20. Ibid., 238–39.

see both subjects in tension as *stereoscopic vision*.

In addition to claiming that metaphors are composed of the sign focus, subsidiary subject, and principal subject, tension theory further affirms that "the difference between the referents of any metaphor must be such that a literal or univocal interpretation of their conjunction would produce absurdity."[21] My wife, in other words, does not stand in the sun with her feet rooted in the soil, photosynthetically sustaining her life. In other words, a metaphor "is implicitly akin to a counterfactual statement."[22] This is the source of the "tension" in tension theory.

Lastly, tension theory posits that metaphor actually creates meaning, or at least reveals antecedent meaning, from the subsidiary and principal subject by "construing the one in terms of the other."[23] This created or revealed meaning is called *transformed assimilation*. It is this transformed assimilation that brings the tension of tension theory into focus: though we construe one subject in terms of another, neither is collapsed into the other.

> If the initial differences between the two referents were not simultaneously preserved, even while the referents are also being transformed into closer alignment, the metaphorical character of the construing process would be lost. The possibility of comprehension of metaphorical construing requires, therefore, a peculiar and rather sophisticated intellectual ability which W. Bedell Stanford metaphorically labels "stereoscopic vision": the ability to entertain two different points of view at the same time.[24]

---

21. Ibid., 239.

22. Ibid., 240.

23. Ibid., 242.

24. Ibid., 243.

In sum, the tension of tension theory arises because, "on the one hand, a logical or empirical absurdity stands in apparent conflict with a possible truth. On the other hand, this possible truth may itself depend upon a creative interaction between diverse perspectives which cannot be literalized or disentangled without destroying the kind of insight, truth, or reality which the metaphor provides."[25] Tension theory can thus be illustrated with the diagram below.[26]

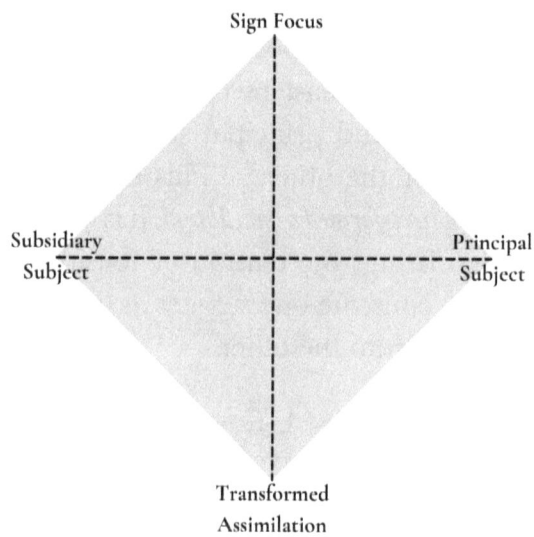

Figure 1: Tension Theory

---

25. Ibid., 244.

26. This diagram is a slightly modified form of the one that Berggren himself provides in the previously referenced article.

Building a Revelational Theory of Metaphor

As stated earlier, our goal is not comparative or strictly evaluative. We are not aiming to judge the validity of tension theory, but only to use it as a foil to better understand our current focus: a revelational theory of metaphor.

To start, we need to clarify what we mean by "revelational" here. Van Til was keen on pressing the truth that all of reality is revelational of God.[27] All words ultimately reveal the God who speaks, so in what sense can we have a "revelational" approach to metaphor? Is our approach to metaphor not revelational by default, since we are working within a world that is exhaustively revelational of God?

In the introduction, we stated that special revelation redefines our understanding of reality. Once we come to see the truth of Scripture and, by the Spirit, are brought to faith in the person of Christ, then we are in the same position that Nicodemus was in: our rebirth demands re-comprehension all of reality according to the Word of God. Nicodemus certainly had a special encounter with the incarnate Christ, but we also encounter Christ in the words of Scripture, since God's words are God's speech, and the Son is tied to that speech.[28] God is always present with his words because words are always present to and derived

---

27. Van Til, *Introduction to Systematic Theology*, 119–36.

28. On the relation between the Word and God's creational words, and the specific words of Scripture, see Vern S. Poythress, "God and Language," in *Did God Really Say? Affirming the Truthfulness and Trustworthiness of Scripture*, ed. David B. Garner (Phillipsburg, NJ: P&R Publishing, 2012), 94–97; Poythress, "Reforming Ontology and Logic," 188.

from *the Word*.[29] In this sense, we all have our Nicodemus experience and are working out that experience in reality.

In light of the above distinction, when we use the phrase "revelational approach," we mean "special-revelational," i.e., biblical. To outline this approach, we will introduce Kenneth Pike's understanding of metaphor, in comparison with tension theory, and then suggest how God's special revelation can shape our approach to metaphor and to all of reality. Through the following pages, we will use John 1:1–5 as a test case, since it offers broadly accessible metaphors: words, life, and light.

Kenneth Pike's Understanding of Metaphor

Pike distinguishes between "central" and "marginal" meanings of morphemes (meaningful linguistic units). For the sake of simplicity, we will consider words in their central and marginal meanings rather than staying strictly focused on morphemes themselves, since words can be a single morpheme or a combination of morphemes.

Now, how do we know what the central meaning of a word is? There are several factors that help us decide. (1) Time: "the central meaning will be one which was learned early in life," thus carrying a certain "primacy."[30] (2) Physicality: the central meaning "is likely to have reference to a physical situation—a physical situation which is early encountered by the child as he learns the language."[31] For

---

29. John M. Frame, *The Doctrine of the Word of God* (Phillipsburg, NJ: P&R Publishing, 2010), chap. 11.

30. Kenneth L. Pike, *Language in Relation to a Unified Theory of the Structure of Human Behavior*, 2nd ed. (The Hague: Mouton, 1967), 600.

31. Ibid., 600–601.

example, my son learned the word *head* by bumping it into a table; he does not yet know the marginal, idiomatic meaning of "having a good head on his shoulders."[32] (3) Explanatory power: "if two meanings are related, the more central is the one in terms of which the other can be explained."[33] Pike offers the humorous example of a boy who thought that *pigs* were properly called such because they were so dirty. The child's mother referenced the word *pig* in the context of eating (*eating like a pig*) or of cleanliness (*filthy as a pig*), before the child had the opportunity to see a pig. So, he had reversed the central and marginal meanings of his peers, classifying the animal according to human habits rather than understanding human behavior as metaphorically tied to the behavior of an animal. (4) Frequency: within communities, central meanings "may occur with greater frequency than any one of the marginal meanings."[34] These criteria are meant to be seen as descriptive guides rather than prescriptive rules. Language, for Pike, cannot be so cleanly compartmentalized. Nevertheless, these criteria can help us discover the central and marginal meanings of a word, and we can also apply these features to phrases and sentences. For instance, "the central meaning of a phrase . . . would first of all be related to the central meaning of its included words. Thus the phrase as a whole, if treated in its

---

32. Note that this also is tied to, and perhaps is derived from, the notion of "observation sentences," i.e., sentences that point out objects or events in one's physical environment. See, Pike, *Talk, Thought, and Thing*, 1–8, and Willard Van Orman Quine and J. S. Ullian, *The Web of Belief*, 2nd ed. (New York: Random House, 1978), 28. Pike was particularly familiar with Quine's work.

33. Pike, *Language*, 601.

34. Ibid.

central meaning, would have its included words understood in their central meanings."³⁵

Now, what does all of this have to do with metaphor? Metaphorical meanings are, for Pike, marginal to the central meanings of words or phrases. And, what's more, they are dependent on the central meanings. Metaphorical uses of words are "dependent or derived" and "develop as an extension of words used in central meanings."³⁶ Here Pike goes deeper than tension theory by laying a semantic and pragmatic, rather than lexical, foundation for metaphor. That does not eclipse the notion of tension, however, as we will see; it merely takes another step backwards to gain perspective on meaning in relation to use.

At this point, Pike introduces an analogy for the way in which words or phrases pass from marginal, metaphorical use to "central-meaning" use, and vice versa. If we imagine that physical reality is a planet and a word used in reference to it is a satellite,

> then the distribution of the satellite in a wider orbit carries with it more energy than its distribution in a narrower orbit. As the satellite loses energy it spirals down into an inner, closer orbit. Let us now assume that the central meaning of a word has reference to an ORBIT. Words occur in particular distributions which are frequent and close to the physical situation which they name directly. If, however, the same word is used in distributions remote from the original distribution, and especially if they are remote from the physical contexts in which the words were first learned by

---

35. Ibid. Note that idiomatic meanings of phrases can sometimes be central, thus bucking the trend outlined above. "Take it easy" does not mean that I want someone one to obtain something in an easy manner; it means "I wish you well" or "don't push yourself too hard."

36. Ibid., 603.

the child, or within which they have their central meanings, these special distributions carry with them a certain kind of "communication energy." These extended symbolic usages, because of their special distributions, have a heavier impact on the listener. . . . If, however, the word is used very frequently in this metaphorical sense, and as such comes in more and more contexts, so that it takes the distributional place of the word which formerly was used for the central meaning relevant to it, the communication energy of this special meaning has been dissipated, and the now "dead metaphor" carries no more impact than an ordinary word in its ordinary central meaning.[37]

Pike's analogy can be illustrated as follows:

Central Meaning

Marginal/Metaphorical
Meaning

Figure 2: Pike's Understanding of Metaphorical Meaning

Note here that Pike is more focused on the *effect* of metaphorical language (what it does) than on its *inner*

---

37. Ibid., 603–604.

structure (what it is). This is one of the reasons why it would not be fair to compare tension theory with Pike's analogy, since the two are serving separate ends.

Keeping Pike's focus in mind, we can see from his orbit analogy that he brings into play two critical features for any understanding of metaphor: (1) physical experience must be adequately accounted for; and (2) metaphorical meaning must have an explanation that is tied to such experience.[38] Remember Van Til's words, "The lower was made for the higher. The lower did not just exist independently of the higher." He links physicality with spirituality; he does not bifurcate them. We need both. But Van Til was also right to point out that a proper understanding of metaphor must also contain a third informant: special revelation. This is where we can supplement Pike's model.

Cornelius Van Til was adamant that we always account for revelation in our understanding of humanity, and that would include the language we use. We have a *revelational metaphysic* and a *revelational epistemology* because we live in a world that is "exhaustively revelational" of the triune God."[39] All that exists, and all that we know about what

---

38. Note Reverend William Jones' emphasis on the figurative language of Scripture, which draws on physical experiences in order to teach spiritual content: "In this sort of language did our blessed Saviour instruct his hearers; always referring them to such objects as were familiar to their senses, that they might see the propriety and feel the force of his doctrine. This method he observed, not in compliance with any customary speech of peculiar to the Eastern people, but consulting the exigence of human nature, which is everywhere the same." This is quoted in Stephen Prickett, *Words and the Word: Language, Poetics, and Biblical Interpretation* (New York: Cambridge University Press, 1986), 215.

39. Cornelius Van Til, *Common Grace and the Gospel* (Nutley, NJ: Presbyterian and Reformed, 1977), 169. With regards to revelational metaphysic, we must remember that God's speech both specifies *what* exists and *how* it

exists comes by way of God's revelation. But it seems this has not yet been worked into our understanding of metaphorical meaning—and we are all the poorer for it. A revelational approach to metaphor would, I argue, be a means of revolutionizing our understanding of language and showing us the richness of biblical revelation.

A Revelational Theory of Metaphor

Here is how a revelational approach to metaphor would work, based on Pike's previous discussion. We begin, as Pike does, with physical experience or central meanings of words.[40] We then have marginal and metaphorical meanings of words, but by the communicative nature of special revelation, God can and has revealed himself in creation with metaphors in a way that has the potential to redefine even our central meanings of words.[41] The most potent example of this is the metaphor of the Son as "the Word" of the Father.

---

exists. Vern S. Poythress, *Redeeming Philosophy: A God-Centered Approach to the Big Questions* (Wheaton, IL: Crossway, 2014), 105. In that sense, ontology is itself linguistic. With regards to a revelational epistemology, Van Til writes, "Since the human mind is created by God and is therefore in itself naturally revelational of God, the mind may be sure that its system is true and corresponds on a finite scale to the system of God." Van Til, *Introduction to Systematic Theology*, 292.

40. These central and marginal meanings of words, again, are already revelational in the sense of being bound up with general revelation. Our focus here, however, is how they are illumined by special revelation.

41. "Revelation is communicative. By revealing himself to human beings, God desires to establish and maintain communion with us and to make this communion between him and us steadily richer." See J. van Genderen and W. H. Velema, *Concise Reformed Dogmatics*, trans. Gerrit Bilkes and Ed M. van der Maas (Phillipsburg, NJ: P&R Publishing, 2008), 24–26.

To begin understanding this metaphor, we start with personal experience. How are words used by others around us? What do we do when we speak? What does it accomplish? There is a plethora of experiential data available to us as we answer these questions. We can gather data from phonetics (sound systems), phonemics (particular sets of sounds within a language), articulation (how sounds are produced physically), graphics (how words are inscribed an arranged in a visual medium), pragmatics (how people use words to accomplish a certain end), ethics (in what senses and by what standards we judge a word to be used with good or evil intentions), etc. There is no shortage of data because words occur in so many different contexts and are used to do so many different things. Drawing on a selected pool of this data, we use both our central and marginal meanings to come to a rough conclusion of what it might mean for *the Son* to be *the Word*.[42] At this point, remember, the metaphor "the Son is the Word" is in an outer orbit, and our curiosity as to its meaning is testifying to what Pike calls its massive "communication energy."[43]

---

42. For example, drawing on a select number of examples from everyday experience, we might gather the expressions "I spoke several words to him," and "I had a word with him." The former is an example of "word" used in its central meaning (graphic and aural significations that reference objects in reality), while the latter is an example of "word" used more marginally, meaning "conversation" or "discussion." Another example of "words" used centrally would be the instruction we give to our toddler when he shouts or grunts if he does not get his way: "use your words."

43. It is important to add that this metaphor, given its referent cannot ever become a "dead metaphor," especially in light of the resurrection of the Son. This adds a whole different dimension to this metaphor that we cannot explore here. But we must note that not all of the metaphors of Scripture fit neatly into Pike's explanation, and he would not expect them to do so. The Son as the Word of the Father is an ever enlivening and enlightening metaphor.

Based on the experiential data we have gathered from numerous "inner orbits," we begin traveling toward the outer orbit that contains the unique metaphor we wish to understand (the Son as the Word of the Father). Perhaps it means something along the lines of the Son being the Father's communication, the expression of his thought, or the communicative action he takes. But this is not where our understanding ends.

Up to this point we have only been considering *human* meaning. When we are told that the Son is the Word of the Father, that metaphor, coming as it does from special revelation, has *divine* meaning, so we look to revelation itself (Scripture) to understand what it could mean for the Son to be the Father's Word. The Son incarnate, Jesus Christ, lived an embodied, self-sacrificial, God-honoring life. He bound himself to a particular community, cared for their physical and spiritual needs, and taught them to give up all things for the sake of the heavenly kingdom and creaturely communion with the Trinity (John 17).

Here again we see that the meaning of the Word is not divorced from physical reality, for we understand the eternal Son by looking at the incarnate Son as he lived among us. It is that knowledge that helps us better understand what it means for the Son to be the Word of the Father. The Son is the perfect and holistic expression of the Father in eternity; he glorifies the Father without end, as does the Spirit, who glories the Son and Father, and so on and so forth. When we think of the Son as the Word of the Father, then we grasp, as much as is possible for finite minds, that "the Father does not distance Himself from the Son and Holy Spirit, and They do not think about separating Themselves from the Father. Rather, each sees Himself in the other and is more preoccupied with the other's good and with His own."[44] By the mutual love each person has for the other persons, we learn that the Trinity is a gapless God, and yet a God who chooses to communicate with himself (internally) and with his creatures (externally). The Son as the Word of the Father means that language for the Trinity is the highest form of communion, showcasing the fact that the persons of the Godhead were, are, and always will be "inextricably intertwined."[45]

But we must still go further. In light of the fact that human language is analogical, we take this understanding of the Word and use it as an illuminating perspective on the current central and marginal uses of the term "word."[46] Words, from our experience, might merely seem to be instruments for information transfer or arbitrary signs in systems that serve only the individual. But if the Word illuminates our understanding, then we begin to see that words comprise the lifeblood of communion and the salt of relationships. They are not arbitrary signifiers for self-serving purposes, but means for communion—means which reveal that we are *communicators* made in the image of the self-communicating God and that we are *with* our words. Here, then, is a revelational model for metaphor.

---

44. Dumitru Stăniloae, *The Holy Trinity: In the Beginning There Was Love*, trans. Roland Clark (Brookline, MA: Holy Cross Orthodox Press, 2012), 42.

45. Daniel F. Stramara Jr., "Gregory of Nyssa's Terminology for Trinitarian Perichoresis," *Vigiliae Christianae* 52, no. 3 (August 1, 1998): 263.

46. If, as Lakoff and Johnson suggest, "the essence of metaphor is understanding and experiencing one kind of thing in terms of another," then we must say that the relationship can always be extended. We understand the Son in terms of the Word, but we also understand words in terms of the Word. George Lakoff and Mark Johnson, *Metaphors We Live By* (Chicago: University of Chicago Press, 2003), 5.

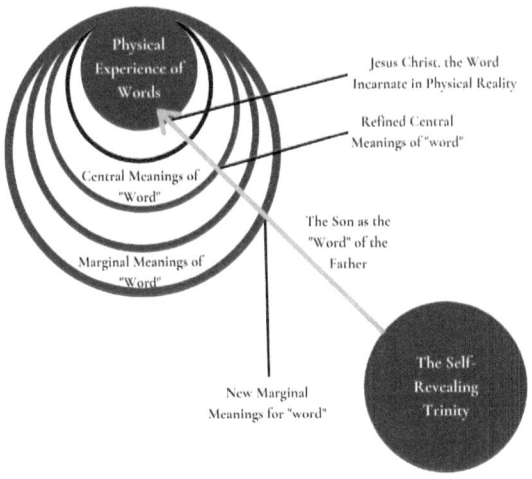

Figure 3: A Revelational Approach to Metaphor

The revolutionary nature of this approach surfaces in two places. First, it challenges what oftentimes becomes the idol of "literal language" with the rich and tangible revealed language of the Bible. Literal language is helpful and has its place, but, as we noted, all of language at its roots is bound up with metaphor. So, language cannot be *purely* literal. In the late 80s, John Frame helpfully noted that "there is no reason to have any general theological preference for literal language over figurative or to assume that every metaphor must be literally explained in precise academic terms. Scripture does not do that. Often, in fact, figurative language says more, and says it more clearly, than corresponding literal language would do."[47] Second, a

---

47. John M. Frame, *The Doctrine of the Knowledge of God* (Phillipsburg, NJ: P&R Publishing, 1987), 227–28. He adds a few pages later that we must also be conscious of the "disanalogy" that is present with every analogy. This refers to the tension phenomenon of tension theory. Note the earlier

revelational theory of metaphor helps us to relate spiritual truth to earthly description, when oftentimes the former is left out of the equation. It does not discount earthly reality by doing so, but it does tell us that there is more to reality than what we see, and that what we see must be understood by what we cannot see (Heb 11:1). Thus, we have a faith-based approach to linguistic meaning.[48] The "Word," then, as God's self-expression—his creative and redemptive speech—is the archetypal meaning for our creaturely use of the term "word." The same applies, we will see, to the concepts "life" and "light."

Thus far, we can see that a revelational theory of metaphor still fulfills the criteria that Pike's model offers, but it goes beyond it to include a role for special revelation, which is critical for those who hold to orthodox Christianity. It affirms that God is deeply involved in human language, not simply because he chooses to be, but because he himself is a communicative being and all that he has made reflects him.

How does this theory engage with tension theory? To be sure, there is a sort of tension in any metaphor. When John tells his readers that the Son is the Word of the Father, we likely see the sign focus, "Word," as it relates to a subsidiary subject (perhaps verbal communication) and a principal subject (the Son). With these two subjects in mind, we *begin* by using stereoscopic vision (viewing both "the Word" and "the Son" simultaneously) to arrive at a

---

quotation from Berggren: "the difference between the referents of any metaphor must be such that a literal or univocal interpretation of their conjunction would produce absurdity."

48. This also means we have a psycho-somatic view of language, which pairs with our psycho-somatic view of people, as *body-spirit* image bearers.

transformed assimilation: the Son is the embodied verbal revelation of the Father. But we do not stop with tension, for one of the reasons such tension arises is because of our effort to maintain the "uni-directionality" of the metaphor. Our goal is only to comprehend the Son in a deeper way, not the term "word." But a revelational theory of metaphor underscores that we understand a great deal about the term "word" in addition to learning a great deal about the Son. Just as a bridge carries traffic in both directions, so metaphors are *bidirectional*. Certainly, an author can and often does have a *primary* focus, and most often focuses on moving the semantic traffic in one direction. John is not primarily trying to instruct us about the nature of human words; rather, he is deepening our understanding of the second person of the Trinity. But that does not mean that the bridge built by the metaphor disallows *secondary* traffic in the other direction. That is the beauty of revelation. It reveals *more* than what we expect or imagine. It does not simply deliver the truth; it overwhelms us with it. This will become clearer as we examine the other metaphors in John 1:1–5, but not before we understand something of the context in which they occur.

Life and Light in Relation to the Word

Because life and light can only be understood in and are determined by their relationship to the Word, a few comments are in order before we further examine "words," "life," and "light" with a revelational approach to metaphor.

It seems apparent that John's main intention in the Prologue is to introduce the subject of the Gospel, namely "(1) the relationship between God and the Word (Jesus); and

(2) the possibility of a close relationship between God and human beings."⁴⁹ Relationship—that is John's concern in the Prologue. In light of this, it would be best to understand "the Word" as conveying, firstly, the "intimate and unique relationship between the Father and the Son."⁵⁰ How exactly do we understand this relationship? Geerhardus Vos suggests that the Son as the Word signifies the Son's rationale "inherent in the speaker," as being the "imprint of [the speaker's] personal existence," and as tied to the speaker by living on in the speaker's consciousness.⁵¹ In other words, the Son *as Word* is bound up with the Father as divine Speaker (and, we should add, with the breath or power used to produce it, i.e., the Spirit). The Son perfectly represents the intimate and personal presence of the Father as Speaker, and is never removed from the consciousness of that Speaker.⁵² Secondly, we should understand "the Word"

---

49. Andreas J. Köstenberger, *A Theology of John's Gospel and Letters*, Biblical Theology of the New Testament (Grand Rapids, MI: Zondervan, 2009), 361.

50. Maksimilijan Matjaz, "The Significance of the Logos in the Relational Aspect of John's Theology," in *"Perché Stessero Con Lui": Scritti in Onore Di Klemens Stock SJ, Nel Suo 75° Compleanno*, ed. Lorenzo De Santos and Santi Grasso (Rome: Gregorian and Biblical Press, 2010), 302.

51. Geerhardus Vos, *Reformed Dogmatics*, vol. 1, *Theology Proper*, ed. and trans. Richard B. Gaffin, Jr. (Bellingham, WA: Lexham Press, 2014), 57. Vos writes shortly before this that "the Word" is primarily designating who the Son is with respect to the Father, and only secondarily who the Son is with respect to us. I would grant Vos' conclusion, but I would immediately add that these cannot be sundered from one another in John's Gospel.

52. This would fit under Lane Tipton's discussion of the triune God as both a uni-conscious being and a tri-conscious being, a concept that originally came from the pen of Cornelius Van Til. See Lane G. Tipton, "The Function of Perichoresis and the Divine Incomprehensibility," *WTJ* 64 (2002): 291–95, and Van Til, *Introduction to Systematic Theology*, 348. The Son is never absent from the uni-consciousness of the Godhead.

as conveying the truth that "the essence of life is a *relation to God.*"⁵³ Thus, when we have faith in the Word, this leads us "to a *relationship*, to the Person. Eternal life is in the knowledge of the Father and the Son (17:3), and whoever keeps the Father's words will come to know the Son and believe in him, and will enter into a relationship with him (17:6–8)."⁵⁴ It is in relationship to this Word that we have life, which brings us to our next metaphorical expression.

The Logos as Life

In v. 4a we read, "In him was life." How are we to understand "life" as residing *in* the Word? Casting this question in the light of the previous discussion, we seem compelled to affirm that life is in *relationship*. This goes against years of philosophical treatment of life and existence (ontology and metaphysics) as categorized by impersonal qualities or attributes. But if the Word, the relational person of the Son, is the origin of life, then existence itself cannot be impersonal. Life is found not in isolated enjoyment of breath and material, but in relationship—both with God and with other people.⁵⁵

---

53. Matjaz, "The Significance of the Logos," 290.

54. Ibid., 293.

55. Aristotelian philosophy has tended to treat ontology in abstraction, as substance and accidents. Aristotle's categorical system provides the illusion of mastery: that we can know what a thing *is* exhaustively. But "no 'ultimate' system of abstract categories reaches down and makes transparent to human reason the foundations of human existence. That is because creation as a whole and every individual creature have their foundation in God's plan, his commands, his governance, and his presence." That presence is a personal presence. So how could life (i.e., existence) itself be impersonal? Poythress, *Redeeming Philosophy*, 137.

This life is best understood in the context of v. 3, "All things were made through him, and without him was not any thing made that was made." The making of life, the bringing forth of creaturely existence, is inescapably relational, for at the dawn of their creation, every creature is bound in continuous relationship to the Word. Vos seems to have captured this decades ago. The Word did not create reality and leave: he remains and relates. In referencing John's intentions for v. 3, Vos observes,

The writer does not look upon the production of the world through the Logos as a past fact, of which the significance and influence ceased with the moment of creation. It is a fact resulting in *a continuous relationship*,[56] for only as such could it offer a reason why the world could and should, under normal conditions, have so known and received the Logos as is implied in both verse 10c and verse 11c. The bare fact that the Logos had a hand in the creation of the world would not of itself have made it easier for the world to know Him; this would result only if the origin of the world through the Logos established a perpetual relation of immanence in the world and proprietorship of the world.[57]

In other words, the creation and giving of life itself presupposed relationship because it comes through the *Logos*. That is why discipleship is not merely a matter of epistemology. It is not *what* you know that makes you a disciple of the Word in the flesh; it is *who* you know. So it

---

56. Italics added.

57. Geerhardus Vos, "The Range of the Logos Title in the Prologue to the Fourth Gospel," in *Redemptive History and Biblical Interpretation: The Shorter Writings of Geerhardus Vos*, ed. and trans. Richard B. Gaffin Jr. (Phillipsburg, NJ: P&R Publishing, 1980), 89.

is quite natural for John to illustrate that discipleship is not a question "about Jesus' teaching. It is him, his life and his concrete relations. The disciple is invited to a relationship with the Lord and nothing else but life with Him makes him a disciple."[58] For the Word to have life *in himself* means that we cannot access life apart from him. Simply by being created (and later by being re-created) we partake in the life that belongs properly to him alone.[59] But it is difficult to realize this without the light of the knowledge of God, which is where we turn presently.

The Logos as Light

So, the *Logos* has life in him, but, apart from the comments just made, what else can we say about that life? John tells us directly, "the life was the light of men." At the outset, we must remember that this light is never independent from or received prior to a relationship with the Word. If a relationship were possible primarily through the light of knowledge, then that would open up the door to the heresy of Gnosticism. Instead, we settle with Vos: "The first thing associated with the Logos-name by the writer does not lie in the sphere of knowledge but in the sphere of power; the first characteristic Logos-product is life, not light."[60]

The light is accessed only through the life. And if that life comes in the form of relationship, would we expect the light to be isolated from this relational context? No, the light

---

58. Matjaz, "The Significance of the Logos," 294.

59. "It is through the Logos that all things were made; it is also through the Logos, become flesh, that all things in redemption were accomplished." Vos, "The Range of the Logos Title," 63.

60. Ibid., 65.

itself is tied to the relational context of life, both before the fall and after the fall. If we assume that light can be understood as "the knowledge of God," then that light has always been with us. For this reason, we interpret v. 10 not as meaning that Christ was in the world by taking on flesh, but that he *was already in the world* before the incarnation as the life-imparting *Logos*, and this naturally fits the context of the following clause: "and the world was made through him."[61] This, Vos thinks, is one of the defining gifts of the Prologue.[62] The light of the *Logos*, then, enters by two windows: the linguistically established natural world and the linguistically transmitted special knowledge of salvation in the one who shines in darkness.[63] In that light, we are able to find the source of life and have relationship with the God who speaks.

A Revelational Approach to Words, Life, and Light

Now that we have a context for these concepts, we can more closely examine them with a revelational approach to metaphor, contrasting them with how tension theory might treat them. Earlier, we noted that God's revelation has the ability to take the metaphors we have—the "second

---

61. This interpretation should be fully credited to Vos. For details in the translation of the past-tense verbs, see Ibid., 84.

62. "It not only vindicates for nature the character of a revealing medium through which God speaks, but also links together creation and redemption as both mediated by the same Logos." Ibid., 90.

63. Prickett notes that "the metaphor that Christ is the 'light of the world' changes not merely the way in which we are to understand Christ, but also the way we understand *light*." Prickett, *Words and the Word*, 217.

orbit satellites," marginal uses of words that are tied to our physical experience or central uses of words—and reshape our understanding of them based on his Trinitarian primacy. In the Trinity we find the archetypal Word, Life, and Light. Creaturely words, life, and light must then be understood analogously and derivatively. Thus, the metaphors *word*, *life*, and *light* in John's Prologue primarily tell us about the second person of the Godhead, but they serve the secondary purpose of illuminating our understanding of our central and marginal uses of these terms.

Words

If the *Logos* is not "an impersonal force," but the personal presence of God himself in the Son, and if human words are analogous to the words God uses in creation and ultimately to "the Word" of John 1:1, then we must reject any impersonal definition of language or of linguistic units.[64] What are human "words" essentially? Are they "vehicles" of thought? Perhaps in some sense, but "vehicle" has mechanical and impersonal connotations. The nature of the *Logos* in John 1:1–5 would seem to call for words to be seen as units of communion. This is not to take away from their signifying function or their various uses in spoken and written discourse. Rather, by calling words "units of communion," I mean to reinforce that all communicative acts, and thus all of the units that comprise them, are ultimately bound up with relationships—the drawing

---

64. Moisés Silva, "God, Language, and Scripture: Reading the Bible in the Light of General Linguistics," in *Foundations of Contemporary Interpretation*, ed. Moisés Silva (Grand Rapids, MI: Zondervan, 1996), 215. Poythress, "Reforming Ontology and Logic," 188.

together of persons, in a way that reflects how the Son, as Word, is inextricably bound up with the person of the Father and the Holy Spirit. Spoken and written language, then, as comprised of groups of words, is trinitarian communion behavior.[65]

Because of the revelational approach to metaphor, in which biblical metaphors recalibrate the central and marginal meanings of words on which they are based, we understand simple phrases and idioms in relation to this communion behavior. For example, we might consider the "central" or "marginal" uses of the term "word" in statements such as "his words were harsh," or "that is not the right word," and how these expressions might be reinterpreted in light of the revelation of the Word.[66] Harsh words are not simply "mean" or "derogatory"; they have potential to disrupt communion between persons. In the world of a communicative being, disruption of communion is a far more serious crime than haphazard derision. A revelational theory of metaphor here accents the weight of words—it is no light thing to break communion. Likewise, the "right word" is then not simply inaccurate, but failing to articulate the precise meaning that is required for the communion of minds, thus biblically recalibrating

---

65. This follows Pike's understanding of language as "behavior," and of words as form-meaning composites. With regard to his tagmemic theory, Ruth Brend reminds us that, "Besides emphasizing that language must be considered in its social context, tagmemics holds as a basic assumption that language, and human behavior in general, is purposeful and meaningful." Ruth M. Brend and Kenneth L. Pike, eds., *Tagmemics, Vol. 1, Aspects of the Field* (The Hague: Mouton, 1976), 86.

66. To start, we might say that "harsh" words are acts of disunion, not merely hurtful expressions. The "right" word is the word that fits the context and accurately signifies meaning so as to foster the process of communion.

the axiom that accuracy is a standard of expression and a criterion for truth. As another example, in the context of communion behavior, the question, "what words did you use?" can refer not merely to lexical choice but to the manner in which the words were spoken, thus shattering the false divide between matter and manner that so often plagues verbal and written discourse.[67] The wall between what we say and how we say it comes tumbling down with a revelational approach to words, for the original Word is more than a thing; the Word is a *person* who not only exists, but exists in a certain way.

Another implication of a revelational approach to the term "word" is our placement of language in relation to reality. Words are commonly relegated to the discipline of linguistics and semantics and only brought into discussions of metaphysics and ontology when they help clarify "non-linguistic" concepts. But if the Word is the one through whom all of creation was brought into existence, then language itself is fundamental to reality and cannot be divorced from any discipline, for the original Word not only accounts for human communication but has actualized the very reality in which communication occurs. This would mean that there is a linguistic underpinning to ontology, science, mathematics, sociology, geology, etc. Everything in creation can be understood through the window of the Word.

How does this approach to the term "word" compare with how it might be treated in tension theory? The true source of the tension in tension theory is its resistance to collapsing the subsidiary and principal subjects into one

---

67. T. David Gordon, *Why Johnny Can't Preach: the Media Have Shaped the Messengers* (Phillipsburg, NJ: P&R Publishing, 2009), 43.

another, for that would allegedly result in absurdity. As mentioned earlier, tension theory would see "word" as the sign focus, "verbal communication" as subsidiary subject and "the Son" as the principal subject, the tension between the latter two perhaps leading us to conclude that the Son is the embodied verbal revelation of the Father. But here we witness the tension of tension theory break down. *The Word as the Son of the Father is a special kind of metaphor because there is no tension between the subsidiary and principal subjects.* Certainly, we use a kind of stereoscopic vision to hold "Word" and "Son" in relationship without collapsing them into one another, but, contrary to tension theory, collapsing them into one another (the Son *is* God's speech) would not result in absurdity. Perhaps proponents of tension theory would then say that this was not a "vital metaphor."[68] But that avoids the issue. It seems, theologically speaking, that in some cases we are meant to collapse the subsidiary and principal subjects into one another for particular purposes. In this case, perhaps one of those purposes is the realization that God always speaks his Son.[69] He spoke him in eternity

---

68. "Where a reduction of the metaphor's cognitive import to non-tensional statements is possible, whether in practice or in principle, then the metaphor is not what I choose to call a vital one." Berggren, "The Use and Abuse of Metaphor 1," 244. Berggren would perhaps view the metaphor of the Son as the Word of the Father to be a "non-vital" metaphor, but theological metaphors require special treatment, for absurdity itself must be understood based on the premise of God's revelation.

69. I say "one of those purposes" because we must also guard ourselves against treating this "collapse" of the subsidiary and principle subjects reductionistically, as if all metaphors reduce to a single meaning in a platonic sense. Metaphors (in fact, many of the features of human language) are *prismatic*—their facets are not meant to be reduced to a single plain but to be appreciated in their rich, n-dimensional diversity. This is so because our perception (and the language we use to express it) is n-dimensional, that is, it has more than three or four dimensions to it. See Kenneth L. Pike, *Tag-*

past, and, as Vos stated above, he spoke him in time at the moment of creation and unwaveringly throughout history. So, the creation of the world through the Logos is "a fact resulting in a continuous relationship." God has not removed himself from the world; he is ever revealed, always communicating with it. The tension, then, is not between the subsidiary and principal subjects of John's metaphor; the real tension is between sinful and restored vision of the same reality. Sinful vision refuses to accept the continual, perspicuous revelation of God in created reality and in Scripture—both of which are products of God's speech, products of the Word. Restored vision sees no tension between the Son and the Word because God's speech is creative and redemptive. In this case, the tension of tension theory would preclude us from unearthing a theological gem.

Life

Following the previous example, how might we re-interpret the central and marginal uses of the word "life"? Looking to the Trinity for the archetypal understanding of *life*, we would first say that life cannot be sundered from the second person of the Trinity. Life is *in him*, not outside of him. True life, then, is a relationship with the Trinity, not a collection of synapses and biological potentialities. There are many people with biological life who suffer from a lack

---

memics, Discourse, and Verbal Art, Michigan Studies in the Humanities 3 (Ann Arbor, MI: University of Michigan, 1981), 18. Largely due to the influence of Plato and Aristotle, we are always struggling to exchange reduction for richness. The latter is not a threat to the stability of meaning, but a complement to it and a testament to the incomprehensibility of the Trinitarian God.

of relationship. Do such people truly have life, or are they living an illusion, as the walking dead (Eph. 2:1, 5; Col. 2:13)? We only have "life," properly speaking, *in the Word*.

If the Word has life *in himself*, then life is not, as stated before, an impersonal category or quality. Life is at all times and places relational—first to the Word who produced it, and second to the creatures who share it. When I say, "My dog's life," I do not mean to express a chain of time encapsulating his animate existence. I mean that he has *Logos*-given existence and relates both to God's creational Word and to the Word of redemption, which is making all things new (Rev. 21:5). The phrase "my dog's life" connotes a relationship, with his environment and with our family. Life never occurs in a vacuum. It exists in a web of relations. So, "life" is never merely breath.

This, again, recalibrates our central and marginal uses of the word "life." Consider the expression, "Get a life." While it is often used merely to relay an insult ("do something productive" or "stop meddling in someone else's affairs"), we cannot exclude the divine meaning of "life" when we hear such expressions. A true life is a life of relationship with the triune God, so to "get" a life means that there is discord in an interpersonal relationship—discord that is ultimately rooted in discord in a divine-human relationship. We must resist the urge to treat problems as purely sociological, assuming that changes in social behavior will help someone "get a life." Matters of the heart are always involved. Getting a life must be situated with a divine-human relationship before sociological behaviors can be modified.

For the Word to have life in himself is for us to have life primarily in him. When we are estranged from him, there is a deep sense in which we are not *alive*. It is for this reason that Paul can refer to people as being *dead* in sins and trespasses (Eph. 2:1; Col. 2:13). Life *is* in relationship with the Father, through the Son, by the power of the Spirit. All of biological life serves that end. Any understanding of "life" that attempts to supersede this relational understanding is, in fact, misconstruing the biblical use of the term.

Tension theory, again, would be limited here. Setting aside, for now, the added complication that the preposition *in* ("in him was life") has a broad semantic range and includes various metaphorical senses, we would have "life" as the sign focus, "existence" as the subsidiary subject and "the Word" as the principal subject, the tension between these subjects leading us to affirm something like, "the Word is the source of existence." This is certainly true, but not nearly rich enough an understanding, and again, the collapsing of these subjects does not end in absurdity.

In terms of richness, while we certainly affirm that the Word is the source of existence, we must be quick to add that the Word also sustains existence. All of reality is still upheld by the word of God's power (Heb. 1:3). God did not speak reality into existence and walk away, as Vos has already shown. He stayed. The Word is responsible for the origin and the continuance of earthly life, all of which is destined to one day bow the knee and confess that Christ is Lord (Phil. 2:10–11). Until that day, the Word is *with us*, even to the end of the age (Matt. 28:20). There is not only a *source* of life; there is a *relationship* of life.

In terms of the tension between the subsidiary and principal subjects, if we collapse "Word" and "life" into one another, we do not end up with absurdity (that the speech of God is alive); we end up with, at the very least, another biblical truth, "for the word of God is living and active" (Heb. 4:12).[70] God's word is not simply propositional; it *does* things.[71] Perhaps most importantly, it pierces the soul, "discerning the thoughts and intentions of the heart" (Heb 4:12). Without such piercing we cannot truly have life, since life is a relationship with the Word.

Light

Light provides an interesting application for a revelational theory of metaphor, since the term is so typically associated with physicality. But yet again, taking the Trinity for our archetypal understanding, we first say that light, as it is bound to the life of the Word, cannot be divorced from its relational context. Light, especially if taken to mean knowledge, is the arena of relationship. God knows himself exhaustively. He is a light unto himself.[72] And only in him do we know ourselves, because the relational life we have with God is "the light of men" (John 1:4). Our light is not

---

70. See the previous note on the prismatic nature of biblical metaphors.

71. This goes beyond the limits of speech-act theory, though the latter can be helpful when understood biblically, as Vanhoozer's work has illustrated. For the limitations of speech-act theory, see Vern S. Poythress, "Canon and Speech Act: Limitations in Speech-Act Theory, with Implications for a Putative Theory of Canonical Speech Acts," *Westminster Theological Journal* 70, no. 2 (September 1, 2008): 337–54.

72. The light that God is surrounded by before the creation of earthly light is a kind of self-referential light based upon which he creates earthly light. See Bruce K. Waltke, *Genesis: A Commentary* (Grand Rapids, MI: Zondervan, 2001), 61; Jacob Milgrom, "The Alleged 'Hidden Light,'" in *The Idea of Biblical Interpretation: Essays in Honor of James L. Kugel* (ed. Hindy Najman and Judith H. Newman; Boston: Brill, 2004), 44; and Mark S. Smith, "Light in Genesis 1:3—Created or Uncreated: A Question of Priestly Mysticism," in *Birkat Shalom: Studies in the Bible, Ancient Near Eastern Literature, and Postbiblical Judaism Presented to Shalom M. Paul on the Occasion of His Seventieth Birthday* (ed. Chaim Cohen et al.; Winona Lake, IN: Eisenbrauns, 2008), 1:127–31.

self-referential knowledge but relational knowledge of the Triune God. Only in his light do we see light (Ps. 36:9). All that is to say John 1:1–5 reveals that the life of the Word precedes the light that we have *in him*, a light that both illumines ourselves and the God with whom we are meant to have communion.

When we seek light, i.e., knowledge, without recourse to our personal relationship with God or with others, is it really light that we are after? And when we see physical light, do we think of it in the context of a relational life, or do we do the opposite? Do we think that life only occurs in physical light, or that light exists to serve our relational life with God? I would suggest that the relational nature of light means that we use physical light, and the metaphorical light of knowledge, only in conscious service of relationships, for true light is relational: it comes about in the relationship we have to the creative and redemptive Word of God.

Again, we let this reshape our central and marginal uses of the word "light." The expression "the light of knowledge," frequently referenced by rationalists and Enlightenment philosophers may have been understood as a set of propositional truths or a system of logic, but the biblical light of knowledge goes far deeper. We do not *possess* knowledge so much as *live in accordance with it*. Knowledge is not merely attained; it is sustained and sustaining in relationship with the life we have in the Word. To know something truly, in this sense, is to act on it with regard to relationships in reality.[73]

---

73. This could be related to Leonard Bloomfield's notion of meaning—which is certainly a part of knowledge—as a situation of speaking and response, or to Wittgenstein's understanding of meaning as use in context, or, in Frame's language, meaning as an expression of God-ordained use, i.e., understanding and responsible use. See Frame, *Doctrine of the Knowledge of*

Physical light is a glorious reflection of Trinitarian light. When we light a candle, turn on a light, or see the sun rise, we are presented with a world of relations that calls for our engagement. Light allows us to function in reality for the sake of accenting and drawing others to its attendant life. How paradoxical it is, then, when we walk into a lit room and insult another person; or when we offer to pray for someone and then blow out a candle and leave her alone (I am guilty on both counts). The light we have is meant to serve the life we were given. All light is not merely phenomenal. It is more than photons. It is always purposively bound up with the life of the Word.

Tension theory, again, while helpful in pointing out that we use stereoscopic vision to hold the "life" and "light" in view at the same time, cannot account for the relational meaning that is conveyed by the metaphor. Light is not to be understood in tension with life, but as bound up with it. We can collapse the subsidiary subject (physical light) into the principal subject (existence) and end up not with an absurdity (light is the sustenance of human existence), but with a community: physical light, as a derivation of the light of God's knowledge, is meant to sustain and serve the relational life of human existence. The Trinitarian God, who has life and light in himself, has condescended and extended that life and light in creation. Our light *is* his life, and our life is *in* his light.

Conclusion and Implications

One of the strengths of a revelational theory of metaphor is

God, 95–97 and *Systematic Theology: An Introduction to Christian Belief* (Phillipsburg, NJ: P&R Publishing, 2013), 660–61.

that it is loose enough to account for the richness of biblical truth. Rather than trap ourselves within a particular, univocal understanding of metaphor, we can draw on the various approaches to metaphor, such as tension theory, as they are informed by special revelation. As promised in the introduction, a revelational approach shows how Scripture illuminates our central and marginal uses of words through the metaphors it offers. Our case study of John 1:1–5 is just one passage among many. Admittedly, these metaphors have a special potency because they are related to the Son of God, not just any element of creation. Nevertheless, the principle would be the same with other passages of Scripture, since the Bible always recalibrates our understanding of reality. There is no part of language that is not affected by our reception of revelation, so we must continue to explore the implications of revelation for language. We are, after all, just like Nicodemus. Being born of water and the Spirit means that, in our growing faith, we continue to work out the implications of a Word-made world.

In ending, perhaps our greatest discovery thus far is that our central and marginal uses of words are not properly understood apart from the trinitarian, revelational context of Scripture, and that all words, many of which seem to be embedded in physical reality, have a spiritual source that runs deeper than we can imagine. The mystery of the self-communing Trinity, once again, challenges us to see all of language as a divinely endowed, derivative behavior. Metaphor, it seems, does more than build bridges between concepts; it builds the bridge between divine and human communication.

The Emic and Etic, Immanent and Economic
Perspectives on Theology from Language Theory

There is an ancient relationship between theology proper and language theory—between what we think about the triune God and what we postulate about the nature of human communication. Ultimately, this is because the Trinity is profoundly linguistic and language is profoundly Trinitarian.[1] The Father, Son, and Holy Spirit have eternally communed with one another in mutual expressions of love and glory.[2] Human image bearers of the Trinity, by analogy, use language to foster communion in a similar way on the creaturely level.[3] Thus,

---

1. There is much literature on the Trinitarian nature of communication, spanning the Catholic and Protestant traditions, but one might begin with Vern S. Poythress, *In the Beginning Was the Word: Language—A God-Centered Approach* (Wheaton, IL: Crossway, 2009). His approach, built upon the thought of Kenneth Pike, is the most methodologically Trinitarian approach I have come across. I address this in the opening chapter of *The Trinity, Language, and Human Behavior: A Reformed Exposition of the Language Theory of Kenneth L. Pike*, Reformed Academic Dissertations (Phillipsburg, NJ: P&R Publishing, 2018).

2. John M. Frame, *Systematic Theology: An Introduction to Christian Belief* (Phillipsburg, NJ: P&R Publishing), 480–81.

3. See Pierce Taylor Hibbs, "Imaging Communion: An Argument for God's Existence Based on Speech," *Westminster Theological Journal* 77, no. 1 (Spring 2015): 35–51; "Words for Communion," *Modern Reformation* 25, no. 4 (August 2016): 5–8; "Closing the Gaps: Perichoresis and the Nature of Language," *Westminster Theological Journal* 78, no. 2 (Fall 2016): 299–322.

when we learn anything about God, we simultaneously learn something about language, and vice versa.

In light of the resurgence of Trinitarian theology over the last few decades, I have found it helpful to resurrect and reapply a somewhat dated set of linguistic concepts from the language theory of Kenneth L. Pike (1912–2000): *emic* and *etic*. While Pike himself never saw the potential application of these terms to Trinitarian theology, I have found them to be quite useful in drawing attention to the communicative nature of God. The aim of this article, then, is to draw on Pike's language theory to show how the emic-etic distinction can deepen our understanding of the immanent-economic categories in Trinitarian theology. In that sense, this article is continuing an informal series of articles I have written on Pike's language theory and its bearing on theology.

Emic and Etic Defined

Kenneth Pike coined the terms *emic* and *etic* several decades ago, and these terms have been widely used in the fields of linguistics and anthropology ever since, even though many who have used them are either clueless or mistaken about their origin.[4] While the terms have a broad semantic range, it is helpful to think of *emic* as *insider* and *etic* as *outsider*.[5] In this sense, the terms represent two perspectives on our

---

4. See Thomas N. Headland's introductory comments on this in Thomas N. Headland, Kenneth L. Pike, and Marvin Harris, eds., *Emics and Etics: The Insider/Outsider Debate*, Frontiers of Anthropology 7 (London: Sage, 1990).

5. Pierce Taylor Hibbs, "Where Person Meets Word Part 1: Personalism in the Language Theory of Kenneth L. Pike," *Westminster Theological Journal* 77, no. 2 (Fall 2015): 371–74.

communicative behavior.[6]

The emic view is oriented to the linguistic community from the inside. Meaningful actions—both verbal and nonverbal—are interpreted according to participant responses and community-driven functions. For example, consider an emic view of the following exchange:

> A: Hello!
> B: Hi; how are you?
> A: *No response—the two persons continue walking past one another.*

Emically, this simple exchange might be viewed as a mutual greeting. In many places where English is commonly spoken, the question "How are you?" is used not to obtain information but to extend a nicety of social interaction (though conservative-minded English speakers protest this trend).

Etically, however, this exchange appears not to be mutual. The non-native English speaker, for example, might interpret person A as offering a greeting and person B as attempting to open a conversation. After all, person B is clearly asking a question, and the words he uses differ from those of person A. The outside observer of a given linguistic community might interpret these two language

---

6. Viola Waterhouse summarizes the emic and etic approaches as follows: "The etic view has to do with universals, with typology, with observation from outside a system, as well as with the nature of initial field data, and with variant forms of an emic unit. The emic view is concerned with the contrastive, patterned system of a specific language or culture or universe of discourse, with the way a participant in a system sees that system, as well as with distinctions between contrastive units." Viola G. Waterhouse, *The History and Development of Tagmemics* (The Hague: Mouton, 1974), 6. See also Poythress, *In the Beginning Was the Word*, 150–152.

units as semantically different, even while many native participants of the language view them as emically the same (i.e., serving the same function, reflecting semantic equivalence, and eliciting the same responses from native participants).

Of course, these concepts are far more complex than this example suggests.[7] However, the example does reveal something basic to the emic-etic distinction: the emic approach to language reflects *immanence* for a particular language community, while the etic approach reflects the *economy* of language—its external appearance—for the outsider. The potential relation to the immanent-economic distinction in Trinitarian theology is apparent here.

Immanent and Economic Trinity

The immanent-economic distinction for the Trinity has long been recognized, inspected, and analyzed by theologians in our day.[8] It is sufficient here only to remind the reader of the largely accepted definitions.

---

7. For details, see Kenneth L. Pike, *Language in Relation to a Unified Theory of the Structure of Human Behavior*, 2nd ed. (The Hague: Mouton, 1967), pp. 37–72. Hereafter I will refer to this work as *LRUT*.

8. See, for example, Fred Sanders, *The Image of the Immanent Trinity: Rahner's Rule and the Theological Interpretation of Scripture*, Issues in Systematic Theology 12 (New York: International Academic Publishers, 2004). For a shorter exposition of one of his central points, see "Entangled in the Trinity: Economic and Immanent Trinity in Recent Theology," *Dialog* 40, no. 3 (Fall 2001): 175–82. Recently, Sanders has also noted the abuse and misunderstandings that these categories have cause by those who use them carelessly. See Fred Sanders, *The Triune God*, New Studies in Dogmatics (Grand Rapids, MI: Zondervan, 2016), 144–53. On the purpose of these categories in highlighting the relationship between the temporal relations of the Trinity to creation and the eternal processions of the divine persons in God, see pp. 112–119.

Put simply, "The *ontological* Trinity (sometimes called *immanent* Trinity) is the Trinity as it exists necessarily and eternally, apart from creation. It is, like God's attributes, what God necessarily *is*. The *economic* Trinity is the Trinity in its relation to creation, including the specific roles played by the Trinitarian persons through the history of creation, providence, and redemption."[9] This is not to say, of course, that the immanent-economic distinction has been embraced uncritically by all theologians. There are important questions regarding the nature and relationship between the immanent and economic Trinity, questions that lead to drastically different theological positions concerning God's identity and freedom.[10] In fact, as Emery and Levering point out, within theological circles "the majority of studies . . . pay attention to the problematic of the unity and distinction between the 'economic Trinity' and the 'immanent Trinity' (or, if one prefers, between the Trinity in its work of creation and grace, and the Trinity in its inner life). The question of the relationships between the Trinity and *history* is often found at the centre of contemporary writing on the Trinity."[11]

Yet, leaving aside for now the specifics of these "relationships," we can in general say that the immanent Trinity is the Trinity as it appears from the *inside*: who

---

9. John Frame, *Systematic Theology: An Introduction to Christian Belief* (Phillipsburg, NJ: P&R Publishing, 2013), 489.

10. Peter Phan introduces some of these questions in Peter C. Phan, "Introduction," in *The Cambridge Companion to the Trinity*, ed. Peter C. Phan (New York: Cambridge University Press, 2011), 16–18.

11. Gilles Emery and Matthew Levering, "Introduction," in *The Oxford Handbook of the Trinity*, ed. Gilles Emery and Matthew Levering (New York: Oxford University Press, 2011), 2.

God is in the intratrintarian relations of Father, Son, and Holy Spirit. The economic Trinity would then be God as he appears to us from the *outside*: in his providential and redemptive work. This is not to say that there is discord between the two. Rather, these concepts help us to express basic human perspectives on who God is—the former being derived or inferred from God's revelation, helping us glimpse into eternity, and the latter being derived both from revelation and from our witness of God's work in history, offering clarity on the meaning and purpose of our temporal world.

Applying the Emic-Etic Distinction to Trinitarian Theology

As noted in the introduction and foreshadowed in the previous section, there is a fascinating correspondence between the emic-etic viewpoints in Pike's language theory and the immanent-economic categories in Trinitarian theology. This correspondence may have implications both for our understanding of God and for our relationship with him as creatures. Let us first understand the emic-etic distinction in Pike's theory more deeply before moving on to explore its potential theological application.

As stated earlier, *emic* can be replaced with the word *insider*, and *etic* with *outsider*. In the context of Pike's language theory, the emic viewpoint sees a given language from the inside, based on the use and responses of native participants.[12] Emic descriptions of language "represent to

---

12. In the late 1980s, Pike also noted the following defining features of emic units: (1) native participants label the unit as appropriate in a given context; (2) emic units can be complex (containing many smaller emic 'sub-

us the view of one familiar with the system and [one] who knows how to function within it himself."[13] Pike notes that the value of the emic is that it (1) helps us understand how a language or culture is constructed as a whole; (2) enables us to understand the personal actors in that culture; and (3) establishes a homogeneous behavioral basis upon we can predict future behaviors.[14] In contrast, an etic description of language "has to do with universals, with typology, with observation from outside a system, as well as with the nature of initial field data."[15] The etic has value in (1) training us to see a broad spectrum of behavior occurring around the world; (2) allowing us to "obtain a technique and symbolism . . . for recording the events of a culture";[16] (3) reminding us that *all* linguists studying a foreign language begin by making only etic observations, many of which will then be adapted to fit the emic patterns of the culture in question; and (4) helping us to focus on smaller areas of emic study while drawing on more widespread etic patterns

---

units'); (3) an emic unit may be referenced with a specific name by native participants; (4) each emic unit must be different from another as judged by the perception or usage of native participants; (5) the emic unit occurs in a relevant place in a hierarchically structured pattern; (6) each emic unit has a relevant occurrence within the total cultural pattern of an individual or society. Pike, "On the Emics and Etics of Pike and Harris," 28–29.

13. Pike, *LRUT*, 38.

14. Ibid., 40–41.

15. Waterhouse, *The History and Development of Tagmemics*, 6.

16. Remember that Pike is coming from a unique context of Bible translation in which linguists were sent into foreign communities with no written alphabet. Thus, using foreign observations to begin building a symbolism was part and parcel of his work in the Summer Institute of Language (SIL).

for comparison.[17] After all, we cannot study everything emically at the same time. We rely on the etic to inform us as we focus on a particular area of emic behavior.[18]

Now, consider the emic in relation to the immanent (or ontological) Trinity. Traditionally, the immanent Trinity is discussed regarding the relations between the divine persons in eternity. The first person of the Trinity is distinguished by his fatherhood and unbegottenness.[19] "The special qualification of the second person in the Trinity is filiation. In Scripture he bears several names that denote this relation to the Father, such as word, wisdom, logos, son, the first-born, only-begotten and only son . . ."[20] The Spirit's "personal property is 'procession' (*ekporusis*) or 'spiration' (*pnoae*)."[21] These incommunicable properties of the divine persons reveal who God is *in himself*, apart from creation.[22]

Another way of understanding the ontological Trinity is to consider it as the *emic* Trinity, that is, the Trinity as the

---

17. Pike, *LRUT*, 40.

18. Pike noted frequently that all people work with a theory that is *directional*; that is, every theory views the world from a particular angle and is selective. We must focus, since we cannot account for all data at the same time. Kenneth L. Pike, *Linguistic Concepts: An Introduction to Tagmemics* (Lincoln, NE: University of Nebraska Press, 1982), 5–7. Only God himself can do that. To God, the entire world is one giant, unfathomably complex emic unit.

19. Herman Bavinck, *Reformed Dogmatics*, vol. 2, *God and Creation*, ed. John Bolt, trans. John Vriend (Grand Rapids, MI: Baker Academic, 2004), 306.

20. Ibid., 308.

21. Ibid., 311.

22. See also J. van Genderen and W. H. Velema, *Concise Reformed Dogmatics*, trans. Gerrit Bilkes and Ed M. van der Maas (Phillipsburg, NJ: P&R Publishing, 2008), 154–158.

ultimate insider community.[23] Only God knows himself—his eternal tripersonal "culture," if you will—exhaustively. God has communicated with himself for all eternity. He is his own linguistic community.[24] What we find in God's speech at creation is a temporal manifestation of an eternal reality. In this sense, at creation we witness "a twofold communication of God—one within and the other outside the divine being; one to the Son who was in the beginning with God and was himself God, and another to creatures who originated in time."[25] The communication "within" God is the eternal generation of the Son, the Word of the Father.[26] This communication (generation) is done in the 'hearing' of the Spirit. We can draw the latter truth from the New Testament, especially from John's Gospel. Reflecting on John 16:13–15, Poythress writes,

> The principal role of the Holy Spirit in these verses is to speak to the disciples of Christ. But we need to notice the basis for that speaking: "Whatever he hears he will speak." The Spirit is first a hearer. And whom does he hear? The subsequent explanation brings in both the Father and the Son. The Spirit hears the Father, and hears about "what is

---

23. We must be careful with our understanding of terms here, since "community" should not be taken in an ordinary sense, as if God were just like three human persons who have fellowship with one another. The persons share the divine essence, so by "community" we mean the intricate relations of the distinct persons of the Godhead, each of whom shares equally in the divine essence.

24. Poythress, *In the Beginning Was the Word*, 18.

25. Bavinck, *God and Creation*, 420.

26. "By generation, from all eternity, the full image of God is communicated to the Son." Ibid.

mine," that is, what is the Son's.[27]

This is an example of how we can take an etic observation (looking at what God is doing in history) and infer an emic truth (who God is in eternity). That the Father eternally utters (generates) the Son in the hearing of the Spirit is what makes intratrinitarian behavior emic. The ultimate purposive language system is the eternal language of the Trinity, for, as Douglas Kelly reminds us, "there is—and has been from all eternity—talk, sharing and communication in the innermost life of God."[28] Certainly, we cannot say much about the details of this language, aside from what Scripture reveals. At the least, Scripture indicates that God has communicated with himself eternally in interpersonal expressions of love and glory. Love and glory constitute the emic language of the Trinity.

Understanding the immanent Trinity as emic brings the communicative nature of God to the fore, and, by extension, shines a light on the basis of all coherent creaturely communication. God in himself, as a being who eternally "speaks," is the ground for all coherent communication outside of himself.[29]

Of course, the Trinity is also *etic*. That is, the actions and behavior of the Triune God are observable to those outside of the eternal and holy insider community of Father, Son, and Spirit. This is typically referred to as the economic Trinity—God in his relationship to creation.

---

27. Poythress, *In the Beginning Was the Word*, 18.

28. Douglas Kelly, *Systematic Theology: Grounded in Holy Scripture and Understood in Light of the Church*, vol. 1, *The God Who Is: The Holy Trinity* (Ross-shire, Scotland: Mentor, 2008), 487.

29. Hibbs, "Imaging Communion."

Within the etic Trinity, as with the emic, there is both unity and distinction. While it is true that "the unity of God is manifested by the fact that the three divine persons are inextricably interconnected in their actions," they are also distinguishable.[30] They each have roles to play in creation and redemption. The Father is the speaker who delivers his creative Word in the life-giving breath of the Spirit. It is the Son, not the Father or the Spirit, who submits himself to the Father's will and dies on a cross. There are distinct personal roles played by each member of the Trinity, even as they are one in knowledge, will, and consciousness.[31]

This etic Trinity is observable to outsiders—to creatures—before and after the fall. However, after the fall, they do not understand God as they should. Romans 1 reminds us that all people know God and have some knowledge of his "eternal power and divine nature" (Rom. 1:20). This God of whom all people know *is* the Trinity. However, Protestants and Catholics alike have always held that knowledge of the Trinity is strictly revealed in Scripture. So, what non-Christians know of the etic God is not rightly understood by them emically; that is, they do not recognize God as the three-in-one, self-contained community in love and glory, for that is only revealed to us in Scripture by the communicative behavior of the Trinity (special revelation). Instead, they might perceive God as a monolithic, non-communicative, abstract entity. God, in other words, must not be perceived only etically, from the outside. He must be perceived *as Trinity*, as the emic three-in-one, communicative and relational God. As Calvin

---

30. van Genderen and Velema, *Concise Reformed Dogmatics*, 158.

31. Charles Hodge, *Systematic Theology* (Peabody, MA: Hendrickson, 2013), 1:461.

said, "[God] so proclaims himself the sole God as to offer himself to be contemplated clearly in three persons. Unless we grasp these, only the bare and empty name of God flits about in our brains, to the exclusion of the true God."[32]

Given the climate of Trinitarian theology in the modern and contemporary eras, we should pause to make a critical point about this emic and etic Trinity. *The emic must undergird the etic*, and, by extension, *the ontological must undergird the economic*. Cornelius Van Til frequently wrote of the "ontological Trinity" as the Christian's grounding presupposition.[33] Why, some readers may wonder, did he throw in the word "ontological"? Why not just say "Trinity"? The decision was, no doubt, intentional for Van Til. Many theologians of his era and ours collapse the ontological or immanent Trinity into the economic Trinity.[34] Doing so not

---

32. Calvin, *Instit.* 1.13.2.

33. See, for example, Cornelius Van Til, *Introduction to Systematic Theology: Prolegomena and the Doctrines of Revelation, Scripture, and God*, ed. William Edgar, 2nd ed. (Phillipsburg, NJ: P&R Publishing, 2007), 59, 73, 124, 197, 198, 353, 364; *Christian Apologetics*, ed. William Edgar, 2nd ed. (Phillipsburg, NJ: P&R Publishing, 2003), 29–30, 39, 43, 128; *The Defense of the Faith*, ed. K. Scott Oliphint, 4th ed. (Phillipsburg, NJ: P&R Publishing, 2008), 37, 38, 100–101, 227, 229, 236, 241, 395–96, 397–98. These page references are taken from the indexes of the respective works.

34. Frame, *Systematic Theology*, 489–90. See also Louis Berkhof, *Systematic Theology*, new ed. (Grand Rapids, MI: William B. Eerdmans, 1996), 83. Fred Sanders has stated the problem concisely: "To tie economic and immanent Trinity together too closely is to collapse the divine being into the world process, to make God's freedom indiscernible, and to saddle the created world with the burden of being God's self-actualization. There is only one Trinity, and that Trinity is truly present in salvation history, in the missions of the Son and Spirit. But that single economic and immanent Trinity is God, and God's freedom must be duly recognized by theological formulations." Sanders, "Entangled in the Trinity: Economic and Immanent Trinity in Recent Theology," 181.

only makes God dependent on creation; it also means that God simply is what he does, and that is a very dangerous ontology, for it destabilizes the being of God and suggests that God does not *have* an identity; rather, he *makes* one, and that can (and should) lead Christians to feel that they are serving a somewhat capricious God.[35]

Rather than leave himself open to this possibility, Van Til repeatedly stresses the necessity of the *ontological* Trinity. This stress makes perfect sense when we consider the emic-etic distinction we have introduced to Trinitarian theology. There would be no etic—no observable reality to outsiders—if there were no emic. There can be no outsider if there is not first an insider. Thus, that the emic Trinity (God in himself) exists necessarily in independence from all else is what *allows* for our apprehension of the etic Trinity in creation and redemption. *To create and redeem, God goes outside of himself*; he goes to outsiders with the offer first of life and then of forgiveness and reconciliation, which alone can enable fallen creatures to be united with the tri-personal God. In salvation, sinful outsiders become righteous insiders—righteous, mind you, because they are clothed in the righteousness of one of the members of the divine emic community: Jesus Christ, the incarnate Son of God (Rom. 13:14).[36] All of this, however, is possible because of the emic

---

35. For background on this issue in Barth's theology, see James J. Cassidy, "Election and Trinity," *Westminster Theological Journal* 71, no. 1 (Spring 2009): 53–81.

36. By using the term "community" with reference to the triune God, I am not aligning myself with social Trinitarianism. There are certainly strands of truth within social Trinitarianism, but there are significant problems as well, namely that the advocates of this position attempt to rationalize the being of God in a manner analogous to that of contemporary Thomistic Trinitarian theology. The latter emphasizes God's unity; the

Trinity. We could not be adopted as sons of God apart from the divine Son. As Garner has put it, we are only "sons in the Son."[37] We are reconciled with the emic Trinity because of the work of the etic Trinity, but the work of the etic Trinity always and everywhere presupposes the emic Trinity. Thus, we can and must say with Van Til that "if we are to have *coherence* in our experience, there must be a correspondence of our experience to the eternally coherent experience of God. Human knowledge ultimately rests upon the internal coherence within the Godhead; our knowledge rests upon the *ontological* Trinity as its presupposition."[38]

There are still other benefits to viewing the Trinity as emic and etic. Some of these can be drawn out of Pike's original statements about the value of each viewpoint. Let us deal with emic first, and then the etic.

We noted earlier three ways in which the emic is valuable for us: it (1) helps us understand how a language or culture is constructed as a whole; (2) enables us to understand the personal actors in that culture; and (3) establishes a homogeneous behavioral basis upon we can predict future behaviors. We can apply these values in some sense to the

---

former, his trinity. Reformed theology, as mentioned earlier, holds to the equally ultimate, mysterious, and incomprehensible relationship of oneness and threeness in God. Nevertheless, as Hodge notes, we have clear biblical grounds in affirming that "The Father, Son, and Spirit are severally subject and object. They act and are acted upon, or are the objects of action. Nothing is added to these facts when it is said that the Father, Son, and Spirit are distinct persons; for a person is an intelligent subject who can say I, who can be addressed as Thou, and who can act and can be the object of action." Hodge, *Systematic Theology*, 1:444.

37. David B. Garner, *Sons in the Son: The Riches and Reach of Adoption in Christ* (Phillipsburg, NJ: P&R Publishing, 2016).

38. Van Til, *Introduction to Systematic Theology*, 59; emphasis added.

emic Trinity.

First, the notion of the emic Trinity helps us to understand God's identity as communicative and tri-personal; that is, as a whole, God is to be understood as *his own linguistic community*, independent from creation. Some contemporary theologians may balk at this because they feel it distances God from his creatures. But actually, the opposite is the case. If God is inherently communicative and personal—if he is, as Van Til put, "absolute personality"—then we relate to him on a level far deeper than we often recognize. What's more, we not only gain insight into the nature of God as communicative and personal; we also gain insight into the nature of creation as relational. By that we mean *creation is fundamentally personal and relational*. In the words of Van Til, "Our surroundings are shot through with personality because all things are related to the infinitely personal God."[39] Every element of creation is related to every other element by the all-controlling plan of a personal God. To God, the entire cosmos is one complex emic unit, known intimately and exhaustively only to him. To put it negatively, there is nothing that exists by itself. Within the created realm, "autonomy" is illusory. Everything is interdependent and related, and everything is dependent on the personal God of Scripture.

Second, just as the emic view of language enables us to understand the personal actors in a given culture, so the concept of the emic Trinity helps us to understand the etic actions of God. I am here doing little more than expanding Herman Bavinck's discussion on the necessity

---

39. Cornelius Van Til, *In Defense of the Faith*, vol. 2, *A Survey of Christian Epistemology* (Phillipsburg, NJ: Presbyterian and Reformed, 1969), 78. For the development of this idea in a counseling context, see Hibbs, "Panic and the Personal God," *Journal of Biblical Counseling* 29, no. 3 (2015): 36–41.

that the Creator God be triune. For Bavinck, "If, in an absolute sense, God could not communicate himself to the Son, he would be even less able, in a relative sense, to communicate himself to his creature. If God were not triune, creation would not be possible."[40] Part of what Bavinck is expressing here is the truth that what we see in the actions of the etic Trinity is grounded somehow in the nature of the emic Trinity. In the words of Gerald Bray, "What God does in time reflects who and what he is in eternity."[41] We have before us, then, a paradigm for more deeply understanding the actions of God in time. Why did God use speech to create the cosmos (etic)? Because he is a personal, communicative being (emic). Why did God adopt us as his children in Christ (etic)? Because the Father has always gloried in the eternal Son (emic) and longs to commune with and glory in his created sons and daughters in eternity future. Why is the Spirit the bond of union for all believers in Christ (etic)? Because the Spirit is the bond of love between the Father and the Son (emic).[42] In sum, the concept of the emic Trinity helps us better understand and appreciate all that God has done to create and redeem. It does this by showing how the emic is the ground for the etic.

Third, as the emic establishes a homogeneous behavioral basis upon we can predict future behaviors, the notion of the emic Trinity gives us confidence in God's promises

---

40. Bavinck, *God and Creation*, 420.

41. Gerald Bray, *God Is Love: A Biblical and Systematic Theology* (Wheaton, IL: Crossway, 2012), 29.

42. See Matthew Levering, "The Holy Spirit in the Trinitarian Communion: 'Love' and 'Gift'?," *International Journal of Systematic Theology* 16, no. 2 (2014): 126–42.

being fulfilled in the future. God does not change (cf. James 1:17). The emic Trinity—who God is in himself—gives us utter surety that God is the same yesterday, today, and tomorrow (Heb. 13:8). Moreover, because God cannot lie (Titus 1:2), we trust that what God has revealed about himself and his desires—all of which is grounded in the emic Trinity—is trustworthy and true. Christians, however, do not even have to "predict future behaviors" for God, because he has revealed his future behaviors to us in his Word. Nonetheless, we can have firm faith in the truth that God's "homogenous behavior" of love, grace, mercy, and justice will be the basis on which his future actions stand.

Let us now deal with the statements Pike made about the value of the etic viewpoint. Pike wrote that the etic has value in (1) training linguists to see a broad spectrum of behavior occurring around the world; (2) allowing linguists to "obtain a technique and symbolism . . . for recording the events of a culture"; (3) reminding us that all linguists studying a foreign language begin by making only etic observations, many of which will then be adapted to fit the emic patterns of the culture in question; and (4) helping us to focus on smaller areas of emic study while we draw on more widespread etic patterns for comparison. We can examine each of these in turn with reference to the etic Trinity.

First, the etic Trinity—God in his external work— helps us to see a broad spectrum of holy behaviors that are imitated on a finite scale by God's creatures. Van Til once wrote, "All of man's acts must be representational of the acts of God. Even the persons of the Trinity are mutually representational. They are exhaustively representational of one another."[43] There is much to unpack here, but at the very least we find in these words a critical implication for us. If all of our behaviors are to be representative of God, then any behavior that can be labeled with the adjective "good"—anything selfless, sacrificial, coherent, graceful, beautiful, loving, kind, wise, etc.—is representative on a finite scale of what is properly (directly or indirectly) rooted in the emic Trinity and worked out in the etic Trinity.

Everywhere, we can observe God's common and special grace manifested in the behaviors of creatures. Sometimes it is easy to relate these behaviors to the etic Trinity, and other times it is not. Studying the expression of God outside himself, however, exposes us to a pattern of behaviors according to which we might judge (or at least begin inspecting) the allegedly good behaviors of creatures. For example, consider an office worker who, despite the criticism of his colleagues, submits to the will of his boss in carrying out a business proposal. What his co-workers view as thoughtless submission or even cowardice is, in fact, vaguely reflective of Christ's voluntary submission to God the Father during his time on earth (Luke 22:42)— a behavior of the etic Trinity. This is not to say that the office worker is a type of Christ, or even that his decision to submit to his boss is essentially holy. On the contrary, he may grumble and wince at the idea of submission! It does, however, tell us that *if* there is anything good in the man's decision to submit, that goodness is ultimately possible and meaningful because of what God has done in creation and redemption. This is but one example of how observing behaviors of the etic Trinity can help us interpret the (supposedly representational) behaviors of God's creatures.

---

43. Van Til, *A Survey of Christian Epistemology*, 78.

Thus, studying the broad spectrum of behaviors in the etic Trinity helps us to inspect and assess the array of mimetic creaturely behaviors in time and space.

Second, we noted that studying the etic allows linguists to "obtain a technique and symbolism . . . for recording the events of a culture." What is the purpose of this symbolism? Symbolization is an attempt to graphically systematize communication. The benefit of this systematizing is that it presents language users with a perceptual organization of the language in focus. The perceptual organization of language then helps language users to make sense of the world around them, since that world is inevitably filtered through that language. Consider a simple example. A man at a gas station watches a teenager grab the purse of an older woman and then flee the scene. As the man fills out a police report, he writes down what he saw. Perceptually, he witnessed one human being lay hold of an object that was attached to another human being and then run in the opposite direction. This is interpreted by the man to be *theft*, and he expresses this with his language, perhaps a sentence such as, "The boy stole the woman's purse and then tried to escape." His language has graphically organized his perception. What's more, it has solidified his understanding of what constitutes as theft. In other words, the symbolization of written language reinforces his interpretation of reality.

Now, what is true of this smaller incident is true for all of us with every experience we have. The symbolism of language—which for Pike is initially constructed from etic observations—helps reinforce our interpretation of the world and its events. A very similar phenomenon happens on a spiritual plain when we consider the etic Trinity as the symbolization of God's redemption in history. God's work in the world gives us a spiritual, perceptual grid through which we interpret all that goes on around us. Take the same experience we just described—the man who witnesses a teenager stealing a woman's purse. We can (and should) interpret that action with reference to the legal system, but on a deeper level, we process the event with *categories of redemption*. That is to say, the boy's theft is not simply a free-will decision by a human agent, a decision which violates the codes of conduct for a given country. The boy's theft is a mark of *sin*. For Christians, his action is a reverberation of Adam's sin of disobedience in the Garden of Eden. The remedy for that sin cannot be merely external—a punishment meted out by a judge in a juvenile court. The remedy must in the end be internal renewal, spiritual rebirth, a heart of stone surgically replaced with a heart of flesh (Ezek 36:26).[44] How do Christians know this? Because of the etic Trinity! What the Father, Son, and Spirit have done in creation and redemption—the long and glorious history of heavenly intervention—lays out our spiritual grid of perception. We understand the world through the symbolism (the historical manifestation of God's work, now inerrantly persevered in Scripture) of the etic Trinity. True, that symbolism is somewhat abstract when compared to a physically represented symbolization of a human language. But the principle still holds. Observing and studying what the etic Trinity has done in creating and redeeming

---

44. Notice here the link between the etic and emic Trinity and the etic and emic spiritual behaviors of creatures. God's creatures are ever striving to have their etic (external behaviors) conform to the Christ-like emic. Christians are in a constant struggle to move from the etic (who they are currently, in the process of sanctification) to the emic (who they truly are in Christ, in intimate fellowship with the emic Trinity). God is the only one whose etic behavior perfectly and exhaustively corresponds to his emic identity.

humanity helps us to "obtain a technique and symbolism . . . for recording the events of a culture." The nuance is that we are now considering this symbolism not as a written language but as a revealed system of interpretation for spiritual realities.

In essence, I am saying that the etic Trinity has "written" reality—both creation and redemption, with the pen of revelation.[45] We use those revelatory markings to perceive

---

45. See Hibbs, "We Who Work with Words: Towards a Theology of Writing," *Themelios* 41, no. 3 (December 2016): pp. 460–76. I draw on this article for what follows. Because all things are essentially linguistic products of the Trinitarian God and mark his presence in the world, there is a sense in which God has written himself in everything. In the words of Dorothy Sayers, we might say that in God's general revelation, he has written his "autobiography," i.e., he has clearly revealed who he is (Rom. 1:19–20). Dorothy L. Sayers, *The Mind of the Maker* (New York: HarperOne, 1987), 89. There is nothing that exists in the world that does not in some sense testify to who God is, and nothing that is not written into his personal plan for history. Oliphint reminds us that "history can be properly defined only in light of what the second person of the Trinity has condescended to do—both in creation generally and for his people more specifically." K. Scott Oliphint, *Covenantal Apologetics: Principles and Practice in Defense of Our Faith* (Wheaton, IL: Crossway, 2013), 64. Sayers adds that in the incarnation, God wrote himself into history as the central character. Sayers, *The Mind of the Maker*, 88. Creation and history are steeped in God's presence because he has written them.

God has also written redemption in his special revelation. The repetition of the Greek word γέγραπται, "it is written," both in the Septuagint and in the New Testament, lends warrant to this conclusion. The term (along with the participial form γεγραμμένα) is often used to express that what God has declared in Scripture must be followed for the redemption of his people (Josh. 1:8; 8:31; 23:6; 1 Kgs. 2:3; 2 Chr. 23:18; Ezra 3:2, 4; Ps. 40:7; Matt. 2:5; 4:6, 7, 10; 21:13; 26:24, 31; Mark 14:21; and others). Such a usage implies the fixity that we commonly associate with the craft of writing. As Hunt, supported by a great number of others in the Reformed tradition, notes, "the very notion of *divine revelation*, the communication of truth that cannot otherwise be known, demands a method of documentation and preservation that goes beyond orality, pictorial representation, dance, or smoke signals.... [only writing] possesses the objectivity and permanency needed

the true nature of human behavior all around us, and that is analogous to the way in which linguists develop a written language for non-literate cultures, the latter helping the language users to organize and process the reality they encounter each day.

Third, the etic has value in reminding us that all linguists studying a foreign language begin by making only etic observations, many of which will then be adapted to fit the emic patterns of the culture in question. Consider this in light of the process that non-Christians go through as they pass from unbelief to Spirit-wrought faith. Because God is omnipresent, non-Christians have no choice but to see God everywhere (cf. Ps. 139:7–12). They witness God working in the world (etic Trinity) without being fully aware that it is the triune Christian God who is at work. Right now, non-Christians are making etic observations about reality. They are witnessing acts of kindness, receiving words of grace and compassion, taking in the splendor and breadth of nature. All of these phenomena are rooted in the etic Trinity. They are gifts of common grace meant to call non-Christians into relationship with the God of glory. And when non-Christians are reborn in the power of the Spirit, they have a newfound understanding of such phenomena. Acts of kindness are not merely self-less acts done for another, which is how the world might define "kindness." Rather, they are actions rooted in the God who loved us *before* we had the chance to love him (John 3:16)—indeed, *while* we were yet

---

to tell the old, old story." Arthur W. Hunt III, *The Vanishing Word: The Veneration of Visual Imagery in the Postmodern World* (Wheaton, IL: Crossway, 2003), 35. Triune writing in this sense brands an object of reality with its author's presence (i.e., God himself). And that presence does not evaporate. It holds. God is always present with his words, bringing them to fulfillment.

sinners (Rom. 5:8).[46] Non-Christians, in other words, make etic observations of reality (observations of the work of the etic Trinity, often mediated through human agents) and then adjust them to the emic understanding they acquire when immersed in the "language" of special grace. It is then that they see the etic Trinity as an outworking of the emic Trinity.

Fourth and finally, we saw that the etic has value in helping us to focus on smaller areas of emic study while we draw on more widespread etic patterns for comparison. None of us is a specialist in everything. We each have our unique role in God's redemptive plan, manifested in the daily work we put ourselves to—as parents, office workers, sales associates, etc. We strive to image Christ in our respective roles, and yet we know that others have roles different from ours. While we aim to move closer in fellowship with the emic Trinity—through the work of the etic Trinity—we make observations about how the etic Trinity is at work in the lives of those who are distant from us. There is a sense here in which another person's life is a foreign country. As outsiders, we make etic observations of purposive behaviors (though we are not always aware of the purposes). We speculate about possible motives for decisions and reasons why events occur in a person's life. In doing this, we are developing etic patterns that may be useful to us in our own lives. We are looking at what the etic

---

46. Note how different this Christian notion of kindness is from the secular mantra, "The more you give, the more you get." While I appreciate the sentiment behind such a statement (people cheered for Paul McCartney when he uttered this statement in an episode of Saturday Night Live some years ago), it is fundamentally flawed. If I do something for someone else *because* I think that later someone will do the same for me, by motive is still selfish, not self-less. It is only if I know that I will gain *nothing* by doing something for someone else that the act is truly self-less.

Trinity might be doing providentially in someone else's life and using that in our own life to interpret similar events. Of course, we can and often do *misinterpret* what the etic Trinity is doing in a given situation, and there is always an element of mystery that remains. But this does not (and should not) stop us from trying to draw on etic observations to deepen our emic (personal) relationship with the triune God.

Let me offer just one example. I have struggled for over a decade with an anxiety disorder. God has taught me much through it and has drawn me closer to himself in the process. I sometimes wonder what other Christians were observing when I was fighting a particularly rough swell of nerves. On one occasion, a co-worker asked me how I was doing. I responded with something like the following. "I've been seeing over and over again that when my life is free of anxiety, I drift away from God and pursue some sort of idol. God always uses the pain of anxiety to draw me to dependence." The co-worker responded simply: "Hmmm . . . I needed to hear that." I do not know exactly why this person replied in this way, but it was evident that what the triune God was doing in my life was of some help to her in her own life. Her observations of the etic Trinity at work in another were then useful in her own spiritual formation. She was drawing on etic observations, in this sense, to help her in her emic relationship with God.

In ending this discussion, I will revisit an earlier point. The emic-etic distinction teaches us much about the Trinity—who God is essentially as communicative and how he has acted to create and redeem the cosmos. Yet, there is also an emic-etic dimension to personal Christian life, and I have hinted at this in the preceding paragraphs. Let me develop it briefly here before concluding the article.

Applying the Emic-Etic Distinction to Creatures

As creatures living in a fallen world, each of us is on a trajectory. Upon birth, we enter the world as observers of the etic Trinity—a God from whom we are estranged because of the inherited sinful nature we have in Adam. We are responsible to this God even if we claim ignorance of him, for we all truly know him (Rom. 1). We are, in this sense, *outsiders* with regards to the divine, redemptive "language" of forgiveness, love, and glory. (This redemptive language is built upon the dialect of pure love and glory that is spoken among the persons of the emic Trinity.) In faith and by God's grace, creatures can move from being etic observers of God's redemptive language to being participants within it—trained in the tongue of reconciliation, beneficiaries of the saving message of Jesus Christ. For Christians, all of life is a movement from the etic to the emic, outside observation to personal participation. That participation climaxes in the indwelling of the persons of the Trinity.

In John 14:23, Jesus says, "If anyone loves me, he will keep my word, and my Father will love him, and we will come to him and make our home with him." When we receive Christ, we invite the Father and the Son to indwell us. And the Spirit is not left out of this indwelling. Paul asks the Corinthians a simple but profound question, "Do you not know that you are God's temple and that God's Spirit dwells in you?" (1 Cor. 3:16; cf. Rom. 8:9) The rhetorical nature of Paul's question is obvious. Christians are creatures *indwelt* by the Father, Son, and Holy Spirit. The tri-personal God lives *in* us. This is the ultimate transfer from etic to emic—though this transfer is not consummated until we enter into glory.

That this paradigm is in place for every Christian is substantiated by Jesus's own earthly ministry. Consider Mark 4:1–13, where Jesus tells the Parable of the Sower.

> Again Jesus began to teach by the lake. The crowd that gathered around him was so large that he got into a boat and sat in it out on the lake, while all the people were along the shore at the water's edge. [2] He taught them many things by parables, and in his teaching said: [3] "Listen! A farmer went out to sow his seed. [4] As he was scattering the seed, some fell along the path, and the birds came and ate it up. [5] Some fell on rocky places, where it did not have much soil. It sprang up quickly, because the soil was shallow. [6] But when the sun came up, the plants were scorched, and they withered because they had no root. [7] Other seed fell among thorns, which grew up and choked the plants, so that they did not bear grain. [8] Still other seed fell on good soil. It came up, grew and produced a crop, some multiplying thirty, some sixty, some a hundred times." [9] Then Jesus said, "Whoever has ears to hear, let them hear." [10] When he was alone, the Twelve and the others around him asked him about the parables. [11] He told them, "The secret of the kingdom of God has been given to you. But to those on the outside everything is said in parables [12] so that, "'they may be ever seeing but never perceiving, and ever hearing but never understanding; otherwise they might turn and be forgiven!'" [13] Then Jesus said to them, "Don't you understand this parable? How then will you understand any parable? (ESV)

Jesus here has formed his own emic community, separate from "those on the outside" (v. 11). The outsiders cannot understand the language that he is speaking; that is, they cannot perceive the meaning of the parable. They are etic observers. However, Jesus's own disciples cannot understand the parable either! He has told them that they have been given "the secret of the kingdom of God," but they do not seem to understand what he means. They have not yet learned the tongue of redemption. If they had, they would have understood that Jesus *himself* is the secret of God's kingdom, for he is the eternal Word, now wrapped in human flesh and calling all people to repent and believe in him. Jesus is himself the promised seed of the woman (Gen. 3:15), the word that is sown in the hearts of men (Mark 4:14). His disciples would realize this only later. At the time of the telling of this parable, they were still on the trajectory from etic to emic; they were outside observers of the redemptive language of God, but not yet native participants in that "culture" of redemption.

The need for all true believers to move from etic to emic—from mere observers of the Trinitarian language of grace to active participants within it—is presented strikingly in the story of Nicodemus (John 3). Here, we learn something very important about this creaturely move from etic to emic: *it is an internal rebirth that is solely God's doing, and it restructures the entire life of the creature.*

Nicodemus came to Jesus after nightfall with the hope of learning more about him. Before he encountered Jesus, the incarnate second person of the etic Trinity, he had carried with him a perceptual grid for reality: a way of understanding the world both physically and spiritually. Everything he perceived and understood was bound together with all the glorious complexity of a Jackson Pollock painting. He knew about fish and finances, death and daylight, sacrifice and sapience. All of what he experienced in his embodied existence was expressed on a single canvas of perception, stretched as tightly as the skin around his knuckles when he struck the wood on the door of the Word.

What happened that night? Nicodemus had come to admit Jesus' divine influence, but then found himself puzzled at this teacher's claim that he must be born again in order to see and enter the kingdom of God (John 3:3, 5), a kingdom that has its own language of grace. Why could Nicodemus not see the kingdom? In essence, Nicodemus did not have Christ at the center of his perceptual canvas. "You need a new canvas," in effect, is what Jesus told Nicodemus.

> You will have to abandon your total thought system and begin to build it all over again. You will have to accept my goodness and power as primary data, and start from there. Like a baby coming into the new world, you will have to learn to live with these facts before you can understand their source or reason. You must learn to accept the revolution this makes in your whole spiritual life without being able at the moment to understand its source any more than the sailor understands the source of the wind that moves his sails.[47]

In other words, Nicodemus would need to be reborn and acquire a new native language—the language of the etic Trinity, the language of redemption. This underscores the point that "Christianity is not an accretion; it is not something added. It is a *new* holistic outlook which is satisfied with nothing less than penetration to the farthest corners of the mind and the understanding."[48]

We know from elsewhere in John's Gospel that this would not happen by Nicodemus's efforts. The truth that Nicodemus needed—the truth that all of us need—was given only by the Spirit of God, the Spirit of truth. Our

---

47. Kenneth L. Pike, "Language and Life 1: A Stereoscopic Window on the World," *Bibliotheca Sacra* 114, no. 454 (April 1957): 56.

48. Kenneth L. Pike, "Prescription for Intellectuals," *Eternity* 8 (August 1957): 45.

transfer from etic to emic happens *internally* by the Spirit of God himself. The Spirit then becomes our language teacher, guiding us through the foreign country of reconciliation and restoration. Thus, Jesus would later tell his disciples,

> When the Spirit of truth comes, he will guide you into all the truth, for he will not speak on his own authority, but whatever he hears he will speak, and he will declare to you the things that are to come. He will glorify me, for he will take what is mine and declare it to you. All that the Father has is mine; therefore I said that he will take what is mine and declare it to you (John 16:13–15).

Only an emic member of the etic Trinity could deliver the truth to Nicodemus . . . and to us. The Spirit opens our hearts to receive the saving Word of the Father. So, our movement from sinners to saints, from etic observers to emic participants in God's triune language of grace, is a work of God in our hearts, and this work restructures all of our life. You might say, then, that when a person becomes a Christian, he learns a new language.

All of this can be summarized in one of Pike's deceptively simple poems, entitled "Emic Circle."

See, and know.
Know, and be.
Be, and do.
Do, and see.
See, and know.[49]

Here is how I interpret this poem in reference to the emic-etic distinction. My rendition is far more clumsy:

---

49. Pike, "On the Emics and Etics of Pike and Harris," p. 45.

Etic, and emic.
Emic, and deeper emic.
Deeper emic, and etically perceived behavior.
Etically perceived behavior, and etic observance of others' behaviors.
Etic, and emic.

As Christians, we move from etic observance of the Trinity in the world around us to emic participation in the Trinitarian language of grace and redemption (See, and know)—a language that is foreign to us. As we are taught that language by the Spirit (John 16:13), who is a native participant in the triune communion of grace, we move closer and closer to communion with the triune God (Know, and be). In that communion, we act as the hands and feet of the body (1 Cor. 12:12–31), working under God's governance to bring others into the linguistic community of redemption (Be, and do). As we carry out these actions, we continue to make etic observations (Do, and see). Each new etic observation (either of God's work or of the daily lives of people), then leads to another opportunity for emic deepening (See, and know).

Conclusion

In this article, I have argued that the emic-etic distinction draws our attention to the communicative nature of the Trinity and deepens our understanding of the tradition immanent-economic categories. This article is meant to be one example of how language theory can serve as a unique window onto theology proper. Though in this discussion I have placed myself in the Reformed tradition, the implications for what I have said are certainly relevant for broader Christendom. Both Catholics and Protestants must continually focus on the communicative nature of the Trinity and use such knowledge to shape and inform their thought and behavior. As Christians reflect on the communicative nature of God and their own movement from etic to emic, they will be better equipped to see the whole world as moving towards a hearth of communion in the God who is a linguistic community unto himself.

Metaphysics, Epistemology, and Language

In this essay, I lay some groundwork for the relationship between metaphysics, epistemology, and language. I have elsewhere referred to this as the MEL triad.[1] After defining this triad in general, it is important to outline its biblical roots before applying it both to the Trinitarian God and to his creatures. Then we can briefly consider a few dangers of secular approaches to the MEL triad, in the work of a contemporary philosopher, John R. Seale, and end by responding to Searle and situating Kenneth Pike's language theory in relation to the MEL triad. I hope to show Pike's language theory is not simply a revision of our approach to communication; it is a revision of our approach to all of human behavior, thought and action included.[2] At the same time, the MEL triad is a massive topic in and of itself, so we must acknowledge at the outset that we can only scratch the surface here. We must focus the discussion on what we need to know for this particular study.

Defining the MEL Triad

The MEL triad, in its most basic expression, simply means that language is bound up with thought (epistemology),

---

1. See Hibbs, "Imaging Communion."

2. I will be considering human behavior an aspect of metaphysics, since behavior is inherently bound up with being. What we do is governed by who we are.

and thought is bound up with being (metaphysics).[3] In other words, language, epistemology, and metaphysics are intertwined and must be understood in conjunction with one another. We cannot understand who we are apart from what and how we think, nor can we understand what we think and who we are apart from language. Any discussion of language presupposes a certain epistemology and metaphysic.[4] Let us draw this out in a bit more detail within a biblical worldview.

With regards to metaphysics, because we are made in the image of the Triune God of Scripture, we are personal, relational beings, just as God is personal and relational in his triunity. As Poythress notes, "The New Testament indicates that the persons of the Trinity speak to one another and enjoy profound personal relations with one another. . . . Personal relationships exist not solely among human beings, but also in divine-human relationships, and even in divine-divine relationships."[5] As creatures bearing the image of the Trinity, we too are personal and relational.

---

3. In addition to being influenced by Cornelius Van Til here, my initial thoughts on the MEL triad were influenced by John Frame's triad of metaphysics, epistemology, and ethics. See John M. Frame, *The Doctrine of the Knowledge of God* (Phillipsburg, NJ: P&R Publishing, 1987), 19, 63, 109. Also see his *Systematic Theology*, 704–05; and *A History of Western Philosophy and Theology* (Phillipsburg, NJ: P&R Publishing, 2015), 24–36.

4. It is critical that we not separate ontology from epistemology. Van Til noted that "God's knowledge is what it is because his being is what it is." Cornelius Van Til, *Christian Apologetics*, ed. William Edgar, 2nd ed. (Phillipsburg, NJ: P&R Publishing, 2003), 26. See also Van Til, *Defense of the Faith*, 56–57; K. Scott Oliphint, *Reasons for Faith: Philosophy in the Service of Theology* (Phillipsburg, NJ: P&R Publishing, 2006), 41, 69n22.

5. Vern S. Poythress, *Redeeming Sociology: A God-Centered Approach* (Wheaton, IL: Crossway, 2011), 24.

Gerald O'Collins reminds us that "authentic personhood does not spring out of one's private experience but is given and received within relationships. To be a person is to be an interpersonal subject, sharing love and giving oneself in love."[6] Yet, the Creator-creature distinction remains at the forefront of this discussion. Human persons are separate subjects, each with a separate consciousness and will, whereas with the divine persons "one consciousness subsists in a threefold way and is shared by all three persons, albeit by each of them distinctively."[7] The Creator-creature

---

6. Gerald O'Collins, *The Tripersonal God: Understanding and Interpreting the Trinity*, 2nd ed. (New York: Paulist Press, 2014), 177.

7. Ibid., 178. Quite a ruckus has been raised by Van Til's claim that the whole Godhead is one Person and that God is both a uni-conscious and tri-conscious being. The latter statement was introduced by Van Til when he discussed the Trinity in his *Introduction to Systematic Theology*. Lane Tipton's article, in my opinion, has clearly revealed what Van Til's (and perhaps Charles Hodge's) primary concern was in using such allegedly heterodox language: a defense of God's incomprehensibility. This was centered in the ancient teaching of perichoresis: the mutual interpenetration of the persons in the Godhead. "Hodge recognizes that the mysteries of God's intratrinitarian existence infinitely transcend the limitations of human reason, particularly in light of the perichoretic relationships. Perichoresis in Hodge's theology involves a description of God's unity which moves beyond a mere unity of essence (i.e., toward a unified person) without compromising the tripersonality of the Godhead, and such a formulation accentuates God's incomprehensibihty." Lane G. Tipton, "The Function of Perichoresis and the Divine Incomprehensibility," *Westminster Theological Journal* 64 (2002): 293. Tipton continues, "it seems clear from Van Til's reflections that he does not intend to replace a traditional Trinitarian formula; instead he wants to supplement a potentially deficient expression of the orthodox formula. . . . The person/essence formulation is accurate and veridical so far as it goes. However, Van Til is convinced that such a formulation, if left as the sole statement of Trinitarian orthodoxy and articulated in a rationalistic manner which fails to take account of perichoresis, simply fails to explain adequately the complexity and richness of orthodox Trinitarian theology." Ibid., 295. See also Tipton, "The Triune Personal God: Trinitarian Theology in the Thought of Cornelius Van Til" (PhD diss., Westminster Theologi-

distinction, however, is not meant to erase mystery from personhood and all its attendant behaviors—especially language. We are not saying, in other words, that mystery exists for divine Persons but not for human persons. In fact, it is precisely because personhood is rooted in the Trinity that all of what we do, think, and say is, upon close examination, permeated with mystery.[8] So, while it is critical to keep the Creator-creature distinction in focus, we must also understand that language will never be reductionistically explained via principles and theories within creation—not because language is too complex, but because it is rooted in an eternal being who is independent from creation and whom we cannot comprehensively understand.[9] That needs to be taken into account when

---

cal Seminary, 2004), 89–113.

For a survey of the church's understanding of "Person" throughout the centuries, especially in light of contemporary Trinitarian theology, see Ángel Cordovilla Pérez, "The Trinitarian Concept of Person," in *Rethinking Trinitarian Theology: Disputed Questions and Contemporary Issues in Trinitarian Theology*, ed. Giulio Maspero and Robert J. Woźniak (New York: T&T Clark, 2012), 105–45. For a concise definition of "person," see William Hasker, *Metaphysics and the Tripersonal God*, Oxford Studies in Analytic Theology (Oxford: Oxford University Press, 2013), 193.

8. Recall the striking statement of Cornelius Van Til in his classroom several decades ago: "We certainly cannot penetrate intellectually the mystery of the Trinity, but neither can we penetrate anything else intellectually because all other things depend on the mystery of the Trinity, and therefore all other things have exactly as much mystery in them as does the Trinity." Cornelius Van Til, "Christ and Human Thought: Modern Theology, Part 1" (lecture, Westminster Theological Seminary, Glenside, PA, n.d.). See also Letham, *The Holy Trinity*, 460; and Hibbs, "Where Person Meets Word Part 1: Personalism in the Language Theory of Kenneth L. Pike," *Westminster Theological Journal* 77, no. 2 (Fall 2015): 357–59.

9. So, in a sense, yes, because it is too complex, and because, with Pike, it cannot be detached from other human behaviors. However, we can treat all

we explore the structure and coherence of language. We are *creatures* handling a *Creator's* gift.

All I aim to affirm in terms of metaphysics is that we are personal, relational, communicative, image-bearing beings who are bound in covenantal relationship with the Triune God. That, in short, is *who* and *what* we are.

Our epistemology follows from our metaphysical identity. Creatures made in the image of the tripersonal God are made to think God's thoughts after him analogically, within a world that is exhaustively revelational of God himself.[10] We do not think univocally (to the same extent and in the same manner as God) or equivocally (as if our thought were inherently unreliable and unstable). Rather, we might say that we think *revelationally*, that is, as creatures informed by God's revelation.[11] Here, once again I mean only to affirm what the Reformed tradition has known as a revelational epistemology.[12]

---

of human behavior from the perspective of *creatures*. In fact, that is precisely what the biblical narrative demands that we do.

10. Van Til, *Defense of the Faith*, 62, 67, 70–71, 183, 376; *Christian Apologetics*, 77; *Introduction to Systematic Theology*, 31, 33, 42, 177–78, 185, 292, 363; *A Christian Theory of Knowledge* (Phillipsburg, NJ: Presbyterian and Reformed Publishing, 1969), 16, 17, 38, 47, 172, 278. See also paragraph twelve of John M. Frame, "A Primer on Perspectivalism," Frame-Poythress.org, accessed May 18, 2016, http://www.frame-poythress.org/a-primer-on-perspectivalism/; and Poythress, *In the Beginning Was the Word*, 268.

11. Oliphint reminds us of the centrality of our imaging behavior. "A person is, in the deepest sense of the word, an image, an *eikon*, made according to the 'pattern' of the Original, the triune God. This means that whatever we are, think, and do, we are, think, and do *as image*. We will never become, at any time and in any way, original." Oliphint, *Reasons for Faith*, 179.

12. For a helpful introduction to what a revelational or biblical epistemology is, see G. K. Beale and W. Andrew Hoffecker, "Biblical Epistemology: Revelation," in *Building a Christian World View*, ed. W. Andrew Hoffecker and

Lastly, regarding language, we need to remember that it is fundamentally communal. Language is, as I have written elsewhere, *communion behavior*.[13] It is the key that unlocks the doors of our minds so that we can relate to other beings.[14] It is not, first and foremost, a tool for information transfer or a self-serving social faculty. It is a behavior that allows interaction and communion with other beings, which of course then leads to more specific uses such as the gathering of information and caring for one's physical and social needs. This behavior traces back to the Trinity, in a qualified sense, of course. The persons of the Godhead communicate with one another in unending reciprocity of love and glory.[15] Their communication fosters perfect

---

Gary Scott Smith, vol. 1, *God, Man, and Knowledge* (Phillipsburg, NJ: Presbyterian and Reformed, 1986), 193–216.

13. Pierce Taylor Hibbs, "Closing the Gaps: Perichoresis and the Nature of Language," *Westminster Theological Journal* 78, no. 2 (Fall 2016): 299–322; and "Words for Communion," *Modern Reformation* 25, no. 4 (July/August 2016): 5–8.

14. "The modern impersonalist worldview thinks of the human mind as a closed room. But when God created us, he intended our human minds to be open rooms in which the Father, the Son, and the Holy Spirit dwell." Vern S. Poythress, *Inerrancy and Worldview: Answering Modern Challenges to the Bible* (Wheaton, IL: Crossway, 2012), 134.

15. On "mutual glorification" of the persons in the Godhead, see Frame, *Systematic Theology*, 480–81; Francis Cheynell, *The Divine Triunity of the Father, Son, and Holy Spirit* (London, 1650), 62; Abraham Kuyper, *The Work of the Holy Spirit*, trans. Henry De Vries (Chattanooga, TN: AMG Publishers, 1995), 542; and Dumitru Staniloae, *The Holy Trinity: In the Beginning There Was Love*, trans. Roland Clark (Brookline, MA: Holy Cross Orthodox Press, 2012), who writes that "the divine essence is only divine when hypostasized in three Persons, because these three have a value and a relationship between Them that deserves and is capable of absolute love" (17). He later notes, "The highest form of love is revealed to us in the unending love between the one and only Father of a unique Son. Yet throughout eternity the love between the Father and the Son has also been directed toward a third

union among distinct persons who share the same essence. We might say that, while our communication attempts to foster communion; Trinitarian communication simply *is* communion.

That, essentially, is the MEL triad. Understanding and applying this triad requires that we keep in mind the Creature-creature distinction, as stated earlier. The triune God *is*, *thinks*, and *communicates* in a way that is qualitatively different from the being, thought, and language of humanity. And yet, this qualitative difference has built into it an analogical correspondence, made possible by the fact that this God chose to create us in his image.

Before looking at an example of how this triad can be misunderstood in secular thought, we need to examine its biblical roots.

Biblical Roots of the MEL Triad

On every page of the Bible, there is some reference, direct or indirect, to who we are, how or what we should think, and how we communicate. In light of this, exploring the biblical roots of the MEL triad is an intimidating venture in its own right. Once again, we must focus our discussion for the purpose of the current project. One passage that brings together the entire triad quite clearly is 1 Cor 2:11–13. I have placed the Greek next to the English translation below to show how I see the MEL triad connected to the original language.[16]

Person who takes joy in the love that each has for the other" (ibid., 55).

16. All Scripture quotations will be taken from the ESV unless otherwise noted.

τίς γὰρ οἶδεν ἀνθρώπων τὰ τοῦ ἀνθρώπου εἰ μὴ τὸ πνεῦμα τοῦ ἀνθρώπου τὸ ἐν αὐτῷ; οὕτως καὶ τὰ τοῦ θεοῦ οὐδεὶς ἔγνωκεν εἰ μὴ τὸ πνεῦμα τοῦ θεοῦ. ἡμεῖς δὲ οὐ τὸ πνεῦμα τοῦ κόσμου ἐλάβομεν ἀλλὰ τὸ πνεῦμα τὸ ἐκ τοῦ θεοῦ, ἵνα εἰδῶμεν τὰ ὑπὸ τοῦ θεοῦ χαρισθέντα ἡμῖν· ἡμεῖς δὲ οὐ τὸ πνεῦμα τοῦ κόσμου ἐλάβομεν ἀλλὰ τὸ πνεῦμα τὸ ἐκ τοῦ θεοῦ, ἵνα εἰδῶμεν τὰ ὑπὸ τοῦ θεοῦ χαρισθέντα ἡμῖν· ἃ καὶ λαλοῦμεν οὐκ ἐν διδακτοῖς ἀνθρωπίνης σοφίας λόγοις, ἀλλ᾽ ἐν διδακτοῖς πνεύματος, πνευματικοῖς πνευματικὰ συνκρίνοντες.	For who knows a person's thoughts except the spirit of that person, which is in him? So also no one comprehends the thoughts of God except the Spirit of God. Now we have received not the spirit of the world, but the Spirit who is from God, that we might understand the things freely given us by God. And we impart this in words not taught by human wisdom but taught by the Spirit, interpreting spiritual truths to those who are spiritual. (ESV)

Notice here the three elements of the triad: (1) a personal being (ἀνθρώπων/θεοῦ); (2) knowledge or thought (οἶδεν/τὰ τοῦ ἀνθρώπου/ἔγνωκεν); and (3) communicative exchange (χαρισθέντα/λαλοῦμεν/λόγοις).[17] Exploring the theological extensions of these features of the text reveals much about both the divine and human structure of the MEL triad.

First, for the triune God, the Father has an eternally generated thought (the Son) that is intimately known by the Spirit, who is *in him* (the Father).[18] This brings to our attention the ancient teaching of *perichoresis*, the intimate

---

17. The "things given to us" by God (χαρισθέντα) implies linguistic revelation, since the truth of salvation has been delivered via special revelation, likewise with the "teachings of the Spirit" (διδακτοῖς πνεύματος).

18. Geerhardus Vos points out that the Son being the Logos of the Father (John 1:1) means that this Word's "rationale is already inherent in the speaker . . . . is an imprint of his personal existence [and] . . . . lives on in

union of the divine persons, such that "each is in each, and all are in each, and all are one."[19] It is this teaching that can be linked to the metaphysical element of the MEL triad for God, since perichoresis is deeply tied to the being of God himself. God *is* the Trinity: three-in-one. Though there is an order in the Godhead, the Father is not the "fountain of deity" or the source of divinity for the other persons.[20] Following John Calvin, we would say that all of the

---

the consciousness [of the Father]." Geerhardus Vos, *Reformed Dogmatics*, Vol. 1, *Theology Proper*, ed. Richard B. Gaffin, Jr., trans. Richard B. Gaffin Jr. (Bellingham, WA: Lexham Press, 2014), 57. See also Calvin, *Instit.* 1.13.7. The Son of God as the Logos of the Father has been a widely studied in Trinitarian theology for centuries, notably strong in the theology of Thomas Aquinas, which Gilles Emery has highlighted. See Gilles Emery, *The Trinitarian Theology of Saint Thomas Aquinas*, trans. Francesca Aran Murphy (Oxford: Oxford University Press, 2007), 180–192.

19. Augustine, *De Trinitate* 6.10. For other definitions of perichoresis, see Augustine, *De Trinitate* 1.18; John of Damascus, *Writings*, 177; Joel R. Beeke and Mark Jones, *A Puritan Theology: Doctrine for Life* (Grand Rapids, MI: Reformation Heritage Books, 2012), 90–91; Collins, *Trinitarian Theology: West and East*, 209–15; Oliver D. Crisp, "Problems with Perichoresis," *Tyndale Bulletin* 56, no. 1 (January 1, 2005): 135–39; Egan, "Toward Trinitarian Perichoresis," 92; Frame, *Systematic Theology*, 479–81; Harrison, "Perichoresis in the Greek Fathers," 59–63; Kelly, *The God Who Is: The Holy Trinity*, 489; Michael G. Lawler, "Perichoresis: New Theological Wine in an Old Theological Wineskin," *Horizons* 22, no. 1 (March 1, 1995): 52–53; Letham, *The Holy Trinity*, 365–66; John McClean, "Perichoresis, Theosis and Union with Christ in the Thought of John Calvin," *Reformed Theological Review* 68, no. 2 (August 1, 2009): 134–35; Randall E. Otto, "The Use and Abuse of Perichoresis in Recent Theology," *Scottish Journal of Theology* 54 (2001): 366; Stramara, "Gregory of Nyssa's Terminology for Trinitarian Perichoresis," 259; Tipton, "The Function of Perichoresis and the Divine Incomprehensibility," 292; Torrance, *The Christian Doctrine of God*, 169–73; and Van Til, *A Survey of Christian Epistemology*, 78.

20. See Henri Blocher, "La Trinité, Une Communauté an-Archique?," *Théologie Évangélique* 1, no. 2 (2002): 3–20.

divine persons are *autotheotes*.²¹ Each of the three persons has eternally carried the full divine essence. So, the entire Trinity—the Father, Son, and Holy Spirit—represents the metaphysical element of the triad. Again, more could be said here, but certainly not less.

With regards to epistemology, as we have said, the Son is the eternal thought or wisdom of the Father, known intimately by the Spirit. The comprehensive or "systematic wisdom of God is found in the Son: 'in whom are hidden all the treasures of wisdom and knowledge' (Col. 2:3; see 1 Cor. 1:30)."²²

This thought of God the Father, however, does not remain dormant in a static or lifeless Godhead. It is eternally spoken (or eternally generated) in the power of the Spirit. Put anthropomorphically, the Spirit is like the breath that produces the utterance (the Son) from the speaker (the Father).²³ All of this happens eternally, for language (communicativeness) belongs to God's essence.²⁴

Thus, the triune God *is*, *thinks*, and *communicates* with himself. He holds eternal and uninterrupted Trinitarian discourse. As George Tavard put it, we might render the

---

21. Calvin, *Instit.* 1.13.8; Tipton, "The Triune Personal God," 101–110.

22. Poythress, *In the Beginning Was the Word*, 265.

23. Ibid., 19–21. This model of the Trinity as Speaker, Speech, and Breath is not meant to downplay the equally important biblical truth that each of the persons of the Godhead is assigned speaking and hearing roles. As Vanhoozer notes, "the gospels assign speaking parts to each of the three divine persons." The Father speaks (Matt. 3:17; 17:5; Mark 1:11); the Son obviously speaks throughout the gospels; and the Spirit speaks through believers (Matt. 10:20). The Son also hears (John 12:49–50), as does the Spirit (John 16:13). Kevin J. Vanhoozer, *Remythologizing Theology: Divine Action, Passion, and Authorship* (New York: Cambridge University Press, 2010), 246.

24. Frame, *Systematic Theology*, 522–24.

beginning of John's Prologue, "'In the beginning was Discourse, and Discourse was with God, and Discourse was divine . . .'"[25] The divine discourse of the Godhead accents the language element of the MEL triad, but discourse also presupposes thought, and, as we noted at the outset, thought presupposes being—in this case, the tripersonal being of God. There is great and deep mystery here, and we could go much further, but the central idea is that the tripersonal God (metaphysics) is filled with the eternal thought of the Son (epistemology) expressed in and through the Spirit (language).

Beyond the bounds of the ontological Trinity, we see this structure take shape in creation and redemption, i.e., in the economic Trinity. The Creator-God carries out the action of creating in a way that gloriously reflects his own communicative nature: the Father speaks the Word in the power of the Spirit in order to manifest reality. Divine sound gives way to earthly substance. The Word and the Breath of the Speaker work conjointly to create, just as, later in the biblical story, they work conjointly to recreate (cf. Gen. 1:26; 2:7; Rom. 8:9–11). In sum, the Triune God's thought finds material expression by the power of his Spirit both at the dawn of time and at the eschatological entrance of eternity—the moment when a creature is bound to Christ in Spirit-wrought faith and thus begins to live a life that will consummate in eternal communion with God himself. All of this comes to be in light of the Speaker-Speech-Breath model, a model reflected in 1 Corinthians 2:11. The Father exhaustively knows his thought (the Son) through the power of the Spirit, "which is in him."

---

25. George H. Tavard, *The Vision of the Trinity* (Washington, DC: University Press of America, 1981), 122.

Second, for creatures made in the image of the Trinity, we *are*, *think*, and *speak* in an analogous manner. This is related clearly to the Speaker-Speech-Breath model, since each of us is a speaker who produces words by our breath. It is in this sense, among many others, that we image the Triune God of Scripture in our being (metaphysics). We are communicative beings, imaging the communicative God.[26]

First Corinthians 2:11–13 draws our attention to human epistemology and language as well. Every person's thoughts are inherently connected to his spirit. In other words, only we ourselves can trace and monitor our own thoughts, as Paul's question makes plain: "who knows a person's thoughts except the spirit of that person, which is in him?" And yet, Paul is also very aware that every Christian's spirit has been infused with the life-giving, regenerative power of the Holy Ghost. That is why he continues in 1 Corinthians 2 by saying that we have received *the Spirit of God*. This Spirit brings into our consciousness thoughts that burn away the dross of sin; the Christian thinks of higher things than he did before his second birth—Christ's glory, communion with the Triune God, spreading the dynamic good news of the gospel to every corner of the earth. These thoughts are Spirit-given and Spirit-driven. We might pause here to remind ourselves of the profoundly Trinitarian nature of salvation, a salvation that has made us new creatures in Christ: we are brought by the Spirit to conform to the image of the Son (Rom. 8:29) in our adoption by the Father (Gal. 4:4–7)! The result of salvation is a new identity, an identity *in Christ* (2 Cor. 5:17). This is related to the metaphysical

---

26. On God as a communicative being, see William M. Schweitzer, *God Is a Communicative Being: Divine Communicativeness and Harmony in the Theology of Jonathan Edwards*, T&T Clark Studies in Systematic Theology 14 (London: T&T Clark, 2012), 11–30.

element of the MEL triad. While it is true that our Spirit-wrought union with Christ has not made us new beings per se, that union has removed the ethical hostility that categorized us as creatures in rebellion (cf. Col. 1:21; Eph. 2:3).

Now, as the Spirit indwells us as new creatures in Christ and sanctifies our thoughts, we impart the spiritual truths we have been taught not with our own words, but with the words of the Spirit. The word, then, is the medium that takes the things "freely given us by God," i.e. God's thoughts, and communicates them to others. We might express what we have discovered in the figures below.

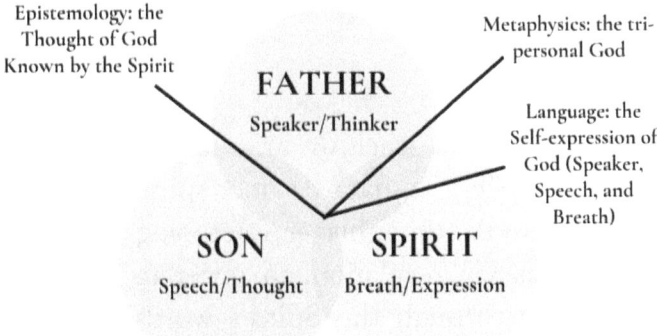

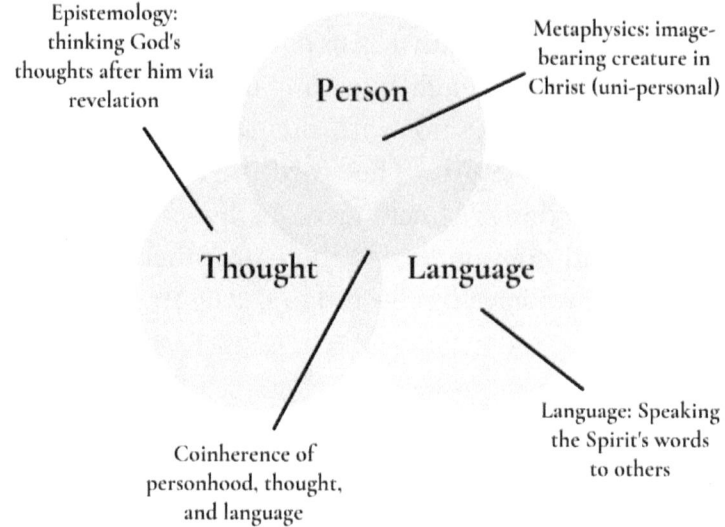

In sum, by God's grace we are made new speakers in Christ (metaphysics), so that we can be spiritually instructed concerning God's thoughts (epistemology), which are delivered to us via revelation, in order to communicate those thoughts through the Spirit's words (language). A reversed paradigm holds for unbelievers as well, but with drastically different consequences. Their spirit is lost, and so their thoughts are confused as they try to suppress the truth (Rom. 1:18), which produces words that, at their best, appear to be wise but which are, in fact, foolish (Rom. 1:22).

Secular Approaches to MEL

Now that we have surveyed a key passage that highlights the MEL triad and have a general understanding of how it applies to the Creator and the creature, we can consider a secular approach to this triad, noting the dangers we encounter. I will then briefly contrast this with Kenneth Pike's language, which will put us in a better position to appreciate his theory and its structure.

We will examine only one figure, since our aim is not to sufficiently survey the field of secular approaches to metaphysics, epistemology, and language—which would be the task of several dissertations. Instead, our aim is to show where an unbiblical view of this triad breaks down.

John R. Searle

John Searle, a prominent philosopher in our time, has written a popular book that summarizes his basic approach to the MEL triad, though he does not refer to this triad as such. His work, *Mind, Language, and Society: Philosophy in the Real World*, has been well received in the field as a concise and cogent presentation of how the three elements in the title engage with one another. For our purposes, we would link "mind" with epistemology and "society" with metaphysics. Linking the categories this way does not change Searle's theory; it simply sets it in a context with which we are already familiar.[27]

We must start by noting the stark contrast between a Christian and non-Christian approach to philosophy,

---

27. Society, in other words, is comprised of people, who exist and act in a certain way, and this has a very close tie with metaphysics.

especially concerning the nature of reality, as reflected in Searle's opening chapter. We have discussed creation as an event of the Triune God of Scripture whereby he speaks creation into being and thus calls it into covenant with himself. Reality, for the Christian, is simultaneously physical and spiritual—physical in the sense that God has spoken substance into being, spiritual in the sense that our lives are lived either in covenantal submission to or rebellion against God and his clear revelation in nature and Scripture.[28] Because the physical world is revelatory of the God who made it, there is a sense in which physical reality cannot be exhaustively known—though it can certainly be studied and examined. Recall the words of Van Til: "We certainly cannot penetrate intellectually the mystery of the Trinity, but neither can we penetrate anything else intellectually because all other things depend on the mystery of the Trinity, and therefore all other things have exactly as much mystery in them as does the Trinity."[29]

Searle, on the other hand, accepts what he calls "the Enlightenment Vision." He affirms that in western civilization there has long been a divide between the physical and spiritual realms. This divide has allowed us to assume

---

28. In Van Tillian terms, we could also say there is an ontological and epistemological component of reality. Ontologically, we are creatures made in God's image, and the rest of creation serves to reveal God in his glory. Ontologically (metaphysically), the Christian and the non-Christian have everything in common. Epistemologically, we are either at enmity with God or are reconciled to him in the person of Christ by the power of the Spirit. In this sense, we *know* reality in a fundamentally different way as compared to the non-Christian. So, we would also say that the Christian and the non-Christian have nothing in common. See Greg L. Bahnsen, *Van Til's Apologetic: Readings and Analysis* (Phillipsburg, NJ: P&R Publishing, 1998), 405–424.

29. See footnote 25.

that "the universe was completely intelligible and that we were capable of a systematic understanding of its nature."[30] While Searle notes the challenges to such an understanding of reality, and further argues that we do *not* "live in two worlds, the mental and the physical, . . . but in one world," he ultimately comes to agree with the Enlightenment vision and aims to "make a modest contribution to" it.[31]

So, what is Searle's contribution? To put it concisely, Searle hopes to affirm a unifying coherence amongst our world, our minds, and our language. Put differently, he wants to stand upon a few basic principles of metaphysics—"external realism" and the "correspondence theory of truth"—to show how our thought and our language engage with that metaphysical base in an understandable way.[32] Of course, our follow-up question would be, how exactly do we understand this engagement?

For Searle, we must first agree that there is a real world out there that exists independently of us (realism). Most people, he seems to suggest, would have little trouble with that claim—aside from marginal philosophers.[33] "Any attempt to find out about the real world at all," he notes, "presupposes that there is a way that things are. . . . That

---

30. John R. Searle, *Mind, Language, and Society: Philosophy in the Real World* (New York: Basic Books, 1998), 2.

31. Ibid., 6. Searle focuses on the physical and relegates the spiritual to the realm of religion, which we can infer is subjective and relative in the common sense of those words.

32. He defines "external realism" as the belief that "there is a real world existing independently of us" and "correspondence theory of truth" as the view that "statements are true if they correspond to, or describe, or fit how things really are in the real world, and false if they do not." Ibid., 13.

33. Searle refutes common critiques of realism on pages 20–37.

is, the negation of this or that claim about the real world presupposes that there is a way that things are independently of our claims."[34] This "way that things are" is not sketched out in detail, but in places throughout his book he reveals his affinity for the hard sciences. What is real to him is what can be empirically verified or rationally expounded based on our experience.

In answer to the Christian's curiosity as to whether or not God is involved with "the way things are," he provides a personal anecdote on the famous atheistic philosopher Bertrand Russell, who once told him that if he were wrong about God, that God really did exist, then when he arrived at the gates of heaven, he would march straight up to God himself and proclaim, "You didn't give us enough evidence!"[35] This anecdote seems to be the most treatment Searle gives to the question of God's existence or involvement in reality. He is concerned with physicality, not spirituality, as his following chapters confirm.[36]

In sum, Searle's basic metaphysical principle is external

---

34. Searle, *Mind, Language, and Society*, 31.

35. Ibid., 37. It is worth noting here, since this is a popular response to the matter of God's existence, that the Christian worldview, especially in the Reformed tradition championed by Van Til, claims that our knowledge of God's existence is not a matter of evidence. It is not a matter of data; rather, it is a matter of the *interpreter* of that data. Perception of truth is not merely a matter of brute facts (since there is no such thing). Instead, it is a matter of the mind and heart of the *person* doing the interpreting, since all of our life is lived either in covenantal rebellion against or submission to the self-revealing Triune God of Scripture. In this sense, we might imagine God's response to Russell: "I gave you all of the evidence, and you refused to see it."

36. Searle includes "mental" states as part of physical reality, as we will see momentarily when we discuss his view of the mind as a "biological phenomenon."

realism, by which he predicates the existence of a reality that is independent of us, a reality that is assumed "by us when we perform many sorts of intentional actions."[37] This metaphysical principle is linked to his acceptance of the "correspondence theory of truth": a view that claims, because there is a real world independent of us, "statements about objects or states of affairs in that world are true or false depending on whether things in the world really are the way we say they are."[38]

Second, and following from his metaphysical principles, he introduces the mind as a "biological phenomenon." He supports the "biological" component of this phrase by emphasizing and expounding upon our *consciousness*. Our consciousness, for Searle, has an "inner, qualitative, and subject nature."[39] First, the inner nature relates to the fact that all conscious activity occurs inside the brain and is related to the vast array of all of our other conscious experiences.[40] These conscious experiences are tied to the real world. Second, the qualitative nature expresses the truth that "for each conscious state there is a certain way that it feels," and this feeling marks each conscious

---

37. Searle, *Mind, Language, and Society*, 39.

38. Ibid., 13.

39. Ibid., 41.

40. "My mental states are internally related to each other in the sense that in order for a mental state to be that state with that character it has to stand in certain relation to other states, just as the whole system of states has to be related to the real world. For example, if I really remember running the ski race, then there must actually have been a running of the ski race by me, and that running of the ski race by me must cause my present memory of it. Thus, the ontology—the very existence of my conscious states—involves their being part of a sequence of complex conscious states that constitutes my conscious life." Ibid., 42.

experience as unique. Third, conscious states are subjective in the sense that "they are always experienced by a human or animal subject. Conscious states, therefore, have what we might call a 'first-person ontology.' That is, they exist only from the point of view of some agent or organism or animal or self that has them."[41]

This last element of our consciousness is particularly important to Searle, for he refutes the critique that because consciousness is subjective (a type of 'first-person ontology'), it cannot be studied with scientific objectivity. On the contrary, he argues that a subjective "mode of existence" is no less real—no less capable of being studied scientifically—than are mountains and glaciers, which have an "objective mode of existence" (i.e., they do not depend for their existence on a conscious subject). He writes,

> Mountains and glaciers have an *objective mode of existence* because their mode of existence does not depend on being experienced by a subject. But pains, tickles, and itches, as well as thoughts and feelings, have a *subjective mode of existence* because they exist only as experienced by some human or animal subject. The fallacy in the argument was to suppose that because states of consciousness have an ontologically subjective mode of existence, they cannot be studied by a science that is epistemically objective. But that conclusion doesn't follow. The pain in my toe is ontologically subjective, but the statement "JRS now has a pain in his toe" is not epistemically subjective. It is a simple matter of (epistemically) objective fact, not a matter of (epistemically) subjective opinion.[42]

Beyond these features of consciousness, the point

---

41. Ibid.

42. Ibid., 44–45.

that Searle ultimately wishes to support in all of this is that "consciousness is a biological phenomenon like any other." It "occurs in the brain in the way that digestion is a biological process that occurs in the stomach and the rest of the digestive tract."[43] In fact, he labels his position on this issue "biological naturalism"—"'naturalism' because, on this view, the mind is part of nature, and 'biological' because the mode of explanation of the existence of mental phenomena is biological."[44]

Note at this point how Searle has attempted to sketch out a metaphysics (external realism) and a component of epistemology (consciousness as a biological phenomenon) in compete isolation from God and his revelation. While earlier in the book, Searle tries to guard himself against the charge of being a materialist, we cannot help but notice how bound up his worldview is with physicality—that which can be measured, calculated, and experienced is "real." Thus, when he comes to his discussion of language, we are not surprised to find him arguing that language is tied to the *intentionality* of the mind as a biological phenomenon. Intentionality, for him, simply refers to the ways in which we relate to our environment and to other people—the main components of physical reality.[45]

For Searle, the intentionality of the mind precedes the intentionality that we often witness in language when

---

43. Ibid., 51.

44. Ibid., 54.

45. Ibid., 85. Searle's view of consciousness is more developed than we can outline here. For details, see his chapter, "How the Mind Works: Intentionality."

we extract meaning from a sentence or utterance.[46] Thus, there is a clear connection between the mind and human language. This mind-language connection, in a broader sense, is obvious to both scholars and laymen. We recognized this connection in our discussion of the MEL triad and its relation to 1 Corinthians 2:11–13. The question we must ask at this point is one we have already answered: "what is the matrix lying behind the connection between the mind and language?" In other words, what is the metaphysical framework within which we understand our thought (intentions) and language? While our answer is, "the tri-personal God of Scripture and his purposeful revelation," Searle's answer is, "the material world" (external realism). This is why he suggests that language has a "derived intentionality," i.e., an intentionality that is traceable to that of the mind, which, Searle has already stated, is a *biological* phenomenon.

Notice, then, that when Searle proposes that "all linguistic meaning is derived intentionality," he is saying something both helpful and dangerous.[47] It is helpful in the sense that it links language to thinking "agents." There is, in other words, no such thing as "pure language"—language that can be isolated from a speaker. (We will discuss this point in more detail when reviewing Kenneth Pike's language theory.) However, it is quite dangerous in that it "naturalizes" language as a biological phenomenon.[48] At first glance, this might not seem so troubling, but remember

---

46. Ibid., 90. Searle refers to the intentionality of language as "derived intentionality," since language is the medium by which we express our original cognitive intentions.

47. Ibid., 93.

48. Ibid., 96.

the system in which Searle is working: it is a system in which all spiritual realities are ignored. We will look at the ramifications of this position momentarily.[49]

We can and should say a bit more about Searle's view of language. The derived intentionality of language is linked to language as a kind of human action. Words are, for Searle, a kind of signifying placeholder for complex human intentions.[50] Here, he is following the well-trodden path of speech-act theory by J. L. Austin and G. E. M. Anscombe. Language is the expression of human intentions via illocutionary acts, and those acts have meaning within particular situations governed by "constitutive rules."[51] We might formulate these rules with the equation, "X counts as Y in C." For example, we could say, "Gold counts as currency in today's developed global market." Gold might not count as currency in a tribal setting, where an element's worth is based more narrowly on its practical function. Based on the above constitutive rule, we could utter the following sentence: "John prefers gold to silver." This assertion has meaning in expressing the agent's desire for something. John, as a human agent living in physical reality,

---

49. It is worth noting that Searle also seems to leave out a discussion of the innately social dimension of language, focusing instead on individual intentionality. This is an important lacuna in his exposition, for people do not "invent" language; they *learn* it from others. Thus, "one of the purposes of language—in fact, a central, predominant purpose—is to be a vehicle for personal communication and communion between God and human beings." Poythress, *In the Beginning Was the Word*, 38. In this sense, the personal, social element of language lays at the base of our understanding of what it is and how it is used. This is one of the reasons why I define language as *communion behavior* and contrast this with more impersonal definitions.

50. Searle, *Mind, Language, and Society*, 132.

51. Ibid., 122–24. These include assertive, directive, commissive, expressive, and declarative acts. Ibid., 148–50.

has a certain desire that can be formulated into a rational thought. This thought is then poured into the mold of his particular human language. Meaning, then, is a matter of thought, which is a matter of interaction with the world. He writes,

> The key to understanding meaning is this: meaning is a form of derived intentionality. The original or intrinsic intentionality of a speaker's thought is transferred to words, sentences, marks, symbols, and so on. If uttered meaningfully, those words, sentences, marks, and symbols now have intentionality derived from the speaker's thoughts. They have not just conventional linguistic meaning but intended speaker meaning as well.[52]

More could be said about speech act theory and Searle's appropriation of it, but we have said enough for our purposes.[53] Let us pause here to summarize Searle's approach to the MEL triad.

In terms of metaphysics, Searle affirms that there is a real, material world in which we dwell, and that this world is engaged with by our minds (epistemology), which form intentional relations with it. These intentional relations can be expressed in language through various illocutionary acts that accurately or inaccurately convey a state of affairs, i.e., the way the world really is, the way a person

---

52. Searle, *Mind, Language, and Society*, 141. Note, once again, that language learning in social settings seems to be ignored. When Searle writes "transferred to words, sentences, marks . . . ," where do these words come from? Are they not learned from others? And if they are, then why is this basic social dimension left out of his discussion?

53. Note the limitations of speech-act theory in Vern S. Poythress, "Canon and Speech Act: Limitations in Speech-Act Theory, with Implications for a Putative Theory of Canonical Speech Acts," *Westminster Theological Journal* 70, no. 2 (September 1, 2008): 337–54.

feels, etc. (correspondence theory of truth). Language is thus bound up with speaker intentionality, which is bound up with our behavior in time and space. We might even summarize Searle's approach to the MEL triad with our initial statement at the outset of this chapter: language is bound up with thought, and thought is bound up with being. Certainly, we might disagree with Searle on various particulars here, but, on the whole, we would agree with him, wouldn't we? No.[54]

A Response to Searl

There are several elements of Searle's approach that are problematic from a Christian perspective. Some of these we have already noted—e.g., the materialist bent of his thought and his essentially atheistic view of reality. For the sake of brevity, we can draw out two central problems: (1) Searle's inability to account for personal diversity and contextual complexity within human communication and (2) the absence of purposiveness and prescriptiveness in his worldview as a whole.

The first problem is in some ways anticipated by the

---

54. Part of the reason for our opposition is that Searle's approach focuses on the autonomous individual consciousness without giving proper weight to our learning of language as a personal, communal behavior. The Enlightenment idea of the autonomous rational mind is problematic in several ways, but perhaps the most important is the way in which it encourages us to think of ourselves as masters of linguistic meaning—a meaning that is controlled by human intentionality. This, once again, leaves God out of the picture. For the Christian, God is the one who creates all meaning, "for from him and through him and to him are all things" (Rom. 11:36).

postmodernist movement.[55] There are many facets of postmodernism that can be interpreted as little more than bold rebellion against structures of authority. However, in God's common grace, postmodernists have reminded us of a truth that has long been ignored in some circles: in the intellectual sphere, humanity has let hubris run wild by presupposing that God-like knowledge of reality is an attainable goal. Much analytic philosophy is built upon the ideal of comprehensive knowledge. This ideal is destructive of Christian truth in several ways (e.g., in ignoring the Creator-creature distinction), and perhaps the most striking piece of collateral damage is blindness to a basic epistemological fact: *every person is rooted in a unique cultural, social, and linguistic context.* Postmodernism drew attention to this, but then made the wrong move of suggesting that *relativity* should replace *normativity*—that because we are all contextual creatures, none of us has access to truth that is normative for anyone else. This is not the case, as all Christians would be quick to claim. There is normative truth that applies to all cultures, societies, and language groups, and such truth is offered only in the inerrant words of Scripture. The triune God has broken through all contexts (historical, geographical, and linguistic) to deliver the one unchanging truth of salvation.[56]

---

55. In my remarks here I am drawing on conversations I have had with Vern Poythress, along with his appendix in *In the Beginning Was the Word*, 362–364.

56. Note, however, that God does not ignore the particularities of cultures. The gospel message is embedded in the Koine Greek language, and the Old Testament Scriptures were brought to people largely through the Hebrew and Aramaic languages. Thus, God does not *bypass* human cultural contexts to deliver his truth; he works *in* and *through* them to express his message and then calls upon his children to proclaim that unchanging truth in other lan-

Yet, we should not overlook the common-grace elements of postmodernism, for such elements are not, in the end, the property of postmodernists; rather, they are the property of the Tri-personal God who has revealed himself in Scripture. We can and should critique Searle for ignoring the basic epistemological fact we noted above—not because postmodernism is true and trustworthy, but because God's Word is true and trustworthy, and postmodernism has stumbled across something already etched on every page of Scripture: the uniqueness of persons.

Let us apply this to Searle's use of speech-act theory. When Searle discusses language as "derived intentionality" and then links this to speech-act theory, he "is not interested in any particular natural language. Rather, he considers a hypothetically enriched language that would have whatever resources the speaker needs. This move to a hypothetical language is certainly an idealization."[57] This idealization in terms of language is closely related to the ideal of comprehensive knowledge that we mentioned earlier. In imagining a universal approach to communication in speech-act theory, Searle is trying to simplify the dynamics and complexity of human language. He assumes that speakers—no matter what their native language is—can either draw on the communicative expressions of their native language or invent new expressions that align with their intentionality. The problem is that

> Real people sometimes have the experience of struggling toward what they mean. They may grope for words, not completely knowing what they are after until they find a

---

guages and contexts.

57. Poythress, *In the Beginning Was the Word*, 363.

way of saying it. Or, even after they have said it, they may sometimes have a dim sense that they expressed themselves inadequately, but they have no idea how to proceed to "invent" ideal linguistic resources that would allow them to grasp even for their own benefit what they are groping after. They are experiencing the limitations of their finiteness and of their own grasp of language.[58]

The point here is that Searle has not given ample attention to these struggles and limitations. Instead, he has tried to *transcend* them by imagining that there is a universal approach to communication that can rise above the particularities and complexities of any specific language or person. We should be able to sense the desire for God-like mastery here.

The plain truth of the matter is that we live in a world that has a plurality of languages and a plurality of unique persons. All of us, Searle included, are rooted in a unique cultural, social, and linguistic context. We can make true observations from our unique context, but we must guard against assuming that our unique context accounts for *all* of the features and functions of *every* language. We are insiders for our own context and outsiders when it comes to other cultural and linguistic contexts.[59] But

> speech-act theory bypasses the distinction between insiders' and outsiders' views of language and culture. That simplification can have potentially disastrous consequences, because a person is undertaking to analyze all languages by

---

58. Ibid., 363.

59. We will discuss this in greater detail when we come to the *emic* and *etic* approaches to language in Kenneth Pike's language theory. For additional background on these terms, consult Poythress, *In the Beginning Was the Word*, 150–152.

analyzing only one (in this case, English). All the discussion is intended to be completely universal. But it conveniently uses English and the broader context of scholarship in the Western tradition as its context for what it hopes will be culturally universal truths. The results are stimulating and suggestive. But the method is unsound anthropologically. We need to check other languages and cultures, in order to find out whether some feature that appears to be salient from our insider's cultural standpoint within English is indeed universal rather than being limited to English.[60]

Not only does Searle fail to account for personal diversity in language; he also does not adequately deal with the contextual complexity of human communication. By relying on speech-act theory, Searle focuses on the propositional content of sentences. For instance, the question, "Are you going to the store?" can be broken down into its propositional content (p) and its illocutionary force (F), expressed by the symbolic notation *F(p)*. This analysis is adequate only for a particularly simple communicative exchange in which one person is trying to elicit information from another person. But introducing some contextual complexity into this situation shows how limited the analysis is. If the person to whom the question is being addressed is sick with the flu, then the questioner may not be simply trying to elicit information; he may instead be challenging the sick person's logic: *why would you go to the store when you have the flu?!* Or the questioner might have an ulterior motive. He may be asking the question to see if the other person would be willing to pick up some additional items at the store for himself. In this case, the question merely serves as a prelude to a request; it is meant to elicit information, but the eliciting of information is bound up with a following

---

60. Ibid., 364.

request—the two cannot be torn apart from each other. Or the questioner may be asking the question to see if he or she will be left alone for an extended period of time. In this case, perhaps the questioner is made anxious by loneliness. Again, there is partial truth to the analysis that the question is eliciting information, but it does not account for the depth of the communicative exchange. It isolates propositions, treating them as autonomous from personal motives and intentions. In other words, the *F(p)* analysis does not help us get at the underlying, contextually embedded motives of the speaker, or the relationship between the speaker and the hearer, or the relationship between the speaker and the surrounding physical environment.

We could provide other examples, but the point is that speech-act theory may not be the best approach to assess the contextual complexity of human communication, and this is no small critique. Each of us is entangled in specific communicative exchanges every day, and these exchanges are often nuanced and complex, bound up with hierarchies of verbal and nonverbal behavior. We will see this when we examine Kenneth Pike's language theory in the following chapter. We may at times attempt to simplify our exchanges by introducing certain concepts into our approach to language, such as the "pure" concepts of speech-act theory—propositions, illocutionary acts, perlocutionary force, etc. These concepts can be helpful when used carefully, but they can also be mishandled. They can be used to suggest that human communication is rather simple and has components that are neatly separable, when in reality this is not the case.[61]

---

61. For examples of the limitations here, see Poythress, *In the Beginning Was the Word*, 366–67.

The second problem is a lack of *purposiveness* and *prescriptiveness* in Searle's worldview as a whole. For Christians, being, thought, and language have the distinct yet broad purpose of helping us to glorify God and work with him by grace to restore the world according to the Word, i.e., the gospel. Who we are as image-bearers (metaphysics) defines how we are to think (epistemology) and how we are to communicate (language). In other words, the *purpose* of our being is necessarily tied to the covenantal nature of reality: in condescending to create the cosmos and to call us into covenantal relationship with himself, God set in place *prescriptive* boundaries for our thought and communication. Ultimately, it is God's Word, special revelation, that sets those boundaries.

Recall Adam and Eve in the Garden of Eden. They were to take God at his word as they interpreted their environment and engaged with it. This fact illuminates both their thinking and language at the time of the serpent's temptation. When the serpent came to Eve and challenged God's words, she and Adam had the epistemological duty of recognizing the falsehood and trickery of that challenge. They were to witness how the serpent's proposal was an example of rebellious thought, encouraging them to break through the covenantal boundaries set by God himself via special revelation (his spoken word). Upon identifying the falsehood and rebellion in the serpent's words, they were to respond by reaffirming the truth and authority of God's words, and thus banish the serpent from God's holy presence. This is exactly what Jesus does when tempted by the devil in the wilderness (Matt. 4:1–11; Luke 4:1–13)! As Satan twists and distorts God's words (Ps. 91:11–12) and puts the challenge to Christ, he responds by proclaiming God's spoken truth (Deut. 8:3; 6:16; 6:13). Christ saw the falsehood of Satan for what it was; the eternal Word, who had taken on flesh, crushed the ancient serpent with the words of his Father, and he then banished Satan from God's presence (Matt. 4:10). Another way of stating this would be to say that who Christ *is* led him to *think* and *speak* in a certain way—a holy, God-honoring way.

What we are witnessing here is the *purposive* and *prescriptive* nature of reality. In both Adam and Eve's encounter with the serpent and Jesus's encounter with Satan, we find that God's ultimate purpose is bound to a prescription for thought and language. God's *purpose*, then, is behind a biblical ontology. The purpose of our being—indeed, the purpose for all of reality—is to glorify God and enjoy him forever (WSC Q. 1). As image-bearing creatures, we are defined by our desire to commune with the God who made us and to steward the created physical world in which we find ourselves.

This means, in short, we would not be able to accept the metaphysical base that Searle is offering. Our metaphysical base is not simply "external realism"—the notion that there is a real world out there independent of our thought and experience. Rather, our understanding of metaphysics is tied to the tri-personal God who has purposively and covenantally created all things and is upholding them by the word of his power (Heb 1:3). Thus, when Van Til says "a fact *is* its function,"[62] he is saying that things *are* not what they are abstractly; rather, they are ontologically defined in terms of their function in God's creative and redemptive plan. While Searle affirms the existence of a real world that

---

62. Cornelius Van Til, *Common Grace and the Gospel* (Nutley, NJ: Presbyterian and Reformed, 1977), 115.

is independent of us, he cannot account for the purpose that is woven into the fabric of that world.

This means not only that he cannot account for the ultimate metaphysical base of reality, but also that the more specific purposes that he attributes to mental phenomena such as consciousness cannot be adequately accounted for. Remember, Searle tries to affirm three features of our consciousness.

> Conscious states are *inner* in a very ordinary spatial sense in that they go on inside my body, specifically inside my brain. Consciousness can no more lie around separate from my brain than the liquidity of water can be separated from the water, or the solidity of the table from the table. . . . Consciousness is also inner in a second sense, and that is that any one of our conscious states exists only as an element in a sequence of such states. One has conscious states such as pains and thoughts only as a part of living a conscious life, and each state has the identity it has only in relation to other such states. . . . Conscious states are also *qualitative* in the sense that for each conscious state there is a certain way that it feels, there is a certain qualitative character to it. . . . There is something that it is like to drink red wine, and it is quite different from what it is like to listen to music. In that sense, there is nothing it is like to be a house or a tree, because such entities are not conscious.
>
> Finally, . . . conscious states are *subjective* in the sense that they are always experienced by a human or animal subject. Conscious states, therefore, have what we might call a "first-person ontology." That is, they exist only from the point of view of some agent or organism or animal of self that has them.[63]

These three features of consciousness, because they are

---

63. Searle, *Mind, Language, and Society*, 41–42. Vern Poythress pointed out to me that Searle's wording here seems to confuse anatomy with consciousness. Consciousness cannot literally be located anywhere.

torn from an ultimate purposive base (the plan and purpose of the triune God), can only be superficially understood. Yes, conscious states occur inside each of us, each has a particular quality, and each is subjectively experienced—but what about the *purpose* of each of these features?

Why is it that human creatures are designed to have inner conscious states? This phenomenon seems to create a lot of communicative problems for a godless worldview. We seem trapped in our own inner consciousness and then must struggle to communicate our inner conscious states to others, or else we risk feeling isolated. Moreover, because Searle does not give any practical relevance to God's existence, we are forced to account for this conscious entrapment with a purely biological explanation. But there is no purely biological explanation. It does not seem biologically necessary for conscious states to be inner rather than outer, i.e., shared by a community. The best explanation that Searle could offer would appear to be that our question of purpose is irrelevant. What does it matter what purpose there might be for the fact that our conscious states are internal? Let us just accept that they are and move forward. Christians are not so easily satisfied.

For the Christian, Scripture seems to offer a few purposes for this inner feature of conscious states. Recall 1 Corinthians 2:11–13:

> For who knows a person's thoughts except the spirit of that person, which is in him? So also no one comprehends the thoughts of God except the Spirit of God. Now we have received not the spirit of the world, but the Spirit who is from God, that we might understand the things freely given us by God. And we impart this in words not taught by human wisdom but taught by the Spirit, interpreting spiritual truths to those who are spiritual.

The inner feature of consciousness appears to be rooted in the triune God himself. The Spirit of God, which is *in him*, knows the thoughts of God. And yet, those thoughts of God are, through the eternal Word, expressed, i.e., communicated. This brings our attention once more to the biblical truth that "the persons of the Trinity function as members of a language community among themselves."[64] The Father's thoughts are known by the Spirit and expressed through the eternal Word: God knows and speaks to himself in an exhaustive and incomprehensible way. In relation to the economy of the Godhead, the Father's thoughts are known by the Spirit and communicated through the words of spoken revelation (which are analogically tied to the speaking of the eternal Word),[65] which have been given to us as God's covenantal creatures. In fact, God has given us *his Spirit* so "that we might understand the things freely given us by God"! And note what happens next: we impart this (the inner, Spiritual thoughts of God) in words taught by the Spirit—the paradigm of inner, conscious knowledge expressed through language moves from the Trinity to his image-bearing creatures, who image God so strikingly through language that they replicate the communicative nature of God in their spreading of the gospel! The purpose of inner conscious states, for Christians, is to foster communion among persons. This happens in qualitatively different but analogically related ways for the divine persons of the Trinity and human persons made in the image of the tri-personal God. Inner conscious states, in other words,

---

64. Poythress, *In the Beginning Was the Word*, 18.

65. Vern S. Poythress, "Reforming Ontology and Logic in the Light of the Trinity: An Application of Van Til's Idea of Analogy," *Westminster Theological Journal* 57, no. 1 (March 1, 1995): 188.

serve the purpose of imaging God. The communication of our conscious states to other persons, then, is not a problem that needs to be solved; it is an imaging behavior that serves God's greater purposes for reconciliation, communion, and personal fellowship.

Similarly, our understanding of the qualitative feature of conscious states is undercut by a godless worldview, but deepened by a Christian worldview. Searle affirms the qualitative uniqueness of conscious states in relation to other conscious states. All of our conscious states, however, are linked. As he writes, "any one of our conscious states exists only as an element in a sequence of such states. One has conscious states such as pains and thoughts only as a part of living a conscious life, and each state has the identity it has only in relation to other such states." In other words, the distinctive quality of each conscious state *both* sets it apart (diversity, plurality) *and* relates it to a complex matrix of other conscious states (unity). If this is the case, then uniqueness and relation must be treated as equally ultimate in our understanding of consciousness. On the one hand, a particular conscious state can only be recognized and understood by its relation to other states (commonality, unity). The taste of a red wine, to use Searle's example, has a distinct quality in relation to the tastes of other wines, the taste of cheese, the sound of a train, the feel of birch bark, etc. Relations help us to distinguish one conscious state from countless others. On the other hand, these relations cannot be emphasized to the extent that commonality trumps individuality. Tasting red wine is not just like hearing the sound of a train but with a few modifications; there is a real distinction between the qualities of these conscious states, even amidst their relations (diversity, plurality). In short, there must be balance in order for us to achieve an adequate understanding of what the "quality" of each conscious state is like—a balance between uniqueness and relations, between diversity and unity. But why is our experience structured in this way? Why does it seem that we misunderstand a conscious state if we overemphasize either its uniqueness or its relations to other conscious states?[66] Searle does not seem to offer an answer to this question.

For the Christian, however, a potential answer can be found in the Trinity: the God for whom unity and plurality are equally ultimate.[67] Van Til and a few other theologians, notably Colin Gunton, have found in the Trinity the ultimate solution to the one-and-many problem.[68] This

---

66. For example, if we overemphasize the uniqueness of tasting a particular red wine, that experience becomes isolated from our other experiences, and because of this isolation, we actually understand the initial experience less, not more. We draw on the known in order to comprehend the new. Conversely, if we overemphasize the relations between tasting that red wine and several other qualities of other conscious states, then we risk losing our unique understanding of that conscious state. We cannot understand the new if we force it into the category of the known and refuse to see its particularities.

67. "The unity and the diversity in God are equally basic and mutually dependent upon one another." Van Til, *Christian Apologetics*, 25. "In God the one and the many are equally ultimate. Unity in God is no more fundamental than diversity, and diversity in God is not more fundamental than unity. The persons of the Trinity are mutually exhaustive of one another. The Son and the Spirit are ontologically on a par with the Father." Van Til, *Defense of the Faith*, 48. See also Vern S. Poythress, *Redeeming Philosophy: A God-Centered Approach to the Big Questions* (Wheaton, IL: Crossway, 2014), 57–59.

68. In reflecting on Samuel Taylor Coleridge's *Essay on Faith*, Gunton writes, "If the one, the reality which makes the world what it is, is not merely one—impersonal, mechanical, mere nature—but persons in relation, a unity of free *hypostases* taking their being and particularity from each other, then we may understand how it is that we have a world fit for the creation

ancient philosophical problem is actually at the heart of our current discussion: the notion that both the uniqueness (diversity, plurality) and the relations (unity) of the quality of a conscious state are equally important. Van Til once wrote,

> The unity and the plurality of this world has back of it a God in whom unity and the plurality are equally ultimate. Thus we may say that this world, in some of its aspects at least, shows analogy to the Trinity. This world is made by God and, therefore, to the extent that it is capable of doing so, it may be thought of as revealing God as he exists. And God exists as a triune being.[69]

In other words, that our comprehension of the quality of a conscious state requires *both* uniqueness and relations is a reflection of the Trinitarian God who is *both* one and three. When we ignore the three persons in God, we end up with monism; when we ignore the unity of God, we end up with tritheism. Neither case gives us a true and biblical representation of who God is. These are the classic issues that led to certain heresies in the early church. Analogously, and because the world in many ways reflects the Trinity, when we downplay the uniqueness of the quality of a conscious state, such as tasting a red wine, that quality becomes absorbed into an amorphous mass of other qualities of different conscious states, and so we understand and appreciate it less. If, on the other hand, we

---

and redemption of persons. In other words, we learn from Coleridge not simply that there are analogies to be drawn from the divine to the human person, but that the question of the three in one is also the question of the kind of world we live in." Colin E. Gunton, *The Promise of Trinitarian Theology*, 2nd ed. (London: T&T Clark, 1997), 97.

69. Van Til, *Introduction to Systematic Theology*, 364–65.

exaggerate the uniqueness of a conscious state, we isolate it from our other experiences and thus have trouble truly comprehending it. These phenomena might be categorized as "epistemological heresies," since they falsely represent the workings of the mind (consciousness).

The discussion so far has meant that Christians are in a unique place to recognize both the purposiveness and prescriptiveness of our being and thought: the purpose of our being is to glorify the personal God who has spoken reality into existence and called us into covenant with himself. That is *why* reality exists (both the world and persons), and this broader purpose gives all of reality ultimate meaning, certainly far more meaning than does the notion of "external realism."[70] The purpose of thought is to cognitively image the triune God for whom unity and plurality are equally ultimate. There is also a prescriptive element to both of these pieces. If the purpose of our being is to glorify the speaking God of Scripture (chiefly through hearing and obeying the Father's Word and being conformed, by the Spirit, to the image of his Son), then when we refuse to do this, there is a moral problem. Humans

---

70. This take on metaphysics is the rooted in the nature of reality as Trinitarian. The communion of the Trinity is at the base of all that exists, undergirding every human action by giving it ultimate purpose in relation to God himself. Thus, A. J. Torrance is right to conclude that "a doctrine of the Trinity which takes seriously the mutuality of loving communion opened up for humanity in Christ by the Spirit suggests the ultimate identification of the source of being and the communion of the Trinity. The communion of God is in no sense to be conceived as a qualification of a more foundational category of 'being' or 'substance.' The Triune communion characterizes Reality (Being) at the most fundamental level – it is that in which we live and move and have our being. The communion of the Trinity as such constitutes the *arche* and *telos* of all that is." A. J. Torrance, *Persons in Communion: An Essay on Trinitarian Description and Human Participation* (Edinburgh: T&T Clark, 1996), 258.

do not simply *exist*; rather, they exist *as covenantal creatures of the triune God*, and that means that there is a certain way in which they are called to *be*, i.e., to live. Likewise, if the purpose of our thought is to image the Trinity and thus to avoid lapsing into an epistemological form of monism or tritheism, then when we fail to think this way, or if we reject the God in whom such an epistemological framework is rooted, then, once again, we have a moral problem. The purposiveness of being and thought is inextricably bound up with the prescriptiveness of being and thought. Who we are and how we think is not a matter of realism, or a matter of biological phenomena; it is a matter *imaging*—imaging the Trinity who is both three and one, and who has called us into covenant with himself.

More could certainly be said about Searle's take on metaphysics and consciousness, but at this point we must move on to the final element of his triad: language.

Our critique of Searle's view of language has to do with a more general critique of speech-act theory. "Speech-act theory, like any theory, is selective in its attention to human behavior."[71] This selectivity is not in itself problematic; a problem would only arise if such selectivity left out something that is essential to our understanding of communication. This, unfortunately, is what commonly happens with speech-act theory. Proponents of speech-act theory tend to atomize human communication and reduce it to a limited set of verbal actions (assertives, directives, commissives, expressives, declarations). This marginalizes the importance of context and the complex hierarchical structure of language, along with the rest of human behavior. As Poythress notes,

---

71. Poythress, "Canon and Speech Act," 338.

The decision to start with atomic propositions is a decontextualizing move, and all such moves are problematic when, as is the case with human language, context is essential to meaning. In this case, the context includes the complexity of human beings, who are the speakers and conversationalists, and the complexity of their environment, which includes world history and the God who rules it.[72]

Context and complexity emerge, for Poythress as well as for Kenneth Pike, when we broaden our focus to include what Pike called "behavioremes." A behavorieme is simply a segment or piece of purposive human activity,[73] which is structured in a certain way and fits into a complex, culturally-specific system. Speech acts, in this sense, would only constitute a small group of simplified behavioremes, leaving more complex behavioremes out of the discussion. But notice what this does to our understanding of human communication.

Take, for example, the declaration of a basketball coach in the fourth quarter of a playoff game: "He was fouled!" From the perspective of speech-act theory, this declaration would be analyzed primarily in terms of the speaker and hearer (perhaps the referee), and also, secondarily, in terms of the player who was fouled and the other player who allegedly committed the foul (this would be more closely related to the correspondence theory of truth, i.e., whether a foul was actually committed). The first step of analysis would involve the judgments and perspectives of both the coach and the referee. For Searle, this would include an examination of both the speaker

---

72. Ibid., 339.

73. Kenneth L. Pike, *Language in Relation to a Unified Theory of the Structure of Human Behavior*, 2nd ed. (The Hague: Mouton, 1967), 121.

meaning (what the speaker intended to communicate) and the sentence meaning (the meaning of the grammatical or syntactic structure, in relation to the speaker's intention);[74] a consideration of what, exactly, the speaker wanted the hearer to understand;[75] and the illocutionary force of the speech act as well as its perlocutionary effects.[76] The second step would involve assessing the truth value of the coach's declaration, in relation to the contextually embedded rules of the basketball game. In other words, we might question whether a foul was, in fact, committed, and we would make our judgement based on our understanding of the context (which would include what Searle labelled "constitutive rules") as well as our physical observations. These analyses would certainly be fruitful, revealing much about the coach's intention and the nature of his message, and perhaps even about the basketball game itself, but we would be limited by the atomizing goals of speech-act theory. Our focus would remain only on that speech act, not on the surrounding human behaviors that led up to it or the ones that followed it, or the ones that were occurring at the same time. With such a narrow focus, we would indeed miss out not only on our understanding of the broader context, but, in particular, on our understanding of how the coach's utterance is related to and informed by that context. For instance, was the speaker's intention to point out a fault in the refereeing, or was he primarily concerned with protecting his player from physical harm, or was it both?

---

74. Searle, *Mind, Language, and Society*, 140. We will see later on why distinguishing between speaker meaning and sentence meaning is problematic. See Hibbs, "Where Person Meets Word: Part 1," 374–377.

75. Searle, *Mind, Language, and Society*, 145.

76. Ibid., 136–39.

We would need to see more of the game and learn about the coach's relationship with his players in order to draw a conclusion. Or, was the coach's declaration part of a larger ploy to retain the attention of the referee for future use? In other words, was the declaration an authentic critique of the referee's decision, or was it merely one element of a verbal game that was meant to draw the referee onto his side so that later in the game he would be able to argue for a more important call?[77] Now we are getting deeper into the context of the basketball game and even touching on the coach's motives, and the latter has a moral dimension to it. Yet, we have not even considered the player's actions. Was the player trying to draw a foul by exaggerating his body movements (which is all too frequent in professional sports) or was he legitimately restrained in his movement by his opponent? And if the player was exaggerating in order to lure the referee into making a call, how does that affect the meaning of the coach's declaration? And what about the referee? Is not his decision to *not* call the foul embedded in a pattern of making certain calls for certain reasons? Do you see the complexity that emerges when we examine the context of this allegedly simple speech act more closely? The reductionism of speech-act theory

---

77. I can attest to this from my own life experience in playing the sport. Arguing about a call that is relatively unimportant can have the effect of producing a feeling of guilt in the referee for not making that call. Later in the game, that residual guilt might encourage the referee to execute what is commonly referred to as a "make-up call," i.e., a call that is meant to make up for the one he missed earlier. All of this, of course, is part of the emic (insider) structure of the sport and is not visible to those who are unfamiliar with the game. On the contrast between etic and emic, see Hibbs, "Where Person Meets Word: Part 1," 372–74.

can thus blind us to important information that colors our understanding of a given utterance.[78] In the example above, it might be misleading to label the coach's speech act as a pure declaration, and even if we do so, we will likely not appreciate the significance of the declaration if we refuse to look at the complexity of the surrounding context.

Now, contrast the approach of speech-act theory with that of Pike, as expressed through Poythress' work. Note how Pike's language theory looks at the broader context (the complex behavioreme of a basketball game) and appreciates its complexity.

A basketball game is a complex behavioreme. It has three interlocking dimensions. First, it has a unity or identity, and *contrasts* with other types of games and other types of activity. We can speak of its *contrastive-identificational* features. Second, it has *variation*. That is, there are many different basketball games that differ in detail. Third, it is *distributed* within larger contexts of human activities—a series of games in a season, and other human activities during the same day.

> Speech-act theory focuses primarily on the contrastive-identificational features that characterize particular kinds of behavioreme. But what becomes of the distributional aspect of these behaviaremes? Small speech acts are embedded ("distributed") within larger groupings of human behavior. Speech-act theory does encourage reflection about contextual conditions that may be necessary for the happy execution

---

78. I believe that such reductionism is tied to the notions of mastery and autonomy. If we reduce situations in their complexity, we can imagine that we have a godlike control of the meaning and significance of an element of language. So, there is a theological danger that comes along with speech-act theory. On the notions of godlike mastery in human thought, see Poythress, *In the Beginning Was the Word*, 246–47. Poythress, *Redeeming Philosophy*, 104, 120, 242.

of a speech act. . . . But because of the focus on atomic propositions, there is little attention to the way in which behavioremes can be embedded in larger behavioremes in a hierarchical array, and how several smaller purposeful human actions may together accomplish a larger purpose.[79]

Poythress' words point toward our previous contextual questions. The utterance of the basketball coach is *embedded* in the larger context of more complex behavioremes—the series of offensive plays made by the particular player and the defensive responses of his opponent; the ongoing conversation between the coach and the referee; the pattern of calls that the referee has made in that quarter and in the rest of the game; the other actions occurring simultaneously with the speech-act; the actions of the other players that have occurred before it (and will occur after it); the pattern of discussions that the coach maintains throughout the season with various referees; etc. The complexity is staggering, but that does not mean it should be ignored. Rather, we should attempt to account for all that we can in order to carefully understand a particular utterance more fully, knowing all the while that the triune God has complete control and exhaustive knowledge of all of these hierarchically embedded and complex behavioremes and is using them to accomplish his purposes.

What's more, after we have gleaned what we can from considering the complexity and hierarchical embedding of various behavioremes, we can refocus on the original utterance in terms of its contrastive-identificational features, its variation, and its distribution. This, again, would offer us a richer understanding of the meaning in context. We can keep our observations here brief, since a

---

79. Poythress, "Canon and Speech Act," 340.

fuller exposition of Pike's language theory will follow in the subsequent chapters.

The utterance "He was fouled!" has what Pike called *contrastive-identificational features*.[80] In other words, it has both contrasts with and similarities to other units of language that are comparable in structure and function, and these contrasts and similarities serve to set this particular linguistic unit apart from others. We might find contrasts and similarities in terms of grammar, phonology, and reference.[81] For example, the utterance "He was fouled!" is similar to and different from other grammatically parallel syntactical structures following the pattern *subject + verb in the passive voice*: "He was pushed," "He was hit," "He was held," etc. The commonality amongst all of the examples is the syntactical structure, which is used to show an action reflecting back upon the subject. The particular verbs in each example, however, set the utterances apart from one another, since each verb has various other structures and collocations that can accompany it. For example, we can follow the verb "hit" with an inanimate object such as "ball," but we cannot do so with the verb "foul," since that verb (in this specific sense) must take an animate object; we can *foul a person*, but we cannot *foul a ball*, if by that we mean "commit an illegal act against the ball."

In terms of variation, each linguistic unit has "features . . . which may change *without causing the loss of recognizability*

---

80. Kenneth L. Pike, *Linguistic Concepts: An Introduction to Tagmemics* (Lincoln, NE: University of Nebraska Press, 1982), 42–51.

81. We will explore this in greater detail in the following chapter. For an overview of the grammatical, phonological, and referential hierarchies, see Ibid., 69–106.

of the unit."[82] In other words, we could remove or change certain features of the utterance "He was fouled!" without eradicating the basic meaning of the unit. For instance, we could accent each of the different words in the utterance:

HE was fouled!
He WAS fouled!
He was FOULED!

None of these varied pronunciations would alter the fundamental meaning of the linguistic unit, though it would certainly nuance that meaning in some way.[83]

Lastly, we could examine the utterance with reference to larger patterns of occurrence in discourse, since "reference to successively larger patterns of occurrence, to a larger *universe of discourse*, is necessary if one is to know the significance of a person, a thing, or a word."[84] How many times, for example, was the utterance "He was fouled!" made in that basketball game? In other words, is this a game in which many fouls are being called or a game in which relatively few are being called? Or, we might look at the pattern of pronunciation for this utterance when it is delivered by this particular coach. Does the coach usually yell out this complaint (signaled by the exclamation point) or does he often just call the referee over and speak to him quietly? There are many ways to look at this unit's *distribution* in larger patterns—each of them would be revelatory of

---

82. Ibid., 52.

83. The first might focus our attention on *who* was fouled, the second on *the fact that* he was fouled, and the third on the *action* being carried out.

84. Pike, *LC*, 60.

details we might not have considered.[85]

Let us save our rigorous exposition of Pike's language theory and its advantages for the following chapters. What we have seen is a sufficient response to the shortcomings and simplicity of speech-act theory. This is not to say that speech-act theory is useless, but only that it is limited and has the potential to blind us to the richness and complexity of human communication. This concludes our response to John Searle, but we should summarize our findings.

In terms of the MEL triad, we found that Searle's metaphysical principles (external realism) and his epistemology (his exposition of consciousness) lack a theoretical base that can account for the purpose or prescription required for a coherent worldview. Without the triune God behind our understanding of being and thought, we cannot account for the purpose of reality or our cognitive processing of it. Searle and his sympathizers can offer only limited observations of phenomena that are void of ultimate meaning because they are interpreted in isolation from (in fact, in rebellion against) the triune God who is lord of all meaning. In terms of language, we saw how the complexity and depth of language can easily be ignored by the restricted focus of speech-act theory, and we were able to glimpse how Pike's theory might begin to account for the richness and complexity of human communication.

We end this essay by drawing on what we have found to note a relationship between language theory and theology proper—a relationship that was already discussed in the

---

85. Pike notes that we can examine a unit (1) as a member of a "substitution class," (2) as part of a structural sequence, or (3) as a point in a system. Ibid., 62–65.

Introduction. It is this relationship that I believe obligates us to consider Pike's language theory as felicitous with the Reformed doctrine of the Trinity.

Theologically, we would affirm that God is God *of all*. This claim might seem juvenile, given the context of this project, but it is worth restating in more specific terms. The speaking God of Scripture is God of all in the sense that he is the Creator of being, thought, and language (MEL). He has spoken reality into being and interpreted that reality exhaustively in relation to himself. He has also revealed the truth of this reality to his creatures via speech: this is what we find faithfully and masterfully set forth in Scripture. It is in this sense that God has "thought" about all that exists (he has interpreted the meaning of all things in relation to himself) and has then given us the means to think his thoughts after him. One of the ways in which we engage with God and the world and thus come to a deeper knowledge of him and a fulfillment of the covenantal obligations we have is through communication—language. Thus, there are inextricable bonds between being, thought, and language that can be traced back to the Trinity. All that exists, is thought, or is communicated is interrelated and bound to the triune God and the purposes he has for whom and what he has created. This means that we can take any of the elements in the MEL triad and look *through* it to understand something of God and his creation, including ourselves. How we view language, then, is paramount in shaping our understanding of reality (including the God who made it) and thought. Our theory of language is not simply an addendum to our worldview; it directs and shapes our worldview, broadening or restricting our perspective. It does this because, as we have seen in studying the MEL triad, language reflects thought and thought reflects being.

So, we need a language theory that, as much as possible, accounts for being, thought, and language since we are aiming to understand and more deeply commune with the triune God of all. This does not, as we will see, eschew the notion of mystery from language, thought, and being. In fact, it underscores it, but it does so in a way that more felicitously reflects the Trinitarian God who spoke all things into existence, interpreted all things, and communicates exhaustively with himself.

That, in sum, is where Pike's language theory has a distinct advantage, for though his theory is focused on language, it bleeds into our understanding of thought and being (the latter including human behavior) and thus becomes formative in broadening our view of reality and the God who shapes it so that we might more fully know him and commune with him. Of course, Pike's theory also leaves room for mystery, since all of reality is undergirded by a God who is incomprehensible to his creatures. That fact in of itself might be part of the reason why Pike's theory has not been embraced as passionately as the theories of others; sinful creatures are bent on control and mastery, fixity and absolute rationalism. Any theory that fundamentally opposes such desires is unpopular, to say the least.

A Linguistic Perspective on Divine Persons

There are no truly simple questions in theology, but there are many that appear to be. The "simple" question that has preoccupied me for some years is this: *What is a divine person?* For any informed theological reader in our time, a panoply of responses inundates the mind: "subsisting relation," "real relation," "mode of being," "mode of subsisting," "center of relationship," "oppositional relation," and so on.[1] The surge of trinitarian theology over the last few decades reminds us that there is no lexical shortage. Undoubtedly, the global church has deepened its awareness of the divine persons and is ever working to defend and further articulate how those three persons constitute one God.[2] Yet, even in the midst of all of the debates—quandaries over the nature

---

1. A helpful resource for background on the church's understanding of 'person' throughout its history can be found in Douglas Kelly, *Systematic Theology: Grounded in Holy Scripture and Understood in Light of the Church*, vol. 1, *The God Who Is: The Holy Trinity* (Ross-shire, Scotland: Mentor, 2008), pp. 493–518.

2. We do well to remember that "Scripture itself does not use technical terms for God's oneness and threeness, and . . . it is not always concerned with terminological precision in describing the relations of the three persons." John M. Frame, *Systematic Theology: An Introduction to Christian Belief* (Phillipsburg, NJ: P&R, 2013), p. 481. The historical terms that the church uses to reference God's oneness (essence, substance) and God's threeness (persons, relations, modes of subsistence) are helpful in guarding against heresies such as Sabellianism and tritheism, but the terms themselves are on a lower level of the authoritative hierarchy from that of Scripture.

of analogical language, skirmishes among social and classical trinitarians—it can be easy to behave as if our understanding has reached its climax at certain points of dogmatics.[3] But, as John Murray wrote many years ago, "However epochal have been the advances made at certain periods and however great the contributions of particular men, we may not suppose that theological construction ever reaches definitive finality."[4] In this spirit, I ask two questions, the first intellectual and the second practical: (1) Has our understanding of divine persons adequately accounted for the way in which God is portrayed in Scripture as the three-in-one divine speaker? (2) Does the terminology we currently employ in our definitions of divine personhood help us to better worship and commune with the Trinity?

Perhaps we could answer these questions afresh if we take up a linguistic perspective on divine personhood, one that is rooted in Scripture. That is what I aim to do here. A linguistic perspective does not exclude other historical perspectives on divine personhood; it merely helps us to see more of the truth about who God is. In response to the simple question, "What is a divine person?" I would like to offer an equally simple answer: *a divine person is one who speaks bearing a divine incommunicable property*.[5] Thus, the triune

---

3. An example of one of these "skirmishes" is captured in Wesley Hill, "Divine Persons and Their 'Reduction' to Relations: A Plea for Conceptual Clarity," *International Journal of Systematic Theology* 14, no. 2 (April 2012): pp. 148–60.

4. *Collected Writings of John Murray* (Edinburgh: Banner of Truth, 1982), 4:7–8.

5. This is related to a comment made by Eugen Rosenstock-Huessy, who once wrote that the name "God" means "he who speaketh; he who enthuses man so that man speaketh." Eugen Rosenstock-Huessy, *The Origin of Speech* (Norwich, VT: Argo Books, 1981), p. 5.

God is the three-in-one divine speaker who is everywhere and always addressing his creatures in general and special revelation. Any novelty in this answer is illusory, for the speech of God has long been recognized as a distinguishing mark of his being.[6] In fact, I will begin by taking up the thought of the very church father who coined the term "person" with reference to the Trinity: Tertullian.

In what follows, after interacting with Tertullian and a modern figure of Reformed orthodoxy (Charles Hodge), I survey a few passages of Scripture from the Old and New Testaments, arguing that speech can be seen as an important means by which God is revealed as both one and three. In other words, speech seems to be essential to our understanding of God as one being in three persons.[7] I end by responding to potential objections and suggest the benefits that this perspective may have in relation to our communion with and worship of the triune God.

Before I begin, let me be clear from the outset: this article is *not* intended to supplant traditional trinitarian language as found in the historic creeds and confessions. It is meant to complement that language and help us to better appreciate the communicative nature of the Trinity in our concrete experience.

---

6. See, for instance, the recent study by William M. Schweitzer, *God Is a Communicative Being: Divine Communicativeness and Harmony in the Theology of Jonathan Edwards*, T&T Clark Studies in Systematic Theology 14 (London: T&T Clark, 2012).

7. On speech as an essential attribute of God, see Frame, *Systematic Theology*, pp. 519–24.

The Nature of Definitions

Before revisiting Tertullian, it is important to say a few words about the nature of definitions and how they function in human language. It is very easy to assume unknowingly a *univocal* approach to definitions. A univocal approach is one that seeks to reduce the meaning of a phrase or term so that our understanding of it is allegedly exhaustive and mirrors God's own understanding. We know, on the surface, that this is impossible. Our understanding cannot perfectly match God's understanding, for that would make us divine. We are limited. That simple statement needs to affect the way in which we approach language in general and definitions in particular.

I suggest that instead of viewing definitions only as static *particles*—that is, as encoded and analogically related information units, capable of being fully enveloped by the minds of finite creatures—we view them also as *waves*, progressively instantiated throughout human history and thus acquiring additional nuances of meaning, and as *fields*, webs of lexical and conceptual associations that expand with time and help us better relate to God and to one another.[8] A definition, in short, can be viewed as a particle (a relatively static semantic "thing"), as a wave (acquiring nuances of meaning as the word or concept continues to be used by God's creatures), and as a field (expanding its associations with other words and concepts as history progresses). We cannot *master* any of these components of a

---

8. My approach is modeled on the linguistic theory of Kenneth L. Pike. I am specifically drawing on his particle, wave, and field observer perspectives. See Kenneth L. Pike, *Linguistic Concepts: An Introduction to Tagmemics* (Lincoln, NE: University of Nebraska Press, 1982).

definition, though we can certainly know something about them and use them in discourse.

The point of all this is to suggest that *we must think of definitions being used by persons*, not existing in some sort of isolatable semantic space.[9] By thinking in this way, we can avoid univocism in our approach to definitions and focus instead on how God is using definitions to help us know and serve him more faithfully. So, when I offer a linguistic perspective on a definition for divine persons, I have a truly *analogical* approach in mind: one that recognizes our finitude from the outset and sees this not as a threat to academic inquiry but as a means to inquire felicitously within our creaturely limitations.

Tertullian's Passing Comment

Let us start with Tertullian. In his famous treatise *Against Praxeas*, Tertullian makes a passing gibe at his debate partner. As he discusses the divine persons referenced in John's Gospel, he writes, "How many Persons do you think there are, self-opinionated Praxeas, if not as many as there are voices."[10] It is easy to gloss over this comment, and some scholars would advise us against reading too much into it.[11]

---

9. This, again, is rooted in Kenneth Pike's language theory, where he makes the biblical point that all observation and understanding begins with *persons*, not with things.

10. Tertullian, *Against Praxeas* 23.4.

11. For instance, David Brown, "Trinitarian Personhood and Individuality," in *Trinity, Incarnation, and Atonement: Philosophical and Theological Essays*, ed. Ronald J. Feenstra and Cornelius Plantinga Jr. (Notre Dame, IN: University of Notre Dame Press, 1989), p. 54. Brown cautions us against reading the patristic fathers out of context. Here, however, I believe we are not skewing Tertullian's message, since he discusses the concept of speech with reference

But the fact that Tertullian often references God's speech in this treatise as a behavior that marks the divine persons suggests that we should take it more seriously.[12]

Tertullian makes a connection between *voices* and *persons*. Three distinct voices (Latin *voces*) indicates three distinct persons. This should not be too surprising to us, given the fact that the church has long understood rationality to be a mark of divine personhood, and speech certainly presupposes rationality.[13] Though I agree with Colin Gunton that rationality should not be the primary means of identifying divine personhood, one cannot sideline rationality either.[14] And herein lies part of the value in defining a divine person as "one who speaks bearing a divine incommunicable property": rationality can and must be bound up with relationality. We are not forced to choose one over the other, and thus we can join the emphases of recent classical and social trinitarians, the former focusing on an Augustinian sense of the person as a rational being, and the latter focusing on the Cappadocian sense of the

---

to the Trinity throughout this work. To say that divine persons have voices is thus not truly a passing comment; it adds to what he has already said about the Son being the Word of the Father.

12. See chapters 5, 11, 12, 21, 23, and the end of 28.

13. For a brief and selected history of the use of 'person' in trinitarian theology, see Ángel Cordovilla Pérez, "The Trinitarian Concept of Person," in *Rethinking Trinitarian Theology: Disputed Questions and Contemporary Issues in Trinitarian Theology*, ed. Robert J. Woźniak and Giulio Maspero (London: T&T Clark, 2012), pp. 105–45.

14. Colin E. Gunton, *The Promise of Trinitarian Theology*, 2nd ed. (London: T&T Clark, 1997), pp. 83–99. Gunton argues against the primacy of rationality in defining persons, pushing instead for *relationality*. In this article, I hope to combine both features of personhood, since the concept of speech combines rationality and relationality.

person as a concrete relational entity.

If we follow Tertullian's lead and associate the divine persons with their respective voices, this might shed light on another notion recurring in trinitarian debates: the consciousness of God. Traditionally, orthodox theologians have been quick to defend the claim that God is a uni-conscious being. The divine persons, in the words of Charles Hodge, "are one God, and therefore have one mind and will."[15] Hodge, however, ties this *unity* of consciousness to the doctrine of perichoresis, the interpenetration of the *three* distinct persons. As Lane G. Tipton notes, "In the diversity of intratrinitarian life, Hodge takes perichoresis to entail a single will and mind in the Triune God. Perichoresis leaves the tripersonality of God intact, yet he affirms that the *three* persons nonetheless have *one* mind."[16] The three divine persons, therefore, seem to have a kind of self-consciousness that is wholly *interdependent*.[17] In other words, while we can and must affirm that there is only one will in God, and thus one consciousness, we must be equally vigilant in affirming the interdependent self-consciousness of each divine person, such that the will of God remains unified.[18] So, there is a sense in which the Trinity is *both* a uni-conscious being *and* a tri-conscious being.[19] This, again,

---

15. Charles Hodge, *Systematic Theology* (Peabody, MA: Hendrickson, 2013), 1:461.

16. Lane G. Tipton, "The Function of Perichoresis and the Divine Incomprehensibility," *Westminster Theological Journal* 64 (2002): p. 292.

17. This is critical to maintain, since three *independent* centers of self-consciousness would represent the heresy of tritheism.

18. Tipton, "The Function of Perichoresis and the Divine Incomprehensibility," pp. 295, 305.

19. Cornelius Van Til, *Introduction to Systematic Theology: Prolegomena and the*

should not be surprising, since a divine speaker would have to be self-conscious in some sense. The Father must know that it is he, and not another, who is speaking to the Son (Matt. 3:17), and the Son must know that it is he, and not another, who is speaking to the Father (John 17). Likewise, the Spirit must know that it is he, not the Father or the Son, who is speaking to the disciples of Jesus (Luke 12:12; John 16:14). Speakers by nature are self-conscious; the very production of speech requires it. But the divine speakers are *dependently so*. In other words, when the Father is speaking to the Son, the Son and Spirit are indwelling the Father and thus have pure access to the Father's self-consciousness, such that the Father's self-consciousness is not exclusive of the other divine persons. When the Son speaks to the Father, the Father and the Spirit indwell him, and so they too have pure access to the Son's self-consciousness. The same goes for the Holy Spirit. That is to say, self-consciousness with the divine persons does not imply individualism (exclusivity), but it does imply individuation, what we might call an *individuation of openness*.[20] By this, I simply mean that the divine persons are distinct but are also self-consciously and exhaustively open to one another.

In this light, it is fascinating to see how Charles Hodge describes the divine persons *as speakers*, for it accords with what we have been discussing.

> The Scriptural facts are, (a.) The Father says I; the Son says I; and the Spirit says I. (b.) The Father says Thou to the Son, and the Son says Thou to the Father; and in like manner

---

Doctrines of Revelation, Scripture, and God, ed. William Edgar, 2nd ed. (Phillipsburg, NJ: P&R, 2007), p. 348.

20. Brown, "Trinitarian Personhood and Individuality," p. 49.

the Father and the Son use the pronouns He and Him in reference to the Spirit. (c.) The Father, Son, and Spirit are severally subject and object. They act and are acted upon, or are the objects of action. Nothing is added to these facts when it is said that the Father, Son, and Spirit are distinct persons; for a person is an intelligent subject who can say I, who can be addressed as Thou, and who can act and can be the object of action. The summation of the above facts is expressed in the proposition, The one divine Being subsists in three persons, Father, Son, and Spirit.[21]

Notice here that Hodge affirms the creedal language of three persons "subsisting in one essence," and yet he also offers evidence for the distinctiveness of persons according to their communicative abilities, to say "I" and refer to the other divine persons as "Thou" or "He."

Drawing together Tertullian and Hodge, we can begin by saying that a divine person is *one who speaks*, and this is perfectly consistent with the historical teaching that the divine persons are rational agents who share the one divine essence. However, this does not mean that the divine persons are three repetitions of one speaker, since each speaker is distinguished from the others by an incommunicable property (unbegottenness, begottenness, and spiration).[22] Thus, the Father is one who speaks as the eternally unbegotten, the Son is one who speaks as the eternally begotten, and the Spirit is one who speaks as the one eternally proceeding from the Father and the Son. That much must be kept in place.[23] The persons are

---

21. Hodge, *Systematic Theology*, 1:444.

22. Kelly, *The God Who Is: The Holy Trinity*, pp. 494–97.

23. In other words, this linguistic perspective on divine persons (speech) should flow from the distinctness of each person in terms of what we might

distinct speakers with distinct incommunicable properties, so our definition of divine persons must be nuanced: *a divine person is one who speaks bearing a divine incommunicable property*, a property which does not in any way threaten the essential unity of God.

While this definition does not in any way require the abandonment of traditional terminology, a linguistic perspective on divine persons does add a new dimension to trinitarian dialogue, for we must now relate this view of divine persons to the unity of God, as every orthodox theologian is enjoined to do. In the following section, we will see that God *in his unity* is also one who speaks, albeit in a different sense. This is problematic only if we are not willing to affirm the equal ultimacy of the oneness and threeness in God.[24]

As the next section will affirm, perhaps one of the greatest benefits of this definition for divine persons is that it is drawn directly from Scripture.[25] Let us now look to selected passages in Scripture that have given rise to this

---

call the divine *manner* of their speech. The Father speaks *as the unbegotten*. The Son speaks *as the eternally begotten*, and so forth. It is, admittedly, quite difficult to say what this means precisely. How does the Father speak in an unbegotten manner? We are reaching the boundary of our reasoning here. I would nevertheless claim that it is necessary to make this point in order to guard against modalism, which would suggest that the three persons do not have distinct voices and are merely varied instantiations of one voice.

24. This point was championed by Cornelius Van Til and frequently referenced throughout his corpus.

25. "The gospels assign speaking parts to each of the three divine persons." Kevin J. Vanhoozer, *Remythologizing Theology: Divine Action, Passion, and Authorship* (New York: Cambridge University Press, 2010), p. 246. The Father speaks (Matt. 3:17; 17:5; Mark 1:11); the Son speaks throughout the New Testament; and the Spirit speaks through believers (Matt. 10:20). The Son also hears (John 12:49–50), as does the Spirit (John 16:13).

definition, first noting that God in his unity is one who speaks.

The Speaking God of Scripture: One and Three

From the very outset of Scripture, God is identified through his speech and is marked as a unified speaker. It is clear that God's first actions with regards to creation are utterances and that humanity is first addressed by God himself.[26] This divine-human dialogue runs throughout the Old Testament and comes to striking manifestation in the New. The one speaking God from the Old Testament is more clearly revealed as the *three-in-one* speaking God with the coming of Christ and the Holy Spirit. The passages below highlight this progressive revelation. In what follows, I have been very selective. Much more could be said about each passage, and many other passages could be referenced. For the sake of brevity, I will focus only on the element of divine speech in each passage and how that speech serves to identify God for his people, first as one and then later as three.

---

26. I will not develop anything in this article with regards to speech-act theory. That work has been done by others, such as Nicholas Wolterstorff, *Divine Discourse: Philosophical Reflections on the Claim That God Speaks* (New York: Cambridge, 1995) and Kevin J. Vanhoozer, *Is There a Meaning in This Text? The Bible, the Reader, and the Morality of Literary Knowledge* (Grand Rapids, MI: Zondervan, 1998). In my opinion, speech-act theory is limited in its application to divine speech, and it tends to oversimplify communicative behavior. See Vern S. Poythress, "Canon and Speech Act: Limitations in Speech-Act Theory, with Implications for a Putative Theory of Canonical Speech Acts," *Westminster Theological Journal* 70 (2008): pp. 337–54.

Genesis 1–2

Creation is linguistic, grounded in divine speech. God brings the world into being with jussives: *let there be*. The inception of creation is thus marked from the outset by speech, and this speech comes from a unified being, signaled by the singular subject of the Hebrew verb form translated as "and God said." However, it is also well known that the writer uses the first-person plural with reference to God at the creation of Adam.[27] I still believe that the most natural reading of this usage, based on the rest of the canon, is as a foreshadowing of trinitarian revelation, i.e., that God is three persons who commune with one another. So, at the dawn of creation in general, we have one divine speaker.[28] As the psalmist writes, "By the word of the LORD the heavens were made, and by the breath of his mouth all their host" (Ps. 33:6).

---

27. Waltke outlines the six options we have for interpretation: (1) the plural is a remnant of ANE myth in which God is addressing other gods. This is untenable given that the Pentateuch opposes polytheism at every corner. (2) The plural is directed towards a host of previously made creatures (this still ends up relying on polytheistic tendencies that do not comport with the Genesis account). (3) The plural is honorific, like the form אֱלֹהִים, but Waltke notes that this form is elsewhere attested by nouns, not pronouns. (4) The plural is, in Gesenius' language, "a plural of *self-deliberation*," though no other instance supports this view. (5) The plural is a reference to the Trinity. This view would be supported by later NT texts, even though Waltke argues that this violates the boundaries of grammatico-historical interpretation. (6) The plural refers to the heavenly court that surrounds God's throne. See Bruce K. Waltke, *An Old Testament Theology: A Canonical and Thematic Approach* (Grand Rapids, MI: Zondervan, 2007), pp. 212–13.

28. I have elsewhere referred to this as the *consciousness model* of the Trinity: the Father speaking the Son (the eternal Word) in the power of the Holy Spirit. See Pierce Taylor Hibbs, "Language and the Trinity: A Meeting Place for the Global Church," in *Redeeming the Life of the Mind: Essays in Honor of Vern Poythress*, ed. John M. Frame, Wayne Grudem, and John J. Hughes (Wheaton, IL: Crossway, 2017), p. 190.

Yet, at the creation of man we are also introduced to a plurality of speakers capable of taking self-counsel, which aligns with later New Testament revelation.

God's creation is juxtaposed with Adam's first divine encounter, an encounter mediated through speech:

> And God blessed them. And God *said* to them, "Be fruitful and multiply and fill the earth and subdue it, and have dominion over the fish of the sea and over the birds of the heavens and over every living thing that moves on the earth." And God *said*, "Behold, I have given you every plant yielding seed that is on the face of all the earth, and every tree with seed in its fruit. You shall have them for food. And to every beast of the earth and to every bird of the heavens and to everything that creeps on the earth, everything that has the breath of life, I have given every green plant for food." And it was so. (Gen. 1:28–30; emphasis added)

Adam meets God through the latter's condescension in language.[29] It is God's speech that establishes a relationship with humanity and serves as a means by which his creatures come to know him and his commands.[30] In the primeval quietude of Adam's existence, divine-human dialogue enabled him to know his maker as the divine *speaker*. God was, for Adam, "he who speaketh; he who enthuses man so that man speaketh."[31] This is especially critical for Adam because for a time God was his only conversation

---

29. For a philosophical treatment of "Son-Condescension," see Nathan D. Shannon, "Son-Condescension and the Logic of Theology," *Neue Zeitschrift Für Systematische Theologie Und Religionsphilosophie* 59, no. 2 (2017): pp. 245–64.

30. God's establishing a relationship with Adam through speech is a manifestation of how the Father establishes and then redeems his relationship with humanity through the Word, the second person of the Trinity.

31. Rosenstock-Huessy, *The Origin of Speech*, p. 5.

partner. Adam's knowledge of God was bound up with his knowledge of himself as an imaging speaker.

Adam subsequently used his abilities as an imaging speaker to carry out the task of naming the animals, following God's command in Genesis 2:19–20, and then he speaks in deep gratitude for the gift of his wife (2:23), taken from his own body. From one speaker comes another speaker.

In Genesis 1–2, it is beyond debate that God is marked by his speech and then, in his relationship with creatures, is presented as the divine, authoritative speaker. God is, for Adam and Eve, one who speaks with divine authority. The serpent, of course, is also one who speaks, which perhaps makes him the craftiest creature in the garden (Gen. 3:1), but he does not speak with divine authority. Quite the opposite: he speaks with creaturely, rebellious authority, which is no authority at all. His speech is a counterfeit of truth, meant to deceive and destroy.[32]

The Patriarchs (Gen 12, 26, 28)

After the Fall, God continues to present himself and to be known by the patriarchs as the one who speaks. The calling of Abram begins with the same verb form that we encounter in the creation account.

> Now the LORD *said* to Abram, "Go from your country and your kindred and your father's house to the land that I will show you. And I will make of you a great nation, and I will bless you and make your name great, so that you will be a blessing. I will bless those who bless you, and him who

---

32. On Satan as a counterfeit, see Vern S. Poythress, *God-Centered Biblical Interpretation* (Phillipsburg, NJ: P&R, 1999), pp. 167–75.

dishonors you I will curse, and in you all the families of the earth shall be blessed." (Gen. 12:1–3; emphasis added)

Abram has communion with God through *speech*. Yahweh reveals himself verbally, making himself known as the one who speaks with divine wisdom, truth, and authority. Abram's subsequent action is then based on his trust in verbal communication with this divine speaker.

It is the same for Abram's promised offspring, Isaac. "And the Lord appeared to him and *said*, 'Do not go down to Egypt; dwell in the land of which I shall tell you. Sojourn in this land, and I will be with you and will bless you, for to you and to your offspring I will give all these lands, and I will establish *the oath that I swore* to Abraham your father'" (Gen. 26:2–3; emphasis added). Here, Yahweh not only directs Isaac through speech but also reminds him of the speech he delivered to his father. As was the case for Abraham, Isaac's action in heeding the speech of Yahweh is based on his trust in verbal communication from the divine speaker. Thus, Isaac acts in accordance with God's speech precisely because God has revealed himself verbally as the one who speaks with supernatural authority. Theologians often call attention to God's covenantal relationship in these passages, and that is certainly necessary, but we tend to overlook the significance of the fact that the covenant was mediated through speech, by a divine speaker.

The pattern with Abraham and Isaac holds true for Jacob in his vision of the great ladder stretching from earth to heaven. Yahweh stands above that ladder and once more presents himself through speech.

"I am the Lord, the God of Abraham your father and the God of Isaac. The land on which you lie I will give to you and to your offspring. Your offspring shall be like the dust of the earth, and you shall spread abroad to the west and to the east and to the north and to the south, and in you and your offspring shall all the families of the earth be blessed. Behold, I am with you and will keep you wherever you go, and will bring you back to this land. For I will not leave you until I have done what I have promised you." (Gen. 28:13–15)

These passages suggest what may seem to be obvious to us: for the patriarchs, God was presented through speech as the divine, covenant-making, authoritative speaker. God's repeated verbal revelation is what enables the patriarchs to have a personal relationship with him.[33]

Exodus 33:18–19

Later in the unfolding narrative of Israel, God has a very special encounter with Moses, the one with whom he had developed a longstanding relationship through speech (particularly Exod. 3:4–6; 5–11; 16:4–8; 19:1–9). After interceding for the people because of their heinous idolatry, Moses lays down a bold request. "Moses said, 'Please show me your glory.' And he said, 'I will make all my goodness pass before you and will proclaim before you my name "The LORD." And I will be gracious to whom I will be gracious, and will show mercy on whom I will show mercy'" (Exod. 33:18–19). Notice here the very same elements we have seen in the creation account and in God's encounters with the patriarchs: God is presented as the divine speaker

---

33. Note also that according to Romans 1 God's general revelation also establishes a relationship between mankind and God, for creation everywhere reveals him. This relationship, however, is one of covenantal condemnation, not personal communion.

bearing the highest authority. This is complemented by God's promise to proclaim not his power and greatness, but his *name*. Certainly, God reveals his power and greatness to Moses through this encounter, but God is not concerned that Moses *see* something. In fact, God plainly tells Moses that no man can see his face (Exod. 33:23). Rather, he is concerned that Moses *hear* something: his name, the unique marker of his divine speech.

God's revelation of his name is a profound act. Herman Bavinck writes, "A name is a sign of the person bearing it, a designation referring to some characteristic in which a person reveals himself or herself and becomes knowable."[34] God becomes *knowable* through his name, through his self-given, divinely authoritative verbal title. Once again, we see that God is revealed to his people through speech. He becomes knowable through his name, that is, through the verbal mark by which he is addressed and by which he reveals himself as divine speaker.

The Prophets: "Thus says the LORD"

Though the formula "Thus says the LORD" occurs early in Scripture, especially in the book of Exodus, it is most often associated with the prophets, those who were tasked with delivering the message of the divine speaker to a people hard of hearing.

One example should serve to illustrate the point I wish to make. In Jeremiah 23, the prophet is grieving over the moral corruption of the people. After promising to judge Judah and make Jerusalem a heap of ruins (9:11), God

---

34. Herman Bavinck, *Reformed Dogmatics*, vol. 2, *God and Creation*, ed. John Bolt, trans. John Vriend (Grand Rapids, MI: Baker Academic, 2004), p. 97.

delivers an exhortation through the mouth of the prophet: "Thus says the Lord: 'Let not the wise man boast in his wisdom, let not the mighty man boast in his might, let not the rich man boast in his riches, but let him who boasts boast in this, that he understands and knows me, that I am the Lord who practices steadfast love, justice, and righteousness in the earth. For in these things I delight, declares the Lord'" (9:23–24). The expression "Thus says the Lord" always serves to remind the reader of the source of the communication. The one who speaks is not the prophet himself but the divine, authoritative speaker, whom we met on the first page of Scripture. That divine, authoritative speaker is telling his people the only thing worth boasting about: understanding and knowing him. Recall that Bavinck declared that God is only *knowable* through his name. In other words, God is only knowable through verbal address, through dialogue—a dialogue initiated by God himself. The only thing that is worthy of a boast is the true testament to a verbal relationship with the divine speaker.

The passages we have noted above treat God in his unity as a divine speaker. But there are texts throughout the Old Testament that also indicate plurality in God.[35] In fact, later New Testament revelation compels us to conclude that the one divine speaker from the Old Testament is really the Father speaking through the Son in the power of the

---

35. Of course, as every Reformed theologian who has written on the Trinity points out, there are many Old Testament foreshadowings of the Trinity. See, for instance, Robert Letham, *The Holy Trinity: In Scripture, History, Theology, and Worship* (Phillipsburg, NJ: P&R, 2004), pp. 17–33. What is in the background for the Old Testament comes to the foreground in the New.

Holy Spirit.[36] The divine speaker of the Old Testament is, in his essence, triune. As Camden Bucey put it recently, "God is just as much essentially one as he is essentially three, and vice versa."[37] Theologians are often tempted to prioritize God's unity or his trinity, but both must be held as irreducibly fundamental. What we have in redemptive history is a panorama of God's self-revelation that shifts *emphases* as we move from the Old Testament to the New. God has always been and will always be essentially three-in-one, but the emphasis in the Old Testament is on God's unity while the emphasis in the New Testament is on God's trinity. That is where we turn next.

In the New Testament, the focus on the unity of the divine, authoritative speaker from the Old Testament is exchanged for a focus on trinitarian communication and agency that includes differentiation of persons. Of course, there are also a number of references in the New Testament that present God as one speaker, carrying on the usage of the Old Testament. But in the New Testament, this Old Testament usage is complemented by the equally important portrayal of God as three speakers.

Matthew: A Clear Distinction of Speakers

When we come to the Gospel of Matthew, we find in more

---

36. For an overview of how this applies to Genesis 1, see Vern S. Poythress, "God and Language," in *Did God Really Say? Affirming the Truthfulness and Trustworthiness of Scripture*, ed. David B. Garner (Phillipsburg, NJ: P&R, 2012).

37. Camden M. Bucey, "The Trinity and Monotheism: Christianity and Islam in the Theology of Cornelius Van Til," in *Redeeming the Life of the Mind: Essays in Honor of Vern Poythress*, ed. John M. Frame, Wayne Grudem, and John J. Hughes (Wheaton, IL: Crossway, 2017), p. 176.

explicit terms not one divine speaker, but three. This is a profound but organic development in God's self-revelation. In place of the many references to a singular divine speaker, we have a focus on the Father, the incarnate Son, and the Holy Spirit as distinct speakers. This is clear in passages such as Matthew 3:16–17, "And when Jesus was baptized, immediately he went up from the water, and behold, the heavens were opened to him, and he saw the Spirit of God descending like a dove and coming to rest on him; and behold, a voice from heaven said, 'This is my beloved Son, with whom I am well pleased.'"[38]

The incarnate Son is already obviously a speaker from the outset of Matthew's Gospel, but we might overlook the fact that the heavenly Father is carrying on discourse not just with the human nature of Christ, but with his *person*. The person of Christ includes both his human and divine natures, and it would be arbitrary to distinguish when God the Father is addressing Christ's human nature and when he is addressing his divine nature. Natures do not speak to each other; *persons* do. So, the discourse at Christ's baptism is not simply a discussion between God and the incarnate Son; it is not simply discourse from divine to human, as we might assume. Upon closer dogmatic inspection, it is also divine-divine discourse: the eternal Father speaking in history to the eternal Son. This makes perfects sense in light of the fact that in Matthew's Gospel (and in the others) "we find Jesus speaking of God as Father with unparalleled intimacy."[39] The unparalleled intimacy is rooted in the

---

38. Elsewhere in the Gospel of Matthew, especially with the "fulfillment formulas," God is referenced as one divine speaker.

39. Brandon D. Crowe, "The Trinity and the Gospel of Matthew," in *The Essential Trinity: New Testament Foundations and Practical Relevance*, ed. Brandon

eternal divine relationship between the Father and the Son. That relationship is not put on hold during the incarnation. The Holy Spirit, who descended from the heavens in the form of a dove as Jesus emerged from the Jordan River, is also marked as a divine speaker. In the very next chapter in Matthew, the Holy Spirit is said to have "led" Jesus into the wilderness. Our understanding of language is typically narrower than it should be.[40] Though lexically there is nothing here that says the Spirit speaks, conceptually it is difficult to conclude otherwise. The concept of leading requires some sense of communication between the Spirit and Jesus, and this conceptual affirmation of communication between the persons of the Son and Spirit is confirmed at the end of the Gospel, where, interestingly, baptism is the context once again. "Go therefore and make disciples of all nations, baptizing them in the name of the Father and of the Son and of the Holy Spirit" (28:19). The Holy Spirit is given a distinct name, and a distinct name implies a distinct speaker (just as earlier we saw that a distinct voice implies a distinct speaker). This assumption is validated in Luke's Gospel, where the Spirit is said to communicate with believers. "And when they bring you before the synagogues and the rulers and the authorities, do not be anxious about how you should defend yourself or what you should say, for the Holy Spirit will teach you in that very hour what you ought to say" (Luke 12:11–12). The Spirit, as teacher,

---

D. Crowe and Carl R. Trueman (London: Apollos, 2016), p. 26.

40. I have always followed Kenneth Pike's understanding of language as an "aspect of human behavior" that is structurally integrated with the rest of what we do as humans. See Kenneth L. Pike, *Language in Relation to a Unified Theory of the Structure of Human Behavior*, 2nd ed. (The Hague: Mouton, 1967); and *Linguistic Concepts: An Introduction to Tagmemics* (Lincoln, NE: University of Nebraska Press, 1982).

will communicate (i.e., "speak") to believers in a manner analogous to the way in which he communicated with the Son. The Spirit, then, is recognized with the Father and Son as a distinct divine speaker, one who holds the same supernatural authority in his speech.

John 16 and 17

In John 16, the writer opens with Jesus addressing the disciples, telling them about the persecution they will face from those who "have not known the Father" (16:3). Jesus then promises to send the Holy Spirit (16:7). We might pause here and recognize that only a distinct person can be known or acted upon. Bringing together what we earlier saw in Charles Hodge and later noted from Herman Bavinck, we can say that a speaker becomes *knowable* through his name, and can be addressed and acted upon by other communicative agents. In Vos' words, the three divine persons "assume objective relations toward each other, address each other, love each other, and can interact with each other."[41] That is what we see here. The Spirit is being distinctly recognized as a divine speaker who will be sent by the Son and will subsequently communicate with Jesus' disciples, convicting the world concerning sin, righteousness, and judgement (16:8–10).

A few verses later, we find out something else about the Spirit: "When the Spirit of truth comes, he will guide you into all the truth, for he will not speak on his own authority, but whatever he hears he will speak, and he will declare to you the things that are to come" (16:13). The Holy Spirit is

---

41. Geerhardus Vos, *Reformed Dogmatics*, vol. 1, *Theology Proper*, ed. and trans. Richard B. Gaffin, Jr. (Bellingham, WA: Lexham Press, 2014), p. 43.

both divine addressor and addressee.[42] The Spirit takes what he hears, presumably from the Father, and communicates it to the followers of Christ in an instance of what Köstenberger refers to as "trinitarian collaboration."[43] This both distinguishes the Spirit as divine speaker and reassures us that this distinction does not threaten the unity of God. As Carson puts it,

> Just as Jesus never spoke or acted on his own initiative, but said and did exactly what the Father gave him to say and do . . . so also the Spirit *speaks only what he hears*—a point elucidated in vv. 14–15. As Jesus' absolute but exhaustive obedience to his Father ensures that he is not to be taken as either a mere mortal or as a competing deity, but as the very revelation of God himself, so also the Spirit, by this utter dependence, ensures the unity of God and of the revelation God graciously grants.[44]

These verses from chapter 16, then, clearly mark the Holy Spirit as a divine speaker on par with the Father and the Son.

Chapter 17 then brings into focus the communication

---

42. This is to be understood in accordance with his title as *paraclētos*. "Whatever the precise meaning of *paraclētos*, it is undoubtedly a human personal image. Evidently, Jesus himself is a *paraclētos*, and the Spirit, in this role, another such (14:16). The Paraclete teaches, reminds, testifies, convicts, guides, speaks, declares (14:26; 15:26; 16:8, 13–15)." Richard Baukham, "The Trinity and the Gospel of John," in *The Essential Trinity: New Testament Foundations and Practical Relevance*, ed. Brandon D. Crowe and Carl R. Trueman (London: Apollos, 2016), pp. 104–05. Notice here the verbal elements of each of the actions Baukham lists.

43. Andreas J. Köstenberger, *A Theology of John's Gospel and Letters*, Biblical Theology of the New Testament (Grand Rapids, MI: Zondervan, 2009), p. 245.

44. D. A. Carson, *The Gospel According to John*, Pillar New Testament Commentary (Grand Rapids, MI: William B. Eerdmans, 1991), p. 540.

between the Father and the Son. In verse 5, we read that the Son has been glorified in eternity with the Father, before the world began.[45] Then in verse 8, we read that Christ has given his disciples "the words" of the Father. Carson writes, "Here *words* renders the Greek *rhēmata*, neither Jesus' teaching as a whole nor his itemized precepts, but his actual 'words' or 'utterances.'"[46] This again highlights both the Father and the incarnate Son as divine speakers who, as we saw earlier, enjoy a relationship of unparalleled intimacy.

Though the survey and treatment of New Testament texts above is embarrassingly brief, it nevertheless points out that each distinct person of the Godhead is presented as a divine speaker, and, what's more, a divine *hearer*. The Father hears the Son, the Son hears the Father, the Spirit hears the Father and the Son. This trinitarian communication is an important behavior that serves to carry forth the plan of salvation, the *pactum salutis*, which was forged by these same divine persons in eternity past.

Our survey of selected Old Testament and New Testament texts leads us to conclude that God's speech is both uni-personal and tri-personal. God speaks in his unity: the Father speaking the eternal Word in the power of the Spirit to both create and redeem. God also speaks in his trinity: the Father speaking to the Son and Spirit, the Son speaking to the Father, the Spirit hearing from the Father and Son and speaking to the followers of Christ. There is, in other words, equal ultimacy of unity and trinity in God in terms of speech. We cannot reduce God either to bare

---

45. I consider the eternal exchange of love and glory among the divine persons to be a kind of speech, though certainly in a sense that is very different from our common understandings of verbal behavior.

46. Carson, *The Gospel According to John*, p. 560.

unity or to bare trinity. God is the *three-in-one speaker*.

Defining a divine person as "one who speaks bearing a divine incommunicable attribute" thus accords with biblical revelation. As one speaker, God is the Father speaking through the Son in the power of the Spirit. As three speakers, the divine persons are Father, Son, and Spirit speaking and listening to one another in what we might term an *I-thou-he communion*. This communion is possible because of the eternal distinctness each person maintains by his divine incommunicable attribute.

Potential Objections

There are, of course, various objections one might raise to my definition of divine persons. Though I do not believe anything I can say in this article will preclude strong reactions of discontent, I will offer brief responses to three potential objections.

The definition is too broad and does not clearly distinguish the persons from the essence. Part of the appeal of traditional dogmatic language for divine persons (subsisting relation, mode of subsistence, etc.) is their *perceived* precision of meaning. (However, recall what we noted earlier about the nature of definitions.) This precision has served the church in combatting heresies of various stripes. However, the fine lines of a precise definition are not so fine under closer scrutiny. A cursory glance at the word "subsist" in the *Oxford English Dictionary* reveals that, semantically, the word does not even come close to the hairline specificity that some would like to claim for it. In other words, it is not the clear-cut semantic "particle" that theologians treat it as. At best, it seems to indicate something close to "exist," but that meaning is somewhat "fuzzy," for lack of a better term.

A similar issue can be raised with the word "subsistence." These words, like all words, have a core meaning that is generally understood (particle), but they also have fuzzy semantic boundaries in their continued usage (wave) and a network of associative relationships with other words throughout history (field), each of which colors their meaning.[47] This is not a threat to their value or semantic stability, but merely accents the truth that we cannot be masters of language in any God-like sense. We should instead focus on how definitions can be useful to us in our relationship with God and with others. Given that fact, if "one who speaks bearing a divine incommunicable property" is too broad, the same critique might be turned against nearly every other definition of divine personhood. All definitions in human language simply cannot have a scientific precision that perfectly parallels God's exhaustive knowledge of himself and the world that he has made. There is mystery in definitions, just as there is mystery in God. No amount of analytical rigor will alter that fundamental biblical affirmation, for it is, in essence, an affirmation of the Creator-creature distinction.

I am sure, of course, that some theologians hold fast to the alleged clarity in distinction between *person* and *essence* that the older dogmatic views of divine personhood seem to suggest. But here I bring up once more the fact that "Scripture itself does not use technical terms for God's oneness and threeness, and . . . it is not always concerned with terminological precision in describing the relations of

---

47. I am here following Kenneth Pike's triad of particle, wave, and field perspectives on lexical semantics.

the three persons."⁴⁸ In light of this, we should be wary of those who cling to the language of historical theology, and even to the language of the creeds themselves, with a penchant to treat them as supremely authoritative or inerrant. Creedal language is very important in articulating what Scripture teaches and has served a high purpose of unifying the church around a core of articulated beliefs. But creedal language must not be treated on the same level of the authoritative hierarchy as Scripture. There is only one inerrant, supremely authoritative book, and the creeds were written to serve the truth of that book, not to be taken as theological perfections. This is not meant to perpetuate the "no creed but the Bible" mentality. We all have a creed of one kind or another, and the historic creeds are vitally important to the church and our theological heritage.⁴⁹ Nevertheless, we cannot *equate* the creeds with Scripture in terms of their authority. In this article, I have tried to account for the distinction between unity and plurality in God by noting the way in which the Trinity can be viewed as one speaker and as three speakers in distinct senses, thus preserving the relationship between unity and plurality that the language of historical theology also aims to preserve. But even beyond all this, we must continue to affirm that our creatureliness precludes our exhaustive understanding of *all* language. Any claim to have a perfectly precise, exhaustive understanding of language is a claim to be God.

The definition cannot adequately be related to the orthodox system of trinitarian dogma. It might be argued that the perspective I have offered on divine persons causes problems for other

---

48. Frame, *Systematic Theology*, p. 481.

49. See Carl R. Trueman, *The Creedal Imperative* (Wheaton, IL: Crossway, 2012).

areas of trinitarian dogma. If we perceive the divine persons as speakers, do we not run the risk of tritheism, at worst, or embrace social trinitarianism, at best? We then face a host of dogmatic dilemmas dealing with the will of God, his real and essential unity, and even the redemptive work of the Son and Spirit on behalf of the Father. Understanding a divine person as "one who speaks bearing an incommunicable property" seems to avoid these problems. I have tried in this article to explain how the divine persons are dependently self-conscious agents who share the same divine essence. As such, the divine will is one, and yet the three persons distinctly serve that one will. They are distinguished from one another not essentially, but by an incommunicable property. This guards against the critique that a linguistic perspective on divine persons threatens the essential unity of God. It also assures that the there is no warring of wills in the Godhead, since the persons share the same will. There is nothing that the Father wills that the Son and the Spirit do not also will. In sum, this definition does not pose any significant problems to our orthodox theological system of trinitarian dogma. Instead, it provides another way of understanding divine persons, one that accords with what is taught in Scripture and helps us discern how we might better commune with the triune God, which I will touch on in the conclusion.

The definition does not guard against univocity in understanding the term "person" as applied to God and man. Theologians are rightly circumspect when using language in reference to God and to man. Words and concepts do not apply to God in the same way that they apply to man, and yet there is correspondence on some level. If a divine person is one who speaks bearing a divine incommunicable property, then a human person is one who speaks bearing a created incommunicable property. Now, let me explain this a bit. Each human person is unique. That is what I mean when I say that we each have some "incommunicable property." I will forever be distinct from my brother, my wife, my pastor, my colleagues, and so on. Where does that inviolable personal distinction come from? It must come from God or else there would be no grounds for it. We do not have the personal properties that belong to the divine persons (unbegottenness, begottenness, and spiration), for they are *divine* and share the same essence. Yet, we find an analogous distinctness in human persons as creatures who communicate in a manner all their own. Each human person speaks distinctly from that God-given identity that only he or she bears. The analogy between human persons and divine persons, as I have argued, comes to glorious manifestation in the concept of speech.

Conclusion

Recall from earlier in the article how the nature of definitions (from a particle/wave/field perspective) pushes us to see our limitations as finite creatures. Rather than trying to master definitions with utter precision (which is something only God can do anyway), we should instead focus on how we can *use* our limited grasp of definitions to grow closer to God and better conform to the image of Christ. A linguistic perspective on divine persons helps us to do that. It tells us simultaneously how God is three *persons* and how we are finite *persons*. God is three persons as three speakers, each bearing a divine incommunicable property. We are persons as created speakers, each bearing a unique created identity that is given voice through our use of language.

Thus, we are brought to see *speech* as a fundamental means of communing with God (through prayer) and with other people, who are made in God's speaking image. We can readily *use* a linguistic perspective on divine personhood in our relationships, both with God and with others.

This approach to defining divine persons, in my opinion, avoids the problem of univocity, since we are not positing the same thing about God as we are about man. God is the three-in-one speaker with divine, supernatural authority. God's eternal language with himself is, surely, on a different plane than that of human language. Yet, God is essentially one who speaks, one who holds discourse with himself. And so humans, as image bearers, are those who hold discourse with God. We are human persons as we receive and interpret communication from the Trinity, both in general and special revelation. As Carl Trueman once put it, "To be human is to be one who is addressed by God."[50]

Let us return to the questions posed at the outset: (1) Has our understanding of divine persons adequately accounted for the way in which God is portrayed in Scripture as the three-in-one divine speaker? (2) Does the language we currently employ in our definitions of divine persons help us to better worship and commune with the Trinity? Defining a divine person as "one who speaks bearing a divine incommunicable property" answers the first question.

The second question can be answered quite readily, for we use *speech* to worship and commune with God through

---

50. Trueman, p. 62.

prayer.[51] If we approach the divine persons as speakers, and the entire Godhead as a speaker in a different sense, then we are in a perfect place to communicate with the God of Scripture. That is no small thing. Communing with God is the end of the Christian life. If we can biblically define divine persons in a way that helps us to worship and communicate with God more effectively, why not make the attempt to do so? This article serves as my attempt.

---

51. Carl R. Trueman, "The Trinity and Prayer," in *The Essential Trinity: New Testament Foundations and Practical Relevance*, ed. Brandon D. Crowe and Carl R. Trueman (London: Apollos, 2016), pp. 199–214.

What's in a Word? The Trinity

Literature has a way of drawing out our curiosity. In the second scene of *Romeo and Juliet*, Shakespeare had his leading lady ask a now famous question: "What's in a name?" Juliet was no philosopher of language; she only posed the question because family reputations were getting in the way of romance. Still, the question has drawn attention over the years in linguistics, particularly signification, and for good reasons. Names can seem purely conventional, and yet they are deeply meaningful in their sundry contexts.

We might expand Juliet's question to "What's in a word?" Theologians, I argue, should be especially fascinated by this, for the answer goes back to the very nature of God. That is what I aim to show in this article.

Now, let me start by saying that the question, "What's in a word?" is not the same as "What *is* a word?" Many philosophers of language have spent years developing an answer to the latter. Entailed in that question is a word's *meaning*. In the twentieth century, Wittgenstein (in his later work) suggested that "the meaning of a word is its use in the language."[1] For Saussure, "the meaning of a term is defined by its position in the system of language of which it is a part."[2] A word, for most structural linguists, was a

---

1. Ludwig Wittgenstein, *Philosophical Investigations*, trans. G.E.M. Anscombe, 4th ed. (Malden, MA: Wiley-Blackwell, 2009), p. 25.

2. John M. Frame, *A History of Western Philosophy and Theology* (Phillipsburg, NJ: P&R Publishing, 2015), p. 501.

signifier arbitrarily tied to that which it signified. For poststructualists and deconstructionists, a word was a sign that could only refer to other signs, making a labyrinth of signification.[3]

"What's *in* a word?" is a more mysterious question. It moves beyond discussions of signification to address what (in fact, *who*) makes a word *work*. What is the raw communicative "stuff," for lack of a better term, that gives words semantic value in a societal context? What makes it possible for them to reference the world, to strike an audience, to be effective in communication from person to person? My answer to these questions is as terse as it is tantalizing: the Trinity. The Trinity is *in* every word of human language, upholding it, governing it, allowing it to function in all of the contexts that God himself has ordained for it.[4]

The Divine Roots of Language: A Speaking God

To establish this answer, we must begin by understanding something of the nature of God himself. Eugen Rosenstock-Huessy once wrote that the name "God" means "he who

---

3. For a critique of this movement, see Kevin J. Vanhoozer, "A Lamp in the Labyrinth: The Hermeneutics of 'Aesthetic' Theology," *Trinity Journal* 8 (1987): pp. 25–56. See also Kevin J. Vanhoozer, *Is There a Meaning in This Text? The Bible, the Reader, and the Morality of Literary Knowledge* (Grand Rapids, MI: Zondervan, 1998), but compare Vanhoozer's approach to that of Vern S. Poythress, *In the Beginning Was the Word: Language—A God-Centered Approach* (Wheaton, IL: Crossway, 2009), p. 376, who notes that "the Father is like the Signified, the Spirit is like the Signifier, and the Son is the Word, in whom Signified and Signifier are eternally united and mutually indwelling."

4. This article expands on a discussion in a previous work, "Closing the Gaps: Perichoresis and the Nature of Language," *Westminster Theological Journal* 78, no. 2 (Fall 2016): pp. 315–17.

speaketh; he who enthuses man so that man speaketh."[5] This definition of God might seem too broad or simplistic, but I believe it is biblically informed. The very first thing we learn about God in Scripture is that he creates through *speech* (Gen. 1:1).

Theologians past and present have noted that this communicative nature of God is one of his most striking traits. Douglas Kelly remarks, "The true God is not silent; He talks."[6] Reflecting on Augustine's work, Lewis Ayres writes, "From eternity God speaks his Word, the Word in whom he determines all that will be."[7] John M. Frame has even advocated that we treat speech as an essential attribute of God, and I would concur.[8] God *is* one who speaks—both to himself in three persons (in a holy language that goes beyond human comprehension) and to his creatures. We can conclude with Kevin Vanhoozer: "Christian orthodoxy believes that God is essentially the one who communicates himself to others in Trinitarian fashion."[9]

This means that the roots of language, what I have elsewhere called *communion behavior*, are in God, not in

---

5. Eugen Rosenstock-Huessy, *The Origin of Speech* (Norwich, VT: Argo Books, 1981), 5.

6. Douglas Kelly, *Systematic Theology: Grounded in Holy Scripture and Understood in Light of the Church*, vol. 1, *The God Who Is: The Holy Trinity* (Ross-shire, Scotland: Mentor, 2008), 487.

7. Lewis Ayres, "Augustine on the Trinity," in *The Oxford Handbook of the Trinity*, ed. Gilles Emery and Matthew Levering (New York: Oxford University Press, 2011), 123.

8. John Frame, *Systematic Theology: An Introduction to Christian Belief* (Phillipsburg, NJ: P&R Publishing, 2013), 519–24.

9. Vanhoozer, *Is There a Meaning in This Text?*, 161.

man.[10] God speaks because he is "one who speaketh." That is his nature. We speak because we have been spoken to; we address others because we have been addressed by God himself and have been created in his speaking image.[11]

I often encounter the objection that God's "language" cannot be compared to human language. Can we even call intratrinitarian discourse "language" in any recognizable sense? Is not God's eternal discourse on a different plain than human discourse? I can sympathize with the sentiment and concerns of such questions. The problem is that we unnecessarily restrict our definitions for terms when the expansion of those definitions is warranted by Scripture and serves a worthwhile end. In Scripture, we encounter references to divine personal interaction among Father, Son, and Holy Spirit. This is not only alluded to in passages such as 1 John 4:8, "God is love," but is also directly communicated in John 17:5, which draws our attention to an eternal glory that the Son received from the Father *before the world began*. The Father, Son, and Spirit have eternally exchanged expressions of love and glory with one another. Because of the clear correspondence to human language, which is often used to express love and honor (the latter being a derivative of glory), why should we not see intratrinitarian discourse as a kind of language? The fact that we cannot say much about this divine language should not dissuade us from understanding it *as* language,

---

10. "Closing the Gaps," 303; "Words for Communion," *Modern Reformation* 25, no. 4 (August 2016): 5–8.

11. Rosenstock-Huessy is helpful here in reminding us that imperatives lie at the ancient heart of language. As he puts it, we are *vocatives* before we are *nominatives*. We are addressed as *thou* before we can address others as *I*. See Rosenstock-Huessy, *The Origin of Speech*, pp. 51–54, 90, 100–101, 112–113.

for when we do, we have a revealed foundation upon which to build our knowledge and use of human language.

In this article, I begin by noting the relationship between Genesis 1 and John 1:1, drawing some conclusions about language as part of the *imago Dei* before looking specifically at how every word of human language images the Trinity via two triads: classification/instantiation/association, and grammar/phonology/reference.[12] Thus, I aim to draw on Kenneth Pike's language theory and its theological application by one of his former students, Vern Poythress, to show how each of these triads mentioned above is rooted in the Trinity. Thus, every word is revelational of and dependent on the persons of the Godhead and their coinherence. The Trinity, in this sense, is *in* every word a creature can utter.

Genesis 1 and John 1:1

Let us begin by reminding ourselves of the relationship between John 1:1 and Genesis 1.

"In the beginning was the Word" (John 1:1). Readers would be hard-pressed to miss the contextual parallel here with Genesis 1. This parallel strongly suggests an analogous relationship between this Word and the words God spoke at creation.[13] John 1:1, by alluding to the Genesis account, "indicates that God's own Trinitarian nature lies behind

---

12. I am leaving out a discussion here of the particle, wave, and field observer perspectives, which Kenneth Pike developed early on in his language theory. See Kenneth L. Pike, *Linguistic Concepts: An Introduction to Tagmemics* (Lincoln, NE: University of Nebraska Press, 1982), pp. 19–38.

13. Vern S. Poythress, "Reforming Ontology and Logic in Light of the Trinity: an Application of Van Til's Idea of Analogy," *Westminster Theological Journal* 57 (1995): p. 188.

the particular words that he spoke, both words to create the world and words addressed to human beings." So, as we have said, "Language runs deep. It is deeper and older than humanity. God spoke even before there were any human beings."[14]

There is, in other words, a binding relationship between the eternal Word of the Trinity and the temporal words spoken at creation:

> John points out an analogy between the one eternal Word on the one hand and, on the other, the many particular words, that is, creational words, that God spoke according to Genesis 1. The many particular words rest ultimately on the involvement of the eternal Word in God's acts of creating the world. . . . The eternal Word is the archetype, the original speech of God. The words God spoke to create are derivative, but still in harmony with this eternal Word, who was active in creation.[15]

Human language *follows after* God's use of language in creation. And, since all meaning and coherence resides in the Godhead, it follows that if human language is to be meaningful and coherent, it must be an analogue of divine communicative behavior. Certainly, this human analogue will be bound within the confines of creaturehood. Yet, God himself ordained these confines, so he is free to work through and within them. That is precisely what he does in revealing himself.

Kenneth L. Pike (1912–2000) developed a Trinitarian language theory that we can rely on to help to explain this.

---

14. Vern. S. Poythress, "God and Language," in *Did God Really Say? Affirming the Truthfulness and Trustworthiness of Scripture*, ed. David B. Garner (Phillipsburg, NJ: P&R Publishing, 2012), p. 95.

15. Poythress, "God and Language," pp. 95–96.

To begin, we might say that God dwells in his own "emic community," i.e., a self-referential 'insider' community—in this case, a heavenly one.[16] Yet, God chose to create human emic communities in such a way that there could be correspondence between his own eternal emic community and those of his creatures, just as there is correspondence between the eternal Word, the words God uttered at creation, and human words uttered thereafter.[17] Based on the archetype of his own emic community, his own divine cultural structure,

> God chose to reveal Himself within a particular culture, through a particular culture, by means of events occurring in that particular culture. He made His message concrete by incarnating it in an emic structure, rather than by a series of lectures delivered by messengers aloof from and not a part of the revealing cultural medium.
> .... The problems of imparting a message across an emic barrier lying between heaven's communication system—whatever that may be—and man's verbal system involved the restructuring of the initial message into the target emic system. The message restructured into human speech had

---

16. An emic community might be thought of as 'monocultural' because it only perceives internal relations of a person or culture. Pike, "A Stereoscopic Window on the World," *Bibliotheca Sacra* 114, no. 154 (April 1957): p. 145. God's emic community must be understood as qualitatively different from human emic communities, since the divine persons share one essence and since God created and exhaustively knows all other finite emic communities among humanity.

17. "As part of the result of man's being created in the image of God, the communication system of God and that of man are not disjoint. The implication here is that by creation God has made man's language sufficiently like his own internal communication system, whatever that may be, that man's is a pale reflection of his own and allows talk across the barrier in both directions." Pike, "The Linguist and Axioms Concerning the Language of Scripture," *Journal of the American Scientific Affiliation* 26, no. 2 (June 1974): p. 48.

to be cast into the molding limits of noun, verb, lexicon, and sentence structures—in short, into a Hebrew-Greek structural grid—while retaining its conceptual integrity and the faithfulness of its intended impact.[18]

Pike is here calling our attention to the analogous, corresponding relationship between God's communicative behavior (i.e., language) and that of humanity. God, as Lord of all emic communities, chose to take the emic message of revelation and particularize it for his creation, initially in language, and then consummately in the flesh and bone manifestation of his own Son, who, as the eternal Word, was always the grounds for linguistic revelation in the first place.

There is still no doubt, for Pike, that God's own divine communication and that of man are literally worlds apart, but the distance has been bridged by God's own decision to create us *in his image*. That means that all human communication is through and through reflective of and tied to this image. We were created *by the Word* in God's image—the image of the ultimate communicative being. If "in the beginning was the Word," and it was through this Word that God created all things, then that Word would be unintelligible to us were we not made with a communicative capacity that corresponded in some way to that which exists in God himself.

At this point, we can link the *imago Dei* to the linguistic metaphor that we have been discussing from John 1:1, "In the beginning was the Word." Why, Pike asks, would Scripture contain such a metaphor?

Because there, perhaps, above all else directly accessible

---

18. Pike, "A Stereoscopic Window," pp. 152–153, 154.

to science, we can study one characteristic in which we are in the image of God—we can *talk*. And in the beginning was *the One who could talk!* Not just a set of rays of energy ready for a big bang; not a pantheistic sum of non-focused non-personal elements; not a vague spirit of impersonal goodness; but the Personal-One-with-Language.[19]

John's linguistic metaphor illuminates an important facet, perhaps the core, of the *imago Dei*. We speak not simply because we were spoken *to*, but because we were spoken *through* the Word of the speaking God.[20] But here is where we need to make an important clarification. "In the beginning was the Word" requires not that we tie all human words solely to the original Word, but that we tie all words to the divine, emic community that produced them. That is, we must tie all particular human words to the Trinity. This is what I call *Trinitarian particularism*. It is this concept that I believe can help us understand how each word in human language reflects the Trinity.

---

19. Pike, "Morals and Metaphor," *Interchange* 12 (1972): p. 231.

20. "With regard to God's speech . . . the real question is not 'How can God speak (since he does not have a body?)' but 'How can *we* speak?' The answer to this is: We are made in the image of a God who speaks. . . . The biblical narrative presents human language not precisely as a gift created by God for Adam but as a powerful attribute that is (1) intrinsic to God's own being and activity, (2) clear evidence of the fact that Adam and Eve were distinctive creatures made in God's image, and (3) inseparable from the mandate to Adam and Eve to rule creation." Moisés Silva, *God, Language and Scripture: Reading the Bible in the Light of General Linguistics*, in *Foundations of Contemporary Interpretation: Six Volumes in One*, ed. Moisés Silva (Grand Rapids, MI: Zondervan, 1996), pp. 206, 208.

Trinitarian Particularism: Classification, Instantiation, and Association

Before getting to the terminology of Pike and Poythress concerning the former's language theory and how it is rooted in the Trinity, we must remind ourselves that the Trinity is a fellowship. Meaning and cogency rest in divine community, not isolation. Functionally restricting meaning and cogency to the second person of the Trinity (the Word) would ignore the linguistic implications of the Trinity being a divine, self-communicating being who, in creation and redemption, extended a gracious hand to mankind so that he might join that holy company as an imaging servant. It is not the Word that breaks into language to lend it truth and meaning; it is the entire Trinity that supports and engages with human language at every moment in history. The triune God certainly does bring special meaning and power to language through the person of Christ, but he also did so before the Son became incarnate and after the incarnate Son ascended. The Trinity as divine emic community, then, is the bedrock of human communication.[21]

In light of this, when we consider human language, we must account for the doctrine of *perichoresis* or *circumcessio*, namely, "the mutual indwelling of the persons: the Father in the Son and the Son in him (John 10:38; 14:10–11, 20;

---

21. I hope readers would understand that "community" here must be understood distinctly from any ordinary "human" sense. God is not a community of three separate substances, but a community of three self-conscious but dependent persons in one substance. "Community" as applied to God takes on a new meaning that can and must transcend human understanding. Once we claim to understand precisely what "community" means with regards to the Godhead, we have allowed rationalism to slither into our theological epistemology.

17:21), both in the Spirit and the Spirit in both (Rom. 8:9). To see Jesus is to see the Father (John 14:9), for he and the Father are one (10:30). . . . All three persons are involved in all the works of God in and for creation."[22] All three persons are also involved in God's work of redemption. Christ says, "I and the Father are one" (John 10:30); Christ is "the truth" (John 14:6), but he leaves for his followers "the Spirit of truth" (John 14:17). In light of this mysterious and ultimately incomprehensible relationship, while we certainly note the distinction of the persons in the Godhead and the work associated with each one, we cannot ever wholly divorce the sufficiency and work of one person from that of the other two.[23] Augustine championed this doctrine some fifteen hundred years ago.

> Whether we hear then "Show us the Son," or whether we hear "Show us the Father," it comes to the same thing, because neither can be shown without the other. They are indeed one, as he tells us, *I and the Father are one* (John 10:30). . . . Nor is the Spirit of each separable from this unity, . . . the Holy Spirit which is given the proper name of *the Spirit of truth, which this world cannot receive* (John 14:17). For the fullness of our happiness beyond which there is none else, is this: to enjoy God the three in whose image we were made. That is why [Scripture] sometimes speaks of the Holy Spirit as if he would suffice by himself for our bliss, and he does suffice

---

22. Frame, *Systematic Theology*, pp. 477–78.

23. With regards to our knowledge of the Trinitarian persons, "each of the persons bears the whole divine nature, with all the divine attributes. Each is *in* each of the others. So you cannot fully know the Son without knowing the Father and Spirit, and so on. Although the three persons are distinct, our knowledge of each involves knowledge of the others, so that for us knowledge of the Father coincides with knowledge of the Son and Spirit." John M. Frame, *Selected Shorter Writings* (Phillipsburg, NJ: P&R Publishing, 2014), 1:10.

by himself, for the good reason that he cannot be separated from the Father and the Son—just as the Father suffices by himself because he cannot be separated from the Son and the Holy Spirit, and the Son suffices by himself because he cannot be separated from the Father and the Holy Spirit.[24]

We cannot divorce the Word from the Father who speaks it and the Spirit whose breath upholds it. The Word does not exist in a vacuum; it *was spoken*, which, in the divine linguistic community, requires an articulator (the Father), a matter articulated (the Son), and the breath necessary to carry the articulated matter to a destination (the Spirit).

This truth leads to three initial observations, each of which is tied to Kenneth Pike's language theory as it found new expression in the work of Vern S. Poythress.[25] First, the Speaker of the Word is the self-identified Father, who always reveals himself as Speaker in the biblical witness. Especially in the Old Testament, God identifies himself before and after delivering a command or statement (Gen. 15:7; 28:13; Exod. 6:2; Lev. 18:2ff.; and many others). So, the Father is clearly *classified* as God.[26]

---

24. Augustine, *De Trinitate* 1.17–18.

25. Poythress's book *In the Beginning Was the Word* and related articles draw heavily on the language theory of Kenneth Pike.

26. Poythress, "Reforming Ontology and Logic," p. 192. This term represents Pike's concept of *contrast*. See Pike, *Linguistic Concepts*, pp. 42–51.

Poythress uses the terminology of aspect to refer to the *classification, instantiation*, and *association* of God—all of which are ultimately incomprehensible. "The classificational aspect is an expression of God's distinctiveness as God, and of the distinctive work of the Father, which is incomprehensible. The instantiational aspect is an expression of the plurality of Persons in the Godhead and of the unique work of the Son in the incarnation, which is incomprehensible. The associational aspect is an expression of the mutual indwelling and coinherence of the Persons of the Trinity, and of the unique

Second, the Word is the *instantiation* of the Father—the concrete manifestation or *variant* of God's essence, not only eternally but also in time and space.[27] Thus, the Word come in the flesh says to his disciples, "Whoever has seen me has seen the Father" (John 14:9). The Father cannot be seen, or else death would come to those who saw him (Exod. 33:20). Yet, the Son can and has been seen. The Son is the concrete *instantiation* of God.[28]

Third, the Spirit that carries the Word is the Spirit of both the Father and the Son, binding them in *association*. The Father works by the Son—who himself was born by the Spirit (Matt. 1:18)—and through the Spirit in us (Rom. 8:9–11). He is the Spirit of both the Father (Gen. 1:1–2; 41:38; Exod. 31:3; 1 Sam. 11:6; Isa. 61:1) and the Son (1 Pet. 1:11). The Spirit is not only involved in creation (Job 33:4), but in recreation (1 Cor. 15:45). In short, he *associates* the Father and the Son, the Speaker and the Word, in unbroken fellowship.[29]

Perichoresis demands we recognize that none of these persons—Father, Son, or Spirit—exists in isolation from the other two, and each shares qualities with the others.[30]

---

work of the Holy Spirit, which is incomprehensible. The relation among the three aspects is incomprehensible, since it analogically represents the relation among the Persons of the Trinity." Poythress, "Reforming Ontology and Logic," p. 193.

27. Poythress's use of *instantiation* represents Pike's *variation*. See Ibid., pp. 52–59.

28. Poythress, "Reforming Ontology and Logic," p. 191.

29. Poythress, "Reforming Ontology and Logic," pp. 190–191.

30. Frame adds that the concept of *perspective*, when applied carefully, can be helpful here. He notes that though we might be tempted to think of each of the persons of the Godhead as *mere* "perspectives," that would be mis-

The Father, Son, and Spirit are all *classified* as God—each is wholly divine. Each is also a particularization of God, or, in the language of orthodoxy, a person of the Godhead. That is to say, each is a unique *instantiation* of the one divine being. Lastly, each person intimately *associates* with the other two. So, the Speaker, Speech, and Breath of the Trinity cannot be wrested from their relationships with one another.

This profound truth is reflected in every particular word of human language.[31] Consider the sentence, "There is a stone on the driveway." The "there is" structure in English is used to introduce a delayed subject, so we can rewrite the sentence as, "A stone is on the driveway." Each of these words has elements of classification, instantiation, and association.

First, each word can be classified grammatically according to its part of speech and function in the sentence. "A" is classified as an indefinite article, used to introduce one of a set of count nouns, which is the classification for "stone." The verb "is" would be classified as a linking verb, relating the subject and predicate. "On" is classified as a preposition, often used to relate two nouns. "The" is classified as a definite article, here suggesting that the reader or listener knows which driveway is being referenced. Lastly,

---

leading and trend toward Sabellianism. We can say, however, that "if the three persons are not *mere* perspectives on the Godhead, they nevertheless *are* perspectives. They are more than perspectives, but not less. For as I have indicated, each of the three persons bears the whole divine nature, with all the divine attributes. Each is in each of the others." Frame, "A Primer on Perspectivalism," frame-poythress.org, accessed September 30, 2014, http://www.frame-poythress.org/a-primer-on-perspectivalism/.

31. Though I use the English language in my examples, this theory would apply to all languages. Kenneth Pike worked with many languages throughout his lifetime, as did his students. His theory thus found application not just in Indo-European dialects but in many languages across the globe.

"driveway" is another member of a set of count nouns. So, each word in a sentence has a classification—an identity that contrasts it with the linguistic units of other groups (in this case, other parts of speech). This is analogous to the way in which the Father is classified as God throughout Scripture. Even Jesus makes this classification apparent when he speaks of the Father.[32]

Each of the words in the sentence is also an instantiation, a unique variant or occurrence of that form. This is especially clear in speech. Each time this sentence is spoken, we encounter a unique instantiation of each word. The speed at which one person's vocal chords vibrate differs from that of his neighbor; the pitch or intonation used in pronunciation will vary ever so slightly, and even the longevity of each articulated sound will not be precisely identical from one speaker to another. In fact, even for the same speaker there is nuance and variety. I never say my name precisely the same way twice. Recording equipment would pick up differences in consonant and vowel sounds, intonation, and so on. These instantiations of the words we speak do not mean that the words we speak are *essentially* different. Rather, they are essentially identical but nevertheless unique manifestations. This is analogous to the way in which the Son is essentially one with the Father but personally distinct from him and from the Spirit. The Son is a unique manifestation of the divine essence, the perfect image of the Father.

Lastly, each of the words in the sentence is bound up with associations to other words and to other real-world

---

32. See, for example, Mark 10:18; John 4:34; 6:38; 5:19–20. In these verses, Jesus makes a clear distinction between himself and the Father, though this distinction does not necessitate that he and the Father are not essentially one. He would affirm the latter in other places such as John 10:30.

referents. "A" is a singular, but it is bound up associatively with plural nouns, which contrast with it. We know singularity in relationship to plurality. "Stone" is intelligible to us by its relationship to other similar but different sounds. When we hear the long "o" vowel, we know that this word is not the same as "stain" or "stun." The real-world referent for this noun is also understood associatively. We know what a stone is only in relation to other parts of the physical world. It has a relationship in density to other elements such as sand or water; its feature of hardness places it in relationship to other hard objects such as metal or wood. The same can be worked out for the linking verb "is." In terms of semantics, we understand this word in relation to other verbs that could go with this subject, such as "appears to be," "seems to be," or "lies." All of these words also have grammatical associations—groups of similar words with which they fit or in relation to which they become intelligible. These webs of associations in sound, reference, and grammar are analogous to the associative relationship that the Spirit eternally maintains with the Father and the Son. In the Spirit, the Father and Son are eternally associated with one another.

Perichoresis also comes into play here, since each of the words in the sentence we examined has a classification, instantiation, and association simultaneously. Yet, these three features do not constitute three separate linguistic units. There is *one* linguistic unit, but three ways in which the unit can be viewed and analyzed. This is analogous to the way in which God is one being in three persons. Of course, the analogy breaks down at a certain point, which it must, since no earthly image of the Trinity can adequately represent the fullness of God. But the analogy, as far as it goes, is quite striking. If we look closely enough, we can see the classification, instantiation, and associations of every word in human language. Because these features are rooted in the Trinity, there is a sense in which we can see the Father, Son, and Spirit upholding every word of human language. This is the first sense in which we can say that the Trinity is *in* every word.

Trinitarian Particularism: Grammar, Phonology, and Reference

The second sense in which we can say that the Trinity is in every word has to do with three hierarchies in language: grammar, phonology, and reference. We hinted at these in the previous section. There is a sort of perichoretic relationship among the grammatical, phonological, and referential hierarchies of any given language.[33] These hierarchies are also rooted in the persons of the Godhead.

Grammar is notoriously difficult to define. At the least, we can say that grammar is a complex system of rules by which words can be combined with other words to form

---

33. Pike, *Linguistic Concepts*, pp. 13–15. "We would insist upon the interlocking of the hierarchies, with 'certain points or regions at which some of the units of the hierarchy *are* coterminous, or co-nuclear, in order for the units of the various hierarchies to be relevant to one another,' and that we therefore deny any totally-separate view of three hierarchies. We leave them only sufficiently independent to have identities of their own within the interlocking total fusing system." Pike, *Language in Relation to a Unified Theory of the Structure of Human Behavior*, p. 475. For examples of the interlocking grammatical, lexical, and phonological hierarchies, see pages pp. 567–580. For an example of overlapping hierarchies, see page 101. See also Poythress, *In the Beginning Was the Word: Language—A God-Centered Approach* (Wheaton, IL: Crossway, 2009), pp. 263–264.

larger linguistic units.³⁴ We rely on the grammatical rules of our native language to communicate, and one of the important goals of communication is the conveyance of *wisdom*.³⁵ The biblical concept of wisdom is too rich to unpack here, but wisdom is generally understood to be knowledge *applied*. That is, wisdom refers to our putting to use what we know. How do we *act* in the world based on the truths to which we have committed ourselves? When understood in these terms, growth in wisdom can be understood as the goal of humanity—a goal which we have fallen far short of, but a goal which has been perfectly achieved by the Son of God on our behalf.

The Son *is* the wisdom of God the Father.³⁶ His life is the systematic display of how God wants us to act in the world so as to bring him glory and honor. This applies not only to the incarnate Son's speech, but also to his action. And this is an important point. We must relate language to the rest of human behavior, as Kenneth Pike did. For him, language was not a detached medium or social faculty; rather, it was a *phase* of human behavior that was fully integrated with all that we do. He writes,

> Language is behavior, i.e., a phase of human activity

---

34. I am here leaning on the definition for grammar provided in Randolph Quirk et al., *A Comprehensive Grammar of the English Language* (New York: Longman, 1985), p. 12.

35. On our access to and reception of wisdom, see Vern S. Poythress, "The Quest for Wisdom," in *Resurrection and Eschatology: Theology in Service of the Church*, ed. Lane G. Tipton and Jeffrey C. Waddington (Phillipsburg, NJ: P&R Publishing, 2008), pp. 86–114.

36. "But we preach Christ crucified, a stumbling block to Jews and folly to Gentiles, but to those who are called, both Jews and Greeks, Christ the power of God and the wisdom of God" (1 Cor. 1:23–24).

which must not be treated in essence as structurally divorced from the structure of nonverbal human activity. The activity of man constitutes a structural whole, in such a way that it cannot be subdivided into neat "parts" or "levels" or "compartments" with language in a behavioral compartment insulated in character, content and organization from other behavior. Verbal and nonverbal activity is a unified whole, and theory and methodology should be organized or created to treat it as such.[37]

When we understand language as integrated with nonverbal human activity, we see that linguistic units can be structurally substitutable in function for other similar units of human behavior.[38] Raising a hand is substitutable with the word "hello." Looking at another person while putting on your shoes may be substitutable for the sentence, "I'm getting ready." The intimate relationship between language and nonverbal human behavior is not often appreciated in academic treatments of language, so we tend to segregate language from other activities. But Pike argues that when we do so, we do not accurately represent either language or nonverbal human behavior as they function in the real world.

We can and should, then, see language and human behavior as much more closely connected, even to the degree that human actions sometimes function, in a sense, as bits of grammar. All of the units of our behavior, whether verbal or nonverbal, *communicate*, and they do so in a structurally complex behavioral system that has the purpose of displaying and conveying wisdom.

---

37. Kenneth L. Pike, *Language in Relation to a Unified Theory of the Structure of Human Behavior*, 2nd ed. (The Hague: Mouton, 1967), p. 26.

38. Ibid., pp. 26–27, 30–32. Pike goes on to note that verbal and nonverbal behavior are mutually dependent on each other.

Now, think of all of the thousands of behavioral units that made up a single day in the life of Christ: greeting his mother in the morning, tying the straps of his sandals, putting on his outer garment, calling the name of one of his disciples, reciting a passage of the Old Testament to his followers, eating a meal, praying to his Father, visiting and healing a sick child, offering praise to God, walking from house to well and well to house, from village to village, from town to town. Putting together all of these behavioral units, both verbal and nonverbal, would give us something of a "grammar" of his life for that day. His actions and words fit together holistically so as to represent the systematic wisdom of God the Father. Every action, every conversation, every sentence, every clause, every word—all of it fit together so as to be a perfect and systematic representation of his Father's wisdom, his Father's will for how we should act in the world. In this broader sense, grammar—a complex system of rules by which we combine smaller behavioral units to form larger ones—is upheld and redeemed in the systematic wisdom of God the Father manifested by the Son. Grammar, in other words, is really all about the Son of God and his articulated behavior. Grammar is *rooted* in him.

In a similar way, phonology is rooted in the Holy Spirit. "The primary aim of *phonology* is to discover the principles that govern the way sounds are organized in languages, and to explain the variations that occur."[39] While phonetics examines all possible speech sounds, phonology "studies the way in which a language's speakers systematically use

---

39. David Crystal, *The Cambridge Encyclopedia of Language* (New York: Cambridge University Press, 1987), p. 160.

a selection of these sounds in order to express meaning."[40] There are many elements that go into producing sounds— the vibration of vocal chords, the shape of the mouth, the placement of the tongue and teeth and lips, etc. However, foundational to all of these elements is *breath*. Inhalation precedes the production of sound, and exhalation supports and empowers the sounds as they go out from the speaker to the listener. Breath is the reservoir of sound.

Throughout Scripture, the Holy Spirit is closely associated with the "breath" of God. This is evident in the Trinitarian manner of creation through speech: "By the word [Son] of the Lord [Father] the heavens were made, and by the breath [Spirit] of his mouth all their host" (Ps. 33:6). From Genesis 1 onward, the Spirit is bound up with the life-giving power of God. As Poythress notes, "the third person of the Trinity is named 'Spirit' partly to suggest a close relation between him and the picture of the 'breath' of God."[41] It is the life-giving power of the Spirit that enables living creatures to produce sound. Those sounds are meaningful in the context of any given language. This is what we see in Acts 2 when the Holy Spirit comes upon all of the various language groups: "And they were all filled with the Holy Spirit and began to speak in other tongues as the Spirit gave them utterance" (Acts 2:4). The Spirit gave each language user *meaningful* utterances. The speakers were not babbling; they were "telling in [their] own tongues the mighty works of God" (2:11). In other words, the Spirit was solely responsible for providing meaningful speech sounds to each speaker so that they could all proclaim the great

---

40. Ibid., p. 160.

41. Poythress, *In the Beginning Was the Word*, p. 20.

works of God.

We can conclude that the system of speech sounds in a given language ultimately relies on breath, and human breath ultimately relies on the life-giving breath of the Holy Spirit, who has a vital role in redemption precisely in this sense: that he gives meaningful utterances (a divine phonology that transcends people groups) to God's people. Phonology is thus *rooted* in him.

Lastly, the reference or content of our words is rooted in the Father. Though deconstructionists such as Derrida derided our ability to refer to the real world with our words, most people would have no problem admitting that, practically, words can and do refer to the real world. This concept is sometimes called *logocentrism*.[42] What's more, the content or reference of our words is driven by our purpose or intent. Every unit of language has a communicative purpose, and that purpose is controlled by the speaker. The speaker, we might say, has a plan that language allows him to carry out. He uses language to reference the world around him and to convey meanings so that he can execute his plan.

However, our plans as finite creatures are limited. In fact, our concrete communicative plans would be void of meaning if they were not rooted in an eternal plan that gave them intrinsic value with regards to that plan. This plan is the plan of God the Father. The referential subsystems of human language are meaningless in isolation from the reference of the Father's certain plan. In order for creatures to do anything meaningful, they must be mimetic.

---

42. Logocentrism, in brief, "stands for the harmonious alliance between reality, thought, and language." Vanhoozer, *Is There a Meaning in This Text?*, p. 60.

Mimesis—not creativity—is the core of creaturehood. And for this reason "human purposes using the referential subsystem imitate God's purposes, and more specifically the purposes of God the Father."[43]

In sum, we have the Father, Son, and Spirit standing behind human language in grammar (systematic wisdom), phonology (breath-induced utterances), and reference (communicative plans or purposes).

> God's activity in speaking has its ultimate foundation in his Trinitarian character. The plan of God is the plan preeminently of the Father. The systematic wisdom of God is found in the Son: "in whom [Christ] are hidden all the treasures of wisdom and knowledge" (Col. 2:3; see 1 Cor. 1:30). And the Holy Spirit is like the breath of God that empowers his specific utterances.
> Thus the utterances of human beings display an image of the Trinitarian character of God.[44]

Furthermore, we cannot separate the Father, Son, and Spirit; they are essentially one. Likewise, we cannot ever separate the hierarchies of language that depend upon them. Every unit of language has, simultaneously, a role in the grammatical, phonological, and referential hierarchies. Thus, we can see the Father, Son, and Holy Spirit in every word, every unit of human language, by recognizing the grammatical, phonological, and referential features of these words, noting how such features point back to the Trinitarian God of language.

We can end with an example. Consider the word "stone" referentially, from the sentence, "A stone is on the driveway."

---

43. Poythress, *In the Beginning Was the Word*, p. 267.

44. Ibid., p. 265.

The word "stone" points to an identifiable referent that contrasts it with other physical referents (classification). A stone is not a table, nor is it the sky. Yet, within that identity, there is variation, particular manifestations of the one identity that do not threaten its essential meaning: a red stone, a blue stone, soapstone, sandstone, etc. (instantiation). None of this would make any sense, however, unless stones were part of a complex web of relationships within a larger system (association). The word "stone" does not simply float in space; it is spoken by a *person* who can also speak other words that signify elements of the physical environment. So, with every referential unit of human language, there is identity, variation, and distribution. These features are creaturely analogues of the classification, instantiation, and association of the Word and his perichoretic relationship with the Father (Speaker) and the Spirit (Breath).[45]

---

45. In Pike's words, "If one seeks for linguistic analogies for some facts of the Christian Trinity, the identificational-contrastive structure with its basic priority of meaning and purpose and communication from individual to individual would be suggested as illustrative of the relationship of the person of God the Father to the Trinity as a whole—inasmuch as ultimate purpose seems to reside in Him (Eph. 1:9, 11), He has taken the initiative to communicate and to reveal Himself to us (Heb. 1:1–2), and the Sonship of Christ implies the Father's priority of rank in some sense (John 14:28; Col. 1:15). On the other hand, as the manifestation structure of linguistic units is the audible, concrete form which can be directly apprehended by us, and is the medium through which all linguistic meaning is communicated, so the second person of the Trinity, the Son, was made concretely available to the senses of man, to be seen, heard, touched (Col. 1:15; 1 John 1:1) and it was through the manifested Word become flesh (John 1:1, 14) that the purposes of God were effected (John 1:3). Similarly, as the distributional-functional structure in the sentence forms the matrix within which the words of the sentence occur, in formal units that are obscure and hard to find of themselves because of their function in making vividly present before us the more concrete sounds and lexical units, so the third person of the Trinity may perhaps be viewed as the structured distributional personal matrix for the work of God (as the Spirit works in us with the love of God which "is

The word "stone," in addition to playing a role in the referential hierarchy, is also part of overlapping and interlocking grammatical and phonological hierarchies. What is the grammatical function of "stone"? We do not know unless we know something about the phonological and referential contexts. If it occurs as a noun in the sentence, "There is a stone on the driveway," then it is a delayed subject, likely pronounced with falling intonation (phonology), and referring to a dense physical object (reference). But the referential context still leaves us open to various semantic purposes for the sentence. Are no rocks meant to be on the driveway? Is the speaker merely making an observation? Is the statement made with reference to another object so as to help another person find something, an earring, perhaps? We need to know more about this sentence in its context of discourse. But even within that context, if we change the pronunciation or the referent, we have a whole new situation. If the word "stone" is shouted, we may be dealing with a warning of some sort. The same occurs if the grammatical function alters or if the reference is changed. The grammatical, referential, and phonological hierarchies or "subsystems," as well, are tied to the persons of the Godhead, as noted above.

All of this is to say that human language is tristructural in a way that images the Trinity on a creaturely level.[46] Our

---

shed abroad in our hearts by the Holy Ghost." Pike, "Language and Life 4: Tristructural Units of Human Behavior," *Bibliotheca Sacra* 114, no. 456 (January 1958): pp. 42–43.

46. See Pike, "Tristructural Units of Human Behavior." Poythress notes that "human language and human words are dependent upon God's language. Trinitarian speech is necessarily Trinitarian, trimodal, and coinherent. Human speech is dependent. Since it provides access to real knowledge of God, it is necessarily trimodal and coinherent by analogy." Poythress,

words have classifications, instantiations, and associations in the grammatical, phonological, and referential hierarchies in a completely derivative and dependent sense. It is in this sense that every word is an analogical microcosm of the coinherence of the Godhead. The Trinity is *in* every word. That is why our words function in their various communicative contexts.

Conclusion

Trinitarian particularism is nothing more than the ubiquitous support and engagement of every unit of human language by the *entire* Trinity at every point in history. This has implications for theologians who might wish to separate God from human language, as if God were too holy a being to engage with human words. Quite the contrary: God is everywhere upholding our words, and the incarnation is a fitting testament to this truth.

It was Georg Hamann who said that "the Holy Spirit set forth for us a book for his Word, wherein like a fool and a madman, like an unholy and impure spirit, he made for our proud reason childish stories and contemptible events into the history of heaven and God."[47] Hamann's diction is poetic, perhaps hyperbolic, but it gets at the heart of the matter. God can, if he wishes, lead us to holiness through what seems to be unholy—he can unveil the universal truth of redemption in particulars that *seem* to us to restrict his freedom. In fact, this is precisely what redemptive history

---

"Reforming Ontology and Logic," p. 195.

47. James C. Livingston, *Modern Christian Thought*, vol. 1, *The Enlightenment and the Nineteenth Century*, 2nd ed. (Minneapolis, MN: Fortress Press, 1997), p. 73.

suggests: it is the story of a God who came to dwell among and redeem the unholy by working not in isolation from them but *among and through them*;[48] hence the beautifully terse title of God's Son: Immanuel.

Notice how the incarnation draws our eyes to the holy entering into the unholy, which has implications not just for our understanding of human words, but for our understanding of Scripture. Abraham Kuyper and Herman Bavinck wrote that God's Word takes the form of a lowly servant: "As the Logos has not appeared *in the form of glory*, but in the form of a servant, joining Himself to the reality of our nature, as this had come to be through the results of sin, so also, for the revelation of His Logos, God the Lord accepts *our* consciousness, our human life *as it is.*"[49] Scripture, in both its appearance and its message, parallels the very human and divine nature of Jesus Christ.[50] What's more, the mysterious concinnity of the divine and human natures of Jesus Christ is indicative of the God who holds

---

48. "Jesus in his incarnation accepted the constraints of human language, just as he accepted constraints as to walking in time and place in a body." Pike, "The Linguist and Axioms," 47.

49. Abraham Kuyper, *Principles of Sacred Theology*, trans. J. Hendrik De Vries (Grand Rapids, MI: William B. Eerdmans, 1963), p. 479. Herman Bavinck also picks up on this in *Reformed Dogmatics*: "The bearer of the ideal goods of humankind is language, and the sarx of language is the written word. In making himself known, God also adapts himself to this reality. To be able fully to enter the life of humankind and for it fully to become its possession, revelation assumes the form (morfh) and fashion (schma) of Scripture. Scripture is the servant form of revelation." Herman Bavinck, *Reformed Dogmatics*, vol. 1, *Prolegomena*, ed. John Bolt, trans. John Vriend (Grand Rapids, MI: Baker Academic, 2003), p. 380.

50. "The form of Scripture, as well as its content, is both truly divine and truly human, with God as the primary author." Gaffin, *God's Word in Servant Form: Abraham Kuyper and Herman Bavinck on the Doctrine of Scripture* (Jackson, MS: Reformed Academic Press, 2008), p. 23.

a mysterious concinnity of universals and particulars in his triunity. Our particularism, then, must be Trinitarian, for even in the Word is indelibly marked by his triune emic community. When we begin with Christ as the Word, we begin with the Father and the Spirit, the Speaker and his Breath.

Moreover, if Scripture is revelation in servant form, there is also a sense in which the Word is present in every single word of the Bible.[51] Every specific word in Scripture is an incarnate corollary of the second person of the Trinity.[52] In fact, it shows just how deeply the Trinity has permeated temporal reality in order to redeem it. Surely this gives new meaning to the truth that God upholds all things by the word of his power (Heb. 1:3).

---

51. This is the case especially if we view words as Trinitarian, each one having a speaker (Father), a form (Son), and God's powerful and meaningful presence (Spirit) behind it.

52. In discussing the words of special revelation, Frame calls this the *linguistic model of the Trinity*: "the Father is the speaker, the Son the Word, and the Spirit the breath that conveys the word to its hearers." John M. Frame, *The Doctrine of the Word of God* (Phillipsburg, NJ: P&R Publishing, 2010), p. 125. This can be extended, if we are careful, to the rest of human language. Scripture is certainly in a league of its own as the salvific message of God, but our words are analogously Trinitarian in the sense that our speech parallels the members of the Trinity: we as speakers (creaturely analogues of the Father) deliver words (creaturely analogues of the Son) to hearers by the power of our God-given breath (a creaturely analogue of the Spirit). This coheres with the truth that "God has impressed his Trinitarian character on language. Whenever we use language, we rely on what he has given us. We also rely on the mutual indwelling of the persons of the Trinity. Because of this indwelling, our use of language holds together. In the use of language, we live in the presence of God who through the Spirit gives us life and through the Spirit empowers our use of language. Tacitly, we are trusting in God's faithfulness and consistency and wisdom. This is true even when non-Christians use language. But they have suppressed awareness of their dependence on God, as Romans 1:19–21 indicates." Poythress, *In the Beginning Was the Word*, 22.

Put differently, there is no such thing as 'merely human words.' In our own use of words, we rely on and reflect the divine linguistic fellowship that spoke the eternal Word in the power of the Spirit. Our communicative behavior rests on the presence and coinherence of the Godhead. And so we return to the question at the beginning of the article: what is *in* a word? The Trinity.

Subject and Name Index

A

analog 11, 14, 16, 83
analogical 9, 24, 29, 44, 47, 97, 118, 119, 132, 138, 159, 160, 164, 168,
　　185, 196, 197, 198, 224, 281, 326, 329, 381
Aristotle 180, 192, 193, 194, 229, 237
Artistotle
　Aristotelian 96, 180, 189, 192, 195, 196, 229
Augustine 102, 107, 124, 147, 148, 149, 150, 167, 169, 283, 358, 366, 367
autonomy 73, 77, 78, 81, 82, 83, 98, 106, 107, 125, 134, 190, 258, 318

B

Bavinck, Herman 5, 6, 33, 48, 141, 174, 178, 251, 258, 341, 346, 382
behavior 6, 7, 8, 9, 11, 13, 14, 15, 16, 17, 18, 19, 21, 23, 25, 26, 28, 29, 31,
　　34, 35, 39, 40, 41, 43, 44, 45, 48, 53, 54, 55, 58, 59, 61, 63, 64, 65,
　　66, 68, 69, 70, 73, 78, 80, 81, 82, 85, 86, 87, 88, 90, 92, 93, 94, 95,
　　96, 100, 103, 104, 105, 106, 107, 118, 120, 122, 123, 132, 134, 135,
　　151, 173, 177, 178, 180, 181, 182, 183, 185, 187, 188, 189, 190,
　　195, 197, 198, 199, 212, 217, 234, 235, 238, 243, 246, 250, 251,
　　253, 254, 260, 261, 263, 265, 273, 274, 275, 279, 280, 297, 299,
　　304, 310, 314, 315, 318, 324, 330, 335, 345, 348, 359, 361, 363,
　　373, 374, 375, 384
Berkhof, Louis 24, 33, 111, 143, 145, 255
Bray, Gerald 19, 101, 259

C

Calvin, John 33, 48, 108, 113, 141, 142, 143, 144, 146, 171, 255, 283, 284
Carson, D. A. 109, 110, 114, 347, 348
coherence 25, 28
communion 3, 4, 6, 25, 30, 31, 100, 101, 103, 106, 108, 109, 119, 122,
　　125, 126, 134, 135, 136, 138, 139, 159, 163, 164, 165, 166, 173,
　　175, 176, 179, 181, 182, 188, 189, 209, 221, 223, 224, 233, 234,
　　235, 241, 244, 273, 274, 280, 281, 285, 286, 297, 309, 310, 313,
　　327, 339, 340, 349, 358
communion behavior 106, 173, 234, 235, 280, 297, 358
consciousness 307
　Conscious 105, 153, 294, 307
contrast, variation, and distribution
　contrast 4, 42, 56, 75, 207, 210, 250, 289, 297, 317, 318, 367, 371
　distribution 40, 41, 42, 58, 59, 79, 90, 97, 129, 130, 151, 152, 218, 319,
　　321, 379

variation 40, 42, 44, 59, 62, 79, 152, 160, 318, 319, 320, 368, 379
covenantal 4, 21, 32, 73, 74, 75, 77, 172, 178, 180, 181, 182, 183, 187,
    191, 192, 279, 290, 292, 305, 309, 314, 323, 339, 340
Creator-creature distinction 8, 25, 176, 277, 278, 300, 350
creature 4, 8, 14, 15, 18, 25, 32, 73, 85, 104, 115, 118, 119, 176, 178, 179,
    184, 188, 191, 229, 230, 259, 270, 277, 278, 281, 285, 289, 300,
    338, 350, 360

D

Derrida, Jacques 206, 207, 377

E

emic and etic
  insider 56, 58, 245, 249, 252, 253, 256, 303, 317, 362
  outsider 56, 57, 59, 245, 247, 249, 256
epistemology 7, 8, 9, 10, 29, 30, 75, 78, 96, 97, 200, 220, 221, 230, 275,
    276, 279, 284, 285, 286, 288, 289, 295, 298, 305, 322, 365

F

forgiveness 6, 256, 268
form-meaning composites 62, 65, 66, 69, 82, 234
Frame, John M. 9, 28, 37, 104, 123, 133, 150, 157, 164, 186, 192, 216,
    225, 244, 276, 279, 325, 336, 343, 356, 358, 366, 383

G

Gaffin Jr., Richard B. 5, 18, 85, 104, 188, 230, 283
general revelation 4, 5, 34, 35, 47, 48, 69, 70, 88, 89, 94, 95, 140, 145, 146,
    169, 170, 221, 264, 340
God
  Father 7, 9, 23, 29, 30, 84, 90, 93, 94, 98, 101, 102, 103, 108, 109, 110,
    111, 114, 115, 119, 120, 121, 122, 123, 124, 125, 126, 127, 130,
    131, 133, 134, 139, 140, 141, 142, 143, 145, 150, 159, 160, 161,
    162, 163, 164, 165, 166, 167, 169, 172, 174, 175, 179, 183, 184,
    186, 187, 188, 206, 208, 209, 222, 223, 224, 226, 227, 228, 229,
    234, 236, 239, 244, 249, 251, 252, 253, 254, 257, 259, 261, 263,
    268, 272, 280, 282, 283, 284, 285, 286, 306, 309, 311, 313, 330,
    332, 333, 334, 336, 337, 343, 344, 345, 346, 347, 348, 349, 352,
    357, 359, 365, 366, 367, 368, 369, 370, 371, 372, 373, 375, 376,
    377, 378, 379, 380, 383
  Holy Spirit 7, 9, 23, 29, 74, 101, 102, 103, 108, 110, 123, 139, 140, 142,
    143, 145, 162, 163, 164, 165, 166, 167, 175, 184, 223, 234, 244,
    249, 252, 259, 268, 280, 284, 332, 335, 336, 343, 344, 345, 346,

    347, 359, 366, 367, 368, 375, 376, 377, 378, 381
  Jesus Christ 23, 27, 61, 90, 165, 167, 223, 256, 268, 382
  relational 8, 9, 22, 28, 29, 81, 141, 151, 152, 156, 164, 169, 175, 179,
    180, 181, 209, 212, 229, 230, 231, 232, 238, 239, 240, 241, 242,
    254, 258, 276, 279, 331
  Son 7, 9, 23, 27, 29, 30, 90, 93, 94, 98, 101, 102, 103, 108, 109, 110,
    114, 115, 119, 120, 121, 122, 123, 124, 125, 126, 127, 130, 131,
    133, 134, 139, 140, 141, 142, 143, 145, 150, 161, 162, 163, 164,
    165, 166, 167, 169, 172, 174, 175, 178, 179, 183, 184, 186, 187,
    188, 191, 208, 209, 215, 222, 223, 224, 226, 227, 228, 229, 233,
    234, 236, 237, 239, 243, 244, 249, 252, 253, 254, 255, 256, 257,
    259, 263, 268, 280, 282, 283, 284, 285, 286, 311, 313, 330, 332,
    333, 334, 336, 337, 343, 344, 345, 346, 348, 349, 352, 357, 359,
    363, 365, 366, 367, 368, 369, 370, 371, 372, 373, 375, 376, 378,
    379, 382, 383
grace 6, 7, 29, 74, 97, 248, 260, 261, 265, 266, 268, 270, 271, 272, 273,
  288, 300, 301, 305
grammatical 21, 40, 42, 50, 55, 64, 81, 82, 86, 129, 131, 137, 138, 316,
  320, 371, 372, 373, 378, 380, 381
Gunton, Colin E. 312, 330

H

hierarchy 41, 42, 49, 81, 325, 351, 372, 380
Hodge, Charles 33, 42, 43, 141, 174, 254, 277, 327, 331, 332, 346
hypostasis 51, 52, 53, 188, 189

I

imago Dei 35, 48, 70, 104, 172, 195, 197, 198, 360, 363, 364

K

Kelly, Douglas 102, 143, 175, 209, 253, 325, 358
Köstenberger, Andreas J. 110, 228, 347

L

language 7, 1, 4, 6, 7, 8, 9, 18, 19, 20, 21, 22, 24, 26, 27, 29, 30, 31, 34, 35,
    36, 37, 38, 39, 40, 41, 44, 45, 47, 48, 49, 50, 51, 52, 53, 54, 55, 56,
    58, 60, 61, 62, 63, 64, 65, 66, 68, 69, 70, 71, 73, 74, 75, 80, 81, 82,
    85, 86, 87, 88, 90, 92, 94, 96, 97, 100, 103, 104, 105, 106, 107, 117,
    118, 120, 128, 129, 131, 132, 133, 135, 136, 138, 139, 151, 152,
    168, 172, 173, 174, 175, 176, 177, 178, 180, 181, 182, 183, 185,
    186, 187, 188, 189, 190, 191, 192, 195, 197, 198, 199, 200, 202,
    204, 206, 207, 209, 210, 217, 220, 221, 222, 224, 225, 226, 233,

234, 235, 236, 241, 243, 244, 245, 246, 247, 249, 250, 253, 257, 258, 260, 262, 263, 264, 265, 266, 268, 269, 270, 271, 272, 273, 275, 276, 277, 278, 279, 280, 281, 282, 284, 285, 286, 288, 289, 291, 295, 296, 297, 298, 299, 300, 301, 302, 303, 304, 305, 306, 309, 314, 315, 318, 320, 322, 323, 324, 326, 327, 328, 329, 333, 336, 337, 345, 349, 350, 351, 352, 354, 356, 357, 358, 359, 360, 361, 362, 363, 364, 365, 367, 369, 372, 373, 374, 376, 377, 378, 379, 380, 381, 382, 383
language as covenantal 180
language as representational 183
Letham, Robert 22, 37, 101, 141, 175, 342
Lewis, C. S. 22
linguistic ontology 171, 195

M

meaning, control, and presence 123
metaphor 75, 86, 104, 190, 204, 206, 208, 209, 210, 211, 212, 215, 216, 221, 225, 236, 243, 364
metaphysics 4, 7, 8, 28, 96, 189, 192, 193, 207, 229, 235, 275, 276, 279, 285, 286, 288, 289, 291, 295, 298, 305, 306, 313, 314
mystery 36, 42, 43, 177, 179, 195

O

O'Collins, Gerald 19, 277
Oliphint, K. Scott 8, 9, 16, 34, 48, 68, 89, 140, 255, 264, 276

P

particle, wave, and field
 field 29, 39, 40, 41, 47, 48, 49, 56, 59, 81, 90, 105, 135, 141, 151, 152, 154, 155, 156, 157, 158, 161, 164, 169, 246, 250, 289, 328, 350, 353, 360
 Observer Perspectives 151, 159, 168
 particle 40, 41, 49, 59, 80, 81, 90, 95, 105, 141, 151, 152, 153, 155, 156, 157, 158, 160, 164, 168, 169, 328, 349, 350, 353, 360
 wave 40, 41, 49, 59, 81, 90, 105, 141, 151, 152, 153, 154, 156, 157, 158, 161, 162, 164, 168, 169, 328, 350, 353, 360
perichoresis 19, 24, 42, 43, 44, 66, 92, 107, 108, 109, 111, 112, 113, 114, 115, 116, 117, 118, 119, 120, 121, 122, 123, 126, 128, 130, 131, 135, 136, 138, 139, 164, 166, 167, 168, 170, 175, 176, 183, 277, 282, 283, 331, 365
personalism
 personal 7, 21, 23, 25, 29, 35, 37, 38, 39, 46, 47, 48, 60, 61, 64, 65, 69,

86, 88, 92, 93, 106, 111, 117, 118, 119, 130, 133, 142, 147, 160, 161, 162, 163, 164, 173, 175, 180, 182, 184, 185, 186, 187, 188, 189, 190, 191, 193, 195, 196, 198, 199, 200, 201, 209, 222, 228, 229, 233, 241, 250, 251, 254, 256, 257, 258, 259, 264, 267, 268, 276, 279, 282, 292, 296, 297, 299, 301, 303, 304, 306, 309, 310, 313, 340, 347, 348, 353, 359, 364, 379
phonological 40, 42, 55, 79, 81, 129, 131, 320, 372, 378, 380, 381
Pike, Kenneth L. 33, 34, 39, 40, 41, 49, 51, 58, 62, 66, 68, 69, 90, 99, 104, 105, 128, 141, 150, 152, 153, 173, 190, 199, 205, 212, 216, 234, 236, 244, 245, 247, 251, 271, 278, 315, 320, 328, 345, 360, 361, 374
Poythress, Vern S. 7, 9, 19, 28, 37, 38, 55, 100, 104, 152, 157, 173, 178, 179, 192, 206, 208, 215, 221, 240, 244, 276, 280, 298, 309, 311, 335, 338, 343, 357, 360, 367, 373

R

reductionism 38, 43, 60, 62, 158, 317, 318
resurrection 23, 72, 161, 222
revelation
  general revelation 5, 6, 35, 66, 70, 74, 88, 89, 90, 94, 95, 141, 145, 146, 170, 171, 204, 206, 210, 215, 216, 220, 221, 223, 226, 243, 254, 264, 282, 305, 327, 354, 383
  special revelation 5, 6, 35, 66, 70, 74, 88, 89, 90, 94, 95, 141, 145, 146, 170, 171, 204, 206, 210, 215, 216, 220, 221, 223, 226, 243, 254, 264, 282, 305, 327, 354, 383
Rosenstock-Huessy, Eugen 326, 357, 358

S

Sapir, Edward 54, 55, 56
Schaeffer, Francis 22
Searle, John R. 289, 291
simplicity 11, 12, 14, 17, 89, 216, 322
speaker, speech, and breath 20, 120, 126, 127, 134, 135, 136, 138
speech 3, 4, 5, 7, 8, 9, 10, 11, 13, 14, 16, 18, 19, 20, 21, 23, 24, 26, 27, 28, 30, 31, 40, 44, 52, 55, 58, 60, 81, 98, 120, 121, 124, 126, 127, 128, 131, 132, 133, 134, 135, 136, 138, 161, 172, 178, 179, 180, 181, 182, 183, 186, 194, 195, 196, 200, 215, 220, 226, 236, 237, 239, 240, 252, 259, 297, 298, 301, 302, 303, 304, 314, 315, 316, 317, 318, 319, 322, 323, 327, 329, 330, 332, 333, 334, 335, 336, 337, 338, 339, 340, 341, 346, 348, 353, 354, 358, 361, 363, 364, 369, 370, 373, 375, 376, 377, 380, 383
speech-act theory 240, 297, 298, 301, 302, 303, 304, 314, 315, 316, 317, 318, 322, 335
Staniloae, Dumitru 134, 187, 280

T

Tertullian 327, 328, 329, 330, 331, 333
Tipton, Lane G. 19, 43, 102, 176, 228, 277, 331, 373
Tolkien, J. R. R. 22
Torrance, T. F. 33, 103, 116, 143, 164, 166, 177
trialogue 20, 23, 86
trinitarian structure 35, 39, 69, 94, 97, 147
Trinity
　economic Trinity 19, 23, 123, 177, 248, 249, 253, 255, 285
　immanent Trinity 19, 23, 101, 122, 127, 176, 248, 251, 253, 255
　ontological Trinity 33, 34, 68, 95, 100, 140, 146, 149, 248, 251, 255, 256, 257, 285
tristructural 39, 40, 90, 128, 129, 152, 380
Turretin, Francis 5, 11, 12, 13, 16, 107, 113, 160, 161, 162, 165

U

unity and diversity 15, 26, 42, 169, 184

V

Vanhoozer, Kevin J. 19, 24, 113, 176, 206, 207, 284, 334, 335, 357
Van Til, Cornelius 8, 12, 13, 26, 27, 29, 33, 34, 36, 37, 38, 42, 43, 44, 47, 68, 69, 77, 78, 79, 95, 96, 103, 108, 117, 118, 119, 120, 122, 124, 132, 133, 140, 144, 145, 146, 147, 152, 157, 164, 168, 172, 175, 176, 181, 183, 184, 187, 190, 191, 193, 194, 196, 197, 198, 199, 201, 204, 208, 209, 211, 215, 220, 221, 228, 255, 256, 257, 258, 260, 261, 276, 277, 278, 279, 283, 290, 292, 306, 309, 311, 312, 331, 334, 343, 360
Vos, Geerhardus 228, 230, 282, 283, 346

W

Waltke, Bruce K. 20, 21, 86, 240, 336

Z

Zizioulas, John 107, 188

www.ingramcontent.com/pod-product-compliance
Lightning Source LLC
Chambersburg PA
CBHW022042160426
43209CB00002B/44